The Heralds' Memoir, 1486–1490

Court Ceremony, Royal Progress and Rebellion

RICHARD III & YORKIST HISTORY TRUST

PUBLICATIONS

In Association with Sutton Publishing:

The Crowland Chronicle Continuations 1459–1486. Edited by Nicholas Pronay and John Cox, 1986

Richard III: Loyalty, Lordship and Law. Edited by P. W. Hammond, 1986; reprinted 2000 *

York House Books 1461–1490. Edited by Lorraine Attreed, 2 vols, 1991 *

The Household Books of John Howard, Duke of Norfolk, 1462–1471 and 1481–1483. Reduced facsimile reprint with a new introduction by Anne Crawford, 1992 *

The Hours of Richard III. Anne F. Sutton and Livia Visser-Fuchs, 1990; reprinted 1996

The Politics of Fifteenth-Century England. John Vale's Book. Edited by Margaret L. Kekewich, Colin Richmond, Anne F. Sutton, Livia Visser-Fuchs and John L. Watts, 1995 *

In Association with Shaun Tyas ('Paul Watkins'):

The Alien Communities of London in the Fifteenth Century. The Subsidy Rolls of 1440 and 1483–4. Edited and introduced by J. L. Bolton (1998)

The Merchant Taylors' Company of London: Court Minutes, 1486–1493. Edited by Matthew Davies (2000)

The Beauchamp Pageant. A facsimile edition, edited and introduced by Alexandra Sinclair (2003)

The Estate and Household Accounts of William Worsley, Dean of St Paul's Cathedral, 1479–1497. Edited by Hannes Kleineke and Stephanie R. Hovland (2004)

The Heralds' Memoir 1486–1490. Court Ceremony, Royal Progress and Rebellion. Edited by Emma Cavell (2009).

* The stock of these four titles is also available from Shaun Tyas

THE HERALDS' MEMOIR 1486–1490

COURT CEREMONY, ROYAL PROGRESS AND REBELLION

EDITED BY
EMMA CAVELL

RICHARD III AND YORKIST HISTORY TRUST

in association with

SHAUN TYAS
DONINGTON
2009

© Emma Cavell and Richard III and Yorkist History Trust 2009

Published
SHAUN TYAS
(an imprint of 'Paul Watkins')
1 High Street
Donington
Lincolnshire
PE11 4TA
on behalf of
Richard III and Yorkist History Trust

ISBN
~~1 900289 938 (ten digits)~~
~~978 1 900289 931 (thirteen digits)~~
978 1 900289 86 3

Typeset, subedited and designed from the disc of the author
by Shaun Tyas

Printed in Great Britain by the MPG Books Group, Bodmin and King's Lynn

CONTENTS

Acknowledgements — vi

List of Abbreviations — vii

Illustrations — x

INTRODUCTION

The Heralds
1. The Office of Arms — 1
2. Heraldic Activities — 4
3. Heraldic Narratives — 12
4. Creation of the Memoir — 19
5. The Court and Campaigns of Henry VII, 1486–90 — 25

The Manuscript
1. Composition — 43
2. Date — 55
3. The Author — 57
4. Transmission — 60
5. Editorial Method — 66

EDITION OF THE MEMOIR — 68

Glossary — 186

Select Bibliography — 194

Index — 205

ACKNOWLEDGEMENTS

Since I began my Masters research many years ago under the watchful eyes of Professor Michael Bennett and Dr Megan Cassidy-Welch at the University of Tasmania, I have received support and encouragement from a great many people, not least from Michael and Megan, who patiently supervised the dissertation on which this book is based. I am also grateful to Professor Rod Thomson for his assistance in matters of palaeography, and to my friends, at the University of Tasmania for their kindness, encouragement and assistance throughout the course of my degree: Dr Liz Freeman, Dr Hamish Maxwell-Stewart, Dr Stefan Petrow, Dr Margaret Lindley, Anthony Ray and Andrew Richardson. The MA thesis itself, which involved considerable overseas research, would not have been possible without the financial support of the Tasmania Research Scholarship board, the Faculty of Arts, and the School of History and Classics at the University of Tasmania. For his guidance in converting a rather crude Master thesis into a publishable text I owe a debt of gratitude to Professor Tony Pollard, without whose thorough criticisms and encouragement, I may never have completed the book. I cannot thank him enough. Thanks must also go to Maurice Keen, who supplied several key references and took the time to read over portions of my work; to Garter King of Arms and the heralds of England for granting me access to their manuscripts; and to Robert Yorke, archivist of the College of Arms, for his assistance and for allowing me to continue work with the heralds' manuscripts after closing time. I would also like to acknowledge the assistance of the staff of the British Library, and especially of Ann Payne, former manuscripts superintendent, for her guidance. Last but not least, thank you to Davide Cargnello for his work as a proof-reader in the final stages of the book's preparation, and also to Dr Juliane Kerkhecker and Dr Richard Ingham for some last-minute corrections to my Latin and Old French transcriptions.

Emma Cavell

LIST OF ABBREVIATIONS

Add.	Additional.
André, *Vita*	Bernard André, 'Vita Henrici Septimi' in *Memorials of King Henry the Seventh*.
BJRL	*Bulletin of the John Rylands Library*.
BL	British Library.
Black Book	'The Black Book' in *The Household of Edward IV: the Black Book and Ordinance of 1478*, ed. A. R. Myers (Manchester, 1959).
Bodl.	Bodleian Library, Oxford.
CCR	*Calendar of Close Rolls*.
CFR	*Calendar of Fine Rolls*.
Chroniques de Adrien de But	*Chroniques relatives à l'Histoire de la Belgique, sous la Domination des Ducs de Bourgogne*. Vol. I, *Chroniques de Religieux des Dunes*, ed. Kervyn de Lettenhove (Brussels, 1870).
Coll. Arms	College of Arms, London.
CPR	*Calendar of Patent Rolls*.
Croyland Chronicle	'Fourth Continuation of Croyland Chronicle' in *Ingulph's Chronicle of the Abbey of Croyland*, ed. H. T. Riley (1893).
CSP Venice	*Calendar of State Papers and Manuscripts, Relating to English Affairs, Existing in the Archives and Collections of Venice, and in Other Libraries of Northern Italy 1202–1675*, ed. R. Brown et al. (London, 1864–1947; repr. 1970).
e.s.	extra series.
Econ. HR	*Economic History Review*.
EETS	Early English Text Society.
Eg.	Egerton.
EHR	*English Historical Review*.
Fabian, *New Chronicles*	Robert Fabyan, *New Chronicles of England and France*, ed. H. Ellis (London, 1811).
Ford, thesis	Lisa Ford, 'Consiliar Politics and Administration in the Reign of Henry VII', unpublished PhD thesis, University of St Andrews (2001).

Hall, *Union*	Edward Hall, *Union of the Two Noble Families of Lancaster and York*, facsimilie edn (Menston, 1970).
HMC	Historical Manuscripts Commission.
HMSO	His/Her Majesty's Stationary Office.
Holinshed, *Chronicles*	Raphael Holinshed, *Chronicles of England, Scotland and Ireland*, ed. V. F. Snow, 6 vols (repr. New York, 1965), vol. 3.
JBAA	*Journal of the British Archaeological Association.*
JBS	*Journal of British Studies.*
JMRS	*Journal of Medieval and Renaissance Studies.*
JSA	*Journal of the Society of Archivists.*
Julius B. XII	BL, Cotton MS. Julius B. XII.
KB	Knight of the Bath.
KG	Knight of the Garter.
Leland, *Collectanea*	*Joannis Lelandi Antiquarii De Rebus Britannicis Collectanea*, ed. T. Hearne, 6 vols (London, 1770).
LP	*Letters and Papers Illustrative of the Reigns of Richard III and Henry VII*, ed. J. Gairdner, 2 vols, RS (London, 1861–3).
LRC	William Say, *Liber Regie Capelle*, ed. W. Ullmann (London, 1961).
Materials	*Materials for a History of the Reign of Henry VII*, ed. W. Campbell, 2 vols, RS (London, 1873–7).
McGee, thesis	C. E. McGee, 'A Critical Edition of the First Provincial Progress of Henry VII', unpublished PhD thesis, University of Toronto (1977).
Memorials	*Memorials of King Henry VII*, ed. J. Gairdner, 2 vols, RS (London, 1858).
Molinet, *Chroniques*	*Chroniques de Jean Molinet, 1474–1506*, ed. G. Doutrepont and O. Jodogne, 3 vols (Brussels, 1935–7).
MS/S	Manuscript/s.
n.c.e.	new complete edition.
n.s.	new series.
TNA	National Archives, Kew (formerly the Public Record Office).
NMS	*Nottingham Medieval Studies.*
o.s.	original series.
OHR	*A Collection of Ordinances and Regulations for the Government of the Royal Household made in divers reigns from King Edward III to King William and Queen Mary: Also Receipts in Ancient Cookery*, printed for the Society of Antiquaries (London, 1790).

LIST OF ABBREVIATIONS

Olver, thesis	P. C. Olver, 'Tudor Royal Progress', unpublished MA thesis, University of Swansea (1984).
Paston Intro and Supp.	*The Paston Letters, 1422–1509 A.D. Introduction and Supplement*, ed. J. Gairdner, 3 vols. (Westminster, 1901).
Paston Letters and Papers	*Paston Letters and Papers of the Fifteenth Century*, ed. N. Davis, 2 vols (Oxford, 1971–6).
Paston Letters, n.c.e.	*Paston Letters, A.D. 1422–1509*, ed. J. Gairdner, n.c.e, 6 vols (London, 1904), vol. 3.
Peerage	G. E. Cokayne, *The Complete Peerage of England, Scotland, Ireland, Great Britain and the United Kingdom*, ed. V. Gibb, et al., 12 vols (1910–59).
PMLA	*Publications of the Modern Language Association.*
PO	*Proceedings and Ordinances of the Privy Council of England*, ed. N. H. Nicolas, 7 vols (London, 1834–7), vol. 4.
RP	*Rotuli Parliamentorum.*
RS	Rolls Series.
Somers Tracts	*The Somers Collection of Tracts*, 2nd edn, ed. W. Scott (London, 1809), vol. 1.
Sutton and Hammond, *Richard III*	*The Coronation of Richard III: the Extant Documents*, ed. Anne F. Sutton and P. W. Hammond (Gloucester, 1983).
TRHS	*Transactions of the Royal Historical Society.*
VCH	*Victoria County History.*
Vergil, *Anglica Historia*	*The 'Anglica Historia' of Polydore Vergil, A.D. 1485–1537*, ed. D. Hay, Camden Soc., n.s. 74 (1950).
Wagner, *HH*	A. R. Wagner, *Heralds and Heraldry in the Middle Ages: an Inquiry into the Growth of the Armorial Function of Heralds*, 2nd edn (Oxford, 2000).
YHB	*York House Books, 1461–1490*, ed. L. Attreed, 2 vols (Stroud, 1991).

ffe Ao to
mj

the feast of Easter Anno 4 Hen 7

The kyng kept this ester at hertford whare at that
season the reverent fader In god the lord Fox pope
did the divine service and on saint georges day also
and on the morne he songe the mas of requiem and
of the brethern of the garter ther was therll of
of derby the lord Scrope and sir richart Tunstall
This season ther came In to this londe a gracate ambassade
frome the kyng of romains that is to saye don ladron
de guavara the vicounte of puversalle a doctor
called mester lewys And mester pierre le pussant
and also a noder ambassade In thar companye that
came frome the kyng of portyngall wherfore the
kyng sent for the lorde John morton then archebyshope
of canterbury and chaunceluer of englonde for to
have his counsell and advis And also ther had bew
an ambassatour of the kyng of naples as long as the
kyng had lyen at hertford and at that season ther
was the quene The lady the kyngs moder Therle
of derby Therle of essex Therle of ormond Sir
Richart gilford Sir Raynold bray Sir thomas lovell
Sir charles somerset Sir Richart haulte Sir John
Ryseley The kyngs Almoner The kyngs secretary
And the lorde bothewell a scottysheman. And also
this same ester the kyng of denmarkes oncle called
yonker gerrard was sworne the kyngs servannt
And on saint vitalles day the xxviij day of aprill
was slayne therle of northumberlonde besides
Thurske besydes blackamor esse Tydyngs hereoff
had the kyng sone answerde all the abovesaide
ambassatours and on the xxvijth day of may departed
frome hertford towardes the northe and lay that
nyght at Dunstable acompaynyed with the bishop

Jhs

The morners sat w'in the barrers as acustumed. Whiche
were for that nyght S' Edmond Carew S' John
arundell of the west S' William Sandys. William Courteney
John Roo sergeant at the lawe ./ At tymes acustumed by
officers of armes w't a high voyce saydt ye shall pray for
the sowle of the Right noble lord William Courteney Erle of
Devon &c./ The dirige doon The morners went to a place
for them ordeyned at the cloisters ende where they hadd
spyces and wyne. The corpes was wached all nyght by hys
knyghts and squyres/ and thus depted for that nyght./

On the morowe at vij. at the clocke began the furst
masse whiche was of our Lady songen by the prior of the
place in defaute of a prelatt

The ij. masse of the trinite songen by the provinciall of
the blak fryres

The iij. masse whiche was of Requiem Songen by Doctor
ffitz James bisshopp of london in pontificalibz. To the whiche
came the popes ambassadour The lord Richard ffox bisshopp
of Winchester executors of the defunct./ The lord marquis
of Dorsett principall morner S' Thomas Knevet S' John arundell
S' Thomas Inglefeld S' William Sandys./ at the offryng tyme
The marquis Dorset offerd a noble for the masse peny. whiche
was delivered hym by S' Thomas Knyvett acompanyed w't all
the odir morners and soo retorned to his place./ Then garter
delivered his cote of armes to S' Thomas Knevet and to S' John
arundell. Whiche did offre hit to the bisshopp. The sheld was
offerd by S' William Sandys and S' Thomas Inglefeld. S' Thomas
Knevet and S' John arundell offerd the sweerde. John Roo and
John Stuke offerd the helme and crest. Then was his harneys
offerd by S' Edmond Carew. Whiche was armed in harneys of the
defunct tarryyng at the churche ende rydyng on a courser holdyng
a spere in his hand the point downward The courser trappd w't
a trapper of his harneys led by S' John arundell & S' William
Sandys havyng officers of armes before them. Rode till he came

Garter

And oder and esquiers for the bodie Edward Blount
Saue philipp harry pudsey john croker nycholas ky
ston // the kynge in al this fest wer no robes of
astate but der gownes of riche clothis of gold and
in especiall j gowne which was wrought by the
ladyes in the Toure and richely furred wyth
sabuls // on new yeris day the kyng rewardid
his officers of armes as he ys yerly acustumed
Item the quen gaue the forty shyllinges
Item my ladye the kynges moder xxs̄ // It̄
the reuerent fader in god the bishope of exet
xxs̄ // It therll of derby xxs̄ // Item
therll of essex j nobill Item therll of ormond
2 nobl's Item the kynges chamberleyn xs̄
Item the lord daubey xls̄ // and as of old
acustumed garter kyng of armes desired and
besaut the kyng to all them thankynges and
after cryed ther largess on the the iiij day
the ambassatours of spayne dyned at the
kynges borde and the officers of armes had
ther largess as they wer acustumed this crist
mas j saw no disgysynges and but right few
plays but ther was an Abbot of misrule that

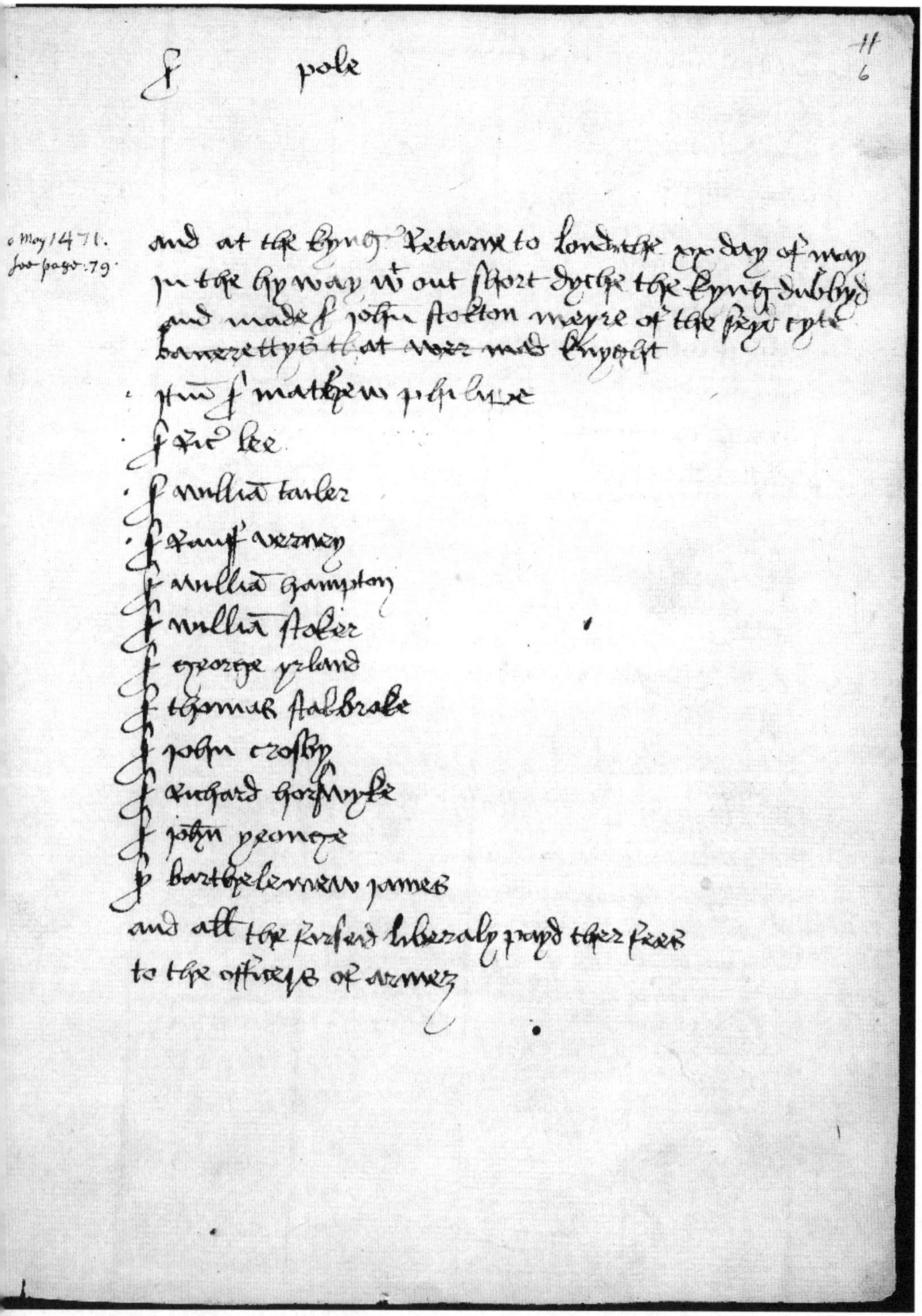

§ pole

6 May 1471.
See page 79.

and at the kyng[es] Returne to london xxi day of may
in the hy way w't out short dyche the kyng dubbyd
and made S' John stokton meyre of the pepull ryte
banerettys that were made knyg't

· hen S' mathew philipe
· S' Ric lee
· S' willm tailer
· S' Rauff verney
· S' willm hampton
· S' willm stoker
· S' George yrland
· S' thomas stalbrok
· S' John crosby
· S' Richard gardyner
· S' John yeonge
· S' bartholomew james

and all the forsaid liberaly payd ther fees
to the officers of armez

Image 4:
The hand of John Writhe.
'Wriothesley's Heraldic Collections', volume 4: *Wrythe's Book of Knights*. BL, MS. Add. 46354, fol. 6.

ffirst Esqwyers knyghte and then the barons of the Cheqwer
and lorde Chefe of Armes And then all thabbots and busshops
in they Copis or Robes of parliament al on the Right syde And the
Barons in they Robes And therles in their Robes of astate S ....
the great Chamberlayn which was in his parliament Robe was
al on the lefte syde And aft them went nexst they .... the duc
and garter and the meyr of london next before the Constable
And marshall And when the quene was comyn into the hall
they went into the white hall and so to the .... chambre And in
the meane tyme the hygh and mighty prince duc of .. ford
in A gowne of clothe of golde Richely furred on a goodly .....
Richely trapped w[i]t[h] A trapper enbrodered w[i]t[h] Red Rose A border of
golde ..... he ... or arme pyssed w[i]t[h] Red dragons A longe
white Rodd in his hand A Rich cheyne about his nek
And therle of derby so lorde sensely And constable of Inglond
also in A Rich gowne furred w[i]t[h] sables And woolg stach cheyne
of golde many folde about his nek also his courser Richely
trapped And armed that is to say ye ry[gh]t golde in the first
quarter A lyon gold[es] havyng A mannes hede in A bycokett of
..... And in the ... a lyon of sables And the trapper sore Right
curiously wrought w[i]t[h] the same And the mannes hede w[i]t[h] the
bicokett stonde w[i]t[h] the saddle And he gadder staff of
offys in his hand And therle of notingm .... Rode also on a noth[er]
Courser Richely trapped in A trapper of cloth of ye gold borderd
w[i]t[h] ...... And his pety staff of his offys in his hand
.... there in great estate Rode about the hall And marshall
therle marshall had great plenty of his ..... w[i]t[h] tippid stavis
to voyde the people for the preys was so great and .... that

THE HERALDS

The Office of Arms

The fifteenth century witnessed a great many important developments in the nature and status of the English herald and his office which were to have a profound effect upon his activities. These changes were not confined to the heraldic body in England, but were linked to the broader socio-political backdrop against which the officers of arms operated.[1] Thus, in July 1415, only three months before the battle of Agincourt, Henry V reinvigorated the chivalric Order of the Garter, and from this action followed the creation of the office of Garter King of Arms *c.* 1417 and the appointment to the position of one William Bruges, then Guyenne King of Arms.[2] The energetic Bruges was soon to contend that he had been granted fixed primacy in the office of arms in England – a position which had formerly rotated among the English kings of arms according to individual seniority and/or royal favour[3] – and he accordingly petitioned the king for the establishment of certain rights for his new office under letters patent.[4]

Given Henry V's abiding interest in French affairs, it is not improbable that he sought to create in Garter King of Arms a counterpart, both practical and symbolic, to the role played by 'Montjoye King of Arms of Frenchmen' in the complex theatre of war diplomacy.[5] As chief messenger in the exchange of threat and

---

[1] The best general history of the English heralds is A. R. Wagner, *Heralds of England. A History of the Office and College of Arms* (London, 1967). See also Wagner, *HH*; H. S. London, *The Life of William Bruges, the First Garter King of Arms* (London, 1970); N. Denholm-Young, *History and Heraldry, 1254–1310. A Study of the Historical Value of the Rolls of Arms* (Oxford, 1965); A. R. Wagner, 'Heraldry', in A. L. Poole (ed.), *Medieval England*, new edn, 2 vols (Oxford, 1958), i, pp. 338–81; H. Chesshyre, 'Heralds on Parade', *British Heritage*, 5.6 (1984), pp. 44–51.

[2] William Bruges was Chester Herald from 1398 to *c.* 1413 and Guyenne King of Arms to 1415. He died in 1450 and was succeeded in the office of Garter King of Arms by his son-in-law, John Smert.

[3] Wagner, *HH*, p. 36; idem, *Heralds of England*, p. 57; London, *William Bruges*, App. X, 'Doyens of the Office Arms before Garter', pp. 92–4. For contemporary references to senior kings of arms in England, see esp. *Oeuvres de Froissart publiées avec les variantes des divers manuscrits*, ed M. le Baron Kervyn de Lettenhove, 25 tomes (Brussels, 1867–77), xvii, p. 566; xv, p. 122.

[4] London, *William Bruges*, App. IX, 'William Bruges's Petition to Henry V', pp. 88–92 and esp. items 3, 7, 22, pp. 90, 92; Wagner, *Heralds of England*, p. 40.

[5] See especially J. Ferguson, *English Diplomacy: 1422–1461* (Oxford, 1972).

entreaty, and grand referee at the negotiating table, Montjoye appears to have performed a ceremonial and honorific function above that of the other heralds of France and unmatched in England before the creation of Garter King of Arms. The regular conversation with France made necessary by long-term Anglo-French hostility, and by Henry V's campaigns in particular, opened the way for the transfer of ideas regarding the body of men who were increasingly called upon to take part in the diplomatic intercourse. As far as the English heralds were concerned, too, the imitation of their French brethren, then more prosperous and more successful, must have seemed a desirable course of action.

The influence of French models upon the character of the new office of Garter King of Arms is, moreover, indicative of a unique internationalism of outlook and conduct that had come to characterise the heraldic professions in England and France. By 1400, if not earlier, the diplomatic status and immunity of English and French heralds was widely recognised, and the heralds regarded themselves in some sense as part of an international fraternity, bound by like interests and a common professional code.[6] At the opening of the fifteenth century, however, the heralds of both nations appear to have been of widely varying status and reputation, and there was some feeling among the more critically-minded officers of the time that their profession had fallen prey to the evils of abuse. This was particularly the case in France, where the vagabond herald thrived and where Anjou King of Arms and Sicily Herald, in turn, wrote scathingly of the over-abundance of pursuivants in France and the permeation of the office by 'spies, liars and disloyal tale-tellers'.[7]

If the heraldic troubles in England embodied in Bruges's petition to Henry V were less by comparison to those in France, there is nevertheless evidence of a similar concern for the reform of the office of arms in England. Although they had to wait more than half a century for their own legal incorporation, the English Crown heralds were already a cohesive, specialist organisation that clearly stood to benefit from the French example.[8] Bruges's own petition called for stricter royal control over the profession in England and closer monitoring of the character and conduct of its practitioners, as well as for the introduction of royal largess at the principal feasts of the year, in deliberate imitation of the practice in France.[9] Yet, despite Bruges's valiant attempts to secure great privilege and power to his new office (for Bruges's petition was, indeed, greatly concerned with his own *ex officio* authority),[10] and despite the potential for the establishment of a senior herald

[6] Wagner, *Heralds of England*, p. 43.
[7] Wagner, *Heralds of England*, p. 45; Bodl., MS. Rawlinson C. 399, fols 76–80; Wagner, *HH*, pp. 41–5.
[8] A. R. Wagner, *The Records and Collections of the College of Arms* (London, 1952), p. 9.
[9] London, *William Bruges*, App. IX, 'Petition', item 20, p. 92.
[10] London, *William Bruges*, pp. 17–18 and App. IX, 'Petition'; *The Antiquary*, 16 (December, 1887), p. 5.

with fixed powers over the developing heraldic hierarchy in England, there appears from the first to have been difficulty in the position of Garter King of Arms *vis à vis* the other kings of arms of England. Unlike Norroy and Clarenceux King of Arms, who exercised authority north and south of the Trent respectively, the non-provincial Garter King of Arms, his jurisdiction 'broad but dangerously ill-defined', boasted 'only the dignity of his connection with the Order of the Garter and the House of Lords and a vague suzerainty over all England which he found difficult to make of any effect.'[11] Royal priorities lay elsewhere at this time and three centuries were to pass before the disputed limits of his jurisdiction were fixed.[12]

Nevertheless, the institution of Garter King of Arms and William Bruges's petition to Henry V were followed within a few years by certain positive steps toward the reform and regulation of the body of heralds in England, including the king's own strictures against the wearing of coats of arms by unqualified persons in June 1417.[13] By the end of January 1420, a chapter of the kings of arms and heralds of England held at Rouen had further resolved that a common seal be created and that the officers of arms swear to uphold a set of resolutions then formulated: all heralds thereafter appointed were required to take an oath of obedience to the constitution before partaking of largess, fees and other rewards.[14] The tendency toward corporate existence exhibited at this time was sustained by three aspects of the heralds' activities: the partition of fees paid to the office as a whole, the regulation of professional conduct, and the preservation of their books of record. As A. R. Wagner rightly noted, the last two of these could hardly have been effected without it.[15]

In the late 1470s, Richard duke of Gloucester, Constable of England and active co-supervisor of the heralds since 1469, promulgated a series of ordinances which emphasised the heralds' duties in recording noble and knightly deeds.[16] In what was perhaps the earliest formal directive for the documentation of ceremonial by English heralds it was decreed that:

> all manner of solemn occasions, solemn acts and deeds of the nobility, those concerned with the deeds of arms as well as others, be truthfully and indifferently recorded ...[17]

[11] Wagner, *Heralds of England*, p. 65; Denholm-Young, *History and Heraldry*, p. 61.
[12] Wagner, *HH*, p. 63.
[13] Wagner, *Heralds of England*, p. 66.
[14] Wagner, *Heralds of England*, p. 68; London, *William Bruges*, App. XII, 'Minutes of a Chapter of English Heralds held at Rouen on 5 January, 1420', pp. 98–107.
[15] Wagner, *Heralds of England*, p. 69.
[16] These ordinances have traditionally been attributed to the duke of Clarence, brother of Henry V, Steward of England and Constable of the Army. See Wagner, *HH*, pp. 59–63 and, for doubts on the role of Clarence, idem, *Heralds of England*, pp. 67–8. The text of the ordinances is printed in Wagner, *HH*, App. C, 'Ordinances of Thomas, Duke of Clarence, for the Government of the Office of Arms', pp. 136–8.
[17] Translation from A. F. Sutton and L. Visser-Fuchs, *Richard III's Books: Ideals and Real-*

The concept was neither original nor peculiarly English. Froissart, Anjou King of Arms, and Dame Prudentia in the fictitious *Débat des Hérauts* had each had something to say about the recording of deeds of arms by heralds in the fourteenth and early-fifteenth centuries.[18] Nevertheless, as Sutton and Visser-Fuchs have pointed out, each generation needed reminders,[19] and the formalisation of this requirement perhaps marked a new departure for the heralds.

On 2 March 1484, Richard III, sometime duke of Gloucester, granted the English officers of arms their first charter of incorporation.[20] Like so many of London's craft guilds, the heralds were moving with the times in the prosperous and pomp-rich capital, and they appear to have enjoyed the king's favour. Like the minstrels before them and perhaps too the inns of court, the act of incorporation, extending as it did to all heralds of England, allowed them strict control over their craft and the right of veto over would-be practitioners. Yet, the charter's primary purpose was probably to qualify the twelve royal heralds for their corporate ownership of the manor house of Coldharbour in the city of London. Formerly inhabited by royalty, Coldharbour House provided a meeting place for the royal heralds, workrooms for the kings of arms, and a common library for all. Its grant to the English heralds was a mark of royal recognition and its importance to the 'advancement and cultivation of their faculty' is inestimable.[21] As principal king of arms, Garter John Writhe was granted the oversight of the manor house and of the sizeable and rapidly growing library held therein.

Heraldic Activities

The officers of arms of the Yorkist Crown were essentially liminal functionaries, who operated both within and outside the structures of the royal household and were able to move with relative ease between the institution's several departments. At court their ceremonial duties were paramount: they organised and supervised coronations and other royal events, and presided over the celebration of the solemn feasts of Christmas, Easter and the like. Away from court they worked as genealogists, and as surveyors and correctors of armorial bearings, and they had frequent business in the Court of Chivalry under the Constable and Mar-

---

ity in the Life and Library of a Medieval Prince (Stroud, 1997), p. 185.

[18] *Chroniques de J. Froissart*, ed. Siméon Luce, Société de l'histoire de France, 15 vols (1869), i, p. 209; Bodl., MS. Rawlinson C. 399, fols 77v, 79; *Le Débat des Hérauts d'armes de France et d'Angleterre*, ed. L. C. A. Pannier and M. P. H. Meyer (Paris, 1877), p. 1. I am grateful to Maurice Keen for drawing these examples to my attention.

[19] Sutton and Visser-Fuchs, *Richard III's Books*, p. 185.

[20] *CPR*, 1476–85, p. 422; BL, MS. Cotton Faustina E. I, fol. 2 (printed with facing translation in G. D. Squibb (ed.), *Munimenta Heraldica 1484–1984*, Harleian Soc., n.s., 4 (1985), pp. 14–19).

[21] Wagner, *HH*, p. 95.

INTRODUCTION: THE HERALDS

shal of England.²² In addition royal heralds, and occasionally their seigneurial counterparts, were employed outside the palace in tasks which were nevertheless undertaken on behalf of the king and his advisors.

Disappointingly little is said of the heralds in the extant literature of the late Plantagenet household.²³ Alone of the surviving documents the discursive *Black Book* of the household of Edward IV reveals that the heralds of the Crown had customary occasional duties at court, falling on the principal feast days of All Hallows, Christmas Day, Easter, St George's Day and Whitsunday, as well as at the solemnities of coronation, baptism, marriage, creation and funeral, and even for their own inductions.²⁴ In part-payment for their duties, English heralds were entitled to an allowance and privileges at the expense of the king and court: as early as 1415 William Bruges had declared it customary for Garter King of Arms to dine apart in the king's hall, with the ordinary officers of arms seated at their own table and the pursuivants at the varlets' table.²⁵ In addition to food in the hall, officers of arms received so-called *bouche of court* – a commons of bread, ale, candles and fuel, typically supplied to household officers of sufficient standing to be lodged within the palace itself. Kings of arms received provision for their horses.²⁶ For much of the fifteenth century, too, select heralds were seemingly in attendance at court at all times for the royal household ordinance of 1445 testifies to the continued presence of three *herlautz*.²⁷

---

[22] M. H. Keen, *The Laws of War in the Later Middle Ages* (London, 1965), p. 16 and chapter 3; Wagner, *Heralds of England*, pp. 37–9.

[23] The household ordinances for the years 1445 and 1478, the household provisions of 1471, and the *Black Book* of the household of Edward IV are printed in *The Household of Edward IV: the Black Book and Ordinance of 1478*, ed. A. R. Myers (Manchester, 1959). A household ordinance for the year 1454 is printed in *PO*, vi, pp. 220–33 and in *OHR*, pp. 13–24, where it is incorrectly dated to 1455. There also survive ordinances for the households of George duke of Clarence, Princess Cecily (mother of Edward IV), and Prince Edward (son of Edward IV) in *OHR*, vi, pp. 87–105, 25–33, 35–9, and for Richard III's household in the North in C. A. Halsted, *Richard III as Duke of Gloucester and King of England*, 2 vols (London, 1844), ii, p. 524.

[24] Myers, *Black Book*, item 51, p. 130.

[25] London, *William Bruges*, App. IX, 'Petition', articles 6–8, pp. 90–1. Kings of arms generally received a knight's service at dinner, and Garter a baron's service; Wagner, *Heralds of England*, p. 97; *The Antiquary*, xvi, p. 5. The officers of arms of Edward IV were entitled, on feast days, to dine in the hall according to the marshal's seating arrangement; *Black Book*, item 51, p. 130.

[26] *Black Book*, item 51, p. 130; E. K. Chambers, *The Elizabethan Stage*, 2 vols (Oxford, 1923; repr. 1967), ii, p. 51.

[27] 'Ordinance of 1445', in Myers, *Household*, p. 70. Since the Ordinance of 1478 chiefly represents a series of *addenda* for defects in the Ordinance of 1445, it may be assumed that its silence on the matter of the officers of arms implies the continuance of the heralds' waiting function at court during the latter half of the fifteenth century.

Despite modern difference of opinion on the relationship between the officers of arms and the fifteenth-century royal household,[28] it seems that the heralds' duties at court increasingly resembled, even encroached upon, certain aspects of the work of the king's chamber. Simultaneously the centre of power and the most direct expression of the king's style and personality, the chamber was that great complex headed by the chamberlain and centred around the king's dwellings. By the fifteenth century it comprised a number of specialist and individually articulated organisations and it had its central component in the non-affiliated personnel of the knights, esquires of the body, carvers, cupbearers, and sewers, gentlemen and yeomen ushers, and yeomen, grooms and pages of the chamber.[29] The collective function of the chamber staffs lay not merely in politics, 'but partly in the enactment of show of ceremonial "magnificence", partly also in those group activities which fostered a sense of courtly culture with its distinctive mores'.[30] While the chamber's many businesses included the financial, political and administrative, it determined above all the shadow cast by the king's household on both the socio-political realm of England and the external world at large. This had scarcely ever been more the case than during the reign of Edward IV.

An increase in their own formal responsibilities at the Edwardian court, combined with the need to keep abreast of the difficult ceremonial and chivalric developments of the fifteenth century, were almost certainly the primary factors urging the English Crown heralds toward the keeping of detailed notes and descriptive accounts of the events in which they took part and for which they received fee. It is from surviving heraldic accounts and supplementary evidence that we learn much about the English heralds' activities and preoccupations during the fifteenth century. The accounts of Lord Scales's ride through the streets of London in 1467 before his combat with Antoine, 'Bastard' of Burgundy, the nuptial procession of Princess Margaret of York in Bruges in 1468, the creation of the Lord Gruthuse as earl of Winchester in 1472, and the christening of Princess Bridget in 1480 each accords the officers of arms conspicuous and elaborate processional roles.[31] Hav-

[28] See for example Chambers, *Elizabethan Stage*, i, p. 33; Wagner, *Heralds of England*, p. 125; D. A. L. Morgan, 'The house of policy: the political role of the late Plantagenet household, 1422–1485', in D. Starkey et al., *The English court: from the Wars of the Roses to the Civil War* (London and New York, 1987), p. 33; R. F. Green, *Poets and Princepleasers. Literature and the English Court in the Late Middle Ages* (Toronto, 1980), pp. 34–7.

[29] Morgan, 'House of Policy', p. 33.

[30] Morgan, 'House of Policy', p. 34. See also, D. Starkey, 'Representation through Intimacy. A Study in the Symbolism of Monarchy and Court Office in Early Modern England', in I. Lewis (ed.), *Symbols and Sentiments. Cross-cultural Studies in Symbolism* (London, 1977), pp. 187–224; M. Vale, *The Princely Court. Medieval Courts and Culture in North-West Europe, 1270–1380* (Oxford, 2001), pp. 56–68.

[31] 'Marriage of the Princess Margaret, Sister of Edward IV, A.D. 1468', in S. Bentley (ed.), *Excerpta Historica*, pp. 223–39; 'Account of the Ceremonial of the Marriage of the

ing assisted the marshal at coronations since the thirteenth century, too, the officers of arms were also integral to the processions that accompanied the crowning of fifteenth-century English monarchs.[32]

The heralds' appearance in processions like these, typically bearing the coat of arms of the king or nobleman for whom the occasion was held, not only integrated them into the ceremonial they were required to supervise, but also proclaimed the legitimacy of the procession and the authority of its principal protagonist. Moreover, the very inclusion of the royal heralds in these processions effectively signified the omnipresence of the English Crown. This was especially notable in the heraldic noble funeral, where the presence of the royal heralds was, according to one historian, 'a salient reminder to all present of the origins of aristocratic power.'[33]

Of course, far more complex duties also informed the royal heralds' participation in ceremonial rights of passage like marriages, coronations, christenings, funerals and elevations to knighthood. In royal and noble funerals of the second half of the fifteenth century, their pre-eminent function was to marshal the procession itself and carry the armour of the deceased.[34] In the earliest surviving evidence of the heralds' role in the funeral *cortège*, an account of the re-interment of Richard Neville, earl of Salisbury, and his son Thomas in February 1463, the chariot bearing the corpses toward the town of Bisham was accompanied by two kings of arms and two heralds, one at each corner of the hearse, wearing Salisbury's coat of arms. During the singing of the dirge that same day, and in the ritual of presentment and offering on the morrow, Garter and Clarenceux Kings of Arms, Windsor and Chester Heralds, and other officers of arms of the Crown each enacted a special ritual. At the ceremony's end the coat of arms, shield, sword, and helm and crest were laid upon the tomb.[35] Such was the splendour of this event

---

Princess Margaret, Sister of King Edward the Fourth, to Charles Duke of Burgundy, in 1468', ed. Sir Thomas Phillipps, *Archaeologica*, 31 (1846), pp. 326–38; 'The Record of Bluemantle Pursuivant, 1471–1472', in C. L. Kingsford, *English Historical Literature in the Fifteenth Century* (Oxford, 1913), pp. 378–83; 'Princess Bridget', ed. P. E. Routh in *The Ricardian*, 3.49 (1975), pp. 13–14.

[32] The contribution of John Smert, Garter King of Arms, and of his fellow officers to the coronation of Elizabeth Woodville in 1465 was liberally rewarded: *The Coronation of Elizabeth Wydeville, Queen Consort of Edward IV, on May 26th, 1465*, ed. G. Smith (London, 1935). See also the account of the coronation of Elizabeth of York in Julius B. XII (pp. 131–52).

[33] C. Gittings, *Death, Burial and the Individual in Early Modern England* (London and Sydney, 1984), p. 174.

[34] Wagner, *Heralds of England*, p. 106. This duty appears originally have belonged to noblemen and knights before the introduction of heralds to the funeral *cortège*: M. Vale, *War and Chivalry. Warfare and Aristocratic Culture in England, France and Burgundy at the End of the Middle Ages* (Athens, Georgia, 1981), p. 90.

[35] BL, MSS. Harley 6069, fols 34–35, Arundel 26, fol. 33, Add. 38174, fols 22–22v; Coll. Arms

that it entered books of precedent as the model for the burying of an earl in the latter half of the fifteenth century and continued to inform English heralds for more than fifty years.[36]

The heralds' specialisation in armorial bearings, and in the genealogical concerns with which the science of armoury was linked, also formed the basis of pictorial records which became more sophisticated toward the end of the fifteenth century but which had their genesis in the earliest period of heraldry. Surviving English rolls of arms date from the reign of Edward I and, in the early days at least, a great many heralds were likely to have been better at pictorial representation than written record. It has been suggested that the lavish Neville funeral described above was the occasion of the creation of the so-called Salisbury Roll of Arms, a pictorial and genealogical record glorifying the ancestors and alliances of several earls of Salisbury. The great compilation to which the Salisbury Roll of Arms now belongs, *Writhe's Garter Book* (compiled 1484–88), also contains a vivid, blow-by-blow pictorial 'essay' on the creation of knights of the Bath, a work which both depicts the ritual ceremonial for which it was created and guides its future replication.[37]

The ancient arena of war was equally compelling for the officers of arms of Yorkist England, and it continued to draw them not only into the mire of the battlefield itself, or at least onto the field's outskirts, but increasingly also into the exclusivist worlds of diplomacy and chivalry that accompanied the militarism. Heralds on the battlefield were expected to take down extensive lists of participants and casualties of war, that is to:

> inquire in the day of battle who has shown prouesse and courage, in act or in counsel, and to record the names of the dead and the wounded, and whether they were in the van or the rear ... that there may be honour to whom honour is due.[38]

Elsewhere, they were instructed to observe banners and ensigns on the field; to exhort the lords of their own party to honourable conduct; to withdraw to a safe vantage point to observe the battle; to announce the victory; to help bury the dead; and to carry prisoners' requests.[39] By the time Henry VI and Edward IV were

---

MSS. I.5, fols 7–7v; I.11, fol. 35v, I.15, fol. 215v; 'The Beryinge of an Erle', in *Antiquarian Repertory*, comp. F. Grose and T. Astle, n.e., ed. E. Jeffrey, 4 vols (London, 1807–9), i, pp. 314–17; 'Henry VII's Ordinances', in *OHR*, pp. 131–3. See also D. Rowland, *An Historical and Genealogical Account of the Noble Family of Neville* (London, 1830), p. 83.

[36] A. Payne, 'The Salisbury Rolls of Arms, c. 1463', in D. Williams (ed.), *England in the Fifteenth Century. Proceedings of the 1986 Harlaxton Symposium* (Woodbridge, 1987), p. 187. The account was still being copied by English heralds in the first half of the sixteenth century. See especially the transcript in Coll. Arms, MS. M6, fols 79v–80.

[37] MS in the possession of the Duke of Buccleuch, formerly BL, MS. Loan 90.

[38] BL, MS. Stowe 688, fol. 79v.

[39] Coll. Arms, MS. M.19, fol. 140.

INTRODUCTION: THE HERALDS

engaged in the struggle for the throne, English royal heralds numbered among the compilers of newsletters dispatched from the field in haste, often before complete casualty lists or outcome of the campaign were known. There can be little doubt that the heralds' expertise in the science of armoury served them well in the aftermath of combat, when the faces of the slain must scarcely have been recognisable.

Officers of arms of the Crown also performed basic messenger service, an early heraldic function doubtless greatly encouraged by the ongoing civil strife of the middle decades of the fifteenth century.[40] Although the prominence of noble factions in England's internecine warring meant that the Crown officers often had to compete with the likes of Mowbray Herald and Lesparre Pursuivant, Garter John Smert (d. 1477) became an active messenger and war-correspondent to both Henry VI and Edward IV.[41] His lower-ranking colleagues were frequently employed as battle-messengers and letter-carriers.[42] During the infamous siege of Bamburgh Castle in 1464, the incumbent of the now defunct royal office of Chester Herald, together with the seigneurial Warwick Herald, carried communications to and from the rebellious Sir Ralph Grey.[43]

On the international stage the heralds' messenger service roughly translated into an ambassadorial function, and evidence attests to a number of diplomatic excursions undertaken by royal heralds of Yorkist England. Although the distinction between heraldic diplomacy and their more traditional function of messengers of war and peace is in many cases largely academic, weighty diplomatic responsibility numbered among the heralds' legitimate duties as early as the reign of Edward III. It continued to inform their sense of identity well into the reign of Henry VIII. Courier service and the accompaniment of ambassadors remained the

---

[40] For discussion of the heralds' messenger services in the royal household during the fourteenth and early fifteenth century, see P. Chaplais, *English Diplomatic Practice in the Middle Ages* (London and New York, 2003), p. 136.

[41] Mowbray Herald belonged to the duke of Norfolk and Lesparre Pursuivant to the duke of Exeter. Mowbray and Lesparre, together with Buckingham Herald, were instrumental in the mediations between Yorkist and royal forces at the battle of St. Albans in 1455: 'An account of the first battle of St. Albans from a contemporary manuscript', ed. J. Bayley in *Archaeologia*, 20 (1824), pp. 519–23; C. A. J. Armstrong, 'Politics and the Battle of St Albans, 1455', in C. A. J. Armstrong, *England, France and Burgundy in the Fifteenth Century* (London, 1983), p. 4; B. P. Wolffe, *Henry VI* (repr. London, 2001), pp. 132, 152, 164–5, 318.

[42] Similar roles seem to have been undertaken by Scottish heralds, as demonstrated in *British Library Harleian Manuscript 433*, ed. R. Horrox and P. W. Hammond, 4 vols (Gloucester, 1983), iii, pp. 48, 50.

[43] *Warkworth's Chronicle of the first Thirteen Years of the Reign of King Edward the Fourth*, ed. J. O. Halliwell, Camden Soc., o.s., 10 (1839), pp. 36–9. Heralds were also openly and symbolically involved in Grey's degradation. See F. Pilbrow, 'The Knights of the Bath: Dubbing to Knighthood in Lancastrian and Yorkist England', in P. R. Coss and M. H. Keen, *Heraldry, Pageantry and Social Display in Medieval England* (Woodbridge, 2002), pp. 195–218.

heralds' most common diplomatic duties during the fifteenth century – indeed, officers of arms were regarded as the normal diplomatic couriers by the reign of Henry VI – yet they did on occasion have powers, instructions or letters of credence.[44] A white rod symbolised their unique personal immunity from war and reprisals.[45]

The dramatic rise of the heralds in the middle years of Edward III's reign and the development of *le noble office d'armes* as an efficacious international confederacy was in large measure consequent upon the heralds' diplomatic and military excursions from the mid-thirteenth century onwards, and likewise upon their role as 'professional exponents of an international code of manners, that of knighthood or chivalry'. The tenets of this code defined conduct in peace and war, in truce or formal defiance, and in the treatment of prisoners.[46] Henry VI employed Fleur-de-Lis Herald to treat with the French, while Garter John Smert appears to have specialised in Anglo-Burgundian affairs under Edward IV.[47] Moreover, the chivalric Order of the Garter was integral to the foreign policy of English kings, and the incumbents of the office of Garter King of Arms, from William Bruges in the early fifteenth century to Thomas Wriothesley under Henry VIII, undertook many international excursions. Certain of these missions, most notably the investiture of foreign princes with the insignia of the Garter, were attached directly and exclusively to the Order.[48]

By the latter half of the fifteenth century heralds also presided over that complex chivalric spirit that governed the mock-warfare of the tournament in the fifteenth-century. If employment as messengers and marshals of the *praeludium bellorum* tournaments of old had numbered among the English heralds' most

---

[44] Ferguson, *English Diplomacy*, pp. 166–7; Wagner, *HH*, pp. 37–8; *LP*, ii, pp. 292–7; Horrox and Hammond, *Harl. 433*, iii, p. 71; R. de Maulde, 'Les Instructions diplomatiques au Moyen-Age', *Revue d'histoire diplomatique*, vi (1892), p. 433; Chaplais, *English Diplomatic Practice*, p. 140. See also Upton's, *De studio militari*, most recently printed in C. G. Walker, 'An edition with introduction and commentary of John Blount's English translation of Nicholas Upton's *De studio militari*', unpublished D.Phil. thesis, Oxford University (1998), which suggests that a herald was 'to initiate negotiations for peace and matrimonial alliance between princes and to report faithfully his missions.' One late fifteenth-century illustration depicts the 'Ambassador of Britain' as a herald of the English Crown: Wagner, *Heralds of England*, p. 15.

[45] Keen, *The Laws of War*, pp. 109, 194–6; Chaplais, *English Diplomatic Practice*, pp. 16, 139.

[46] Wagner *Heralds of England*, p. 43; Chaplais, *English Diplomatic Practice*, p. 139.

[47] Adrian Ailes, 'Heraldry in Medieval England: Symbols of Politics and Propaganda', in Coss and Keen, *Heraldry, Pageantry*, p. 93; W. H. Godfrey et al., *The College of Arms* (London, 1963), pp. 40–1. Examples of heralds on international missions from 1375–1402 are cited in Chaplais, *English Diplomatic Practice*, pp. 139–40.

[48] Hugh E. L. Collins, *The Order of the Garter, 1348–1461: Chivalry and Politics in Late Medieval England* (Oxford, 2000), p. 162.

primitive functions (a duty they shared with the minstrels), by c. 1450 they had long been involved in the development of formal tournament organisation, and were now stewards and judges of the pageantic, courtly *hastiludes*.[49] The chivalric culture which reached its apogee under the Valois dukes of Burgundy exerted an irresistible pull on King Edward IV of England and his court, and was spectacularly manifest in the Anglo-Burgundian feats of arms of the 1460s and '70s. In 1467 the great Smithfield tournament between Anthony Woodville, Lord Scales and brother-in-law to the king, and Antoine, count of La Roche, served as a pretext for the conclusion of the marriage negotiations for Margaret of York and Duke Charles 'the Bold'. The following year the magnificent *Pas de l'Arbre d'Or* was held in honour of the wedding. Such occasions were lavish, their ritual formalities and minute rules of procedure each supervised, on both sides of the Channel, by those 'experts pour déterminer les règles du combat et pour contrôler les armes et les armures des combatants.'[50]

Occasions like the Anglo-Burgundian tournament at Smithfield in the summer of 1467 must also have furthered the flow into England of ideas regarding the heralds' own profession. As was the case in English society at large, French models had now largely ceased to guide the increasingly corporate-minded English heralds who doubtless saw more that was instructive in the company of heralds serving the ceremonially avaricious dukes of Burgundy. The highly institutionalised court of Charles the Bold appears to have included a college of heralds, complete with five or six kings of arms (including Garter's counterpart *Toison d'or*), seven or eight heralds, and four pursuivants.[51] Closely associated with the Order of the Golden Fleece, the ducal heralds had organised, supervised, and recorded court pageantry and chivalric display for some hundred years before Charles the Bold's accession.[52] Perhaps, too, the renewed importance of the tournament on a

---

[49] Wagner, *Heralds of England*, pp. 2–5; Juliet R. V. Barker, *The Tournament in England, 1100–1400* (Suffolk and New Hampshire, 1986), pp. 3, 14, 102, 104, 108, 144; David Crouch, *Tournament* (Hambleton and London, 2005), pp. 63–5. The emphasis on the pageantry of the later tournament is discussed in detail in Barker, *Tournament*, chapter 5, pp. 84–111.

[50] C. A. J. Armstrong, 'L'échange culturel entre les courts d'Angleterre et de Bourgogne à l'époque de Charles le Téméraire', in Armstrong, *England, France and Burgundy*, p. 406; S. Anglo, 'Anglo-Burgundian Feats of Arms: Smithfield, June 1467', *Guildhall Miscellany*, 2:7 (1965), p. 272; Vale, *War and Chivalry*, pp. 67–8, 70, 85; R. Vaughan, *Valois Burgundy* (London, 1975), p. 177.

[51] Vaughan, *Valois Burgundy*, p. 97; idem, *Charles the Bold: the Last Valois Duke of Burgundy*, new edn (Woodbridge, 2002), p. 193; J. Calmette, *The Golden Age of Burgundy: the Magnificent Dukes and Their Courts*, new edn (London, 2001), p. 229.

[52] In 1430 Jehan Lefèvre, a herald of Duke Philip 'the Good', wrote a detailed, quasi-official account of his master's marriage to Isabel of Portugal: Vaughan, *Valois Burgundy*, p. 177. In 1473 the famous meeting at Trier between the duke of Burgundy and Emperor Frederick III became the subject of a widely disseminated narrative, known

scale not seen in England since the reign of Edward III heightened the urgency and envy with which the English heralds, and Anglo-Burgundian specialists like John Smert in particular, observed their ducal peers.[53]

By the time the heralds of the English Crown received their first charter of incorporation in 1484, they had reached new importance and skill in their work for the English court. They were the acknowledged masters of ceremonial in a practical sense and the publicity and marketing officers for an institution increasingly concerned with its public image, and they were uniquely responsible for the genealogical and armorial expertise on which were founded the badges and emblems that proclaimed the ascendancy of the House of York.[54] Indeed, their own incorporation has elsewhere been linked with the importance of ceremonial to the Yorkist kings of England.[55] The contrast between the heralds' activities under Edward IV and Richard III and their work under Henry VI is striking, as is the absence before the 1460s of anything like the corpus of narrative accounts that bulked large under the Yorkist kings. If the 'administrative mechanisms' by which the heralds' manifold skills were 'harnessed to the needs of public-image making' at the Yorkist court are not entirely evident to the modern observer, there is nevertheless a clear sense in which the heralds themselves required a reliable body of materials for the regulation of their manifold preoccupations.[56] The expectation that the heralds would keep some form of written record of events at court had been signalled in the late 1470s, if not earlier.

Heraldic Narratives

The narrative records penned by the English heralds belong to a distinct and important genre of which relatively little has been said by present-day scholars. While great interest was shown during the nineteenth and early twentieth centuries in the historical utility of certain individual narratives, scholars have adopted a dismissive approach to the writings as a group, as was demonstrated in 1913 by C. L. Kingsford's reference to 'little [for the Yorkist period] of a strictly contemporary character, except some records of state ceremonies drawn up by heralds or court officials'.[57] There have been only two modern articles dealing with the

---

in England less than twelve months later: *Paston Letters and Papers*, i, p. 592; Vaughan, *Charles the Bold*, pp. 141–4.

[53] The account of the marriage celebrations for Richard duke of York in 1477 demonstrates the influence of Burgundian armorial developments upon the English tournaments: G. Kipling, *The Triumph of Honour: Burgundian Origins of the Elizabethan Renaissance* (The Hague, 1977), pp. 123–5.

[54] Anglo, *Images*, pp. 29–30.

[55] C. A. J. Armstrong, 'The Inauguration Ceremonies of the Yorkist Kings and Their Title to the Throne', in Armstrong, *England, France and Burgundy*, p. 73.

[56] Anglo, *Images*, pp. 30.

[57] Kingsford, *English Historical Literature*, p. 178. See also M. H. Keen, 'Chivalry, Heralds

INTRODUCTION: THE HERALDS

subject of an heraldic narrative genre.[58] Yet, the corpus of extant heraldic accounts from the second half of the fifteenth century represents not only a valuable source of materials for the study of court life and heraldic preoccupation at the time, but also a critically important context for our understanding of the court memoir edited below.

Often little more than a sequence of memoranda written in the vernacular and bound by a loose narrative thread, many of the extant heraldic accounts appear to be 'unpublished', in-house reports not designed for a readership outside the body of English heralds and their associates, and housed in manuscripts that range from scribal fair copies to the roughest of note-books compiled in the heralds' own hands. They are typically created from notes made at the event, and several of the surviving accounts still contain blank spaces for names, dates and further details; others are supplemented by memory or hearsay; most are compiled in the unadorned, slightly repetitious language of minutes or journal entries; almost all appear to have functioned in the first instance as works of record or precedent in the 'complex and contentious world of ceremony and chivalry'.[59] As one modern scholar has already pointed out, the extant corpus of heraldic narrative accounts may be divided into a number of different subject categories,[60] and these categories clearly also derive from the manifold preoccupations of the English heralds during the fifteenth century and earlier.

Several of the heralds' narratives which survive today are closely associated with their duties on the field of battle. It is perhaps not surprising that battle narratives number among those few surviving texts that pre-date the first reign of Edward IV, for the exercise of the heralds' traditional battlefield duties must have been greatly encouraged by that 'broken sequence of battles, murders, executions, and armed clashes between neighbours' that beset fifteenth-century England.[61] Among the heralds' duties in war was the recording of the names of participants and of the injured and the dead, and on occasion such lists were worked into loose accounts of the battles for which they were compiled. In certain cases these lists and accounts appear to have functioned as newsletters dispatched from the field even as casualties were still being identified.

---

and History', in R. H. C. Davies and J. M. Wallace-Hadrill (ed.), *The Writing of History in the Middle Ages: Essays Presented to Richard William Southern* (Oxford, 1981), pp. 393–414.

[58] G. A. Lester, 'Fifteenth-Century Heraldic Narrative', *Yearbook of English Studies*, 22 (1992), pp. 201–12; idem, 'The Literary Activity of Medieval English Heralds', *English Studies*, 71 (1990), pp. 222–9. The subject is also addressed in Sutton and Visser-Fuchs, *Richard III's Books*, esp. pp. 178–84.

[59] M. J. Bennett, *Lambert Simnel and the Battle of Stoke* (Gloucester, 1987), p. 10.

[60] Lester, 'Heraldic Narrative', p. 202.

[61] K. B. McFarlane, 'The Wars of the Roses', in K. B. McFarlane, *England in the Fifteenth Century. Collected Essays*, ed. G. L. Harris (London, 1981), p. 231.

An account of the first battle of St. Albans in 1455, between the forces of Henry VI and those of the duke of York and the earls of Warwick and Salisbury, is characteristic of such reports.[62] Written up very soon after the event, it comprises a summary of King Henry's strategy, a list of those assembled on either side, the text of letters carried between the contending parties, a version of the speech of the duke of York to his council of war, a summary of the skirmish itself, a list of the slain (including the duke of Somerset and the earl of Northumberland), a list of the injured (the king, struck in the neck with an arrow), a brief list of the craven who fled the field (the earl of Wiltshire and others), and a notice of the resolution of the conflict. So soon after the battle was this report dispatched that the list of casualties to hand lacked for twenty-five names 'not [y]et knowen'.[63]

In contrast, it was a comprehensive list of the battle-dead at Tewkesbury in 1471, together with precise details of their places of burial, that found its way into the *Chronicle of Tewksbury Abbey* soon after its compilation, and was almost certainly the work of a herald on the field, and ostensibly one with Lancastrian sympathies.[64] The dead included Prince Edward, 'slayne and buryed in ye mydste of ye covent quiere in ye monastery ther', Edmund duke of Somerset, captured and beheaded, and Thomas Courtenay earl of Devon, Lord John Somerset and Sir Humphrey Audley, each killed in the fray. The deposed Queen Margaret and the Princess Anne were among those brought before King Edward and pardoned in the aftermath of the battle.[65]

Another, more detailed, account tells of Edward IV's suppression of rebellion in Northumberland in 1464.[66] As a series of loosely-linked memoranda, this account comprises a description of the siege of Bamburgh and the deployment of ordnance, a verbatim account of the exchanges between Chester and Warwick Heralds and the rebellious Ralph Grey, and a graphic version of the speech of the earl of Worcester, Constable of England, in condemning Grey to public degradation and execution.

Peace-time matters were also the focus of heraldic reportage, especially from the latter half of the fifteenth century. The record for the years 1471 and 1472, left by an unknown incumbent of the office of Bluemantle Pursuivant, is of interest for its description of domestic and foreign affairs in England, and for the apparent inti-

---

[62] Bayley, 'First Battle of St. Albans', pp. 519–23. This account may well have been compiled from, or alongside, the list of combatants at St. Albans located among the Paston papers compiled by Gairdner. See *Paston Letters*, n.c.e., pp. 29–30.
[63] Bayley, 'First Battle of St Albans', p. 523.
[64] 'From a Chronicle of Tewkesbury Abbey, 1471', in Kingsford, *English Historical Literature*, pp. 377–8.
[65] Halliwell, *Warkworth's Chronicle*, pp. 29–30.
[66] Coll. Arms, MS. L.9, fols 19v–20 (in the hand of Thomas Wriothesley, d. 1534) and L.15, fols 32–33v (in the hand of Robert Glover, d. 1588); BL, MS. Harley 6069, fol. 60; Halliwell, *Warkworth's Chronicle*, pp. 36–9.

INTRODUCTION: THE HERALDS

macy of its compiler with the daily life of the court.[67] Comprising a number of brief, bald notices, together with passages of more detailed description, Bluemantle's record is chiefly concerned with the activities of King Edward's court: the celebration of Christmas in 1471 and New Year and Epiphany in 1472; the departure from Winchelsea of the English ambassadorial party (with Bluemantle among them) in April 1472, and its arrival on the Continent; Bluemantle's own ride to meet Charles the Bold; and finally the reception of Louis de Gruthuse in England and his creation as earl of Winchester. As a piecemeal composition, apparently compiled from eye-witness detail over a two-year period, the record of Bluemantle Pursuivant is characterised by a notable rawness of reportage and heterogeneity of subject matter.

By far the most numerous and diverse of the surviving heraldic accounts from the latter half of the fifteenth century are records of individual ceremonies or public events in which the heralds took part and for which they received payment. Coronations, christenings, marriage celebrations, state visits, tournaments and other associated festivities, each organised and supervised by the officers of arms of the Crown, and occasionally also by private heralds, provided abundant grist for a herald-recorder's mill. From the list of short notes on the baptismal procession for Princess Bridget (1480) to the numerous funeral narratives of the house of York, to the lengthy, blow-by-blow accounts of the marriage festivities of Margaret of York (1468) and Richard duke of York (1477), the extant accounts vary greatly in length, style and descriptive elaboration.[68] Those records that survive doubtless also reflect the differing priorities and calibre of their authors.

The extant accounts of Yorkist marriage festivities recall the ceremonial detail, the identity and appearance of chief participants, and the fantastic *pas d'armes* with which royal marriages were typically celebrated during the reign of Edward IV. The account of the marriage of Margaret of York is probably the work of a herald attendant upon the princess herself, and it traces her experiences during the weeks preceding her marriage, as she made her stately progress from London to Stratford Priory with a great company of noble persons, offered her devotions at Canterbury, resided at Margate, sailed into the harbour at Sluys and, finally, married the Duke of Burgundy on the morning of Sunday 10 July, 1468. While Princess Margaret's herald deliberately omitted from his account the nine days of jousting at Bruges which followed the wedding (these were reportedly described in a French account by Garter), the chronicler of the marriage of Richard duke of York

---

[67] BL, MSS. Julius C. VI, fols 255–9 and Add. 6113, fols 101–7; 'Bluemantle Pursuivant', pp. 379–88. Four men are known to have held the office of Bluemantle Pursuivant in the time of Edward IV, Henry French or Franke, Richard Champneys, Thomas Hollingworth and Roger Bromley: see Godfrey et al., *College of Arms*, p. 193.

[68] Routh, 'Princess Bridget', pp. 13–14; Phillipps, 'Marriage of Princess Margaret', *Archaeologia*, pp. 326–8; Bentley, 'Marriage of Princess Margaret', *Excerpta Historica*, pp. 223–39.

to Anne Mowbray in 1478 dwelt at length upon the feats of arms performed by Sir Anthony Woodville, Earl Rivers, in honour of his nephew's marriage.[69]

The funeral narratives commence with notice of the date and place of the person's death, together with a memorandum of the dressing, embalming and spicing of the corpse, and of its display to the lords of the realm.[70] Lavish detail informs the description of the dressing of the body and hearse, from the rich cloths and silken cords used to wrap the deceased to the intricate heraldic devices proclaiming the dead person's station and pedigree. In the case of the extant accounts of the re-interment of Richard duke of York in 1476, the focus is on the exhumation of the bones and/or upon the wooden effigy of the deceased.[71] In the solemn procession from the place of embalming to the place of burial, a journey which often took many days, careful note was made of the order in which people processed, of those who took part in the watch and the offering, and of the manner in which the procession came into the place of service. Alone of the surviving funeral narratives, an account of the burial of Edward IV in 1483 is prefaced by an excerpt from a contemporary (presumably heraldic) guide to hosting a noble funeral.[72]

Similarly, the account of the double coronation of Richard III and Anne Neville in 1483 provides not only 'the names of the Dukes Erelles Lordes and Knightes that were at the Crownacion of kinge Richard the iijde and Queene Anne' but also the appearance of the principal participants, the order of the procession to the Abbey (with details of who carried the regalia and who performed which office), and notes on the coronation, coronation banquet and the challenge by the king's champion.[73] What little is said of the crowning and anointing is imperfect and confused, probably owing to the writer's lack of familiarity with, or disinterest in, the church proceedings.[74] In contrast to the fullness of the Ricardian account, the coronation of Elizabeth Woodville, Edward IV's queen, was captured by a herald whose principal concern appears to have been roles and processional order of noble participants, and the extant report bears little embellishment.[75]

---

[69] Bentley, 'Marriage of Princess Margaret', *Archaeologia*, p. 337; 'Narrative of the Marriage of Richard Duke of York with Ann of Norfolk, the 'Matrimonial Feast', and the Grand Justing, A.D. 1477', in *Illustrations of Ancient State and Chivalry from MSS Preserved in the Ashmolean Museum*, ed. W. H. Black (London, 1840), pp. 25–40.

[70] 'Funeral of Edward IV', ed. J. Gairdner in *Letters and Papers Illustrative of the Reigns of Richard III*, ed. James Gairdner, HMSO, 2 vols (London, 1861–3; repr. 1965), i, pp. 3–10.

[71] *The Reburial of Richard Duke of York, 21–30 July 1476*, ed A. F. Sutton and L. Visser-Fuchs, The Richard III Soc. (1996), pp. 13, 20, 31.

[72] Gairdner, 'Funeral of Edward IV', p. 3.

[73] Sutton and Hammond, *Richard III*, pp. 270–82.

[74] Sutton and Hammond, *Richard III*, p. 255.

[75] Still briefer and less adorned is the record of the christening of Princess Bridget. Although it opens with a familiar introductory notice of the day and place of the event,

INTRODUCTION: THE HERALDS

Heraldic narratives were compiled as much for record and precedent as out of the heralds' interest in their subject material; their proliferation after the mid-century may arguably be linked with a need to bolster ceremonial memory from the 1460s onward, and their increase in scope under Edward IV and Richard III consequent upon the heralds' developing expertise and practical responsibilities at the Yorkist court. Precision and detail were paramount, and those accounts that survive today are strikingly derivative of the eye-witness experience of the writer and his closeness to the events he describes. Indeed, the conditions under which the late-fifteenth-century herald laboured to give effect to his record-keeping skills were akin to those of a modern journalist. William Ballard (d. *c.* 1490), March King of Arms, claimed that his efforts were frustrated by the throng of sightseers at the marriage celebrations of the duke of York in 1478, while only ten years earlier the chronicler of Margaret of York's marriage celebrations in Bruges had found himself caught in rain 'that cam so fast that I myght not wryte the certeinte of the presentacions'. Others also mentioned difficulties in reporting what they saw.[76]

In most cases, however, the officers of arms were well placed to see, and the standard of accuracy with names, dates and the minutiae of ceremonial and secular ritual was high. The surviving accounts are broadly similar in preoccupation, arrangement of material and style, and great attention is paid throughout to the heralds' roles in the events depicted.[77] Questions of procedure and precedent, remarks on omission, error or confusion, and general comment and complaint are typically included, suggesting that these records represented the very context for raising and resolving ceremonial issues. Lists of names are frequently arranged in hierarchical order under category of rank and gender; later one also finds knights grouped into retinues. Such lists not only enabled the ready compilation of newsletters or dispatches from the field, but also facilitated the registration of reward and fee-payment to the heralds. As the century wore on, too, the Crown's absorption of the heraldic fraternity doubtless rendered these lists an increasingly

---

this account offers only a list of the chief participants in order of appearance and a statement of each person's role in the baptismal procession: Routh, 'Princess Bridget', pp. 13–14.

[76] Black, 'Marriage of Richard Duke of York', p. 131; Phillipps, 'Marriage of Princess Margaret', *Archaeologia*, p. 331. In addition, Princess Margaret's herald had difficulty describing the pageants because the mime was too subtle for him (p. 328), while a large crowd prevented the herald at the funeral of Edward IV from adequately recording the offerings: Gairdner, 'Funeral of Edward IV', p. 10.

[77] In only two cases has the author explicitly identified himself as a herald, but elsewhere careful note is made of the place of officers of arms in the funeral *cortège* and other processions, to the identity by office title of those heralds performing ritual and ceremonial duties, to the rewards and payments received by heralds, and to such details as 'Mr Norry cryed ye larges in iij places of the hall, because Mr Garter had an impediment in his tonge': Kingsford, 'Bluemantle Pursuivant', p. 384.

valuable source for the Crown's awareness and supervision of potential public servants.[78]

Many of the heralds' narratives are also supplemented by oral report and hearsay, public proclamation, official and quasi-official written documents, and other works originating from both within and outside the body of heralds in the service of the English Crown.[79] Moreover, great similarity between certain of the ceremonial accounts and the details set out in contemporary prescriptive guides for the regulation of the same events, a number of which were also created or owned by officers of arms, suggests that the heralds sometimes assembled their narrative accounts with the assistance of the latter documents.[80] The inclusion of what appear to be portions of prescriptive text in the English narrative of the reburial of Richard of York and the account of Edward IV's funeral, and a similar type of statement incorporated, perhaps accidentally, into the account of the coronation of Richard III not only indicates a common origin for these two types of record, but further supports the notion that ceremonial accounts were compiled at least partly for guidance. Indeed, the occasion of Richard duke of York's reburial in 1476 was prepared with a wealth of manuals, inventories and more, a great number of which survive today.[81] Presumably an eye-witness account written at, or immediately after, an event allowed for a certain flexibility of practice not possible in general, prescriptive guidelines.

With the expansion in scope and ambition of heraldic record-keeping at the Yorkist court, it is scarcely surprising that the line between heraldic record and chronicle is sometimes hard to draw. Although no English herald is known to have written a full-scale chronicle of the sort penned by Jean le Fèvre (d. 1468), *Toison d'or* King of Arms to the duke of Burgundy, newsletters and dispatches compiled by heralds on the battlefield frequently served the propagandist designs of government-employed chroniclers during the Wars of the Roses and may well hold the key to the origins of both English and Continental narrative sources, including Vergil's *Anglia Historia*, Warkworth's *Chronicle* and Molinet's *Chroniques*; the resemblance of chronicles like these to the heralds' records is strikingly suggestive of the input of Yorkist and early Tudor heraldic memoranda.

---

[78] C. Carpenter, *Locality and Polity. A Study of Warwickshire Landed Society, 1401–1499* (Cambridge, 1992), p. 92.

[79] See for example 'St Albans', pp. 519–23 and Halliwell, *Warkworth's Chronicle*, pp. 36–9.

[80] Numerous texts for the regulation of ceremonial generally or for the organisation of specific events circulated within the body of heralds in England during the latter half of the fifteenth century. See for example, 'The maner of makynge Knyghtes aftar ye custome of England in tyme of peace, and at the coronacion, that is to say, Knyghtes of the Bathe', in J. Gairdner (ed.), *Three Fifteenth Century Chronicles* (1880), pp. 106–13.

[81] Sutton and Visser-Fuchs, *Reburial*.

INTRODUCTION: THE HERALDS

If chivalric history did not generally flourish in fifteenth-century England two heraldic accounts devoted specifically to feats of arms – an early fifteenth-century depiction of the tournament victories of Richard Beauchamp, earl of Warwick, and an account of the Smithfield combat between Anthony Woodville, Lord Scales, and the Bastard of Burgundy – are more consciously literary compositions. The former account, again written up soon after the event, describes in flattering terms Richard Beauchamp's victories against three French knights, whom he fought disguised as *le chivaler vert*, *le chivaler gryse* and *le chivaler attendaunt* respectively.[82] The account of the Smithfield combat preserved in the *Grete Boke* of Sir John Paston is still more complex. A 'clever assemblage of documents' compiled over a two-year period, the account includes letters of challenge, the minutes of a meeting held in advance to determine the rules of combat, specifications for constructing the lists, as well as the more typical descriptive memoranda and a roll-call of participants' names.[83] The Beauchamp and Smithfield narratives clearly reflect the twin heraldic interests in martial prowess and legendary heroes like Arthur, Roland and Gawain. These were also factors that urged the staging of elaborate tourneys in which Richard earl of Warwick fought the 'green knight' of Arthurian Romance. With the flowering of the full-scale tournament during the fifteenth century and the proliferation of literary monuments celebrating these events, it is not surprising that English royal heralds occasionally worked the articles of challenge and their own eye- witness memoranda into more polished pieces.

Creation of the Memoir

The royal heralds of England enjoyed the use of Coldharbour for little more than a year. King Richard perished on Bosworth Field in August 1485, and his body – 'dyspoylid to the skyn, and nowgth beying left abouth hym, soo much as wold covyr his pryvy membyr' – was trussed like a hog and borne, bloodied and filthy, to a church in Leicester.[84] The cancellation of King Richard's acts by his supplanter, Henry Tudor, left the heralds once more without a corporate home, their common library in disarray, and several of the royal heralds without employment.[85] Garter John Writhe, Clarenceux Thomas Holme and John Water, York Herald, were temporarily suspended, or resigned, from office at the beginning of the reign; it might have been due to Holme's personal loyalty to Richard III that for him alone of the royal heralds no tabard was prepared before King Henry's coronation. With the repossession of Coldharbour by the Crown, the office of Garter King of Arms, to which the governance of the house and library had been attached,

[82] H. N. MacCracken, 'The Earl of Warwick's Virelai', *PMLA*, 22 (1907), pp. 597–607.
[83] BL, MS. Lansdowne 285, fols 29v–43.
[84] *The Great Chronicle of London*, eds A. H. Thomas and I. D. Thornley (London, 1938), p. 238.
[85] TNA, E404/50(328); *RP*, vi, p. 336; *Materials*, i, p. 406; Wagner, *Heralds of England*, p. 134.

relinquished the only tangible expression of its authority.

The English heralds may have remained legally a corporation, however, despite the loss of their corporate residence. Even as Writhe and others fell from grace, Henry Tudor brought his friend Roger Machado, Richmond Herald, onto the Crown establishment and made him a King of Arms.[86] Officers of arms continued to receive livery and a stipend from the Crown, began to be appointed by patent as the kings of arms had long been, and from late 1487 became subject to a novel roster system apparently designed to ensure their attendance at court in fixed rotation.[87] The new king can have had no small need for the heralds' ceremonial expertise, for (despite Professor Elton's assertions to the contrary) the new royal court appears to have been from the first the very model of measured splendour that the court of Edward IV had been.[88] That magnificence was not only fitting but necessary for the new court can be seen in the 1485 Act of Resumption, which declared that

> your Honorable Houshold ... must be kept and borne Worshipfully and Honorably, as it accordeth to the Honour of your Estate and your said Realme, by the whiche your Adversaries and Enemyes shall fall into the drede wherein heretofore they have byne.[89]

At a glance the heralds' practical responsibilities at the early Tudor court remained much as they had been under the Yorkist kings of England. Officers of arms continued to marshal and supervise, and to participate in, fifteenth-century coronations, baptisms, funerals, creations, feasts, state visits and ceremonial processions.[90] On occasions these events also became the subject of pictorial records, for contemporary statements refer to illustrations of the creation of knights of the Bath in 1487, on the eve of Queen Elizabeth's coronation, and of the queen's own coronation procession the following day.[91] The former document has been tentatively identified as the elaborate series of illustrations which survives in a manuscript belonging to the duke of Buccleuch, and which clearly depicts the heralds'

---

[86] Wagner, *Heralds of England*, pp. 134–5 and 137–8. The reign also saw the institution of the ordinary pursuivants Rouge Dragon and Portcullis, Wallingford Pursuivant for the Prince of Wales, and five new garrison pursuivants: Wagner, *Heralds of England*, p. 56; below, p. 181.

[87] *CPR*, 1485–94, pp. 137, 177; Wagner, *Heralds of England*, pp. 97–9.

[88] G. R. Elton, 'Tudor Government: the Points of Contact. III. The Court', *TRHS* (1976), p. 212; M. van Cleave Alexander, *The First of the Tudors. A Study of Henry VII and His Reign* (London, 1981), p. 156; S. B. Chrimes, *Henry VII*, new edn (New Haven and London, 1999), p. 306; Myers, *Black Book*, p. 48

[89] *RP*, vi, p. 336.

[90] See for example the 'Little Device' emended for the coronation of Henry VII, in BL, MS. Eg. 985, fols 1–11, 41; 'The Christenynge of Prince Arthure, sonne to Kynge Henrie ye VII at Sent Swithins in Winchestar', in Stowe, *Three Fifteenth Century Chronicles*, pp. 104–5; Coll. Arms, MS. L8, fols 17v–19.

[91] Below, pp. 131, 138.

INTRODUCTION: THE HERALDS

own roles.[92] Although the compilation of armorial charts and other pictorial or diagrammatic records was one of the English heralds' earliest functions few, if any, of the extant illustrations of court ceremonial pre-date the reign of Henry VII.

Notices of the broadcasting of proclamations by English royal heralds also appear more frequently in the records of the new reign and, if not due entirely to chance survival, it is possible that this was an heraldic duty for which Henry VII found especial use in the early, formative years of his rule. The scope of subjects for which the Crown heralds issued proclamations at this time was broad, ranging from coronation announcements to the declaration of disciplinary regulations in the town and army in times of war.[93] Proclamations such as these appear to have been issued in both oral and written form.[94]

Henry Tudor also made much use of the diplomatic expertise developed by individual members of the heraldic fraternity. Roger Machado, Richmond King of Arms and sometime Norroy was sent, possibly as a fully accredited ambassador, on several delicate missions: in 1489 he travelled to Spain and Portugal to treat for a marriage between Prince Arthur and Katherine of Aragon, and in 1490 he was twice on assignment in Brittany.[95] John Writhe, Garter King of Arms, was evidently absent from court in September 1486 on business important enough to take him away from Prince Arthur's christening. The Memoir alone mentions four separate international embassies in which English heralds took part and several occasions when foreign herald-diplomats were present at the English court.

Roger Machado was also an accomplished commentator who kept careful account of his diplomatic missions in 1489 and 1490. He, like John Writhe and other members of the heraldic fraternity of the 1480s, must have been fully qualified to undertake the sort of field journalism that had been practised by the English heralds for much of the fifteenth century. Although it is difficult to determine the extent to which the heralds' 'on-road' duties had crystallised by 1485, or to which the twin heraldic duties of reportage and official or quasi-official excursion had merged, the Memoir itself points to the importance placed by Henry VII and/or his heralds on the compilation of descriptive memoranda from within the touring royal entourage.

---

[92] Wagner, *Heralds of England*, p. 138, plates X–XII.

[93] Reference to very early proclamations issued by heralds, specifically in relation to the 1306 ordinances on trial by combat issued by Philip IV of France, may be found in Coll. Arms, MSS. L.6, fols 4–9 and L.10*bis*, fols 36v–45.

[94] See especially *Tudor Royal Proclamations*, ed. P. L. Hughes and J. F. Larkin, 3 vols (New Haven and London, 1964–9), i, p. 3–4, 17; R. W. Heinze, *The Proclamations of the Tudor Kings* (Cambridge, 1976), pp. 65–84.

[95] Below, p. 163; Wagner, *Heralds of England*, p. 138; Wagner, *HH*, p. 38. For Machado's journals of his missions see *Memorials*, pp. 157–222, 328–389. Letters of instruction for his mission to Brittany in 1494 are printed in *LP*, ii, pp. 292–6. See also Godfrey et al., *College of Arms*, pp. 79–80.

Thus it may at first seem curious that, despite the great expertise and prominence of individual heralds in 1485 and the rich professional inheritance to which they were collective heirs, the number of narrative records that survive for the first five years of the reign of Henry VII are very few indeed: an account of the king's coronation, a short series of preparatory memoranda anticipating the creation of Arthur Prince of Wales in 1489, a set of notes compiled at the christening of Prince Arthur in 1486 but available only in sixteenth-century copies, and the Memoir. This fact may seem curious, that is, until it is acknowledged that the key to the shortage of independent heraldic narratives from the early years of the reign of Henry VII probably lies in the very existence of the Memoir.

* * *

By far the most extensive and heterogeneous of all the surviving heraldic narratives of the fifteenth century, the Memoir recounts the activities of Henry VII and the royal court from the spring of 1486 to the first months of 1490, and is unique in its inclusion of virtually all the topics discussed above. It begins with a lengthy account of Henry Tudor's first progress into the northern and western provinces of the realm, and proceeds variously through descriptions of the occasional and seasonal festivities at the English court, ambassadorial excursions to and from court, rebellions, and even – albeit cursorily – the king's recreational pursuits. The great scope of this 60-folio narrative may alone explain the dearth of similar narratives of the period 1485–90.

The proximity of the royal heralds to the Memoir's creation and the eye-witness character of much of the text's constituent subject material is clear. The chronicler of the banquet which followed the installation of Archbishop Morton in January 1487 pronounced it the best managed feast he had ever seen, while the herald who accompanied the king on progress in 1486 announced his own departure from the royal entourage at York after the feast of St George.[96] Great attention is paid throughout to the activities and experiences of the officers of arms, to the minutiae of largess and reward received, and to office particulars like the creation of Wallingford Pursuivant for the Prince of Wales in 1489.[97] The displeasure of at least one herald-recorder is evident in a memorandum for Christmas 1488, when it was noted that 'ther wer many lordes moo in the courte, some comyng and some goyng, which yave no rewardes to the officers of armes'.[98] Even the Queen appears to have aroused heraldic ire for the perceived paucity of her largess on New Year's Day 1487.[99]

The Memoir also contains several supplementary references to works created or owned by English heralds, namely pictorial records of the coronation of Eliza-

[96] Below, p. 82.
[97] Below, pp. 99, 151–3, 179.
[98] Below, p. 163.
[99] Below, p. 107, n. 247. The statement to this effect was later cancelled.

INTRODUCTION: THE HERALDS

beth of York, the heralds' register in which were recorded the New Year's Day gifts of 1487, and two books said to contain, respectively, accounts of the feast of the installation of John Morton and at least the first stage of the king's military response to the murder of the earl of Northumberland in 1489.[100] Further material was imported from sources originating outside the office of arms, but to which the heralds appear to have had direct access. The account of the queen's coronation in November 1487 includes a verbatim copy of the Latin commission for the discharge of the office of Steward of England, as well as transcripts, in both English and French, of petitions to coronation service lodged by the great estates of the realm and presumably preserved among the muniments of the Court of Claims.[101] Elsewhere, verse and proclamation are incorporated into the text, and in one case at least, that of the Worcester pageantry, the herald-recorder must have had access to a written exemplar, for the shows in question were never actually performed.[102]

Like the account of the Smithfield combat in 1467, the Memoir might also be termed 'a clever assemblage of documents',[103] so diverse were the experiences and sources that contributed to its creation. Indeed, it is difficult to escape the sense that the Memoir represents the deliberate amalgamation of all materials compiled or gathered by the royal heralds during the four years in question. Created under some form of editorial policy, that of 'licence and correction', the Memoir was nevertheless fundamentally a working document unsuitable for publication as it stood. Retaining blank spaces for names, dates and other details omitted at the time of writing-up, as well as the marks of error, alteration and annotation, it bears all the characteristics of an internal, office report produced primarily for record and precedent. Palaeographical evidence suggests that it continued to be used as a working document for heralds and antiquaries in the succeeding centuries. Perhaps the Memoir was envisaged as a novel, extended form of record, and derived in some measure from the same initiative as the 1487 roster for the heralds' waiting at court.[104]

The theme and purpose of legitimisation were arguably the principal threads which bound the Memoir to the early years of the reign of Henry VII and account, at least in part, for its unusual size. In the new year of 1486, Henry Tudor's thirst for national approval was equalled only by the heraldic fraternity's own quest for acceptance by the nascent regime. The officers of arms had staked their reputa-

---

[100] Below, pp. 105, 108, 130, 136.
[101] Below, pp. 121–7.
[102] Below, pp. 83–8, 159–60. Similarly, the list of the fifty or so dishes served at the queen's coronation feast appears to have been copied from a written menu or inventory, while the disciplinary regulations proclaimed in the town and royal army during the campaign of 1487 are printed in full: below, pp. 142, 143–4, 112–13.
[103] Lester, 'Heraldic Narratives', p. 206.
[104] See below, p. 25.

tion and the development of their craft on that complex, mutually-dependent relationship between the royal household of Yorkist England and the increasingly elaborate world of ceremony and chivalry. They had ridden high in the favour of Edward IV and Richard III, and certain of them appear to have fostered personal relations with King Richard, a generous patron of their corporation. It is possible that the heralds were viewed by contemporaries as an organ of the Yorkist or Ricardian household. Whatever Henry Tudor's own attitude to the fraternity, or toward individual practitioners, the officers of arms may have felt themselves in danger of becoming a casualty of the new royal will, a will that was bent on the twin aims of self-promotion and the eradication of the former king's legacy. Therein also lay an opportunity for the royal heralds.

The new king must have been at least partly assured of the heralds' utility by their remarkably full attention to the organisation and documentation of ceremonial events at court. There is a very real sense in the Memoir of a concern to codify and formalise chivalric practices at court, an aspiration which may also have extended to the improvement of the heralds' own record-keeping during these years. Procedural issues are closely monitored, and problems, questions and comments raised in the Memoir. In 1487 the chronicler of the queen's coronation recorded a colleague's opinion that the horse of estate should have followed the henchmen in procession, and not the other way round as had actually occurred. At the feast that followed, however, the dishes conveyed to the archbishop of Canterbury were chiefly borne by esquires, as was fitting. Changes of procedure, such as the re-routing of the baptismal procession at Prince Arthur's christening due to inclement weather, helped highlight precedents and anomalies, while on certain occasions instructional memoranda were included for explanation and guidance: 'it is not the custume to crye noman of the chirche, nor no lower degre than a vicount, withoute it bee the stewarde or the chambrelayn.'[105]

If the impressive line-up of notables at court and on campaign affirmed the acquiescence of the ruling elites in the Crown's demands, its documentation by the royal heralds arguably served to reinforce the process. The meticulous cataloguing of names evident in the Memoir not only aided Crown supervision of its public servants, as Christine Carpenter suggests, but also indicates the heralds' own integration into the mechanism of the new regime. Nor could the Yorkist or Ricardian backgrounds of certain individuals have escaped the attention of the heralds any more than it had the king, and it was well to record the participation of individuals like the earl of Lincoln on critical occasions. As far as the heralds were concerned, too, their pressing preoccupations at once compelled them to monitor their own remunerations, to regulate and perhaps reform their manifold duties at court, and to demonstrate their loyalty to the king, not only by participation, but also by methodical documentation and satisfactory report.

[105] Below, pp. 104, 134, 142, 152.

INTRODUCTION: THE HERALDS

The link between the Memoir and the early years of the reign of Henry VII becomes still clearer when one takes into account the layers of production involved in the Memoir's creation, *viz.* its apparent compilation from draft notes, and the evidence of amendment and alteration still visible on the pages of the original manuscript. Most strikingly, the editorial policy governing the creation of the Memoir is unconsciously evoked by the cancellation of a potentially inflammatory statement regarding the queen's largess; this and other contemporary corrections to the text suggest supervision and deference to a higher authority. Moreover, the accounts of the first provincial progress, the Stoke campaign, the northern rising of 1489, the queen's coronation, and the creation of Arthur as Prince of Wales each includes lists of names that were clearly systematised during the writing-up process: social hierarchy prevails, and in a number of cases names are set out in column format and/or grouped according to gender and even retinue.

The interaction between the royal heralds and the Crown at this juncture is difficult to determine. Yet, so measured is the record of the 1489 rising (for example) and so cautious was the new king during the early years of his reign, that it is difficult not to suspect the influence of the bureaucratic and shrewd Henry Tudor on the heralds' conduct, if not on the execution of the Memoir itself. In November 1487 a meeting of the officers of arms at the chapter house at Windsor determined a fixed pattern for the heralds' waiting at court.[106] The king signed a bill requiring the ordinance to be kept. Although the exact pattern of heralds' waiting prior this time is unknown, it is unlikely that a formal rota had ever been in place and more probable that only a general system had been observed.[107] The innovation of 1487 may or may not have come directly from the king, but it certainly complemented the royal agenda and reflects the kind of omnipresent efficiency with which the new regime was launched. Equally, the initiative might have belonged to the heralds, as an aspect of corporate improvement or specifically to ingratiate themselves with the new king. What ever the case, the roster's implications for heraldic conduct and record-keeping are clear.

The Court and Campaigns of Henry VII, 1486–90

There can be little doubt that the creation of the Memoir was informed by the mutually compatible needs of king and herald discussed above. With his first

---

[106] Wagner, *Heralds of England*, p. 97. The roster system was as follows: December and half January: Garter, Windsor and Bluemantle; half January and February: Clarenceux, Carlisle and a pursuivant appointed by Clarenceux; March and half April: March, Chester and Rouge Dragon; Half April and May: Richmond King, York and Falcon; June and half July: Garter, Windsor and Bluemantle; half July and August: Clarenceux, Carlisle and a pursuivant appointed by Clarenceux; September and half October: March, Chester and Rouge Dragon; half October and November: Richmond King, York and Falcon.

[107] See for example, 'The Ordinance of 1445', in Myers, *Household*, p. 70.

provincial progress in the spring of 1486, Henry Tudor seized the chance to lead a stately and carefully planned tour into the former heartland of the Ricardian regime. This was a critical opportunity for the new and untried monarch to demonstrate his adherence to the requisite princely qualities of piety and magnanimity, and for at least one herald to travel in the royal entourage and record the king's commitment to his duties of office.[108] The Memoir accordingly notes that Henry Tudor performed his Easter devotions in the Minster of Lincoln, rather than in a private chapel, passed his week in daily rounds of devotions, washed the feet of twenty-nine poor men (one for each year of his life), performed the hallowing of cramp rings, and dispensed abundant charity.[109] In York, as in Lincoln, he made a point of hearing divine service in the Minster, and on the return journey he attended regular mass and evensong at Worcester, Gloucester and Bristol.[110]

In the account of the progress, as throughout the Memoir as a whole, the king is depicted amid the 'trappings and qualities of kingship' that were so important in securing acceptance of the Crown's demands.[111] The abundance of cloth-of-gold, velvets and brocades, the display of emblems and devices, and the parading of raiment and riches is described to the finest detail by the eye-witness herald. As the royal entourage neared York in 1486, for example, Henry Tudor was 'richley besene in a gowne of cloth of golde furred with ermyn', and his henchmen resplendent in goldsmiths' work.[112] In York itself the emphasis was on the king's use of the symbols of office to enhance his regal dignity in the public arena, namely his wearing of the crown in the morning and the Garter robes and cap of maintenance at evensong.[113] Returning to London, Henry Tudor is said to have appeared at Whitsuntide in a sumptuous 'gowne of cloth of golde of tissue lynede with blake satene'.[114] Nor was this a case of special pleading by the herald-recorder, for at the time that the king began his first provincial progress in the spring of 1486 the royal wardrobe already contained striking and costly robes resembling those worn on progress, while a letter from the king himself to his wardrobe staff suggests that the satin-lined gown of cloth-of-gold was made expressly for the Whitsuntide appearance.[115]

Yet, it is also clear from the Memoir that the first provincial progress of 1486 was not simply a royal publicity stunt and, if not launched in direct response to an

---

[108] E. Cavell, 'Henry VII, the North of England and the First Provincial Progress of 1486', *Northern History*, 39.2 (September, 2002), p. 188.
[109] Below, pp. 69–70.
[110] Below, pp. 80–1, 88–9, 91–2, 97.
[111] Doig, 'Propaganda and Truth', p. 172.
[112] Below, p. 73.
[113] Below, p. 80–1.
[114] Below, p. 88.
[115] *Materials*, i, p. 419; Cavell, 'Henry VII', p. 190.

INTRODUCTION: THE HERALDS

outbreak of violence, was devoted in part to military concerns. Independent evidence reveals that the king was aware of trouble from the very beginning of the reign, and that that he may have intended from the outset to lead a large armed company to the North.[116] Moreover, by the time the king had begun his Easter sojourn in the cathedral city of Lincoln his fears were being realised, and the Memoir reveals the dramatic increase in the size and fighting capacity of the royal entourage between Lincoln and York. Most notably the herald-recorder describes the arrival of the earl of Northumberland with 'xxxiij knyghtes of his feed men, besides esquiers and yomen', and directly associates the defensive posturing of the enlarged royal entourage between Doncaster and Pontefract with the presence of rebels around Ripon, and the former seat of Neville power at Middleham, in the heart of the North Riding.[117]

Of course the influence of unforeseen circumstances upon the actions of the king and his leading men that spring must account in part for the militaristic aspects of the expedition described in the Memoir. The outbreak of pestilence at Newark-on-Trent, mentioned in passing by the herald-recorder, was clearly beyond anyone's control, while the herald's statement that the royal entourage rode to Nottingham 'withoute any bayting' perhaps indicates that a stop had been intended at Newark or a near-by town.[118] More importantly, the unabated ride from Lincoln to the strategic base of Nottingham not only required the king to divert from a northerly course and move rapidly south-east, but also appears to have been put into action after the Easter revelation of rebellion to the north and south-west of Lincoln.[119] Other alterations to the projected itinerary are also evident.[120]

In addition, the timely arrival in the royal camp of the magnates and their retainers described in the Memoir was also more than just an immediate, practical response to the threat of rebellion, and it is possible that the new arrivals were timed by the king and his advisors to make a formidable impression on the people of the North. Henry Tudor's desire for armed strength was mirrored equally by his need to appear lavishly and constantly attended by great figures of the realm and their retainers. Nor could the English magnate afford to remain at home while the new sovereign toured the countryside, particularly if his past was overshadowed by Ricardian sympathies or support of the Yorkist cause, as was the case with the earl of Lincoln and Lord Scrope of Bolton. Even the earl of Northumberland,

---

[116] *Plumpton Letters and Papers*, pp. 48–9, 64; *Materials*, i, pp. 282–3; P. W. Hammond, 'Opposition to Henry Tudor after Bosworth', *The Ricardian*, 4.55 (1976), p. 28; *Paston Letters and Papers*, ii, pp. 445–6.

[117] Below, pp. 72–3.

[118] Below, p. 70.

[119] Cavell, 'Henry VII', pp. 192, 205. The king may even have returned briefly to Lincoln around 4 or 5 April.

[120] See Cavell, 'Henry VII', pp. 205–6.

who had failed to show his hand at Bosworth, must have felt compelled to demonstrate his support of the new regime, and the Memoir reveals that he brought with him a number of Percy retainers who had probably fought for Richard III at Bosworth.[121]

For their part, the towns and cities along the way greeted the king with a reverence and awe that probably combined genuine sentiment with careful planning. With the notable exception of York's civic muniments, the Memoir is all but alone in providing extended detail of the pageantry arranged by the towns and cities of the first provincial progress, as they sought not only to ingratiate themselves with the new regime through flattery, praise and gentle admonition, but also to articulate a place for the new regime in local and national history. As 'Ebrauk', the mythical founder of York, submitted his 'citie, kee and coroune' to Henry Tudor; where Worcester's 'Janitor' was intended to play upon the traditional themes of the Nine Worthies and notions of Henry Tudor's descent; and with Bristol's invocation of the legendary King Brennius, each pageant articulated a vital connection between a formerly obscure Anglo-Welsh earl and the history of England and the British Isles.[122] Such notions were not purely idealistic, but partly grounded in the financial and legal concerns of a number of civic communities visited by the king in 1486.

When the king set off into East Anglia at the head of an impressive entourage the following March, he began his journey in a similar manner to his first progress. The observance of the feast of Easter in Norwich, the alms giving and attendance at divine service, and even the striking new doublets,[123] must have impressed King Henry's dignity and regal piety upon the townsfolk and herald-recorder alike.[124] The royal entourage was probably already graced with the presence of those men reputed to have passed Easter with the king, including the duke of Suffolk, the earls of Oxford and Derby, and perhaps also the newly-installed archbishop of Canterbury, who was responsible for the Easter services.[125] The Sheen council in February, and the arrival of an embassy from France, must also have brought a number of great magnates and lesser English nobles to the court.[126] Even the defection of John de la Pole, earl of Lincoln, immediately after the council does not appear to have prevented Henry Tudor from conducting himself with the vigorous piety

---

[121] These included: Sir Robert Plumpton, Sir Thomas Mauleverer, Sir William Gascoigne, Sir Robert Ughtred and Sir Martin of the Sea.

[122] Below, pp. 75–6, 87–8, 93–4. See the contemporary conceptualization of Brennius (Brynne) in Robert Ricart, *The Maire of Bristowe is Kalendar*, ed Lucy Toulmin Smith, Camden, n.s., v (1872), p. 10.

[123] *Materials*, ii, p. 122.

[124] Below, pp. 109–11. Before the king and company had set off from Sheen, at least one courtier had predicted some relaxation time in Norwich, and several gentlewomen of Essex had made ready to welcome the king: *Paston Letters and Papers*, i, p. 654.

[125] Below, pp. 110–11.

[126] Below, pp. 108–9; *Materials*, ii, p. 114.

expected of a Christian prince; for if he hoped to gain the support he needed he could ill-afford to neglect his religious obligations at this time. He may have felt, too, that devotion at the ancient and venerated shrine of Our Lady of Walsingham, as made by English kings before him, would bring him favour of the highest order.[127]

The description of the campaign of 1487 contained in the Memoir is a remarkable eyewitness account of the weeks leading up to the battle of Stoke penned, like the account of the first provincial progress, by an individual travelling in the royal entourage; perhaps the same herald was responsible for both. As Michael Bennett has shown, the events of that year, and in particular the activities of the king and his men in the run-up to battle, are otherwise poorly served by contemporary and near-contemporary sources. The London annals, of which the *Great Chronicle of London* is the best known, offer little beyond the basics of the battle, and the work of the poet laureate and court historiographer, Bernard André, is disappointing on the conspiracy and battle. Near-contemporary chroniclers like Molinet and Vergil, and later Hall, Holinshed and Bacon (whose information derives little altered from Vergil), offer much that is historically useful but little in the way of intimate or circumstantial detail.[128] It is in primarily in circumstantial elaboration that the herald-recorder of 1487 excels.

Although the Memoir does not describe the true extent and complexity of the new conspiracy against Henry VII, it nevertheless makes explicit the link between the defensive posture adopted by the king over Easter, through the presence of knights, esquires and the larger part of the eastern nobility, and the activities of the rebels in the Low Countries. As Bennett has pointed out, the pace of the journey described by the herald appears to have changed immediately after Easter,[129] as the king led his entourage 'towards the middes of his realme', riding by Cambridge, Huntingdon and Northampton, and arriving at Coventry in time for the feast of St George.[130] No detail at all is provided for the stops between Walsingham and Coventry, and one assumes that they were hurried. Elsewhere we learn that the king's schedule was so tight that he failed to celebrate the feast of St. George with the Garter knights at Windsor and in consequence aroused the ire of at least two leading magnates.[131] The king cannot have known initially that the

---

[127] Vergil, *Anglica Historia*, p. 21.
[128] Bennett, *Lambert Simnel*, pp. 10–11; R. F. Green, 'Historical Notes of a London Citizen', *EHR*, 96 (1981), pp. 585–9; Thomas and Thornley, *Great Chronicle*, pp. 240–1; André, *Vita*, pp. 49–54; Molinet, *Chroniques*, i, pp. 562–5; Vergil, *Anglia Historia*, pp. 15–27; Hall, *Union*; Holinshed, *Chronicles*; Francis Bacon, *The History of the Reign of King Henry the Seventh*, ed. F. J. Levy (New York, 1972).
[129] Bennett, *Lambert Simnel*, p. 59.
[130] Below, p. 110; Edwards, *Itinerary*, p. 41; Cf. G. Temperley, *Henry VII* (London, 1917), p. 412.
[131] TNA, E404/79/183; *Materials*, ii, pp. 152–3.

rebel contingent was bound for the English Channel,[132] but the Memoir gives no indication of what drew Henry Tudor westward in such haste, alluding simply, if rather ominously, to the daily arrival in the royal entourage of more and more of the king's 'true servants and subjects'.[133]

From 22 April to c. 10 June, Coventry and near-by Kenilworth were the focus of the herald's report, as of royal mobilisation, for the king was evidently already lodged in the strategic city of Coventry and attended by most of the southern magnates when he received news that Lincoln and the rebels had reached Ireland.[134] In Coventry the king enlisted the support of the archbishop of Canterbury and other prelates to condemn traitors and miscreants from their pulpits,[135] and from Kenilworth designated the duke of Suffolk as his deputy for the belated celebration of the feast of St. George at Windsor.[136] With the news of a rebel landing in the north-west of England, the king and his men in Kenilworth were seized with the urgency of muster. A series of disciplinary regulations was proclaimed in the town and army, and a council of war was assembled.[137] Almost certainly present at the Kenilworth council, the herald-recorder details the formation of the royal vanguard, and one assumes he was not in contact with the main battalion, then probably stationed in Coventry. The earl of Oxford was granted leadership of the vanguard, taking on the combined forces of the young earl of Shrewsbury, Viscount Lisle, Lords Grey de Ruthin, Grey, Hastings, and Ferrers of Chartley, together with other bannerettes, bachelors and esquires.[138] The right cavalry wing, also dispatched north as 'foreriders', comprised Sir Edward Woodville (probably leader of his wing), Lord Powys, Sir Charles Somerset, Sir Richard Haute, with further 'gallants' of the king's household. Sir Richard Pole and others made up the left cavalry wing.[139]

In the days leading up to the battle on Saturday 16 June the rapid and heady succession of events guiding the king and his entourage becomes increasingly evident in the narrative. Pimps, prostitutes and other hangers-on were purged from the army in Leicester and Loughborough, while on the evening of Wednesday 14 June malicious rumour-mongers were hanged on the ash tree by Nottingham Bridge; still more troubling must have been the complete failure of the king's marshals and harbingers to find suitable camping grounds in Nottingham that same

[132] Bennett, *Lambert Simnel*, p. 59; *YHB*, ii, pp. 550–1; Vergil, *Anglia Historia*, p. 21.
[133] Below, p. 110.
[134] Below, p. 111. Many of these magnates must have been among the faithful allegedly rallying to the king in or near Coventry.
[135] Below, p. 110; TNA, E404/79/58(213), E404/79/162.
[136] Below, p. 110; G. F. Beltz, *Memorials of the Most Noble Order of the Garter* (1841), p. lxxvii; *Materials*, ii, pp. 142–3, 152–3.
[137] Below, pp. 111–13.
[138] Below, p. 112.
[139] Below, p. 112.

night; and on successive evenings there was panic and pandemonium as terrified men, possibly aware of the defeat of the advance party to the north, fled the royal camp.[140] On the morning of Thursday 14 June further excitement was generated when the king suddenly mounted his horse and charged away with little or no explanation. His purpose, according to the herald-recorder, was to locate the vast retinue of Lord Strange; but his conduct clearly alarmed his assembled army.[141] Bennett points to the king's pressing need to ensure the loyalty of the Stanleyite forces (which the herald felt were more than a match for all the king's enemies), but together these episodes reveal much about the daily difficulties facing the king, and his own conduct under pressure.[142]

Despite the remarkable descriptive detail in the Stoke report to this point, the herald ultimately offers only a bald statement of the outcome of the battle, a single notice of the principal casualties, and a list of bannerets and knights created by the king on the field. The earl of Lincoln, diverse gentlemen, and a great number of English, Irish and Low Country mercenaries were dead; Francis Lord Lovell had been put to flight; and a young boy had been captured, known to the rebels as King Edward VI, but (so the Memoir assures posterity) 'whos name was in dede John'.[143] Given the currency of the name 'Lambert Simnel' in the government records from the end of 1487, it is intriguing that the Memoir should claim the boy's name was John. The compiler of the Leland-Hearne edition of the Memoir certainly felt the herald to have erred, and transcribed the relevant clause as 'whos Name was indede Lambert'.[144] The only other record to provide a contemporaneous note on the episode, the muniments of the city of York, do not give the boy a name at all.[145] Derived from close proximity to the battle itself, and probably independent of the official line, the herald's statement may well offer a unique window through official sources and later chronicles onto the true identity of the boy-pretender. Whether or not the boy was really called John (perhaps the herald's choice of name was tantamount to calling him Joe Bloggs), the evidence of the Memoir clearly suggests that the young pretender was unlikely to have borne the name by which he became known to history, and still less likely to have deserved the identity attributed to him by the rebel faction.[146]

---

[140] Below, pp. 114, 115–16.
[141] Below, p. 115. Polydore Vergil attributes a similar episode to Bosworth in 1485: *Three Books of Polydore Vergil's English History, Comprising the Reigns of Henry VI, Edward IV, and Richard III*, ed. Sir H. Ellis, Camden Soc., o.s., 29 (1844), pp. 217–18.
[142] Bennett, *Lambert Simnel*, p. 82.
[143] Below, p. 117. Another early account of the battle may be found in Vergil, *Anglica Historia*, pp. 24–5.
[144] Leland, *Collectanea*, iv, p. 214.
[145] *YHB*, ii, p. 573.
[146] See esp. Bennett, *Lambert Simnel*, pp. 41–56.

With a little interrogation and the aid of several independent sources, the Memoir yields an impression of the size and élan of the army gathering around Henry VII as he rode from Coventry, through Leicester, Loughborough and into Nottinghamshire to face the rebels. Peers closely associated with the new regime included the dukes of Bedford and Suffolk, the earls of Derby and Oxford, Viscount Lisle, and Sir Edward Woodville, certain of whom probably committed a thousand or more armed men to the royal service.[147] Apart from the earls of Shrewsbury and Devon in the vanguard, the earl of Wiltshire and the lords Hastings and Grey of Powys also numbered among the younger peers recorded as rallying to the royal standard. With the knights and bannerets were Ralph Shirley, Humphrey Stanley, Henry Willoughby, Edward Burgh, William Tyrwhitt, John Digby, Nicholas Vaux and William Norris. In the body of knights and men-at-arms derived from the royal household or aristocratic retinues were experienced soldiers like Sir John Cheney and Sir James Blount, both of whom had proven indispensable at Bosworth.[148] Also present in the royal army were young gallants like Anthony Browne (the king's standard-bearer), Sir Charles Somerset, Richard Pole, James Parker, Robert Brandon and Edward Norris.[149] The king also recruited extensively among the gentry of the north midlands, to say nothing of the billmen, archers and footsoldiers.[150] If not quite the 40,000 men suggested by Molinet, the royal host may have been some 15,000 strong when it crashed headlong into the fray.[151]

In contrast to the circumstantial detail of Stoke narrative, the herald's report of the loyalist response to the violence in North Yorkshire in the spring of 1489 is blander and more orderly in composition.[152] Rendered into retinue-based lists of magnates, knights and county notables for each leg of the king's journey north, the account provides little in the way of descriptive elaboration.[153] Nevertheless, it offers critically important insight into the loyalist mobilisation between Tuesday 12 May and Friday 22 May, and into the composition of the king's army at each stage of the journey, as well as striking testimony to the arrival of knights and esquires. For this reason the original account, contained in Cotton Julius B. XII,

---

[147] Below, pp. 110–12, 114–15; A. Cameron, 'The Giving of Livery and Retaining in Henry VII's Reign', *Renaissance and Modern Studies*, 18 (1974), p. 24; *Paston Letters and Papers*, i, p. 654, ii, pp. 452–3; Vergil, *Anglia Historica*, p. 23 n. 15; Bennett, *Lambert Simnel*, pp. 59, 83.

[148] Below, p. 119; Vergil, *Anglica Historia*, p. 23n.

[149] Below, pp. 112, 119–20; *Paston Intro and Supp*, p. 157. See also Chrimes, *Henry VII*, pp. 48, 49, 327, 336n; Bennett, *Lambert Simnel*, p. 83; ibid, *The Battle of Bosworth* (1985; repr. Stroud, 2000), p. 42.

[150] Vergil, *Anglica Historia*, p. 23n.

[151] Molinet, *Chroniques*, i, p. 564; Bennett, *Lambert Simnel*, p. 95.

[152] Below, pp. 166–71.

[153] Below, p. 166, where the herald refers to the book of the king's 'gystys', which may have contained an alternative narrative of the event.

INTRODUCTION: THE HERALDS

was used by Michael Bennett in 1990 to disprove the long-standing conviction among historians that Henry VII dispatched only a forward battalion under the earl of Surrey to disperse the rebels. The latter interpretation derives from the Leland-Hearne edition, which unaccountably omits several folios detailing the raising of the royal army and its journey north. The neglected memoranda also make it clear that the king left Hertford for North Yorkshire on 12 May, ten days earlier than was traditionally believed.[154]

By way of descriptive information for this episode, the Memoir offers only two separate notices of the punishment of rebels in the final days of the campaign. The first is a notice of the summary execution of six rebels of Pontefract, namely the beheading of two men in the market square, the hanging of a further two in their jacks atop St Thomas Hill facing York, and the execution of the last few in other parts of the town. The second memorandum mentions the quartering of a rebel called 'Blades' in Pavement Square in York, the hanging of various others in diverse parts of the town, and the execution of one 'Warton', strung up in the postern where the rebels had entered the city.[155] Finally, the Memoir notes that on successive days the king pardoned up to fifteen-hundred people, a statement very like that in the *Great Chronicle of London* where many commoners, having aided the rebels, are said to have approached the king with halters about their necks and begged lamentably for forgiveness.[156]

Despite the marked contrast between the accounts of the Stoke campaign and the North Yorkshire rising, attention to the impressive Stanley followings is a notable feature of both. The chronicler of the latter event made a point of the king's review of the company of the earl of Derby in a meadow beside Montsorell, listed some seventy-four knights and esquires in Lord Strange's north-western following, and noted that Sir William Stanley reached the king on the road from Market Harborough to Leicester with many noblemen, adding almost apologetically 'whos names I have not'.[157] Part of the explanation may be found in the Stoke narrative, where the herald-recorded his belief that the combined armies of Lord Strange and his father, the earl of Derby, were more than a match for the rebels. Lord Strange led most of the old Stanleyite connection among the gentry of the northwest; his vastly wealthy uncle William occupied a great network of lands and offices centring on his border castle at Holt, and commanded an impressive following of gentry and yeomanry from South Cheshire, Shropshire and North

---

[154] M. J. Bennett, 'Henry VII and the Northern Rising of 1489', *EHR*, 105 (Jan, 1990), pp. 34–59. The missing folios are provided by Bennett as an appendix to his article, pp. 56–9.
[155] Below, p. 170.
[156] Below, p. 170; Thomas and Thornley, *Great Chronicle*, pp. 242–3. See also *Materials*, ii, pp. 451–2.
[157] Below, pp. 168–9.
[158] M. K. Jones, 'Sir William Stanley of Holt: Politics and Family Allegiance in the Late Fif-

Wales.[158] Given the size and strength of the Stanley followings, and the significance of their contribution to muster on both occasions, it is not surprising that care was taken to list the individual members of the retinues where possible. Moreover, the pattern of Stanley support for the ruling monarch in battle between 1483 and 1487, typically based on a 'close estimate of the military chances',[159] gave their unequivocal commitment to the king's standard in 1489 a resonance that is unlikely to have escaped the herald- recorder's attention.

Like the expeditions and dramatic military campaigns of the early years of the reign of Henry VII, the grand ceremonies and customary annual festivities at court during these years were accorded extensive coverage in the Memoir. The attention of the king and his advisors to public relations and the utility of princely magnificence on progress could be translated into the general and ritual displays encouraged by the birth of a son and heir, the crowning of a queen, the christening of a daughter, the creation of a Prince of Wales, and the annual celebrations of Christmas, New Year and the like. These were the occasions when the pressing needs of government and national security were almost wholly subsumed by the opportunity for near unlimited ceremonial and display, and differentiation according to status in society.[160] As the works of historians like Sydney Anglo, Kay Staniland and J. L. Laynesmith have shown, Henry VII's use of ritual and splendour during the early years of the reign is nowhere more evident than in the Memoir.[161]

When Prince Arthur was christened in September 1486, preparations commenced immediately. As rejoicing took place across Winchester and messengers were dispatched to convey the news to noblemen and towns, the place of baptism was made ready for the occasion.[162] Inside Winchester Cathedral the silver-and-gilt christening font was placed in a prominent position between the capitals of the north aisle; it was raised above seven steps, each covered with red worstead, on a single post of iron; rich red say shrouded the block on which the bishop was to stand; and above all was suspended a large, ornate canopy. The overall effect was a cruciform image.[163] Not far from the choir stood a closet, partially enclosed by

---

teenth Century', *Welsh History Review*, 14 (June, 1988), passim; Cameron, 'Livery and Retaining', pp. 23–4; Bennett, 'Northern Rising', p. 43; Bennett, *Bosworth*, pp. 90–106, 109, 116–17.

[159] S. B. Chrimes, *Lancastrians, Yorkists and Henry VI* (London, 1964), p. 153; Condon, 'Ruling Elites', p. 44; Bennett, 'Northern Rising', p. 44.

[160] J. Huizinga, *The Waning of the Middle Ages. A Study in the Forms of Life, Thought, and Art in France and the Netherlands in the Fourteenth and Fifteenth Centuries* (Harmondsworth, 1955), p. 53.

[161] Esp. S. Anglo, *Spectacle, Pageantry and Early Tudor Policy*; idem, *Images of Tudor Kingship*; K. Staniland, 'Royal Entry into the World', in D. Williams (ed.), *England in the Fifteenth Century. Proceedings of the 1986 Harlaxton Symposium* (Suffolk, 1987), pp. 297–314; Laynesmith, *Last Medieval Queens*, passim.

[162] Below, pp. 101–2.   [163] Below, p. 102.

heavy red tapestry and guarded by yeomen of the Crown, within which burned incense and a warming fire.[164] Nearby, wooden barriers clad in arras cloth had been erected to ward off crowds and mark out a space suitable for the dignity of the occasion.[165] The hallowed waters of the font, blessed by Bishop Alcock, were guarded by knights and esquires for the body. As the Memoir makes clear, very little was left to chance.

Most of the leading magnates were in attendance on this grand occasion. Henry Tudor was able to assign the most prestigious of the baptismal functions to individuals of his own choosing, and on this occasion the role of godparents reportedly fell to his mother-in-law, Elizabeth Woodville, to his trusted companion John earl of Oxford, to his powerful father-in-law Thomas earl of Derby, and to the former Ricardian lately reconciled Thomas FitzAlan, Lord Maltravers. The baptismal procession included the queen's sisters, Cecily and Anne, the young earl of Essex, the Lord Strange, and the most impressive of the Yorkist princes, John de la Pole, earl of Lincoln, pardoned by the king after Bosworth and as yet still outwardly loyal to the new regime. With them processed the seasoned campaigner Sir Edward Woodville and other veterans of the Lancastrian cause at Bosworth like Sir Richard Guildford and Sir John Cheney. The domination of proceedings by the Woodvilles, Yorks and their kin is a remarkable feature of the occasion and its documentation, and is almost certainly indicative of Henry VII's desire both to encourage and publicly display their loyalty to the new regime and to confirm Arthur's place as heir to the Yorkist claim to the throne.[166] Presumably the king was motivated in his choice of principal participants in his son's baptism by considerations of magnanimity and political wisdom alike, and it is instructive that on this occasion, the most significant of christenings for Henry VII, pride of place went not to his own mother, but to Elizabeth Woodville, the former queen of Yorkist England.

The Memoir account of Prince Arthur's christening was designed chiefly to preserve the memory of a triumphant occasion and to ensure the future replication of its ceremonial. Yet, if Henry VII had been 'tempting fate in his greed for symbolism' by arranging for the queen to give birth in the old English capital of Winchester, and by naming his son Arthur, it seems from the Memoir that he made no special effort at propagandising through the media of the ceremony and its reportage. In fact, the heralds' detailed and frank account reveals that things did not run altogether smoothly. In late September 1486, the miserable weather hampered proceedings, for the baptismal procession was compelled to make its way to the church by a different route from that normally followed, passing along the sheltered south wall of the nave to a little door at the western end of the same wall. The grand entrance on the cathedral's west end was evidently considered too

[164] Julius B. XII, fol. 22. Cf. *LRC*, p. 68; *Antiquarian Repertory*, i, p. 354.
[165] Staniland, 'Royal Entry', pp. 303–4. Cf. *LRC*, pp. 68–9.
[166] Laynesmith, *Last Medieval Queens*, pp. 205–6.

exposed to the fierce northern winds:

> And thus they procedede thorough the cloister of thabbey unto a litill door beside the weest ende of the chirche in the south parte of the saide chirche ... for the wether was to cowlde and to fowlle to have been at the west ende of the chirche.[167]

Inclement weather also delayed the return of the earl of Oxford from his capital manor house in Lavenham, Suffolk. Arthur's was a premature birth, in the thirty-fifth week of the queen's pregnancy, and despite the ceremony's postponement for several days, Oxford was unable to make it back in time.[168] The members of the baptismal procession were required to wait three hours or more inside the church, before the king finally ordered the ceremony to begin without the absent earl, who was then less than one mile from Winchester.[169] Oxford burst into the cathedral just in time to accompany the baby to the high altar for presentation and confirmation.

It is instructive, moreover, that despite the tendency among modern authorities to assume that Arthur was always a sickly child, the herald's report gives no indication that delay was inadvisable, despite the early birth. While christenings were usually held soon after the birth, as would be the case with Arthur's sister Margaret in 1489, and were hastily procured when an infant was weak, there appears to have been little anxiety over delaying the ceremony in 1486. Indeed a second, independent christening narrative states unequivocally that Arthur was 'a fayre prince and large of bones.'[170] Although the little prince was never to ascend the English throne, there was clearly nothing in 1486 to indicate that he would not be the fulfilment of his father's dynastic ambition and the much hoped-for 'offspring of the race of kings for the comfort of the whole realm'.[171]

Little more than twelve months later, the knights and peers of the realm were called upon to attend the coronation of Queen Elizabeth, preparations for which had been underway since the end of 1485. Still more than the baptism of a royal child, the coronation enabled the practice of ceremonial and ritual, the expression of the ideologies of queenship, and the fulfilment of specific services by the leading noblemen and gentry of the realm. The English royal heralds at this time were at least partly responsible for the adjudication of conflicting claims to coronation service: the extensive, thirty-one folio account of the coronation contained in the Memoir commences with a transcript of the materials relating to the Court of Claims, namely the summons to the Court, held in the White Hall at Westminster

---

[167] Below, p. 104.
[168] Below, pp. 100, 104–5.
[169] Below, p. 104.
[170] Alnwick Castle, MS. Alnwick 467, fol. 96; 'Cristenynge of Prince Arthure', p. 104.
[171] *RP*, vi, p. 270.
[172] Cf. *Materials*, ii, p. 202 and Chrimes, *Henry VII*, p. 67 where different dates are given for the Court of Claims.

on 19 November,[172] the individual claims to coronation service put forward by peers of the realm, and a copy of the commission issued to Jasper duke of Bedford, John earl of Oxford, Thomas earl of Derby, William earl of Nottingham, and others, to discharge the office of Steward of England at the coronation.[173] These documents were clearly an important aid to the heralds' own memory, and they appear to have been copied verbatim from the materials relating to the Court of Claims that year. The transcripts contained in the Memoir represent one of only a few comprehensive collections of petitions still in existence.[174]

On Friday 23 November, the queen began her pre-coronation journey from Greenwich to the Tower of London, attended by the king's mother, Margaret Beaufort, and innumerable great estates. Amid the colour and commotion of the barge ride along the Thames were 'gentilmanly pajants', devised for the queen's entertainment and perhaps the innovation of Garter Writhe and his team.[175] The mechanical, fire-breathing red dragon on the bachelors' barge, symbolic of ancient Britain, was unprecedented in England and not seen again until the coronation of Anne Boleyn in 1533.[176] Having made a public entry into London several days earlier, Henry VII greeted his wife at the Tower 'as if she were the foreigner and he the sovereign who had always been in England'.[177]

At the Tower, on the eve of the coronation, fourteen young men were created knights of the Bath in an elaborate ceremony not described in the Memoir, but reportedly depicted in an alternative, pictorial record in the heralds' possession.[178] Among those listed as receiving the knighthood were Edward Lord Dudley, whose father had served Richard III as a privy councillor; Hugh Lutterel, a man whose ancestral connections were impeccably Lancastrian, but who was destined to remain disappointed of royal patronage;[179] and Hugh Conway, a former companion in exile of Henry Tudor, and the unfortunate emissary chastised for bearing the news of Lovell's rebellion in 1486.[180] The number of knights listed by the

---

[173] Below, pp. 121–7; *Materials*, ii, p. 202; *CPR*, p. 196.
[174] The others are described in Sutton and Hammond, *Richard III*, p. 245.
[175] Below, pp. 129–30; Anglo, *Spectacle*, pp. 49–50.
[176] Below, p. 129; Anglo, 'British History', pp. 35, 38; 'The noble tryumphaunt coronacyon of quene Anne, wyfe unto the moost noble kynge Henry the viij', in *Tudor Tracts 1532–1588*, ed. E. Arber (Westminster, 1903), pp. 41–51; 'Coronation of Queen Ann, Wife to Henry VIII', *Antiquarian Repertory*, i, pp. 232–37; Hall, *Chronicle*, p. 799; Anglo, *Spectacle*, pp. 247–8. On the topic of the guilds of London and river pageantry, see G. Unwin, *The Guilds and Companies of London*, 4th edn (London, 1963), pp. 267–92.
[177] Laynesmith, *Last Medieval Queens*, p. 90.
[178] Below, pp. 130–1.
[179] D. Luckett, 'Patronage, Violence and Revolt in the Reign of Henry VII', in R. E. Archer (ed.), *Crown, Government and People in the Fifteenth Century* (New York, 1995), p. 156; *CPR*, p. 485; *Materials*, ii, p. 67.
[180] *LP*, i, pp. 234–5; Cavell, 'Henry VII', p. 192.

herald was far fewer than at the coronation of past queens, perhaps, as Laynesmith has suggested, because the king wished to limit (or even mould) the new queen's power base,[181] or perhaps simply because the eldest daughter of the House of York had little need of grand display to assert her social standing in England. Indeed, the impact of the queen's appearance on those present during the vigil of her coronation, and on the coronation day itself, was clearly immense. Yet, even on this occasion, things did not go according to plan, for several spectators were crushed to death as they scrambled to cut pieces from the carpet on which the queen walked.[182] The inclusion of this memorandum not only further precludes the notion that the Memoir offered polished and propagandist accounts, but almost certainly served as a warning for future coronation arrangements. It was not the first time Henry VII's heralds had included a health-and-safety memorandum in their notes.[183]

The English royal heralds were heavily involved in the preparation, marshalling and execution of much of the ceremonial and secular ritual that accompanied Elizabeth of York's coronation in November 1487, as well as in the supervision of the heraldic decorations. In the procession from the Tower to St. Pauls, the suns and white roses of the house of York blazed forth from the caparisons of the henchmen's horses. The latter symbol had been a favoured device of the queen's father, Edward IV,[184] and it is testimony to Henry VII's growing security in the aftermath of Stoke that these Yorkist symbols *par excellence* were allowed so proud and public a display. The following day, before the coronation feast, Jasper Tudor, duke of Bedford and Lord High Steward, rode a horse richly adorned with red dragons and the red roses of the triumphant house of Lancaster.[185] Arguably 'more confident if its own righteousness and legitimacy, more ideologically self-reliant' at the end of 1487, the new dynasty boldly invoked the heraldic badges that proclaimed its new-found permanency.[186]

Despite the fifteenth-century heralds' *ex officio* preoccupation with secular ceremonial, it is curious that the account of the coronation of Elizabeth of York is remarkably detailed and accurate in its description of the liturgical ritual of crowning and anointing. This contrasts with the extant heraldic narratives of the coro-

---

[181] Laynesmith, *Last Medieval Queens*, p. 92.
[182] Below, pp. 136–7.
[183] Following the collapse of a viewing platform inside the church at Henry VII's own coronation, the heralds included in their account a reminder that scaffolding be properly secured: BL, MS. Eg. 985, fol. 42.
[184] Below, p. 134; Anglo, *Images*, p. 77. Wardrobe accounts of Edward IV for the year 1480 reveal the place of these emblems in embroidered designs, and so on. *Privy Purse Expenses of Elizabeth of York: Wardrobe Accounts of Edward the Fourth*, (1830; repr. New York, 1972), esp. pp. 117, 118, 119, 136, 137, 143, 144, 152.
[185] Below, p. 140.
[186] Bennett, *Lambert Simnel*, p. 119.

nations of Elizabeth Woodville in 1465 and of Richard III and Anne Neville in 1483, and suggests that the Memoir heralds made recourse to independent information. The most likely source of their information must have been the members of the chapel royal, with whose work the heralds' own duties appear to have overlapped at times. The result is a blend of the secular and religious not found in analogous heraldic narrative accounts, and an uncommonly full treatment of a fifteenth-century queen's crowning.

Following a description of the banquet, the coronation narrative concludes with an extensive, artificially constructed list of some several hundred individuals grouped into categories of knights, bannerets, lords and ladies. Among those feasting with the queen at Westminster were Lady Margaret Pole, the daughter of the late duke of Clarence and sister to the unfortunate earl of Warwick; Lord Edmund of Suffolk, now effectively heir to the Yorkist claim; the semi-independent northern magnates, Henry earl of Northumberland and Thomas earl of Derby, together with knights and esquires of their affinities (including several reputed to have fought for Richard III);[187] and former knights and esquires of the body to Edward IV.[188] In all, the occasion was attended by some 300 named members of the nobility and gentry, and the actual number may have been far greater.[189] So extensive and systematic is the list of guests, moreover, that it is again difficult to escape the sense that Henry VII recognised the utility of the heralds' reportage for his own surveillance purposes.

There was a brief decline in the spectacular aspect of Henry VII's kingship after November 1487, his regality and liberality displayed only at the customary celebrations and weekly ceremonial routines of the calendar year.[190] These were important occasions nonetheless, and the annual festive seasons brought further opportunities for spectacle, largess, piety and open household, as well as for court plays, disguisings, carols, minstrelsy and other revels.[191] The Memoir's reportage for 1488 in particular is almost wholly devoted to the great feast days of the calendar year.[192] The celebration of New Year involved the crying of largess, a crown-wearing, a sumptuous banquet, and the presence of the queen by her husband's side, a notable feature of the descriptive accounts contained in the Memoir. At the great banquet that season the king and queen sat beneath cloths of estate, the

---

[187] Esp. Sir Marmaduke Constable and Sir Gervase Clifton.
[188] Esp. Sir John Cheney, Sir Walter Hungerford, Sir William Stonor and Sir William Norris. In addition, Sir John Fogge was a former treasurer and privy counsellor for Edward IV.
[189] Below, pp. 145–50.
[190] Anglo, *Spectacle*, p. 52.
[191] Below, pp. 151–61, 162, 164–5, 182–4; TNA, E404/79/311, E404/79/109(263); *Materials*, i, p. 337, ii, pp. 60, 68. See also S. Anglo, 'The Court Festivals of Henry VII: a Study based upon the Account Books of John Heron, Treasurer of the Chamber', *BJRL*, 43 (September, 1960), pp. 12–45.
[192] See esp. below, pp. 151–64.

queen's suspended somewhat lower than her husband's in a gesture presumably calculated to advertise both their unity and the queen's lesser and dependent dignity.[193] The celebration of the feast of St George at Windsor that year was also lavish, perhaps in recompense for the debacle of the previous year. With the full celebrations having been deferred until the weekend, the event spanned the usual three days and saw the queen and Lady Margaret Beaufort issued with matching liveries of the Order of the Garter, specially crafted for the occasion. A 35-line song or poem in rhyme royal was composed for the feast in praise of Henry VII and celebrating the wearing of livery together; whether or not it was composed by a herald, its inclusion in the Memoir certainly underscores the triumph of the occasion.[194]

When Princess Margaret was born in November 1489, the early Tudor court witnessed another of those spectacular state occasions that had enlivened the first two years of the reign. Of the two christening accounts contained in the Memoir, only the latter includes a description of the ritual confinement that preceded the birth. The same lavish textiles as were used for the decoration of the church for Prince Arthur's christening were also considered suitable for the queen's chambers: the inner chamber, where the baby was to be born, was 'hanged and steyled with riche clothe of arras of blew with flourdelisses of golde' and equipped with a great bed and a pallet, above which was suspended a rich cloth-of-gold, velvet and ermine canopy of diverse colours, embroidered with the red roses of the house of Lancaster. The room was further furnished with an altar and relics, and with a cupboard bearing plate for the queen's daily use.[195] Here indeed is a glimpse of the lavish, private, relic-laden and richly symbolic setting of royal childbirth rarely seen by contemporaries, much less by the modern eye. Once prayers had been said for the queen, and the curtains drawn, men were excluded from an essentially private, female world. But for the atypical admission of members of a French embassy, an astonishing privilege indeed, 'no maner off officier' should have entered the queen's chamber 'but ladies and gentilwomen after the olde coustume'.[196] Perhaps, as one historian has suggested, the king wished to impress the foreign visitors with the visual evidence of the success of his rule and the fertility of his queen.[197]

The christening ceremony itself largely followed the format of Prince Arthur's baptism, and the event apparently experienced no hitches like those in 1486.[198] On

[193] Below, p. 154.
[194] Below, pp. 155–60.
[195] Below, pp. 174–5.
[196] Below, p. 175.
[197] Laynesmith, *Last Medieval Queens*, p. 115.
[198] The only statement of notable difference between the two reports was the inclusion in the latter of Garter King of Arms in the baptismal procession, walking just before the Constable. Independent evidence suggests that Writhe had been away on embassy at

this occasion Archbishop Morton was godfather, and the ubiquitous Margaret Beaufort, namesake to the little princess, took her place as one of the godmothers at the font. Also appointed godmother at the font was Elizabeth duchess of Norfolk, whose own daughter had once been married to the hapless boy prince, Richard duke of York. The queen's sister Anne carried the chrismal cloth, and the marchioness of Berkeley carried the child under the canopy, supported by the earls of Arundel and Shrewsbury, and was godmother to the confirmation. Also taking part in the baptismal procession that day were Viscount Welles, the young earl of Essex and Edmund Grey of Ruthin, earl of Kent. Bishop Alcock of Ely, who as bishop of Worcester had hallowed Prince Arthur's font, baptised the princess.[199]

The day before the baby was christened, her elder brother Arthur was created Prince of Wales and earl of Chester and dubbed to knighthood in a ceremony marshalled by the heralds and described in detail in the Memoir.[200] The royal barge that carried Arthur from Sheen on the Friday, filled with lords spiritual and temporal, officers of arms, trumpeters and minstrels, was greeted first at Chelsea by the mayor and crafts of London, and then at Lambeth by the ambassadors of Spain.[201]

On great state occasions and at annual seasonal celebrations the king was surrounded variously by peers, knights, esquires, noble ladies and household officials, each of whom, it seems, was being urgently and impressively bound to the new regime by the ceremonial and ritual of the early Tudor court. Nowhere is this process more evident than in the Memoir. The importance of station and hierarchy to the court in which the Memoir had its genesis is a noteworthy feature of the text, as individuals are typically identified by name, rank, ceremonial function, and occasionally family connection, and as Henry VII strove to advertise his princely dignity and the success of his regime to assembled estates, heralds, visiting dignitaries, and even the humble folk on hand to watch the passing parades.

Few among the court notables are as prominent in the Memoir as the king's own mother, Lady Margaret Beaufort, countess of Richmond and Derby and great-great-granddaughter of Edward III. In 1992 Michael Jones and Malcolm Underwood noted, with reference to the Leland-Hearne edition of the Memoir, that 'Margaret's status at the new royal court and the precedence and honour accorded to her were semi-regal'; the original account brings this out still more fully.[202] Mar-

---

the time of Arthur's christening: *Materials*, ii, pp. 45, 82; Godfrey et al., *College of Arms*, p. 42.

[199] Below, pp. 180–82.

[200] Below, pp. 175–80; See John Writhe's 'Articles concernyng the creacion of my lord prynce', in Coll. Arms, MS. L8a, fols 17v–19.

[201] Anglo, *Spectacle*, p. 52.

[202] M. K. Jones and M. G. Underwood, *The King's Mother: Lady Margaret Beaufort Countess of Richmond and Derby* (Cambridge, 1992), p. 69. A similar observation was made

garet Beaufort is mentioned thirty-eight times in the text, less only than the royal couple, and on almost all occasions she is accorded prominence, if not precedence, in proceedings. She attended Queen Elizabeth on her pre-coronation journey from Greenwich to the Tower and sat at the queen's right hand in the parliament chamber that evening, an action which reinforced the process by which the new regime was both created and advertised.[203] During the anointing and crowning and the banquet that followed she watched over proceedings with the king, hidden from view on a shrouded platform. She was even summoned to Kenilworth, to her son's side, when news of a rebel landing in Ireland broke in May 1487.[204] On Christmas day that same year Margaret was dressed like the queen – clad in a like mantel and surcoat and similarly adorned with a jewelled coronet. During the Garter celebrations of 1488 she wore an identical costume to the queen's own, and was similarly issued with the livery of the order of the Garter, a sign of special standing. This was, as Jones and Underwood note, an aura she deliberately cultivated.[205] Above all, when a daughter was born to the royal couple in 1489, the baby was named Margaret after her grandmother.

---

in the early twentieth century by E. M. G. Routh, *Lady Margaret. A Memoir of Lady Margaret Beaufort, Countess of Richmond and Derby, Mother of Henry VII* (London, 1924), p. 62

[203] Below, pp. 129, 145; Jones and Underwood, *King's Mother*, p. 69; Laynesmith, *Last Medieval Queens*, p. 89.

[204] Below, p. 111; C. H. C. Cooper, *Memoir of Margaret Countess of Richmond and Derby* (Cambridge, 1874), pp. 37–8; Routh, *Lady Margaret*, pp. 67–8; *Letters of the Kings of England*, ed. J. O. Halliwell, 2 vols (London, 1848).

[205] Jones and Underwood, *King's Mother*, p. 69.

THE MANUSCRIPT

Composition

British Library, MS. Cotton Julius B. XII (henceforth Julius B. XII), a composite manuscript volume of diverse historical texts in English and Latin, was bound into its present form after 1621. It has undergone little alteration since that time, and today contains over sixty constituent parts of paper and vellum. The great majority of these components date from the fifteenth and sixteenth centuries, appear to be professional scribal transcripts, and include heraldic materials and narrative accounts, records of land grant and debt payment, petitions and inquisitions, and several items of genealogical interest from the reign of Elizabeth I. Only one item is substantially older: a 13-folio vellum manuscript listed in the table of contents as *Inquisitio de Gubernatione Militum Templi in Anglia*,[1] and written in a clear, early Anglicana script of *c*.1300.[2]

Although the binding process has served largely to mask evidence of the original presentation of the manuscripts, remnants of an obsolete foliation scheme still visible on the *recto* of each leaf indicate that Julius B. XII was created by the sewing together of separate pamphlets. Patterns of wear and discolouration throughout the volume suggest that many of its parts, such as the vellum *Inquisitio*, had a working life outside the present volume: some have been rendered incomplete by loss or damage; others have suffered minor injury; still others have lost something in the re-gathering and cutting of the pages. Several items appear to have been re-bound more than once.

Of the constituent parts of Julius B. XII, the item of interest to the present study is located at folios 8v to 66 and commences: 'A shorte and a brief memory by licence and correccion of the fu[r]st progresse of our souveraigne lorde king Henry the vijth' (henceforth the Memoir). The Memoir comprises three distinctive scribal hands and consists of 58 folios in three makes of paper, watermarked with a crowned star,[3] a unicorn, and a *croix formé*[4] respectively. The chainlines of

---

[1] MS. Cotton Julius B. XII, fols 67–82.
[2] I am indebted to Professor R. M. Thomson for his assistance in the dating of this hand.
[3] This watermark is very similar to watermark no. 6113 in C. M. Briquet, *Les Filigranes*, 2nd edn, 2 vols (New York, 1966), ii, p. 354. Paper of this sort, marked with a crowned star, originated in France and became increasingly common in documents toward the end of the fifteenth century. Samples have been found in the Low Countries and in books published by Caxton.
[4] Similar to Briquet, no. 5457.

the first make of paper stand 23 mm apart, and the crowned star is located in the fifth channel from the outer edge, centred between the top and bottom of the leaf. The crowned star measures 42 mm in height and has eight rays. The second make of paper, beginning on fol. 29, bears much fainter chainlines, and these stand approximately 30 mm apart. Its unicorn watermark spans the third and fourth channels and measures some 97 mm from the tip of its horn to the end of its tail. Where the third scribal hand is present, the paper's chainlines stand 29–30 mm apart, and the watermark also spans the third and fourth channels. This watermark, the *croix formé*, measures 16 mm by 16 mm.

The leaves of Julius B. XII, and hence of the Memoir, were cut to their present size during the final binding and now measure approximately 280 mm by 210 mm, with slight variation at the binding edge. The average writing space on each leaf differs between individual scribes and between portions of text in the same hand. Approximate measurements are: 165 mm by 135 mm for the first scribe, 206 mm by 135 mm for the second, and 210 mm by 140 mm for the third. Where the first scribe has included verse in his work, the lines measure approximately 165 mm by 105 mm. There are an average of 27 lines per page, but fewer where verse is present. Verse is arranged with care: each stanza is indented from the main text and separated from its predecessor and/or successor by an empty line, and each line of verse commences with a majuscule letter.

Although the original number and size of the folio gatherings of the Memoir are no longer apparent, the use of catchwords by the first scribe, as is evident at the bottom of fols 12v, 20v, 28v, 36v and 44v, suggests that the folios in this hand were probably once gathered into groups of eight. The number of leaves bearing a watermark is not equal to those without, however; and the absence of a watermark on fols 16, 17 and 18 would seem to indicate the cancellation of leaves.

Also manifest on several leaves of the first scribe's work are traces of what was probably the earliest foliation scheme applied to the Memoir. The first example of this scheme may be found on fol. 7 of Julius B. XII, which bears the numeral 'iij' in the lower right corner of the leaf. Likewise, fol. 8 has been marked 'iiij'. Along the lower edge of the folios bearing catchwords are traces of lettering which might once have been Roman numerals, but which have been too greatly injured for identification. Moreover, the Latin word *prima* is evident on the bottom edge of fol. 29, and perhaps also on fols 13 and 37, although in the latter two cases the words are no longer legible. Both the Roman numerals and *prima* appear to be in the hand of the first scribe, and are only found on his material. Since the word *prima* on fol. 29 is preceded by the catchword 'the lad' on fol. 28v, and as the posited remnants of *prima* on fols 13 and 37 are also preceded by catchwords, it seems likely that we are looking at a system for marking the beginning and end of each gathering. As mentioned above, fol. 29 also introduces the second make of paper, that marked with a unicorn watermark.

INTRODUCTION: THE MANUSCRIPT

By and large Julius B. XII has been remarkably well preserved. Discolouration and degradation are chiefly confined to the outer edges of each leaf, as is consistent with the wear of any bound material. As far as the Memoir is concerned grime, creases and small tears appear on the bottom right corners of most of the leaves. Several rust-coloured spots and small stains, together with the inky prints of scribes, are evident along the outer edges of several leaves, and on some the text itself has been marred by ink stains. In at least two cases repair or alteration to the paper has caused slight loss of text: a flourish on a majuscule *I* on fol. 18 and the final *p* of 'archbishop' on fol. 40v were incorporated into the binding; and a flourish on a miniscule *h*, on the last line of fol. 21, was obliterated by a small repair. Fading, although minimal, has occurred to the greatest extent in the portion of text produced by the second scribe. Here the lettering has lightened to a brownish shade, perhaps indicating an ink of lesser quality. The legibility of the text is scarcely diminished.

The language of the Memoir is largely unremarkable for a manuscript of late fifteenth-century English provenance, and for a document which most probably originated in the vicinity of London. Few dialectical characteristics are present, although vestiges of a southern orthography may be seen in the use of *eth* and *ith* in the third person singular verb-forms, and in the spelling of the word 'hundreth' on fol. 49 and 'chirch/e' throughout.[5] But for one exception[6] thorn is used only in formal address, where it is rendered *y*, and in all other cases *th* is used. The *sh* construction is used throughout, *f* has been capitalised by a double form of the miniscule, and *o* is lengthened by doubling. The presence of the letter *c* with a soft-*s* sound is frequent, as in 'city', 'certaine' and 'licence'. In several instances a *y* or a dotted-*i* has been employed to distinguish the letter *i* from other minims in an individual word, but no practice is consistently followed. The *y* prefix is used in only two places: on fol. 24, in the statement 'that every man myght drynke ynow'; and in a marginal annotation on the same folio.[7] The infinitive ending *n* is never used, and the present participle always ends in either *yng* or *ing*.

A number of genitive inflections also appear throughout the text, and these are: *s*, *es*, and the mark of suspension for the endings *es* or *is* in both English and Latin. The plural is shown by *s*, *es*, *is*, *z*, *ez*, and the mark of suspension mentioned above. Occasionally a plural noun is written without any mark of inflection, such as 'appurtenance' on fol. 16v and 'thing' on fol. 20. The former example was required by the verse rhyme, but the latter was perhaps simply a scribal error. The usual forms of the third person pronoun in the plural are: 'they', 'ther' and

---

[5] What appears to be an error of transcription in a portion of verse on fol. 14v, namely the use of 'standeth' where the rhyme required 'stands', almost certainly betrays the southern origin of the scribe, if not of the materials from which he copied.
[6] On fol. 45v, in an interlineation, thorn has been rendered *p*.
[7] Julius B. XII, fol. 24, and below, p. 106.

'theym', but the conventional modern spellings of 'their' and 'them' also appear. The most common relative pronouns used are 'which/e' and 'who/m'; 'that' occurs only rarely. The possessive pronoun 'whose' occurs throughout.[8]

The language of the Memoir is also heavily reliant upon French, and examples of derivation ('recountrede') and appropriation ('ouvert/e') appear right the way through the text. A scribal error on fol. 40, where the word 'chamber' is preceded by the cancellation of *s*, suggests that this noun still retained the soft *sh*-sound favoured by the French tongue. In addition, the orthography of a very large number of names and words of French origin, from Lord 'Straunge' to 'observaunce' and 'attendaunce', seems to suggest that these words maintained a pronunciation closer to French than allowed by modern English.

The first scribe (henceforth Scribe A) was responsible for the largest portion of the extant text, namely the account of the first provincial progress of Henry VII and the description of all entertainment and celebrations up to the feast of St. George in 1488. A second scribe (Scribe B) took up the task approximately one quarter of the way down fol. 51, directly after an extended verse relating to the 1488 chapter of the Order of the Garter. A third scribe (Scribe C) continued the narrative from part-way through a description of the creation of Prince Arthur in November 1489 on fol. 60v, and brought the text to its conclusion. Scribe B provides an additional note at the foot of fol. 21v and an emendation against the work of Scribe A on fol. 42. Scribe C's hand also occurs in a marginal annotation on fol. 23, and in several minor corrections against the work of Scribe A on fols 24, 25 and 41.

Certain features of Scribe A's work suggest that the Memoir was created by the copying of earlier written materials, namely misprints resulting from eye-skip (fols 24v, 32 and 40v) and transposition (fols 14v and 38v). In replicating a passage of verse from one of the Worcester pageants, on fol. 14v, Scribe A allowed his eye to fall upon the line directly above, so repeating 'this trespasse'. He corrected his mistake before proceeding. The same scribe was again compelled to correct his own work, on 24v, after mistakenly jumping from the phrase 'and all the prelates that wer ther kyste the saide relique or palle' over the intervening lines to 'al the religiouse people of that house': 'prelates' is thus entered above the cancellation of 'people'. By contrast, an error resulting from eye-skip on fol. 41 went unnoticed by all three Memoir scribes, and in consequence there remains the nonsensical statement: 'And at the right ende of the table ther was ordeynede a stage for kinges of armes *stoode corownede*, heraulde[s] and purservantes, whiche kinges of armes stode corownede and beheld that noble service the wise that they cowed' (my italics).[9]

[8] For some introductory material on Middle English grammar and dialect, see S. Horobin and J. J. Smith, *An Introduction to Middle English* (Edinburgh, 2002); C. Jones, *An Introduction to Middle English* (New York, 1972).
[9] Julius B. XII, fol. 41. I have altered the sentence to: 'And at the right ende of the table

INTRODUCTION: THE MANUSCRIPT

Moreover, a peculiar circumstance on fol. 45v creates the sense that eye-skip has resulted in the permanent loss of material regarding the celebration of New Year in 1488. In a passage relating to the customary crying of largess by the officers of arms on New Year's Day, the monetary gifts awarded to the heralds by each of the senior noblemen and women present have been recorded.[10] After each memorandum is recorded the heralds' cry of largess and the style of the gift-giver. However, in the case of Richard Fox, bishop of Exeter and Lord Privy Seal, the notice of his twenty-shilling gift is immediately and incongruously followed by the style of the queen's sister, the Lady Cecily, Viscountess Welles: *'Largesse de noble princesse la seur de la reigne notre souveraigne dame et vicountesse de Welles'*.[11] Neither the correct response to the bishop of Exeter's donation nor any record of Lady Cecily's gift are given. It appears that Lady Cecily's style was mistakenly imported from later in the copy-text, and that the portion of narrative which belonged between the notices of the bishop's gift and Cecily's style was omitted. Just how much material was lost through this error is uncertain.

The proliferation of minor errors and a greater untidiness of script at certain places in Scribe A's portion of the narrative lend further support to the notion of a copyist reproducing large amounts of text at a time. This scribe has fallen prey to word confusion (this/thus, fol. 39) and letter confusion, writing 'poope people' instead of 'poore people' (fol. 9) and 'ster stode' instead of 'ther stode' (fol. 38). In several cases he has repeated 'of', 'in' and 'have'. He has replicated 'after that' (fol. 40), 'shewed in the' (fol. 46v) and 'byfor the Counstable' (fols 38v–39) – although the latter error was corrected – and he has confused plural and singular forms (fol. 20). On occasions he has also confused English and French, writing '*in* la countie dEssex' (fol. 30v) and, conversely, 'al other lordez *et* ladies' (fol. 24). A similar error was adjusted on fol. 38v. If the former mistake indicates the scribe's easy comprehension of French, or at least of the French material he was transcribing, the latter examples are more difficult to explain. It is, in fact, possible that Scribe A worked from French sources on these occasions.

Ultimately Scribe A did not complete his commission, but the work of his two successors in finishing the text differs only in a few minor matters. Scribe B's hand is more compact than that of Scribe A and has none of the flourishes of his predecessor's script. On occasion his writing strays from the horizontal; at other times he makes use of ruled lines to guide his text. This is especially evident on fol. 53, and where he creates lists of names in column format. Scribe B also favours a slightly different orthographical style from that of his predecessor. Thus he writes 'mouder' and 'ouder', prefers the plural ending *is*, and often writes 'off' instead of

---

ther was ordeynede a stage for kinges of armes, heraulde[s] and purservantes, whiche kinges of armes stode corownede ...'. See below, p. 143.

[10] Below, pp. 151–2.
[11] Julius B. XII, fol. 45v, and see below, p. 152 and n. 538.

'of'. His errors are relatively few and have, in most cases, been rectified, leaving but two cases of repetition (fols 53 and 57v), the misspelling of Stephen ('Sthephen', fol. 60), and two examples of word confusion (on/an, fol. 62 and xij/xxij, fol. 53). He makes only one serious error (fol. 52v), the reasons for which are not apparent, but which has been struck through.[12]

Scribe C's portion of text is markedly shorter than those of his two predecessors and appears to have been rather less carefully executed. He uses no ruled lines, and the spacing between words and lines varies enormously. His orthographical style tends toward that of Scribe B, with a preference for 'off' and the plural ending *is*. Like Scribes A and B, Scribe C makes his own errors of transposition (fol. 62), omission (fols 65, 65v), repetition (fols 61, 61v), and simple carelessness (fol. 62v). Scribe C's contribution also appears to be that of both proof-reader – he rectified an omission by Scribe A on fol. 25 – and editor correcting the work of Scribe A against draft notes. Thus, where Scribe A had noted that 'the king yave great largesse', Scribe C cancelled the sentence, inserted 'no' in the left-hand margin, and placed the following statement in the right margin: 'only but xx li for lake of advertiseme[nt] but ther ben president[l]y ynow to be shewede of C li or a C marces'.[13]

Scribe C may also have been responsible for cancelling a somewhat controversial comment, penned by Scribe A at the foot of the same folio: 'And on newyeres day Thomas Lovell delyverde the kinges and the quenes larges, but for the quen so little a largesse wer any was yeven was ther non in our dayes sene, wherfor I passe over to set the service in boke'.

One further, rather curious, scribal error merits discussion, for it is not confined to one scribe, but made on several occasions by both Scribes A and B. This is the consistent confusion over the Christian name of the bishop of Exeter. On fol. 25v Scribe A has inserted the name 'Richard' above the cancellation of 'John', and on fols 51, 52v and 53 Scribe B has inserted 'Richard' over erasures. In one instance at least, the erased word appears to have commenced with the majuscule letter *J*. On fol. 29, as twice on fol. 45v, the erroneous 'Lord John Fox' remains. It seems likely that the fault lay with the original material from which the complete transcript derived, and that the name 'John' was consistently copied into the text, before being altered to 'Richard' in four of the seven cases.

Of the three hands present in the extant version of the Memoir, the last is the most easily identifiable, and it is with little doubt that of John Writhe, Garter King of Arms from 1478 to 1504. Typically large and untidy, Garter Writhe's highly distinctive secretary hand was, like that of Scribe C, made up of sharp, angular strokes and incomplete letterforms 'rather roughly written',[14] and it scarcely altered

[12] Cancelled is the statement: '... and after, Clarenceux King of Armes and Master John Lacy, clerk of the prive seall to the King of Daunemark'.
[13] Julius B. XII, fol. 24, and see below, p. 106, n. 239.

throughout his long career. As may be seen by the samples provided, there is a striking similarity between the hand of Scribe C and verified samples of Writhe's script.[15]

Moreover, the survival of two further documents in Writhe's hand, now housed at the College of Arms and the British Library respectively, are suggestive of John Writhe's association with the Memoir. The first of these, a manuscript entitled 'The Articles concernyng the Creacion of my Lord Prince', represents a two-folio script for the order of ceremony for Arthur's creation as Prince of Wales in 1489.[16]

The 'Articles' were evidently set down by John Writhe less than a week before the ceremony, as he commences his list with a notice of 'the conveyance of my lord prince from Mortelake to Westmynster uppon Wensday next comyng'. The details provided in the 'Articles' correspond almost exactly to the order of events described in the Memoir account of Prince Arthur's creation. Since John Writhe was then Garter King of Arms, we might assume that he was pivotal in the organization and supervision of the occasion.

The second item of interest is a British Library manuscript entitled *Writhe's Book of Knights* (now BL, MS. Additional 46354) and belonging to a multi-volume set known as 'Wriothesley's Heraldic Collections'. *Writhe's Book* chiefly comprises lists of knights arranged chronologically under the occasion of their creation,[17] together with a record of the fee-payment status of each. The names of knights created between 1487 and 1494, and in the thirteenth year of Henry VII's reign (1497–8), are in Writhe's hand. More particularly, folios 16–19v contain lists of knights made at the battle of Stoke, at Coventry during the summer of 1487, at the coronation of Elizabeth of York, and at the creation of Prince Arthur mentioned above. Since both the order in which the names are written and the several notices regarding the knights' payment status match almost exactly the format and content of the same information in the Memoir, it is probable that one document was created from the other. The presence of some additional notes in *Writhe's Book* alongside the names of Sir Humphrey Savage, Sir Thomas Grey, Sir William Tyrwhitt, Sir Amyas Paulet and others suggest that this work was compiled later than, and perhaps from, the relevant portion of the Memoir.[18]

---

[14] L. Campbell et al., *A Catalogue of Manuscripts in the College of Arms. Collections* (London, 1988), p. 11.

[15] Other verified samples of Writhe's hand are contained in *John Wrythe's Garter Book*, an elaborate manuscript belonging to the duke of Buccleuch, and among the holdings of the College of Arms, e.g. MS. L.8a.

[16] Coll. Arms, MS. L8a, fols 17v–19.

[17] With two exceptions: fols 18v and 19, where lists of names and memoranda have been inserted that are not strictly chronological.

[18] BL, MS. Add. 46 354, fol. 18.

The hand of Scribe B, meanwhile, appears to be that of John Writhe's son Thomas Wriothesley, Wallingford Pursuivant from 1489 to 1504, and then Garter King of Arms until his death in 1534. Unlike that of his father, Wriothesley's own hand varied during his career as a herald, and is therefore more difficult to identify with certainty. Nevertheless, verified samples of Wriothesley's own script resemble very closely the hand of Memoir Scribe B, while Wriothesley's monogram 'Ihc' appears at the top of fols 53 and 53v, together suggesting that this section was written by Wriothesley or – less likely – by his clerk.[19]

Scribe A has not been identified.[20] The more decorative nature of this lettering, particularly the proliferation of flourishes on ascenders and descenders, together with the methodical foliation of the quires on which he worked, suggest that Scribe A was a professional.[21] The presence of a marginal annotation on fol. 24 and several minor corrections in Garter Writhe's hand, and of Wriothesley's additions and emendations on fols 21v and 42, further implies that Scribe A's portion was executed under supervision. Both Writhe and Wriothesley are known to have enlisted the services of scriveners.[22] It is interesting, moreover, that Scribe A was further responsible for the two pamphlets that immediately precede the Memoir in Julius B. XII, and that items two, three and four each follows the one before without the intervention of a blank leaf. It is possible that Scribe A had been engaged in the creation of an heraldic miscellany on behalf of John Writhe, for the articles before the Memoir in Julius B. XII pertain to subjects frequently associated with the English heralds.[23] The picture that emerges is one of a scribal transcription of earlier material, quite possibly draft notes, prepared over a period of several years under the supervision of John Writhe, Garter King of Arms. The transcription was probably begun by a professional scribe in Writhe's employment

---

[19] I owe a debt of gratitude to Mrs Ann Payne, former head of the manuscipts dept. at the British Library, for drawing my attention to Wriothesley's monogram. Wriothesley became a skilful and energetic manuscript-maker, and his work may be found throughout the holdings of the College of Arms: see for example Coll. Arms, MSS. L. 8a and M17.

[20] The nearest match I have yet uncovered is in BL, MS. Cotton Julius B. I. This is a paper manuscript of 102 leaves, measuring 11½" by 8", compiled soon after the death of Edward IV and written throughout in the same hand. It is in large part a chronicle account, primarily copied from older versions. See *Chronicles of London*, ed. C. L. Kingsford (Oxford, 1905), p. xiii.

[21] I am again indebted to Mrs Ann Payne for suggesting the possible professional status of Scribe A.

[22] As in the creation of *Wrythe's Garter Book*. See H. S. London, *The Life of William Bruges, the First Garter King of Arms* (London, 1970), p. 14 and App. XVII 'John Wrythe's Garter Book', pp. 112–13.

[23] Items one and two are genealogical, and item three depicts ceremonial of the early years of the reign of Henry VII. The early foliation scheme described above lends further support to this suggestion.

INTRODUCTION: THE MANUSCRIPT

as part of a compilation of materials pertaining to the heralds' duties or interests. For reasons lost to posterity, however, the scrivener did not complete the Memoir, and it was left to Writhe's son Thomas, then a young pursuivant, and Writhe himself to complete the text. Wriothesley made several emendations to the work of Scribe A, while Writhe's alterations can be seen against the work of both Scribe A and Thomas Wriothesley.

* * *

If the Memoir was the brainchild of Garter John Writhe, then some clue to the text's history prior to its incorporation into Julius B. XII must lie in the troubled history of the holdings of the College of Arms. At the time the transcript was completed, the officers of arms had neither library nor permanent corporate residence after the loss of their house at Coldharbour. The heralds' occupation of Coldharbour had provided each of the principal among them with an individual workroom and a central library for the storage of common books, and during its brief period of operation the house and its contents were supervised by Garter Writhe. Upon the return of Coldharbour to the Crown in 1487, Writhe reportedly gathered together his own books and all those held in common.

During their protracted feud in the 1530s, Thomas Wriothesley as Garter King of Arms and Thomas Benolt, Clarenceux, maintained a bitter difference of opinion on the fate of those items rescued by Writhe. Each claimed that the manuscripts in question lay in the possession of the other. The warring kings of arms both died in 1534, but only Benolt's will was ever located: his books evidently passed first to Thomas Hawley, Norroy King of Arms, and then down the line of successive Clarenceux Kings of Arms.[24] Garter Wriothesley's holdings, on the other hand, probably passed to his son Charles, before being dispersed upon the latter's death as Windsor Herald in 1562. Most were purchased by either Sir William Dethick (York Herald 1570–87 and Garter 1587–1606) or his father Gilbert.[25] From William Dethick many of these manuscripts seem to have passed directly to Sir Robert Cotton (1571–1631). As will be seen, the Memoir was in Cotton's hands by the 1620s.

It is not improbable that the earlier portions of the Memoir, or the draft notes from which it was created, were among those manuscripts originally gathered together by Writhe in 1487 that ended up in the hands of the notorious William Dethick a century later. A hand very like Dethick's own appears in the margin against the account of the Henry VII's first provincial progress. Moreover, by the time the heralds took possession of their new corporate residence at Derby House

[24] An inventory of Benolt's library was compiled after his death, but it does not appear to contain reference to anything like the Memoir or parts thereof. The inventory is printed in Wagner, *Heralds and Heraldry*, 2nd edn (repr. Oxford, 2000), App. F, 'Benolt's Inventory', pp. 150–7.

[25] Godfrey et al., *College of Arms* (London, 1963), pp. 169–70.

in 1564–5 their library had come to include a number of manuscripts once held as private property, and it is therefore possible that the Memoir was among those manuscripts newly deposited into the common holding. As Garter King of Arms, William Dethick had his own quarters at Derby House, and it was here that he entertained fellow members of the original Society of Antiquaries, including Sir Robert Cotton. The overlap of heraldic and antiquarian interests at this juncture is critical,[26] and many of the subjects investigated by the Society's members correspond with matters recorded in the Memoir: the forms of the creation of lords, the ceremonies observed at court, the rules governing the activities of the officers of arms and so on. Indeed, these interests are reflected in almost all of the material now contained in Julius B. XII.

Evidence of provenance suggests that the binder of Julius B. XII was a seventeenth-century antiquary associated with the library of Sir Robert Cotton. Cotton himself is one candidate. All of the constituent manuscripts had evidently made it into Cotton's possession by the early 1620s, during which years Julius B. XII was entered twice in the first substantial catalogue of the library's holdings. The first of these two entries, on fol. 130 of the *Catalogus Librorum Manuscriptorum in Bibliotheca Roberti Cottoni*, 1621, comprises a list of fourteen titles, all of which now are now among the contents of Julius B. XII.[27] The reference 'Julius B.12' was later penciled into the margin alongside the entry.[28] It is very likely that this early version of Julius B. XII was the manuscript Cotton 394, from which Roger Dodsworth made notes *c.* 1620.[29]

The second notice in question (fols 139–40) describes Julius B. XII in the form in which it exists today, and this is almost certainly the earliest extant reference to the present volume. Although it was begun in 1621, the *Catalogus* was not completed in that year, but continued to be augmented during the 1620s.[30] Dur-

---

[26] As discussed in K. Sharpe, *Sir Robert Cotton, 1586–1631. History and Politics in Early Modern England* (Oxford, 1979), pp. 17–48, and in C. E. Wright, 'The Elizabethan Society of Antiquaries and the Formation of the Cottonian Library', in F. Wormald and C. E. Wright (eds.), *The English Library before 1700* (London, 1958), pp. 176–212.

[27] BL, MS. Harley 6018, fols 3–145. The Memoir itself also appears twice in the *Catalogus*: on fols 130r and 139r. The first entry is a short title reference to the account of the progress only; the second refers to the progress narrative and all the other solemnities up to 1490. Given that John Writhe had made the final addition to the narrative over 120 years earlier, the first notice of the Memoir must represent an abbreviated entry for the complete narrative.

[28] The marginal reference 'Julius B.12' can have been added to the *Catalogus* no earlier than the end of the 1620s, at which time the decision was taken to institute the arrangement of volumes under the names of Roman emperors.

[29] Bodl., MS. SC 5086. See also F. Madden et al., *A Summary Catalogue of Western Manuscripts in the Bodleian Library at Oxford* (Oxford, 1937), pp. 958–9.

[30] *Thomas Smith's Catalogue of the Manuscripts in the Cottonian Library, 1696*, ed. C. G. C. Tite (Cambridge, 1984), p. 3.

INTRODUCTION: THE MANUSCRIPT

ing these years the composite volume Julius B. XII was probably compiled once and then re-constituted and entered again into the Cotton Library's first substantial catalogue.

Further circumstantial evidence places Robert Cotton near to the scene of the volume's creation. On fol. 108 of Julius B. XII, the second leaf of an article entitled: 'Edward the 4th's graunte of divers mannors in Cornwall and Kent ...' may be found the signature 'Robert Cotton Bruceus'. The signature coincides with a foliation scheme, now redundant, which took 'Edward the 4th's graunte' as its starting point and encompassed all of the subsequent items to the end of the present volume. Cotton's signature and the foliation appear to be of the same hand. It is therefore clear that Cotton at least owned the signature volume before it was bound into Julius B. XII, and he may well have compiled it. Since Cotton more commonly, but not exclusively, added 'Bruce' to his name after the accession of James I, and from the turn of the century, too, devoted his greatest attention to the augmentation of his library,[31] this volume was probably in his possession little earlier than 1603. Moreover, the signature volume contains a number of the constituent manuscripts from the prototype 'Julius B. 12' (Cotton MS. 394), suggesting that it was compiled between the two versions of the extant volume. The acquisitive Robert Cotton almost certainly oversaw, if not executed, the compilation of all three manuscripts, for most of the binding completed during his lifetime was either his own work or that of an employee.[32] Cotton's reputation for dismantling, constructing and rebinding manuscripts was nothing short of notorious.[33]

The antiquarian, historical and heraldic import of the constituent parts of Julius B. XII is emphasized by a series of marginalia entered in the present volume, some of which were probably already present at the final binding of the volume, with others made by men through whose hands the complete volume passed. Cotton's own hand appears to be among these. The most distinctive of the marginal annotations, a selection of notices in red ink on fols 21v, 22v and 23, betray an interest in the conduct, dress and fees of the officers of arms, and are most probably the work of a herald or of a seventeenth-century antiquary with an interest in heraldic matters.[34] In addition, the material in Julius B. XII is subdivided under headings corresponding to the volume's table of contents. A number of these replace titles, in an Elizabethan hand, which were partially lost during the cutting and rebinding. One such Elizabethan heading, located on the first leaf of the Memoir and introducing the account of the first progress of Henry VII, was not dam-

---

[31] *Smith's Catalogue*, p. 2.
[32] Wright, 'Society of Antiquaries', p. 204.
[33] Cotton viewed his library as a working collection and adopted a utilitarian approach to the arrangement of his manuscripts: Sharpe, *Cotton*, p. 68.
[34] McGee, thesis, p. xcviii.

aged during the binding and compares favourably to samples of the script of Sir William Dethick.[35]

The replacement headings, on the other hand, belong to at least one seventeenth-century hand, and at times this bears very strong resemblance to Cotton's own.[36] Cotton commonly headed manuscripts with new titles, marked them with marginal notes, and bound them with other papers on the same subject.[37]

While it is tempting to assign all of the replacement titles to the one hand, certain of them are less like Cotton's script and might be the work of an assistant or successor. However, neither Richard James, Cotton's librarian from c. 1625, nor Cotton's son, Sir Thomas, can claim responsibility.[38]

The table of contents to Julius B. XII is also of interest. A register of all items contained in the present volume, the table was prepared for Julius B. XII after its final binding in the 1620s: the index to the constituent parts corresponds directly to the volume's penultimate foliation scheme. These numerals, superseded during the nineteenth century, appear to have been inserted by the creator of the table of contents.[39] The table's title, *'Registrum Tractatuum in isto Volumine'*, matches the titles on similar tables of contents in Cotton manuscripts. One such example belongs to Nero D. X, and was most probably produced by a scrivener in the employ of the Cottonian library.[40] The date at which the table of contents was completed is uncertain, but the hand is of the late seventeenth century.

Other than Cotton's signature, there are no other marks of ownership on any of the manuscripts. However, in the latter half of the seventeenth century, Julius B. XII passed through the hands of Dr. Nathaniel Johnston (1627–1705), who on 29 May 1679 inserted a marginal corrigendum regarding the descent of the Savile family of Halifax, Yorkshire.[41] Some 53 years later, in 1732, the volume most probably came into contact with the men employed to assess the condition of the Cot-

[35] See BL, MS. Cotton Faustina E. V.
[36] The later heading 'The offices of John Nevill of Rabye An° 12 R^i. 2', on fol. 262, appears to be in Cotton's hand.
[37] Sharpe, *Cotton*, p. 68.
[38] For samples of Cotton's hand see *British Library Journal*, 18. 2 (1992), pp. 131, 151, 152.
[39] There are two anomalies in this scheme: the numerals between 63–66 have been omitted and 69 repeated.
[40] C. G. C. Tite, '"Lost or Stolen or Strayed": a Survey of the Manuscripts formerly in the Cotton Library', *British Library Journal*, 18.2 (1992), p. 134.
[41] On fol. 304 Johnston wrote: 'Who ever writ this hath been misinformed; for the present Lord Marquis of Halyfax is linially descended from Henry Savile who was rightful heir male to Edward Savile, son and heir of Sir Henry, as from original deed, as may be demonstrated by N: Johnston'. Although a practicing physician, Johnston's greatest interest lay in the antiquities and natural history of Yorkshire, and thirty years of study produced over one hundred volumes of collections. He is known to have borrowed other manuscripts for his own work.

ton collection after the fire at Ashburnham House in 1731.[42] In 1793 Joseph Planta commenced work on restoring the damaged volumes in the Cotton Library, and his descriptive catalogue of the library's holdings was first published in 1802.[43]

Planta's catalogue referred to the penultimate system of foliation in Julius B. XII, that corresponding to the table of contents, and it was perhaps then that the following notice of the errors in the system was inserted: 'Cons fol. 314. Fol. 62=67 omitted. 69+ double'. Much later the entire volume was re-foliated in Arabic numerals, in reference to which the very last page of Julius B. XII gives the final number of folios (316) and the date 20 June 1867. On 26 November 1969 the volume was rebound in half-morocco.[44]

Date

As has been discussed above, the Memoir was probably produced from one or more documents of an origin somewhat closer to the events described. If this is true, then the process of dating the manuscript is made more complex by two closely-related layers of production: that of the original reports or draft notes, and that of the complete transcription.

The process of note-taking and hence of transcription can have begun no earlier than mid-March 1486 and the commencement of the first provincial progress of Henry VII. Similarly, the contribution of Garter John Writhe to the extant transcript, both as the third and final scribe and as supervisor, indicates that the document must have been complete on his death in 1504. The *terminus ad quem* of the transcript may be reduced still further, for at the time of the Memoir's completion Prince Arthur was assumed to be alive and in reasonable health. The extant text cannot therefore have been finished later than 2 April 1502, when the sixteen-year-old prince died. It was almost certainly completed nearly a decade earlier, for the earl of Huntingdon and Sir John Savage, both of whom died in 1491, were also assumed to be living when the account of Prince Arthur's creation in 1489, one of the last events recorded in the Memoir, was set down in its present form.

The posited association of John Writhe and Thomas Wriothesley with the Memoir suggests that the portions of text produced by Scribes B and C may be dated to a time when both father and son were active as heralds. If we assume Wriothesley's earliest heraldic activities to have been as a pursuivant, and since Wriothesley was made Wallingford Pursuivant to the Prince of Wales only on 1 October 1489, it is unlikely that the portion of text in the hand of Scribe B was begun before that time. It is also possible that Thomas Wriothesley worked informally, perhaps as an assistant to his father prior to his appointment as Wallingford Pursuivant.

[42] Sharpe, *Cotton*, p. 83.
[43] *Smith's Catalogue*, p. 9.
[44] McGee, thesis, p. xcii.

Within the text itself lie further clues to the dating of the Memoir, and we are again left with the sense that the narrative now contained in Julius B. XII was produced in several stages. There are a number of references to Sir Edward Woodville, and at least four of these references (fols 26, 48v, 51 and 57v; pp. 112, 156, 160 and 172) are posthumous notices. In the first two cases, the invocation 'whose soul God pardon' directly follows the notice; the third contains a record of Woodville's death in Brittany around Whitsuntide 1488; and the last describes a requiem mass held in his honour in July 1489. By contrast, the notice of Woodville's participation in Prince Arthur's christening in November 1486 (fol. 23; p. 103) does not imply his decease and, if not a scribal oversight, was almost certainly written down while Woodville was still living. It is therefore likely that the greatest portion of the extant transcript, that is all of the material including, and subsequent to, the first posthumous mention of Edward Woodville on fol. 26, was copied into its present form after Woodville's death.[45] The material from the commencement of the narrative to the non-posthumous notice of Woodville on fol. 23 must have been penned before Whitsuntide 1488.

Similarly, when the report of affairs in 1486 and 1487 assumed its final form the slaying of the earl of Northumberland by a fractious mob at Cocklodge near Thirsk, in late April 1489, was not anticipated.[46] But on fol. 53 (p. 165) we find reference to Northumberland's death, and on fol. 57v (p. 172) mention of a requiem mass held in his honour three months later. All the material leading up to the coronation of Elizabeth of York on fol. 43 (p. 146), at which time the earl was apparently still alive, must have assumed its present form before 28 April 1489: fols 26 to 43 of Juius B. XII were presumably set down between c. 27 May 1488 and 28 April 1489. More interestingly, perhaps, fol. 51 (below, pp. 160–1) bears two references to 'the Lord Broke', a title only created in 1491 for Sir Robert Willoughby, who thereby became the first baron Willoughby de Broke. The material from fol. 51 to, say, 63v, where Sir John Savage (d. 1492) is last recorded as living, were probably completed within the year of 1491.

The question, of course, arises as to whether these clues are indicative of the several stages during which the transcript was completed, or of the writing of the draft fragments from which I have suggested the Memoir derives. I am inclined to believe that the evidence points toward the dating of the transcript, since any draft notes from which the Memoir might have derived would have been taken at the events depicted, or immediately thereafter, and are unlikely to contain information to assist the dating process. The remarks implying Edward Woodville's decease probably represent the interpolation of the scribes or supervisor working after Woodville's death, yet suitably close to it for his memory to have remained

---

[45] The dates of Whit Sunday, Whit Monday and Whit Tuesday 1488, were 25, 26 and 27 May.
[46] M. J. Bennett, *Lambert Simnel and the Battle of Stoke* (Gloucester, 1987), p. 142n.

INTRODUCTION: THE MANUSCRIPT

significant.

From the details described above, the following pattern of transcription emerges: the entire document was transcribed between mid-March 1486 and 1502; the portion between fol. 8v (the commencement of the progress description) and fol. 23, on which is given notice of Edward Woodville's participation in Arthur's christening, was completed between mid-March 1486 and Whitsuntide 1488; the text from the first posthumous reference to Edward Woodville on fol. 26 and fol. 43, when the earl of Northumberland was last mentioned alive, were written up between about 27 May 1488 and 29 April 1489. A hiatus in production seems to have occurred soon after this, perhaps because of the death of the first scribe, and work only recommenced with Wriothesley in 1491. The narrative between fols 51 and 63v was written in the year 1491, and the rest was completed no later than the death of Prince Arthur in 1502. There remain substantial gaps between datable segments of the text. The diagram below reveals this pattern.

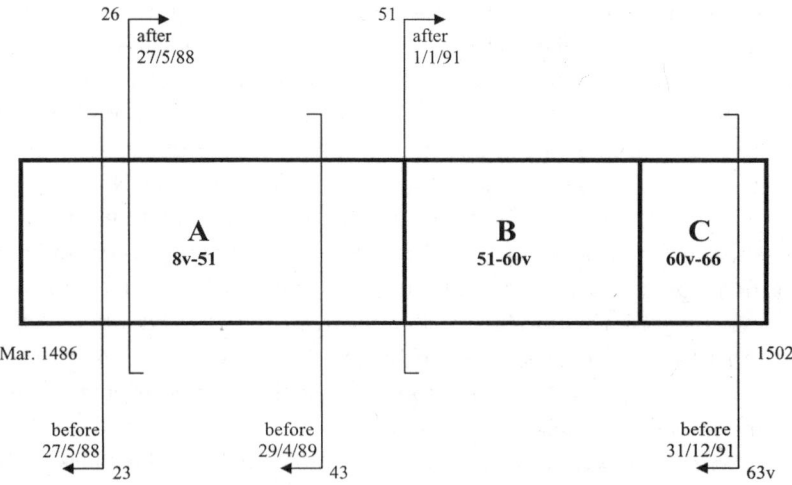

Diagram showing the piecemeal creation of the Memoir.

The Author

Garter John Writhe represents the link that binds the three sections of the complete Memoir, and it is possible that he was the architect and supervisor of a project involving the compilation of several narratives of interest to the English heralds. To that end the opening statement that the progress narrative was written under 'licence and correction' perhaps refers to the *ex officio* power of supervision held by John Writhe as Garter King of Arms.

Beneath the level of transcription things are again made more complicated by the vexed question of the relationship between the original reporter or reporters responsible for the draft notes and the three copyists who worked on the transcription. That the extant narrative derives in large measure from an eye-witness perspective is evident not only in the extraordinary descriptive detail, but also in the occasional references to the author's own eyewitness capacity.[47] Moreover, the input of one or more officers of arms in the service of the Crown, is implied by the text's great preoccupation with the minutiae of largess and reward received by the royal heralds, and with the roles played by the heralds on occasions of state, as well as by cross-referencing with other sources in the possession of the heralds.[48] A single notice of the inauguration of the office of Wallingford Pursuivant in November 1489 may also be seen.[49]

The introduction of a new roster for the heralds' waiting at court probably influenced the general attendance of the officers of arms at court from November 1487 onwards, and it might have provided indication as to who was on duty during which season, if not for the fact that the events described in the Memoir are for the most part those at which the presence of all or most of the royal heralds was typically expected.[50]

In the sections of the narrative covering events not graced by the presence of all heralds, so little detail is given that recourse must be made to other sources. It is far easier to eliminate those royal heralds clearly not present at events described in the Memoir, than it is to be certain of who was responsible for the original information. Of the heralds for whom substantial information survives, we know that Roger Machado, Richmond King of Arms and sometime Norroy, was on embassy in Spain and Portugal between December 1488 and July 1489 and therefore absent from the celebrations of Christmas, New Year and Easter, and at the time of the king's response to Northumberland's murder.[51] In fact, during much of Henry VII's reign Machado seems to have been so preoccupied with diplomatic missions that he agreed for Garters Writhe and Wriothesley respectively to conduct his domestic business.[52] It is therefore possible that he was never greatly available for the recording of affairs in England.

John Writhe was sent on a diplomatic mission to Emperor Maximillian before 24 October 1486, when an order for his prompt payment was issued,[53] and was almost certainly unavailable for Prince Arthur's christening in early November.

[47] Below, on pp. 82–3, is written: 'This doon, I had leve for to depart', followed by: 'At Wytsone even ... I came unto the kinges grace at Worcester, wher as I understande wer ordeynede certeyn pajants like as ensuen, whiche his grace at that tyme harde not'.
[48] Below, pp. 131, 136, 151–2, 166, 183.
[49] Below, p. 179. Other references in the Memoir to the ceremonial and other functions of the officers of arms may be found on pp. 89, 107, 108, 115, 122, 132, 135, 143, 144, 151–4, 158, 163–4, 175–6 and 179–85.
[50] See above, p. 25.
[51] 'Journals of Roger Machado' in *Memorials*, esp. pp. 157–99; Godfrey et al., *College of Arms*, pp. 79–80.
[52] Godfrey et al., *College of Arms*, p. 79.
[53] Godfrey et al., *College of Arms*, p. 42; *Materials*, ii, pp. 45, 82.

INTRODUCTION: THE MANUSCRIPT

Indeed, while the account of Princess Margaret's baptism states that Garter processed ahead of the Constable, there is no reference at all to Garter King of Arms in the description of Prince Arthur's christening.[54] Writhe was likewise sent to Ireland in 1488 and Brittany in 1489:[55] in the former year he was present at court for the celebration of Epiphany in January and the feast of St George in April; in the latter year he had returned to England by November, during which month he and others were admitted to the queen's lying-in chamber and he compiled the program for Princes Arthur's creation.[56] Writhe may himself have been responsible for the descriptive accounts of these events.

In December 1488 Richmond King of Arms, York and Carlisle Heralds, and Falcon Pursuivant were sent on embassy, making them unavailable for domestic duty during the first few months of 1489.[57]

Although originally created York Herald in February 1484, John Water was suspended from office at a date unknown, perhaps as a result of his fidelity to Richard III,[58] and only re-appointed on 25 September 1486. He is therefore unlikely to have accompanied Henry Tudor on his first provincial progress or to have been present at the christening of Prince Arthur on 24 September. Water was sent to France in November 1486, and was again on embassy in 1490.[59] For differing reasons Thomas Holme (Clarenceux King of Arms), Richard Greenwood (Rouge Croix Pursuivant) and John More (Norroy King of Arms), were each variously absent from the major court events of 1486 to 1490.[60]

It is possible that John Writhe was himself involved in some, but not all, of the original note-taking, and that his commitment to the complete transcription was born of this original connection. Beyond this, but one further piece of information might be used to posit a link, albeit speculative, between a Crown herald and an event recorded in the Memoir: a note added by Writhe to his list of knights created at the battle of Stoke in 1487 and set out in *Writhe's Book of Knights*. Alongside the name William Tyrwhitt is written 'as he seythe to Norrey'.[61] Norroy King of Arms was probably responsible for supplying this additional piece of information regarding a knight originating from the north of England. Yet how far recording the 1489 rising in North Yorkshire might have fallen within Norroy's domain, by virtue of his *ex officio* jurisdiction north of the Trent, is uncertain.

---

[54] Below, pp. 100–6.
[55] Godfrey et al., *College of Arms*, p. 42; *Materials*, ii, pp. 296, 437.
[56] Below, p. 175.
[57] Below, p. 164.
[58] Godfrey et al., *College of Arms*, p. 183.
[59] *Materials*, ii, pp. 49–50.
[60] Godfrey et al., *College of Arms*, pp. 183, 211; *Materials*, ii, pp. 438, 470, 472, 474.
[61] BL, MS. Add. 46 354, fol. 17.

Transmission

For several years after its creation, the Memoir remained unaltered and uncopied in the possession of the royal heralds. By the first half of the sixteenth century, however, it had begun serving as a copy-text for a number of private collections. Some time after 1537 an individual scribe compiled a volume of ceremonial and heraldic proceedings of the late fifteenth and early sixteenth centuries (now BL, MS. Eg. 985).[62] In addition to accounts of the coronations of Henry VII and Anne Boleyn, of the christening of Prince Edward, son of Henry VIII, and of the creation of Thomas Howard duke of Norfolk, the scribe has transcribed a large amount of material from the Memoir. These items include the narratives of the coronation of Elizabeth of York, and of the feasts of Christmas 1487, and of Easter and St. George 1488. Since the Memoir's accounts of the first provincial progress and the risings of 1487 and 1489 lay outside the purpose of the Egerton volume, the scribe has omitted them from his transcriptions.

The Egerton scribe's copy is reasonably accurate. His work is neatly written and carefully set out, and generally preserves the content and layout of the passages selected from the Memoir. He was not, however, concerned to create an exact duplicate, rendering 'thirde' as 'iijde' and – conversely – 'vj' as 'sixe', inserting the word 'most' into the phrase 'Elizabeth his most deere wife', changing 'the feste of Alholowes' to 'the feast of all Saintes' and 'the morne after' to 'the morow after', and extending 'the maire' to 'the maire of London'.[63] Minor words such as 'the' and 'and' have been inserted or omitted at random throughout, and a syntactical error in the copy-text corrected.[64] As his work progressed, the accuracy of the reproduction decreased, and there appear additional line-breaks and category headings not present in the Memoir.[65] Lists of abbots, no longer relevant to the mid-sixteenth-century experience, have been dropped, as have seven of the twelve claims to service at the coronation of Elizabeth of York put forward by the peers of the realm in November 1487. The order of these claims was also altered, and the end of the earl of Oxford's petition omitted altogether.

---

[62] 1537 represents the date of the latest events described, namely the accounts of the christening of Prince Edward and the creation of the earls of Hertford and Southampton. Egerton 985 was quite possibly the work of a herald with an interest in ceremony and precedence. Christopher Barker (Richmond Herald 1522–36, Norroy 1536, and Garter 1536–50), was one such herald. Particularly interested in royal ceremony, especially coronations and royal entries, Barker is known to have transcribed a large amount of ceremonial material into his own collections.

[63] See below, pp. 120, 121, 127, 128.

[64] Thus where Julius B. XII, fol. 30v (below, p. 122, n. 351) has 'Whereupon therle of Oxinforde put in his clayme by bylle too *the* bee Chaumbrelayn (my italics), the Egerton Scribe has removed the error.

[65] BL, MS. Eg. 985, fols 14v–15.

INTRODUCTION: THE MANUSCRIPT

One further difference between the two texts is a matter of great curiosity, namely the reintroduction into the Egerton transcript of a cancellation from the Memoir.[66] The lapse in time between the *terminus ad quem* of the Memoir (*c.*1491) and the *terminus post quem* of the Egerton MS. (1537) makes it unlikely that the Egerton scribe transcribed the relevant section from the Memoir prior to the latter document's completion by the Writhe-Wriothesley team. Alternatively, although it has been suggested above that the cancellation was made by one of the three scribes working on the Memoir, it is also possible that the cancellation was made after the completion of both the Memoir and the Egerton transcript. However, in but one case only is there positive evidence of interference with the text of the Memoir after its completion.[67] Perhaps the Egerton scribe either disregarded the cancellation in his copying, or used as his copy-text an intermediary work as yet unidentified and itself made while the Memoir was still under production. The latter suggestion is not entirely improbable.

The ascendancy of the House of Tudor, meanwhile, seems to have generated considerable interest in the christening of Prince Arthur in 1486, and the narrative of the christening incorporated into the Memoir spawned a number of derivative texts during the sixteenth century. Today these narratives are found in the British Library manuscripts Additional 6113 and Stowe 583, and in the College of Arms manuscripts M6 and 1.7.[68]

These five accounts are closely related both to each other and to the text contained in the Memoir, although not one is an exact duplicate of the Memoir narrative. Most notably, where the Julius B. XII narrative belongs to the continuous text of the Memoir, each of the transcripts represents an individual, finite account of the christening.

The two christening narratives housed at the College of Arms were produced toward the middle of the sixteenth century, perhaps for the occasion of the birth and christening of Prince Edward, son of Henry VIII and Jane Seymour, in 1537.[69] Both of the volumes to which these narratives belong bear association with Thomas Hawley (d. 1557, Clarenceux): the transcript contained in MS. M6, a volume entitled *Interments of Queens. Tiltings. Tournaments and Ceremonies*, has been identified as Hawley's own handiwork; MS. I.7, a collection of accounts of

---

[66] Cf. Julius B. XII, fol. 41v (below, p. 144, n. 497) and BL, MS. Eg. 985, fol. 21v, where the latter contains the statement: 'the kinges mynstrells played a song before the queene'.

[67] See the very bottom of Julius B. XII, fol. 58v (below, p. 175, n. 673), where 'Principal' has been inserted into 'Garter King of Arms' in a 17th-century hand.

[68] Bodl. MS. Eng. Hist. C9 contains an index, penned by Dugdale, to 25 volumes formerly in the possession of Sir William le Neve, late Clarenceux King of Arms. Fol. 6v contains notice of a narrative of the christening of Prince Arthur, but to which manuscript Dugdale refers is uncertain.

[69] Edward was the last child born to the Tudor dynasty, although it is just possible that the texts were created in anticipation of the birth of an heir to Mary Tudor in 1550s.

ceremonial of varying ages and hands, was acquired by Hawley during his career as a herald.[70] Of the two, the narrative in MS. I.7 is the more closely related to the Julius B. XII account, and appears to have been transcribed directly from the Memoir narrative or a duplicate. The narrative in MS. M6 was probably transcribed by Hawley from MS. I.7.

On the whole, the I.7 scribe has created an accurate transcript. Although he has inserted an introductory statement and altered the opening sentence of the Memoir, minor orthographical differences represent the greatest diversion between the works. He mimics the layout of the original, generally retains blank spaces for names, and leaves incomplete the following phrase: 'a poost with a ... made of iron.'[71] He has, however, inserted Christian names for the yeomen of the Crown, Rake and Burley, and made several minor adaptations, perhaps for reasons of clarity. Thus, for example, 'was at that tyme at Lanam in Suffolk' becomes 'was not at that time present' and 'above his cremesyn clothede as by fore' becomes 'above him his crysome clothed as above is rehersid'.[72] As was the case with the Egerton manuscript, however, one statement deleted from the Memoir reappears in MS. I.7 (and hence also in M6),[73] once again begging the question of whether an intermediary text, created while the Memoir was still under production, functioned as the true copy-text for MS. I.7.

Where the anonymous scribe of MS. I.7 has adhered to the phrasing and word choice of his copy-text, Hawley has not. The account of Prince Arthur's christening in Hawley's hand is a fair replication of the narrative in the Memoir and, although at least one step removed from the latter, differs to no great degree. It is neatly written and carefully set out, but entertains a slightly different word-choice, orthography and layout. Where the Memoir account and that replicated in MS. I.7 comprise continuous narrative, Hawley has rendered his account as a series of consecutive memoranda, each introduced on a fresh line by the words 'item' or 'and'. Finally, Hawley ends his version with the unique notice: 'And thus Endith the Christenyng of the said noble Prynce Arthur'.

Another version of the christening narrative produced in the first half of the sixteenth century is that on fols 76–79v of BL, MS. Additional 6113, a composite volume entitled *Ceremonies, etc., Edw. III – Eliz. I*. This account may have been occasioned by the christening of Prince Henry, son of Henry VIII and Katherine of Aragon, in 1511.[74] Indeed, the account of Prince Arthur's christening is here fol-

---

[70] Campbell et al., *College of Arms Catalogue*, p. 117.
[71] Julius B. XII, fol. 22 and see below, p. 102, n. 214.
[72] Below, pp. 100, 105; Coll. of Arms, MS. I.7.
[73] Below, p. 106, n. 239: 'The king gave great largess' deleted and altered in the hand of John Writhe.
[74] Printed in *Antiquarian Repertory*, i, new edn (1807–9), p. 353.

INTRODUCTION: THE MANUSCRIPT

lowed immediately by a description of Prince Henry's christening in the same hand and written during the reign of Henry VIII. Again the Arthur narrative is clearly derivative of the Memoir, and again it has a modified opening sentence and an introductory statement not present in the Memoir. The Additional 6113 narrative differs somewhat from the College of Arms versions, however, for the body of the text contains information omitted from MS. I.7 and MS. M6, but present in the Memoir.[75]

Evidence suggests that the Additional 6113 narrative was not transcribed directly from the Memoir, but from some other text. The Additional account alone of the narratives under discussion contains the complete phrase: 'a post with a pyn of yron'. Moreover, the Christian names of several participants in Arthur's baptism, omitted from the Memoir, have again been supplied in Additional 6113. Unlike narratives contained in College of Arms, MSS. I.7 and M6 only the Additional narrative appears to bear correct interpolation. It has 'William', 'John' and 'Nicholas' respectively. Contemporary documentary evidence suggests that Nicholas Knyfton and John Burley were indeed the men to whom the Additional account refers.[76] Rake's Christian name presents more of a problem, however, for it was probably neither 'William' nor 'John', but 'Richard'.[77] If created around 1511, as suggested above, the narrative contained in Additional 6113 was produced at a time when people were still alive who may have known the chief protagonists.

Furthermore, two significant differences between the Memoir and the narrative in Additional 6113 suggest a course of development for the latter. In the first place the notice regarding the king's largess to the officers of arms, cancelled by Garter John Writhe,[78] appears again in the Additional 6113 as in the College of Arms manuscripts. Second, the Additional 6113 narrative contains the notice, not present in the other versions, that Prince Arthur was born around one o'clock in the morning. It also bears a final memorandum, commencing:

> And when the quene shalbe purified she must be rychly besene in tiers and bees [sic] abowt hir necke & in maner of lynyn cloth upon hir bed of estate. And ther shalbe a duches or a countes to take hir down of ye bed ...[79]

---

[75] For example, where Hawley's two narratives state that the earl of Oxford 'was not at that time present', the Additional 6113 narrative, like that contained in the Memoir, has: 'was at that time at Lanam in Suffolk'. Again, where the two College of Arms narratives note that the great gilt ball suspended from the font canopy was 'filled and fringed', the accounts in the Additional 6113 narrative and the Memoir have: 'celed & fryngid' and 'celid and fringede' respectively.

[76] *Materials*, ii, pp. 38–9, 499–500.

[77] *Materials*, i, 405, 533 and ii, 295, 388; *CPR*, p. 31. No-one by the names of either 'William Rake' or 'John Rake' exists anywhere in these sources.

[78] Below, p. 106, n. 239.

[79] BL, MS. Add. 6113, fol. 78v.

and ending with instructions for the creation of a prince as knight of the Bath. This interpolation is perplexing, for it comprises material clearly derived from the kind of prescriptive texts used to regulate ceremonial on these occasions, and seems to anticipate the purification of the queen and the prince's dubbing to knighthood. Although the Additional narrative itself dates from the reign of Henry VIII, it may have been copied from a version of the christening account penned during the four-week period between the baptism of Arthur and the ritual purification of the queen.[80]

The Memoir's christening narrative might itself be based upon an earlier version of the documents now housed in MSS. Alnwick 467 and Lambeth 306.[81] These two very similar texts do not belong to the family of christening narratives described above, but consist of several folios of simple, systematic notices of the order of proceedings and the identity and function of the principal participants in the baptism. The Lambeth account represents a transcript of earlier materials that was produced by John Stowe toward the end of the sixteenth century; the Alnwick transcript belongs to the reign of Mary Tudor. A difference in orthographical styles and several, very minor, variations in expression make it difficult to tell whether Stowe copied from the Alnwick manuscript or whether they are both derived from the same source.

Like the Memoir account, the Alnwick and Lambeth memoranda, listing the gentleman and yeoman ushers, provide the full names of Piers of Wreyton and John Amyas, but do not give the Christian names of Knyfton and Gedding; the same order of names is also observed. In all else they correspond exactly to the detail given in the Memoir, but also offer one or two additional points of detail. While it is possible that this is an independent document produced by another of the royal heralds at Prince Arthur's christening, the similarity of detail and the omission of exactly the same information from both accounts suggests that these may be an example of the very draft notes on which the Memoir was based.

During the seventeenth century another herald produced a version of the narrative of Prince Arthur's christening, and this is now found in the compilation of christening and funeral narratives in BL, MS. Stowe 583.[82] That the Stowe version of Prince Arthur's christening was written up no earlier than the end of the sixteenth century is attested by the age of the paper on which it was written. It is evidently not copied from the Memoir or Additional 6113, but probably from one of the two College of Arms manuscripts, and most likely from MS. M6 or a duplicate.

[80] The Memoir simply proceeds with the brief memorandum: 'And after that the Quene was purified ... the king and quene, my lady the kinges moder and al the court remeved to Grenewhiche': below, pp. 106–7.
[81] MS. Alnwick 467, fols 94v–96 and MS. Lambeth 306, fol. 53. The latter is printed in *Three Fifteenth Century Chronicles*, ed. J. Gairdner, Camden Soc., n.s., 28 (1880), p. 104.
[82] Arthur's christening may be found on fol. 8.

INTRODUCTION: THE MANUSCRIPT

During the eighteenth century,[83] long after the Memoir had been bound into Julius B. XII, another interested party produced an abridged version of the entire Memoir for inclusion in *Baker's Cambridge Collections*, now BL, MS. Harley 7048. The abridgement contains a portion of the progress narrative, together with the descriptions of the feast of Christmas 1487, the receiving of the cap and sword from the pope, the feast of Easter 1487, and the queen's taking to her chamber before the birth of the Princess Margaret. The scribe also included a subheading for the creation of Henry duke of York, an account of which may be found at Julius B. XII, fols 88–103, directly after the Memoir. The transcription was never made. Although he has produced a highly selective version of the Memoir, the 'abridgement' scribe has largely followed the format laid out in the Memoir. He made several minor textual alterations, adopted a more modern orthography, inserted subheadings not present in the Memoir, altered the position of line-breaks, dropped portions of the text,[84] and in several cases substituted the symbol @ for 'and'. His transcript is also subject to the idiosyncrasies of eighteenth-century capitalisation.

The most substantial reproduction of the Memoir is to be found in Thomas Hearne's eighteenth-century edition of John Leland's, *De Rebus Britannicis Collectanea*. The text generally attributed to Leland and printed by Hearne is a fair copy of the entire narrative: but for the omission of fols 30v–33v and fols 53–6,[85] it is largely complete. This version is, however, marred by inaccuracies and eighteenth-century typographical mannerisms. There has been little or no attempt to imitate the original orthography; editorial punctuation hinders, rather than assists, comprehension of the narrative; and the text has been broken into artificial, subtitled divisions. Failure to appreciate standard scribal abbreviations of the fifteenth and sixteenth centuries – compensated for by the use of italics – has resulted in serious errors in the text. Thus the abbreviation p^{i}or, at Julius B. XII, fol. 23, has been rendered '*Por*', rather than 'prior'; the scribal emendation 'halhaloutyde' (All Hallowtide) on fol. 24 has been printed '*Haballutyde*'; and a great number of other words have been rendered in italics because their meanings were considered unclear.

Most intriguing of all is the fact that the Memoir is not actually present in the original volumes of Leland housed in the Bodleian Library, despite Hearne's inclusion of the same in his edition of the *Collectanea*. One clue suggests that the ver-

[83] This scribe's hand belongs to the eighteenth century, although the paper he used, watermarked with a fool's cap, was found in England in the mid seventeenth century.
[84] See for example fol. 252v, where the scribe ends the progress narrative with: '... and that same weke he removed unto Notingham &c', before beginning a description of the christening of Prince Arthur. Fully 25½ folios of Memoir text corresponding to the king's progress have been omitted.
[85] The latter set of missing folios are supplied by M. J. Bennett as an appendix to his article 'Henry VII and the Northern Rising of 1489', *EHR*, 105 (January, 1990), pp. 34–59.

sion of the Memoir was not compiled by Leland at all, but later and possibly by Hearne himself. Thus, a later emendation in a seventeenth-century, 'post-Leland' hand, at Julius B. XII, fol. 58v, has been incorporated silently into the 'Leland-Hearne' edition of the Memoir.[86] It may be that Hearne used a generic title in compiling the *Collectanea*, but supplemented Leland's collection with material from elsewhere. This might also explain the evident lack of familiarity with fifteenth-century scribal abbreviations and word-meanings in the Leland-Hearne text.

Editorial Method

The aim of this edition has been to prepare a text representing, as closely as possible, that contained in Julius B. XII, while also making it accessible to modern scholarship. Where feasible the layout of the Memoir has been retained, although extra paragraph breaks have been inserted to assist the reader. Cases of interlineation and minor scribal emendation have been incorporated silently into the body of the text and mentioned in the footnotes, while significant scribal cancellations are printed in full in the footnotes. Meaningless marks of expansion and/or scribal flourishes are generally ignored, except in extreme cases. Editorial expansions are consistent, even where scribal orthography varies (e.g. the plural and possessive endings es/is). Capitalisation is largely limited to proper nouns, and punctuation has been modernised. The vowel 'u' has been replaced by the consonants 'v' where this is modern practice, but otherwise the spelling of the original has been observed. Latin orisons have been italicised, but the French and English vernacular have not. The heralds' cries of largess and other spoken phrases are given quotation marks. All editorial emendations and additions are enclosed in square brackets and, where deemed necessary, editorial interference has been discussed in the footnotes. Ampersands and Tyronian symbols are typically expanded, except when used at the end of memoranda (in English and French), where they are presented in the form (&c.). Roman numerals appear throughout in their original form.

An historical commentary to the manuscript is given in the footnotes. Events and meanings are explained, and analogous contemporary material and further secondary readings listed. The historical footnotes do not, however, identify all persons listed in the manuscript, as the sheer number of individuals mentioned in the Memoir make this impracticable.

---

[86] John Leland, *De rebus Britannicis Collectanea*, ed. Thomas Hearne, 6 vols (repr., 1770), iv, p. 249.

INTRODUCTION: THE MANUSCRIPT

Stemma showing the possible genesis of, and transcription from, the Memoir, between 1486 and the eighteenth century.

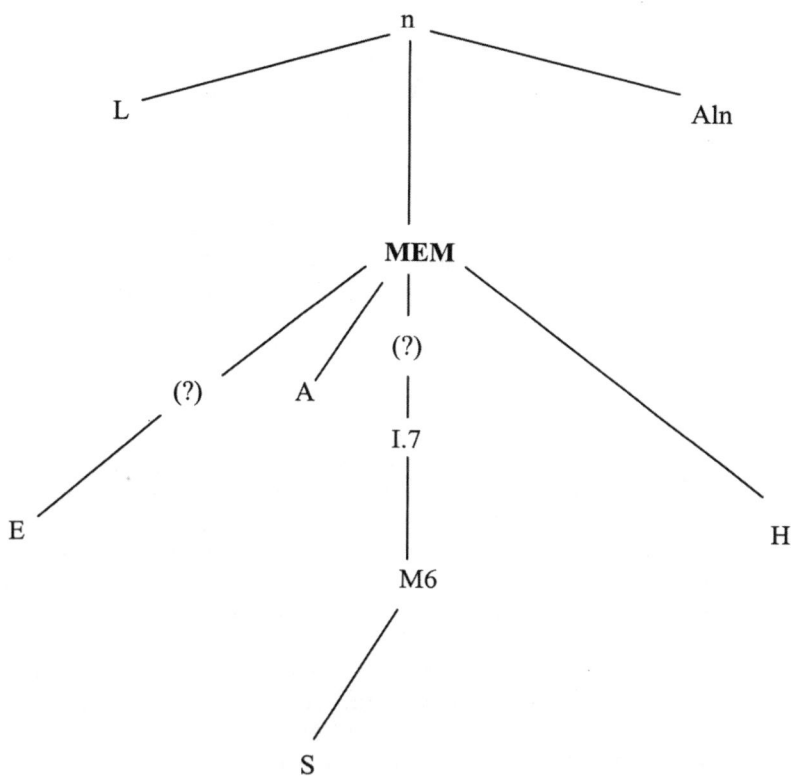

Sigla: A – BL, MS. Add. 6113, fols. 76-9.
Aln – MS. Alnwick 467, fols. 94v-96.
E – BL, MS. Eg. 985, fols. 10v-26.
H – BL, MS. Harley 7048, fol. 252v.
I.7 – Coll. Arms, MS. I.7.
L – Lambeth MS. 306, fols. 53-54.
MEM – the Memoir: BL, MS. Cotton Julius B. XII, fols. 8v-66.
M6 – Coll. Arms, MS. M6, fols. 28-30.
n – draft notes
S – BL, MS. Stowe 583, fols. 8-17.
(?) – hypothetical intermediary MSS.

THE HERALDS' MEMOIR

[f. 8v][1] A shorte and a brief memory, by licence and correccion,[2] of the fu[r]st progresse[3] of our souveraigne lorde king Henry the vijth – after his noble coronacion,[4]

[1] At the top of fol. 8v in an Elizabethan secretary hand, possibly that of Sir William Dethick (Garter King of Arms 1587–1606): 'The goinge of king henry the vijth to Yorke'.
[2] The account of the first provincial progress, if not the entire Memoir, was compiled under some form of official or semi-official sanction, the authority perhaps belonging to Garter King of Arms; however, it was not an official document commissioned by the Crown.
[3] Itineraries for Henry VII may be found in: Ford, thesis, pp. 205–83; Francis Bacon, *The History of the Reign of King Henry the Seventh*, ed. F. J. Levy (New York, 1972), pp. xvii–xx; G. Temperley, *Henry VII* (London, 1917), pp. 411–19; R. Edwards, *The Itinerary of King Richard III, 1483–5* (London, 1983), pp. 40–1 (1485–7 only); McGee, thesis, pp. 245–8 (first provincial progress only). Tudor sources for the first progress include: Vergil, *Anglica Historia*, pp. 11–13; *Croyland Chronicle*, pp. 513–14; Hall, *Union*, 'Henry the vii', fols 4–5; Holinshed, *Chronicles*, pp. 483–4. Recent analysis of the first progress is in E. Cavell, 'Henry VII, the North of England, and the First Provincial Progress of 1486', *Northern History*, 39.2 (September, 2002), pp. 187–207. For general and specific information on Yorkist and early Tudor royal progresses see: Olver, thesis, esp. introd. and ch. 1; S. Anglo, *Images of Tudor Kingship* (London, 1992), pp. 106–12; McGee, thesis, generally; M. J. Bennett, *Lambert Simnel and the Battle of Stoke* (Gloucester, 1987), pp. 36–9; N. Samman, 'The Progresses of Henry VIII, 1509–29', in *The Reign of Henry VIII: Politics, Policy and Piety*, ed. D. MacCulloch (London, 1995), pp. 59–74 (Henry VIII); M. J. Bennett, *The Battle of Bosworth* (1985; repr. Stroud, 2000), pp. 38–41; Edwards, *Itineraries* (Richard III); and C. D. Ross, *Edward IV* (London, 1974), p. viiii (Edward IV).
[4] Westminster, Sun. 30 Oct. 1485. Crowned without his queen. See: 'Empcions and Provisions' in *Materials*, ii, pp. 3–29; the 'Little device' for Henry VII's coronation (adapted from that used by Richard III) in BL, MSS. Eg. 985, fols 1–10, Add. 18669, and Harley 5111, fol. 77; W. Jerdan, *The Rutland Papers*, Camden Soc. (1842), pp. 1–24; *English Coronation Records*, ed. L. G. W. Legg (Westminster, 1901), pp. 220–39. The *liber regalis* and *forma et modus* are printed in Legg, *Coronation Records*, pp. 81–130, 172–90. See also P. E. Schramm, *A History of the English Coronation*, transl. L. G. W. Legg (Oxford, 1937), pp. 88–9 and the catalogue of English *ordines* in his 'Appendix', pp. 233–8. For an eyewitness, heraldic account of the coronation see BL, MS. Eg. 985, fols 41v–48. Secondary analysis includes: S. Anglo, *Spectacle, Pageantry and Early Tudor Policy*, 2nd edn (Oxford, 1997), pp. 10–17; idem, 'The Foundation of the Tudor Dynasty: the Coronation and Marriage of Henry VII', *The Guildhall Miscellany* 2.1 (1960), pp. 1–9; S. B. Chrimes, *Henry VII*, n.e. (New Haven and London, 1999), pp. 58–60.

Cristemas[5] and parliament[6] holden at his paloys of Westminster – towardes the northparties.

In the [xiiijth][7] day of Marche [the king] toke his hors, wele and nobley accompanyede at Seint Johns of London,[8] and rode to Waltham; and from thens the high way[9] to Cambrige,[10] wher his grace was honourably receyvede both of the unyversitie and of the towne. And from thens he roode by Huntingdon, Staunforde and to Lincoln,[11] and ther his grace kepte right devoutly the holy fest of Ester, and full like a cristene prince hard his dyvyne service in the cathedrall chirche and in no prive chapell. And on Sherethursday he had in the bisshops hall xxix poore men, to

[5] Cf. descriptions of the celebration of Christmas 1486, 1488 and 1489, pp. 107, 164, 182.
[6] Mon. 7 Nov. to Sat. 10 Dec. 1485. Writs of summons were issued on 15 Sept: *Materials*, i, p. 6. Several legal problems had to be overcome before the first parliament could assemble, the most awkward being Henry Tudor's attainder; the justices of the exchequer chamber decreed the penalty void by virtue of Henry's assumption of the kingship: Chrimes, *Henry VII*, p. 61. Opened by Archbishop Alcock, then chancellor of England, this parliament involved the attainder of enemies, the release of supporters from attainder, the formal ratification of Henry VII's right to rule, and the vesting of the duchy of Lancaster in his heirs: Sir Robert Somerville, *The Duchy of Lancaster*, 4 vols (London, 1946), i, pp. 260–1; *RP*, vi, pp. 267–84 with extracts printed in *Materials*, i, pp. 110–37. See also J. S. Roskell, *The Commons and their Speakers in English Parliaments, 1376–1523* (Manchester, 1965).
[7] Date of departure not supplied by the scribe, but somewhere between 10 and 14 Mar. *CPR*, 1485–1494, points to the earlier date: documents were issued from Westminster, Ware and Royston on 10 Mar., suggesting that the privy seal was on the move at this time. From 10 Mar. the itinerary suggested by *CPR* corresponds closely to the undated record of the king's movements in the Memoir. Although the chancellor may have been with the royal entourage on its departure from Doncaster (see p. 71 and n. 26), his movements before this time are not verified and the possibility of divergent itineraries for king and chancellor may mislead. The lapse in time between an order's issue and its enrolment add further problems. A royal order dated London, 13 Mar. suggests that the king did not leave the city before that date: *Materials*, i, p. 387.
[8] The priory of St. John of Jerusalem, Clerkenwell; the headquarters of the English Hospitallers until their dissolution in 1540. It was still under construction at the time of the first provincial progress. Copies of royal letters originating from the priory in early Mar. 1486 suggest Henry VII sometimes held court there: *Materials*, i, pp. 344–59. See also *VCH, Middlesex*, i, pp. 193–200.
[9] The main route between Waltham and Cambridge can be see on the map of parliamentary England, 1439 to 1509, in Chrimes, *Henry VII*, pp. 142–3.
[10] The royal entourage reached Cambridge around Thurs. 16 Mar. Cambridge University's *Grace Book A*, ed. S. M. Leathes (1897), p. 202 contains one reference to the royal visit, relating to the provision of 'bread, beer and other victuals' and clearly set down after the event. See also *Annals of Cambridge*, ed. C. H. Cooper, 5 vols (Cambridge, 1842), i, p. 232 for payments to the town treasurers, Robert Ratheby and Richard Holmes, for fish given to the king. This may relate to the progress, as the king was travelling during Lent.
[11] The royal visit is described briefly in F. Hill, *Medieval Lincoln* (Cambridge, 1948), p. 272, as are the earlier visits of Henry VI and Richard III.

whom he humly and cristenly for Christez love, with his noble handes, did wesshe ther fete,[12] and yave as great almes like as other his noble progenitours, kinges of England, have been accustumed aforetyme. And also on Good Friday, after all his offerins and observances of halowing of his ringes,[13] after dyner yave merveolous[14] great summes of mony in grotes[15] to poo[r]e[16] people, besides great almes to poore freres, prisoners and lazares howsez of that countrey. And oon Sherethursday, Goodfryday, Estereven and Esterday[17] the bisshop of that see did the divine service; and everyche of the iij dayes folowing the principallest residencers ther being present did ther divine observance. And the king him silf kepte every day thus, during both the high masse and evensonge in the saide cathedrall chirche.

And that same weke he remevid unto Notingham[18] withoute any bayting, by cause they died[19] at Newark, &c. And the meir and his brethern[20] of Notingham in

[12] The washing of the feet of a select number of poor men, one for each year of the king's age, imitated the actions of Christ and was a traditional part of the observances of Maundy Thursday. Henry VII is recorded as performing the same ritual in 1499: *CSP Venice*, p. 281. For a more detailed account of the Maundy Thursday observances, as celebrated *temp*. Eliz. I, see J. Nichols, *The Progresses and Public Processions of Queen Elizabeth*, 2nd edn, 3 vols (London, 1823), i, pp. 325–27. The practice was evidently also observed by great lords: G. Brennan, *A History of the House of Percy*, 2 vols (London, 1902), p. 20.

[13] The blessing of cramp rings on Good Friday was held to be efficacious against cramp and falling sickness (epilepsy). See M. Bloch, *The Royal Touch: Sacred Monarchy and Scrofula in England and France*, transl. J. E. Anderson (London, 1973), 2.2, pp. 92–107 and R. Crawford, 'The Blessing of Cramp Rings: a Chapter in the Treatment of Epilepsy', in C. J. Singer, *Studies in the History and Method of Science* (London, 1917), pp. 165–87. The Latin service, as used *temp*. Henry VIII, is given in Wilkins, *Concilia*, iv, pp. 103–104, and an English version of *c*. 1685 appears in *Monumenta Ritualia Ecclesiae Anglicanae*, ed Rev. W. Maskell, 3 vols (London, 1847), iii, pp. 335–340.

[14] 'mer' written over an erasure.

[15] A silver coin minted from 1351 to 1662 and valued at 4*d*. See Chrimes, *Henry VII*, plate 10.

[16] Written 'poope'.

[17] Sun. 26 Mar.

[18] Clearly the place where the king marshalled his retinue on progress in 1486: *YHB*, ii, pp. 479–80; *Plumpton Letters and Papers*, p. 65. Payment is registered for 10 Apr. 1486 for the costs of a messenger sent to Lincoln for information on the king's visit: W. H. Stevenson (ed.), *Records of the Borough of Nottingham*, 4 vols (London, 1885), iii, pp. 263–4. The king evidently returned to Nottingham on the way back from York, although the Memoir makes no mention of a second visit: Stevenson, *Records*, iii, p. 264; W. A. Shaw, *The Knights of England*, 4 vols (London, 1906), ii, p. 23. See also Cavell, 'Henry VII', pp. 199, 205.

[19] Probably the plague or 'sweating sickness'. Bubonic plague raged in York in 1485, and a deadly contagion broke out in London in Nov. 1486: *Plumpton Letters and Papers*, p. 67. For a description of the sweating sickness, together with a catalogue of references to the affliction in contemporary accounts, see K. E. W. Busch, *England under the Tudors*, transl. A. M. Todd, 2 vols (London, 1895), i, pp. 23–4, 323n. See also J. A.

scarlet gounes on horsbake, accompanyede with vj or vij^{xx} with other honest men al on horsbake, also receyvede the king a myle by south Trent. And bytwene both **[f. 9]** brigges[21] the procession, both of the frerez and of the pariche chirchez, receyved the king and so proceded thorough the towne to the castell.

And from thens the king[22] the next weke folowing remevede towarde Yorke – at whos remeving therle of Derby, the lorde Straunge, Sir William Stanley with other toke ther leve[23] – and on Satirday came unto Dancaster, wher he abode the Sonday and harde masse at the freres of Our Lady[24] and evensong in the parishe chirche.[25]

And oon the morne the king remeved to Pomfreyte, accompanyed then and sone after[26] with the archebisshop of York, the bisshop of Ely (chaunceller of England), the bisshop of Excester (prive seale); also therle of Lyncolln, therle of Oxinforde, therle of Shrewesbury, therle of Ryvers, therle of Wiltshire, the vicount Wellis, the lorde Percy (whiche came to the king at York), the lorde Grey Rythyn,

---

H. Wylie and L. Collier, 'The English Sweating Sickness (*Sudor Anglicus*): A Reappraisal', *Journal of the History of Medicine*, 36 (1981), pp. 425–45; G. Thwaites et al., 'The English Sweating Sickness, 1485–1551', *New England Journal of Medicine*, 336 (February, 1997), pp. 580–2. The plague and other contagions in England and Europe during the 15th century are discussed in C. Creighton, *History of Epidemics in Britain*, 2nd edn, 2 vols (London, 1965) and J. Hatcher, 'Mortality in the Fifteenth Century: Some New Evidence', *Econ. HR*, 2nd ser., 39 (1986), pp. 19–38.

[20] Richard Alestre, mayor; John Bellyn and John Williamson, sheriffs; Lawrence Lowe, recorder; John Coste and John Howett, chamberlains; Thomas Cost, bridgemaster: Stevenson, *Records*, iii, p. 459.

[21] Probably the bridges crossing the Trent and its tributary, the Leen. Maps of Nottingham and an account of its geography, growth and fifteenth-century economic status are found in K. C. Edwards (ed.), *Nottingham and its Region* (Nottingham, 1966), pp. 364–76.

[22] 'toke' interlineated above but then erased.

[23] The departure of the Stanleys, not anticipated at the start of the journey, may be explained by a commission of 4 Apr: *Plumpton, Letters and Papers*, p. 65; *CPR*, pp. 86–7.

[24] The church of the Carmelites, established in 1350 and housing the famous image of Our Lady of the White Friars or Our Lady of Doncaster. The friary also hosted Henry of Bolingbroke in 1399, Edward IV in 1470, and Margaret Tudor in 1503: *VCH, Yorkshire*, iii, p. 268.

[25] Probably that described by Leland in the 1540s: J. Chandler (ed.), *John Leland's Itinerary. Travels in Tudor England* (Stroud, 1993), p. 524.

[26] The herald's list includes many of the men who were to serve as the king's officers in the north. See R. Reid, *The King's Council in the North*, 2nd edn (Wakefield and Totowa, N.J., 1975), p. 72n. The list was evidently systematised during the writing up of the Memoir, as the names are arranged by rank. Although typically accurate with names and titles, the record errs here on the point of who held the offices of chancellor and bishop of Ely. In March–April 1486 the chancellor of England was John Alcock; the bishop of Ely at this time was John Morton. Morton was appointed archbishop of Canterbury in October 1486 and replaced Alcock as chancellor on 6 March 1487.

the lorde Grey, the lorde fitz Water (stuarde of the kinges howse), the lorde Powes, the lorde Clifforde, the lorde fitz Hugh, the lorde Scrop of Upsale, the lorde Scrop of Bolton, the lorde la Warre, lorde Latymor, lorde Dacre of Gillesland, the lorde Hastinges, the lorde Lumley, the lorde Hussay (chief justice of the kinges benche).

Knyghtes: Sir Richarde Egecombe (countroller of the kinges house), Sir Thomas Burgh, Sir John Cheyny, Sir John Grey of Wilton, Sir George Nevell, Sir John Beauchamp, Sir Walter Hungreforde, Sir Robert Taylboys, Sir Robert Willoughby, Sir Edward Ponynges, Sir Humfrey Stanley, Sir John Savage, Sir Davy Owen, Sir Charles of Somersett, Sir Thomas Cokesay, Sir Robert Poynez, Sir John Amelton, Sir Thomas Markenvile, Sir John Savile **[f. 9v]** (shiref of Yorkeshire), Sir Henry Perpoynte, Sir John Babington, Sir Henry Wenworth,[27] Sir Robert Stirley, Sir Thomas Tempeste, Sir Gerveis of Clifton, Sir John Turburvile, Sir Edmunde Benyngfelde, Sir John a Grisley, Sir Hugh[28] Persall, Sir Nicholl[as] Langforde, Sir Rauff Bygod, Sir John Nevill of Leversege, Sir William fitz William, Sir Thomas fitz William, Sir John Everyngham, Sir Randolf Pigote, Sir Marmaduc Counstable, Sir John Waterton, Sir Robert Rider, Sir Edmonde Hastinges, Sir John Counstable of Holdrenesse, Sir Christofor Moresby, Sir Robert Dymmok, Sir James Danby, Sir Richarde Haute, Sir John Risley, Sir William Say, Sir William Tyler (whiche was sent unto the castell of Midlem).[29]

And by the way in Barnesdale,[30] a litill beyonde Robyn Hoddez ston,[31] therle of Northumbreland, with right a great and noble company, mete and yave his attendaunce upon the king – that is for to say with xxxiij knyghtes of his feed men,[32] beside esquiers and yomen (parte of those knyghtes names as ensuen: Sir [Robert]

[27] –t obscured by an inkblot.
[28] Preceded by the cancellation of 'huh'.
[29] Middleham, Yorks. was a market town with Ricardian associations. See Leland, *Itinerary*, pp. 554, 555, 570–1. A ground plan and history of Middleham Castle are given in *VCH, Yorkshire North Riding*, i, pp. 251–4
[30] A large forest in the wapentakes of Osgoldcross, Staincross and Strafford in the southern region Yorkshire's west riding. It covered over thirty square miles and harboured outlaws from c.1300: McGee, thesis, p. 92.
[31] Robin Hood's Stone, first mentioned in a charter of 1422, lay about a mile south of Barnesdale, near Skelbrook, and approx. 6½ miles north of Doncaster on the east side of the Roman road from Lincoln to York: J. W. Walker, *The True History of Robin Hood* (Wakefield, 1973), p. 14. The location was the meeting place of Henry VII and the earl of Northumberland immediately after Bosworth, and of the subsequent meeting of the earl of Northumberland with Margaret Tudor, on her way to Scotland to marry James IV, in 1503. See also A. H. Smith, 'A York Pageant', *London Medieval Studies* (1946 for 1939), p. 384 and idem, 'Robin Hood', *Modern Language Review*, 28.4 (October, 1933), pp. 484–5.
[32] A surviving order from the earl of Northumberland to several of his fee'd retainers may date from this time: *Plumpton Letters and Papers*, p. 68.

Multon (sumtyme lorde of Seint Johns), Sir William Gascon, Sir Robert Counstable, Sir Hugh Hastinges, Sir William Evers, Sir John Pikering, Sir Robert Plompton, Sir Pers of Medilton, Sir Christofor Warde, Sir William Malary, Sir Thomas Malyverer, Sir William Englisshby, Sir James Strangways, Sir Rauf Babthorpe, Sir Thomas Normanvile, Sir Martyn of the See, Sir Robert Hilliart, Sir Rauf Crathorn, Sir William Bekwith, Sir Robert Utreyte, Sir Thomas Metham, Sir Richarde Quonyers, Sir William Darcy, Sir Stephen Hamerton and Sir William a Stapleston) – and[33] so proceded that same Mondaye to Pomfret, wher his **[f. 10]** grace remaynede unto the Thursday next folowing, at whiche day the king was accompanyed with great noblesse as above saide and merveolous great nombre of so short a warnyng of esquiers, gentilmen and yomen in defencible array;[34] for in that tyme ther wer certeyne rebelles[35] aboute Rypon and Midlem, whiche undrestanding the kinges myght and nere approching within ij dayes disperclede.

And at Tadcaster[36] the king, richely besene in a gowne of cloth of golde furred with ermyn, toke[37] his courser. His henshemen[38] and folowers, also in golde smythez werk, wer richely besene. At the further ende of the brigge foote[39] the shriffes of York,[40] wele accompanyede, mette the king and so procedede and ber ther white roddes afor his grace. And ner hand iij myles oute of Yorke, the maire[41]

[33] 'Pomfrete' written in right margin in the same hand as above, p. 68, n. 1.

[34] This statement resembles a similar assertion in an heraldic account of the 1506 reception of King Philip of Castile: 'A Narrative of the Reception of Philip, King of Castile, in England in 1506', *Memorials*, p. 300. The speed with which the men assembled is somewhat overstated, as the king's intention was known, at least in part, some weeks earlier: *Plumpton Letters and Papers*, p. 64. For some idea of the numbers rallying to the king's banner at this time see the same, p. 64; Williams, 'Humphrey Stafford', p. 182; and the herald's own list.

[35] Esp. Francis, Viscount Lovel, a favourite of Richard III and lord chamberlain of the late king's household, who fled to sanctuary in Colchester after the royal defeat at Bosworth. He subsequently escaped and went north to raise the insurrection to which the herald refers: *DNB*, xii, pp. 172–3.

[36] Initially written 'Tadcastell', and then altered.

[37] 'York' written in the right margin in the same hand as above, p. 68, n. 1.

[38] Probably seven henchmen, the number in the households of both Edward IV and Richard III. The accounts of the city of York for 1486–87 include a payment of 6s. 8d. to the boys, 'voc. Hausmen' [*recte* 'Hansmen'?], who attended the king: *York City Chamberlains' Account Rolls, 1396–1500*, ed. R. B. Dobson, Surtees Soc., 192 (1980), p. 187.

[39] Tadcaster Bridge, on the extremities of York's franchises: *YHB*, ii, p. 482. It was traditional for the sheriffs of a county to greet the king at the boundary of their shires and escort him through the area of their jurisdiction. Here and elsewhere the sheriffs carried their white rods as the symbol of their authority. Cf. the description of the reception of Henry VI at Coventry in *The Coventry Leet Book*, ed. M. D. Harris, EETS, o.s., 4 parts (London, 1907–1913), ii, p. 263 and that of Henry VIII at Lincoln in 1541 in 'Account of King Henry the Eighth's Entry into Lincoln, in 1541', *Archaeologia*, 23 (1831), p. 337.

[40] John Beverley and Roger Appleby. The high sheriff of Yorkshire, John Savile, was in the

of that citie and his brether, with other great nombre of citezeins al on horsbak, receyved the king. And Vavasour, recordre[42] of the same citie, had the speche in bidding the king welcome and also recommaundede the citie and the inhabitauntes of the same to his good grace. And half a myle withoute the gate of that citie, the precessions of al the orders of freres[43] receyved the king; and after theym the prior of the Trinities[44] with his brether, thabbot of Seint Mary Abbey[45] with his covent, the chanoignes of[46] Seint Leonardes,[47] and then the generall procession of[48] al the parisshe chirches[49] of the saide citie, with merveolous great nombre of men, women and childern on foote, whiche in rejoysing of his commyng criden: "King Henry, King Henry!" and saide: "Our Lorde preserve that swete and welefaverde face!"[50]

And at the gate[51] of the citie ther was ordeynede a pajaunt with dyvers personages[52] and mynstrelsyez.[53] **[f. 10v]** And[54] therby stode a king coronede –

---

king's retinue. See *YHB*, ii, pp. 478, 479, 481–5 for an extended programme of arrangements for York's reception of the king. The city intended to outdo its previous efforts and arranged for twice the usual number to accompany Beverley and Appleby at Tadcaster Bridge.

[41] William Chimney, draper, freeman of the city from 1455 and incumbent of several political offices before his death in 1508/9.

[42] For John Vavasour's election as recorder against the king's own wishes, see *YHB*, ii, pp. 478–9. He subsequently gained the king's favour during the rebellion of the earl of Lincoln in 1487: *DNB*, xx, pp. 197.

[43] The White Friars (Carmelites), Grey Friars (Fransiscans), Augustinians, Black Friars (Dominicans), Gilbertines, and the Benedictines of the priory of the Holy Trinity: *VCH, Yorkshire*, iii, pp. 283–96; A. Raine, *Medieval York* (London, 1955), pp. 62–5, 131–3, 202–6, 227–8, 283–7, 298–9.

[44] Robert Hallows: *VCH, Yorkshire*, iii, pp. 389–90; Raine, *Medieval York*, pp. 227–8.

[45] William Sevons, elected prior of the Black Friars in 1485: *VCH*, iii, pp. 107–12; Raine, *Medieval York*, pp. 267–9.

[46] Repeated.

[47] The hospital of St Leonard, York: *VCH, Yorkshire*, iii, pp. 336–345; Raine, *Medieval York*, p. 113–16.

[48] Followed by the cancellation of 'the towne'.

[49] For a catalogue of some 45 parish churches, 17 chapels, 16 hospitals and 9 monasteries see Francis Drake, *Eboracum: or the History and Antiquities of the City of York* (London, 1739), pp. 234–6.

[50] The crowd of children gathered about St. James' chapel was preordained by the city fathers: *YHB*, ii, p. 482.

[51] Micklegate Bar, one of the ancient passageways through the wall around York and a traditional place of reception. The city fathers welcomed visiting dignitaries here in 1482, 1483 and Mar. 1486: *YHB*, i, p. 259; ii, pp. 470, 713. At the time of Henry VII's visit, Micklegate Bar included a built-in house for hire and was fronted by a barbican, portcullis and heavy wooden door with wicket: Raine, *Medieval York*, pp. 26–7; McGee, thesis, p. 108. For a study of medieval royal entries see G. Kipling, *Enter the King: Theatre, Liturgy, and Ritual in the Medieval Civic Triumph* (Oxford, 1998).

THE EDITION

whiche had his speche that folowith – whos name was Ebraucus.

    Ebraucus[55]

O reverende[56] right wis regent of this regalitie
Whos primatyve patron I apper to your presence
Ebrauc of Brytayn I sittuate this citie
For a place to my pleasur of most prehemynence
Herunto I recoursede for moost convenyence
In conforting that by cours of lynyall succession
Myn heirez this my cetie shuld have in possession.

Of right I was regent and ruled this region
I subdued Fraunce and lede in my legeaunce
To you Henry I submitte my citie kee and coroune
To rule and redresse as your due to[57] defence
Nevir to this citie to presume no pretence
But holly I remytte it to your governaunce

---

[52] Probably the citizens required to accompany Ebrauk: *YHB*, ii, p. 482. See also the pageant of King David (p. 79), performed later that day, which was clearly intended to involve a crowd of living people.

[53] Intended to provide angelic harmony, i.e. from the heavens from which the crown descended during the first part of the pageant: *YHB*, ii, p. 482. A heaven full of angelic musicians was a common 15th-century artistic motif, and provided a backdrop to several pageants of the York cycle: Meagher, 'First Progress', p. 52. Minstrels were an important feature of most contemporary entertainment, and music characterised every royal entry from that of Henry V in 1415 to James I in 1603: McGee, thesis, p. 109. See also E. K. Chambers, *The Medieval Stage*, 2 vols (London, 1903; repr. 1996), i, pp. 42–86. Payments to the city minstrels on this occasion are recorded in *Chamberlains' Account Rolls*, p. 187.

[54] Repeated as a Tironian sign followed by the word 'and'.

[55] Inserted in the left margin. Ebrauk of Britain was the legendary founder of the city of York and son of Menpricius the Tyrant. Details of his biography circulating in the late 15th century may be found in Ranulph Higden's *Polychronicon* and Geoffrey of Monmouth's *Historia*. Themes addressed in Ebrauk's pageant include: the transferral to Henry VII of authority over the city of York; the affirmation of the new king's right to rule there [parallels of which may be found in the Worcester pageantry: below, pp. 83–8, and the account of the visit of Henry VI to Exeter in 1452: R. Barnes (ed.), *Liber Pontificalis of Edmund Lacy, Bishop of Exeter* (Exeter, 1847), p. ix]; Bristol's reception of Edward IV in 1461 (Lambeth Library, MS. 306, fol. 132r; Robert Ricart, *The Maire of Bristowe is Kalendar*, ed. L. Toulmin Smith, Camden Soc., n.s., v (1872), pp. xviii n. 43); the reception of Margaret Tudor in Edinburgh in 1503 (Leland, *Collectanea*, iv, p. 289); the people's right to protection from their king (esp. John Fortescue, *De laudibus legum Anglie*, ed. and transl. S. B. Chrimes (Cambridge, 1942), pp. 22, 62); the demonstration of the city's goodwill toward their king; and at least one allusion to the suffering of the city on behalf of Henry VI.

[56] Initially written 'reverdende', before the first –d was cancelled.

[57] 'to' written above a cancelled Tironian symbol.

As a principall parcell of your enheritaunce.

Please it, I beseche you, for my remembraunce
Sith that I am a primatyve of youre progenye
Shewe your grace to this citie with suche habundaunce
As the ruyn may recover into prosperitie
And also of your great grace gif not your ye
Only to this citie of insufficience
But graciously considre ther wille and diligence.

It is knowen in trouth of great experience
[f. 11] For your blod this citie made never digression
[A]s recordeth by the great hurte for blode of your excellence
Wherefor the rather I pray for compassion
And to mynd how this citie, of olde and pure affeccion
Gladdeth and enjoyeth your highnesse and commyng
With hole consente knowing you ther souveraigne and king.

And at the hider ende of House Brigge[58] ther was ordeyned a nother pajaunt,[59] garnysshede with shippes and botez in every side in tokenyng[60] of the kinges landing at Milforde Havyn. And Salamon in his habite roiall crownede hadde this speche as herafter foloweth:

Salamon[61]
Moost prudent prynce of provid provision
Ther premordiall princes of this principalitie

[58] A change of plan from that recorded in the civic muniments, where a shower of rose water had been intended for the entrance to Ouse Bridge, and the pageant of the six Henries at the highest point on the bridge: *YHB*, ii, p. 483. For details of the bridge itself see Raine, *Medieval York*, pp. 207–25.
[59] According to the York civic muniments the second pageant was designed to begin with a council of kings, not described in the Memoir, but alluded to in the first and fourth stanzas of Solomon's speech below: *YHB*, ii, p. 483.
[60] Preceded by the cancellation of 'tokel'.
[61] Inserted in the right margin. The biblical king Solomon was noted for his wisdom and judicial merit. He is used here both to suggest the historical, constitutional and moral legitimacy of the new king's title, and to intercede on behalf of the city. This pageant represents a striking allusion to Henry VII as *ex officio* judge of the realm, complimenting him on his judicial prudence and exhorting him to continue to rule with the wisdom of Solomon: Meagher, 'First Progress', p. 57. The association of the new king with the administration of justice was also a theme of Richard III's northern progress in 1483: *YHB*, ii, p. 729. The pageant's allusion to York's loyalty to Henry VI reflects the same argument used in the city's petition for a reduction of the fee farm rent (*YHB*, i, pp. 390–1), an argument for which Henry Tudor seems to have given the cue: see P. L. Hughes and J. F. Larkin (eds), *Tudor Royal Proclamations*, 3 vols (New Haven and London, 1964–9), i, pp. 3–4.

Hath preparate your reign, the vij by succession
Remytting this reame as right to your roialtie
Ther [are]⁶² kinges conding of your consanguinitie
Full roial and rightwise in rule of ther [regence
And ful lordly thai execute the lawes of ther] legience.⁶³

Sith God full of glorie eternal sapience
Did ensence me Salamon of His affluente grace
Wher thorough I am taken as patrone of prudence
To discusse upon conscience yche judicial case⁶⁴
Revolvyng how with sapience ye have spent your space
To the tyme of this your reign mysteriously
Opteynyng as moost worthy your right not regesly.

Now reigne ye rule ye now your realme right wisely
[f. 11v] By politik providence as God hath enduede
To you souveraigne in sapience, submytting me humbly
Your sage sobre sothfastnesse hath so be shewede
In yche judiciall right this realme to be renewede
Ye be advised moost worthy by graciouse affluence
Submytting to your soveraignetie my septer of sapience.

Beseching you of bountevous benevolence
This your citie to supporte with subsidie of your grace
Thies your noble progenitours recordeth the assistence
Of this citie to the assufferayn in yche tyme and place
Proof makith experience now souveraigne in your space
Of purede witt to your blood of great antiquitie
This your citie is solacede to have your soveraigntie.

And by yonde the brigge, at the turnyng into Quonyeux Strete,⁶⁵ ther was a pajaunt of thassumpcion of Our Lady,⁶⁶ whiche had a speche as ensueth, &c:

---

⁶² Written 'of'.
⁶³ '[regence ... ther]'. This line, omitted altogether by Scribe A, has been taken from the corresponding verse transcript in *YHB*, ii, p. 483.
⁶⁴ Originally written 'cause' before –u was expunged.
⁶⁵ Here was another change in the city's plans, where the authorities had intended an unspecified 'shew' like the rosewater shower at Ouse Bridge; at this point the Memoir describes a pageant of the Assumption of Our Lady, apparently originally intended as the final pageant near York Minster: *YHB*, ii, pp. 484–5. The location of the Assumption pageant at the corner of Coney Street, a traditional wagon stop in the York mystery cycle, disrupts the unity of Hudson's design: McGee, thesis, p. 121. It is impossible to know whether this was a change of plans arising from practical difficulty or an error of reportage or transcription.
⁶⁶ An adaptation of the pageant of the Assumption of BVM, produced by the guild of

Our Lady[67]
Henry sith my Sone as thy Souveraigne hath the sothly assigned
Of His Grace to be governour of His peoplez proteccion
Full specially that thyn heire of pytie bee declynede
I pray thee sith thy people hath me muche in affeccion
My Sonne and my Souveraigne in whom is eleccion
Singulerly this citie hath honourede humbly
And made me ther meane withoute objeccion
In hope of their helpe to have it holly.

What I aske of His Great Grace He grauntith it goodly
[f. 12] As a beme of al bountevous benynge
The His knyght He hath chosen victoriously
To convok and concorde this thy countrey condigne
I the pray in this space.[68]
For this citie is a place of my pleasing
Than have thou no drede nor no doubting
Continuelly her in thy reynyng
I shall shewe to my Sonne to sende thee His Grace.[68]

And in divers places of the citie: hanging oute of tapestry and other clothes[69] and making of galaries from on side of the strete over thwarte to that other; some casting oute of obles and wafers; and sume casting oute of comfettes in great quantitie[70] – as [if] it had been hayle stones – for joye and rejoysing of the kinges commyng. And at the further ende of Conyeux Strete was ordeyned another stage with

---

weavers as part of the York mystery cycle. The cost of the use of the equipment was valued at 4s. 'pro stipendio pagine textorum': *Chamberlains' Account Rolls*, p. 190. Mary probably descended, delivered her speech, and ascended into the pageantic heaven: *YHB*, ii, p. 484. See also E. Waterton, *Pietas Mariana Britannica* (London, 1879), pp. 257–265. The definition of the king's relationship to God in terms of knight-service also appears in several of Lydgate's poems for Henry VI: H. N. MacCracken, *The Minor Poems of John Lydgate*, EETS, extra ser., 107, 192, 2 parts (London, 1911–34), i, pp. 11–12, 58–9, 391–411; R. H. Robbins (ed.), *Historical Poems of the XIVth and XVth Centuries* (New York, 1959), p. 238; and 'Edwardus, Dei Gratia' in F. J. Furnivall (ed.), *Political, Religious and Love Poems*, EETS, n.e. (London, 1903), pp. 4–5. The characterisation of Mary as a mediatrix of mercy was a common motif: C. Brown (ed.), *Religious Lyrics of the XVth Century* (Oxford, 1939); M. Eccles, *The Macro Plays*, EETS, 262 (London, 1969), p. 154; L. T. Smith (ed.), *York Plays* (Oxford, 1885), p. 496.

67 Inserted in the left margin.
68 This line was originally omitted, then inserted in the right margin alongside.
69 Decorative hangings were central to Hudson's plans and a chief expense in York's preparations: *Chamberlains' Account Rolls*, p. 190. See also A. F. Johnston and M. Dorrell, 'The York Mercers and their Pageant of Doomsday, 1433–1526', *Leeds Studies in English*, n. s., 6 (1972), pp. 10–35.
70 Like modern-day confetti or tickertape: Wightman, *Royal Entry*, pp. 94–5. Cf. similar

a pageant,[71] wherin King David stode armede and crownede, having a nakede swerde in his hand, [and] had the speche as ensueth, &c:

> David[72]
> Moost prepotent prince of power imperiall
> Redoubtede in iche region of Christez affiance
> Your actes victorious bith notede principall
> In maner mor noble than Charles of Fraunce
> Sith God so disposith of His preordynaunce
> Like as He yave me myght to devince Goly
> I David submytte to you my swerde of victory.
>
> When I reignede in Jude I know and testifie
> That Ebrauc the noble whiche subdued Fraunce
> In memory of his tryumphe this citie did edefie
> That the[73] name of his nobley shulde have contynuance
> In wittenesse that this citie withoute variaunce
> **[f. 12v]** Was never devincede by force ne violence
> Wherfor I have chosen it for my place to your presence.
>
> Submitting it with thafforce and truth to your excellence
> Beseching your highnesse the more for myn instaunce
> To this your enheritaunce take gracious complacence
> Sith that it [is] your citie not filede with dissaveaunce
> True and bolde to your bloode not dreding perturbaunce
> Whiche causede moost this citie to bee desolate
> Now revivyng in comforte to atteigne your astate.

And from thens the king procedede to the mynster, wher within the west doore tharchebisshop with the dean[74] and processyon of the hole quere of the

---

displays in Bristol, below, p. 96, and for Elizabeth I in 1583: Nichols, *Progresses*, i, pp. 405–406. A recipe for wafers is included in Legg, *Coronation Records*, p. lxxviii.

[71] This pageant took place at the common hall on the south side of Coney Street, at its west end: *YHB*, ii, p. 484. It was probably staged before the hall gates.

[72] Inserted in the right margin. A common character in early pageants and civic receptions, often presented as one of the Nine Worthies: Meagher, '*First Progress*', p. 58; McGee, thesis, p. 126. The pageantic King David submits to Henry VII his sword of victory, describes the respect – held throughout Christendom – for the new king's prowess, sums up the qualities York pledges to his service, and concludes with a plea on behalf of the impoverished city. The latter theme is not necessarily the 'palpable untruth' described by Anglo, *Spectacle*, p. 27, but another reference to the city's support of Henry VI.

[73] Preceded by the cancellation of –t.

[74] Robert Bothe, LL. D., dean from 1477–1487: R. Davies (ed.), *Extracts from the Municipal Records of the City of York during the Reigns of Edward IV, Edward V, and Richard III* (London, 1843), p. 142n.

same mynster receyvede the king as accustumede, and so procedede up into the quere byfor the high auter, wher after the orisons redde by tharchebisshop the king offrede.[75] And from thens the king went and offrede[76] at Seint Williams shryne,[77] and than turned into the quere into the deanes stalle. Tharchebisshop standing in his trone beganne *Te Deum*,[78] &c, whiche by them of the quere was right melodiously songen with organz as accustumede. And after the collect the king went into the paloys,[79] wher he loggede as longe as he was in that citie.

And on the Satirday next folowing, whiche was Seint Georges even,[80] the king harde[81] his evensong in the mynster chirche, having a blew mantell above his sircote[82] and on his hede his cap of maintenance;[83] for he was corowned[84] on the

[75] Another reference to the hierarchical relationship of clergy, king and God. See: Wightman, *Royal Entry*, pp. 111–76; McGee, thesis, pp. 128–30. For an account of the rituals observed at York when Richard III visited in 1483 see J. Raine (ed.), *The Fabric Rolls of York Minster*, Surtees Soc., 35 (London, 1859), pp. 210–11.

[76] Henry IV offered 6s. 8d. in York in 1403: Wightman, *Royal Entry*, p. 175. Henry VII's offering in 1486 probably took the same form: prayer and donation.

[77] Archbishop William Fitzherbert was allegedly poisoned by the sacramental wine not long after his return from exile c.1153; he was canonised in 1284. The stone shrine in the minster choir housed Archbishop William's remains and was still an important local place of pilgrimage at the time of Henry VII's visit: Raine, *Medieval York*, pp. 31, 308; A. Clutton-Brock, *The Cathedral Church of York* (London, 1921), p. 126.

[78] Traditional hymn of thanksgiving, commencing *Te Deum Laudamus*. It was also sung after Prince Arthur's birth and upon Henry Tudor's return to London after Stoke in 1487: below, pp. 107, 128.

[79] The archbishop's palace stood just north of the Minster. Richard III also stayed there in 1483: A. Raine, *Medieval York*, pp. 6, 7, 8, 30, and 221.

[80] 'St Georges Even' in the left margin in a 17th-century hand. Traditionally, all knights of the order of the Garter attended the king on the eve of the feast of St. George (the patron saint of the order) on 23 Apr. This is the only recorded occasion on which the feast was celebrated anywhere but Windsor. See Hugh E. L. Collins, *The Order of the Garter 1348–1461* (Oxford, 2000), esp. pp. 23, 26–7, 193–9 for the religious and secular festivities of these occasions. See also the regulations for the celebration of feast days in the 1493 'Articles' for Henry VII's Household' (*OHR*, pp. 109–33), and the statutes of the order drawn up in 1522 in Beltz, *Garter Memorials*, pp. lxxvi–lxxvii. A copy of the royal warrant appointing the earl of Arundel to be the king's lieutenant at the Garter ceremonies of 1490 may be found in Coll. Arms, MS. L.8a, fol. 3.

[81] 'harde' repeated before the repetition was cancelled.

[82] The mantle and surcoat belonged to the habit of the order of the Garter. The mantle was a blue woollen, sleeveless, full-length garment tied at the throat; the king's mantle was slightly longer, lined with ermine, and probably powdered all over with tiny garters. The surcoat resembled a Roman *tunica*, narrower and shorter than the mantle; it was worn over the vest and under the mantel, and fastened by a girdle. Its colour varied from year to year. The king's surcoat was also furred with ermine: Beltz, *Garter Memorials*, pp. l–lii.

[83] High-crowned hat or cap with flattened top and a broad ermine-lined brim that was turned up to the greatest extent at the front, gradually lessening towards the back: 'The

morn, having thabite of the garters above al other robes of estate. Therle of Oxinforde bare his trayne. Also in the morne the trayne of the mayntell of the garters coverde the trayne[85] of the mantell of astate, and the furre of the astate **[f. 13]** sufficiently shewed.[86] The king kept his estate[87] in the bisshops great hall. Therle of Oxinforde yave attendaunce upon the coroun, havyng also thabet of the garter above thabite of his estate. And Antony Browne sewed[88] that day. And the lorde Scrop of Bolton, by cause he was a knyght of the garter, in both his habitez servede the king of water. Item, Sir David Owen in his habite kervede. Item, Sir Charlez of Somerset in his habite was copeberer. Item, tharchebisshop, whiche ministrede the dyvyne service, sat on the kinges right hande in non other array but as he dayly gooth in. And at that other ende of the kinges borde that day satt noman.

Item, in the forsaide hall were vj tables, that is to say ij in the middez of the saide hall and in every ile ij. At the furst table in the myddez of the hall satt my lorde chaunceller, my lorde privy seale, thabbot of Seynt Mary Abbey, thabbott of Founteyns, tharchebisshops suffragan, with other prelates and the kinges chapeleyns. Item, at the ijde table satt therles of Lincolln, of Shrewsbury, Ryvers, and of Wiltshire; baronez, knyghtes, and esquiers for the body, &c. Item, at the furst table on the right ile of the forsaide hall satt the lorde Scrope, Sir Thomas of Burgh and Sir John Cheyne[89] (knyghtes of the garter), all on oon side;[90] and by neith theym left a voide space; and then other honest persones fulfilled and garnisshed that table. Item, at the ijde table of that ile satt the dean and his brethern with the hole quere of the mynster. Item, at the furst table of the ijde ile next to the walle satt

---

Cap of Maintenance' in Legg, *Coronation Records*, p. lxxxii. See reference to the two caps of maintenance made for Henry's coronation, one of purple velvet and ermine, and one of satin: *Materials*, ii, pp. 3–12.

[84] Of Anglo-Saxon origin, the ritual of crown-wearing marked the major religious ceremonies of the year, and was a device well used by Richard III and Henry VII. The significance of the ritual is discussed in C. A. J. Armstrong, 'The Inauguration Ceremonies of the Yorkist Kings and Their Title to the Throne', in idem, *England, France and Burgundy in the Fifteenth Century* (London, 1983), p. 93. Richard III had also staged a crown-wearing with his wife and son in York soon after his own coronation: *YHB*, ii, pp. 390–1; *Three Books of Polydore Vergil's 'English History'*, ed. H. Ellis, Camden Soc., 29 (1844), p. 190. See also the description of the crown-wearing of both Henry VII and his queen at the celebration of Twelfth Eve, below, p. 163.

[85] –t slightly obscured by an ink smudge.

[86] 'sufficiently shewed' given as catchwords at the bottom of fol. 12v.

[87] See the regulations governing the days of estate in the 1493 'Articles' for Henry VII's Household' in *OHR*, pp. 110–11.

[88] Initially written 'shewed', before –h was cancelled.

[89] 'Cheyne' interlineated above.

[90] Article XI of the statutes of the order of the Garter requires that the Garter knights sit along one side of the table, either according to rank or seniority in their stalls: Beltz, *Garter Memorials*, p. lxxxvi. The overall seating follows the traditional arrangement by estate in 'Articles' in *OHR*, p. 12.

THE HERALDS' MEMOIR, 1486–1490

the mair and his brethen with other citezins in great nombre. Item, at the ijde **[f. 13v]** table of that ile sat the juggez; by neith theym other honest persones.

At the kinges tables ende ther was ordeignede a stage for his officers of armes,[91] whiche at the tyme accustumede cryede his largesse[92] iij tymes: "de treiz haute, treiz puissant, treiz excellent prince, le treiz victorious roy dAngliter et de Fraunce, seigneur de Irland et souveraigne de la treiz noble order, larges", eftsonez thriez larges: "de treiz haute, treiz puissante, treiz excellent prince, le treiz cristen roy de Fraunce et dAngleter", &c as above. Item, Sir John Turburvile, knyght mershall, drewe the surnap;[93] and after dyner was ther the voide. And then the king and the lordez did of ther robez, excepte thabbite of the garter,[94] wherin knyghtes of the same according to ther statutz roode to evensonge[95] and on the morne to the masse of requiem, whiche was songen by the suffragan mytrede. And after masse the king and the knyghtes of the garter went to the chapter house, and ther helde his chapter[96] of the garter.

It is to bee remembrede that on Seynt Georges day thabbot of Seint Mary Abbey redde the gospell, thabbot [of] Fountenz the pistill, the suffragan was croyser and bar tharchbisshope crosse, and all were in pontificalibus. This doon, I had leve for to departe.[97]

[91] 'officers of armes' written in the left margin in the same hand as above, n. 1; the final –es is partially obscured by an ink stain. Presumably denotes all heralds of the Crown not engaged on royal business attended. See the place of the heralds at the coronation banquet for Elizabeth of York in 1487, below, p. 143.

[92] See the description of the heralds' crying of largess at the celebration of New Year's Day, 1488, below, pp. 151–2. See also Wagner, *Heralds*, pp. 93–4.

[93] Denotes the removal of the towel or upper cloth used for washing the hands after meal. See 'The Book of Curtasye', 'John Russells Boke of Nurture' and 'The Boke of Kervynge' in Furnivall (ed.), *Meals and Manners*, pp. 16–17, 92–3, 155–6, 204, 338. An account of the drawing of the surnap of Queen Anne Boleyn may be found in BL, MS. Add. 6113, fols 34–35.

[94] Article IV of the Garter statutes instructs the knights to attend any divine services appointed for the occasion: Beltz, *Garter Memorials*, p. lxxxv.

[95] Article XII of the Garter statutes requires the knights' attendance, on the day following the feast of St. George, at the requiem mass for deceased knights of the order: Beltz, *Garter Memorials*, p. lxxxv; Collins, *Order of the Garter*, pp. 199–200. The achievements of knights who died during the year just gone are offered at the requiem mass, as below, pp. 158–9, in the manner of a funeral. See 'The Burying of an Earle' in *OHR*, pp. 131–2 and accounts of the reburial of Richard duke of York in 1476 in A. F. Sutton and L. Visser-Fuchs, *The Reburial of Richard Duke of York, 21–30 July, 1476* (London, 1996). See also Wagner, *Heralds*, pp. 106–19 for the heralds' roles in the funeral and requiem mass.

[96] The general meetings of the Garter knights provided the occasion for devising or modifying ordinances, correcting offences, and installing new knights. Ideally the chapter was to be held at Windsor on the feast of St. George, although general meetings were also called within six weeks of the death of any member for the election of a replacement: Beltz, *Garter Memorials*, p. lxxxvii; Collins, *Order of the Garter*, p. 26.

THE EDITION

At Wytsone even,[98] at whiche tyme I came to the kinges grace at Worcestre, wher as I undrestande wer ordeynede certeyn pajantes and speches like as ensuen whiche his grace at that tyme harde not, &c:

    Henry VIth[99]
Welcome nevew[100] welcome, my cousyn dere
Next of my blood descended by alyaunce[101]
Chosen by grace of God both fer and ner
To be myn heir in Englande and in Fraunce
[f. 14] Ireland Wales with al the apurtenaunce
Of the hole tytle which I sumtyme had
Al is thyn owne wherfor I am right glad.

I am Henry the vjth sobre and sad
Thy great uncle sumtyme of England king
Full xxxix yeres this realme my silf I had
And of the people had the governyng
Slayne was I martir by great tourmenting
In Chartesey[102] buriede translate unto Windesore
Ther logge I now and arft ther was I bore.

Mek and mercifull was I evermore
From crueltie refreynyng and from vengeaunce
God hath me rewardede largely therfor
And gentil cosyn sith thou hast this chaunce

---

[97] A hand marker in the left margin points to 'to depart'.
[98] Sat. 13 May 1486. The herald reporting on this portion of the journey joined (or rejoined) the royal party after it had been in Worcester several weeks. He managed to secure copies of the Worcester pageants, although these had not been performed.
[99] Written in the left margin as 'RH vjth' in the same hand as above, p. 68, n. 1. The speaker of this pageant, presenting himself as Henry VI, opens with reference to the special relationship between Henry VII and Henry VI, speaks briefly on his own reign and martyrdom, and then moves on to the key theme – an urgent plea for mercy, wisely issued after the city's implication in the Stafford rebellion: Meagher, 'First Progress', p. 63. Henry VI further assures Henry VII of the city's loyalty, and introduces the characters of St. Oswald, St. Wulfstan and the Virgin Mary, each of whom offers a prayer for the king and reiterates the hope that he will rule with mercy and compassion. For further discussion of the themes of this pageant see: McGee, thesis, pp. 145–56, Anglo, *Spectacle*, pp. 29–30; Meagher, 'First Progress', pp. 62–5. On the topic of Henry VI as a Lancastrian saint; see: Anglo, *Spectacle*, pp. 35–43; idem, *Images*, pp. 61–73.
[100] Interlineated above.
[101] Actually written with a superfluous superscript –a over the n.
[102] Henry VI was first interred in the Lady Chapel of the Benedictine Abbey at Chertsey, Surrey, on 22 May 1471. On 12 Aug. 1484, by an order of Richard III, his remains were translated to St. George's Chapel, Windsor.

To be myn heire use wele my governaunce[103]
Pytie with mercy have alwey in thy cure
For by meknesse thou shalt lengest endure.

Advertise wele what founde is in scripture
The Gospell seith whoso right well it markes
Mercifull men of mercy may bee sure
For God Him self this writeth and seith al clerkes
Preferrede mercy above all His werkes
Now for His sake shewe it to free and bonde
And He shall guyde thee both by see and lande.

[f. 14v] And here thou may dere cousyn undrestande[104]
This poore citie with humble reverence
A poore bill have put into myn hande
Be[s]eching[105] me of my benevolence
It to declare to thy magnyficence
Wherto I muste my pitefull herte enbrace
And this procede whos luste is here in place.

Humbly besechith your high and noble grace
Your poore subjectes liegmen and oratours
Wher late befell a lamentable case
A gentilman detected with riottours[106]
Making suggestyon ayenst you and youres
Contryved falsely by his informacion
Shewing so largely by his comunicacion:[107]

That of your grace he had grauntede his pardon
By great charter of lif goodes and landes
Desiring heder to come for his devocion

---

[103] 'pitie' cancelled at the end of this line.
[104] –dre interlineated above.
[105] Written 'Becheching'.
[106] This is the only reference in the Memoir to the rebellion under Stafford. Many of those who joined Stafford and entered Worcester are named in the Coram Rege Roll, Mich. 4 Hen. VII: TNA, KB 27/909, printed in McGee, thesis, Appendix B, pp. 248–53. Stafford's case appears in M. Hemmant (ed.), *Select Cases in the Exchequer Chamber before all the Justices of England*, 2 vols (London, 1948), ii, p. 115–24. For an account of the Stafford rebellion, see C. H. Williams, 'The Rebellion of Humphrey Stafford in 1486', *EHR*, 43 (1928), pp. 181–9. For the defence of one John Collard of Feckenham, who alleged himself duped by Stafford, see *Materials*, i, pp. 434–5. Similar pleas were entered in the king's bench files.
[107] Written 'concacon' without clear abbreviation marks.

To offre at Our Lady[108] wher that she stande[s][109]
By ignorance thus bee they brought in bandes
Beseching you moost mekely or ye passe
Graciously pardon theym this trespasse.

For greatly greven theym both[110] mor and lasse
So many men by oon to be deceyvede
Your oune citie that never pollutede was
Is now defiled for she hath hym receyvede
Your saide subgettes that al this hath perceyvede
[f. 15] Enclyne theymsilf and to your mercy calle
Seing they have a warnyng perpetuall.

And from this tyme after whatever befalle
They will entende to put theym silf in devoure
You for to please both olde yonge great and smale
With al ther service your high grace to recovere
And your saide oratours promysse to pray for ever
For your noble estate and prosperitie
Long to contynue in joye and felicitie.

And now, swete Henry, doo somewhat for me
I stod for vj and now ye stande for vij
Faver thoos folk that fele adversitie
God wille rewarde the therfor high in heven
Now as myghty lyon bere the even
Whos noble angre in his cruell rage
To prostrate people never wolde doo damage.

That he may this with al his counseill sage
Here I beseche the Holy Trynytie
And the swete moder, whiche in her tendre age
Bare God and man in pure virginitie
And ye both seintes of myn affynytie
Oswolde and Wolstan right holy confessours
Pray for my good sone king Henry at al houres.

      [St. Wulstan][111]
Hevenly Fader that art of power moost

---

[108] A statue of Mary, estimated to be ten feet tall, stood over the main altar in the cathedral: Waterton, *Pietas*, pp. 252–3.
[109] Actually written 'standeth', although this does not fit the rhyme scheme.
[110] Preceded by the cancellation of 'this tresspasse'.
[111] Saints Wulfstan and Oswald, as ancient bishops of Worcester, were natural represen-

And thou His Sonne aproprede unto witte
[f. 15v] O thou swete spirite, named the Holy Goost
Thre persones in on Godhede suerly knytt
For King Henry the vij I me submytt
Beseching you to graunte hym in this place
Power wisdome and al soyson of grace.

    [St. Oswald][111]
O Hevenly Lord! Celestiall God durable
Above al kinges having preemynence
Both iij and on and undeseverable[112]
I the beseche for thy magnyficence
King Henry the vij to kepe from al offence
Graunt hym longe liff in vertue the to please
And al his dayes for to reigne in peas.

    [Our Lady][113]
O Eternal God that made al thing of nought
Fader and Sonne and Holy Goost ful preste
Beholde the hande maide whiche they iij have wrought
And namely thou my sone which soke my breste
Henry the vij preserve at my requeste
Englande my dowre to forte rule and guyde
Therby to wynne the blisse that ever shal abide.

    [The Trinity][114]
O Henry moche art thou beholde to us
That thee have reysede by our oune eleccion
Be thou therfor mercifull and graciouse
For mercye pleasith moost our affeccion
Folow king Henry whiche is thy proteccion
As welle in worke as in sanguinitie.

---

    tatives of the city. Oswald had been appointed by King Edgar in 959 and held office until 991; Wulfstan was bishop from 1062 until 1095: *DNB*, xiv, pp. 1217–19; xxi, pp. 1089–91; *VCH, Worcester*, ii, pp. 3–9; H. Thurston and D. Attwater (eds), *Butler's Lives of the Saints*, revised edn, 4 vols (London, 1956), i, pp. 439–40, 121–3.

[112] This sentence should be read as 'both three and one, and undeseverable' in reference to the unity of the Holy Trinity.

[113] Apparently portrayed with the baby Jesus in her arms. The description of England as Our Lady's dowry was a common literary motif, esp. during the early 15th century: Rev. T. E. Bridgett, *Our Lady's Dowry*, 3rd edn (London, 1890); Waterton, *Pietas*, pp. 11–18.

[114] Probably an anthropomorphic representation of the character: McGee, thesis, p. 159. On anthropomorphic representations of the Trinity see especially L. Réau, *l'Iconographie de l'Art Chrétien*, 6 vols (Paris, 1955–9), ii, pp. 19–28.

And in this worlde it wille rewarded bee right welle
If thou serve God in love and drede
[f. 16] Havyng compassion of theym that hath nede
Everlasting joye shalbe thy mede
In Heven above wher al seintes dwelle.

Loquitur Janitor[115] *ad Januam*
Ecce advenit dominator dominus
Et regnum in manu eius potestas et imperium
Venit desideratus cunctis gentibus.
To whom this citie both al and some
Speking by me biddeth hertely welcome
And as I cane welcome I shall expresse
Beseching your grace[116] pardon my simplenesse.

Quis est ille qui venit so great of price?
I thought Noe whiche came late from the flodde
Or is it Jason with the golden flece
The noble mount of riches and of goode
Manly of dede manerly meke of mode
Or it is Julius with the triumphe of victorie
To whom I say 'welcome!' most hertely?

Welcome Abraham which went from his kynnerede
Of al this lande to take possession
Welcome Ysaac that sumtyme shulde have be dedde
And now is heire to his fader by succession
Welcome Jacob opteynyng the beneson
Whiche many yeres dwelled with his ungle true
Fleyng his countrey from drede of Esau.

Welcome Joseph, that was to Egipte sold
[f. 16v] Frely welcome oute of the depe cesterne
Welcome David the myghty lion bolde
Chosen of Gode this realme to rule and governe

---

[115] A fictitious character created by the city. Despite its position in the Memoir, the pageant of Janitor was almost certainly designed to be given first. In a variant on the Nine Worthies theme, the speaker mistakes Henry Tudor for a wide variety of heroes, including Noah, Jason and Julius Caesar (where each statement is supported by a cited parallel between the king and the hero) and emphasises the triumph, virtue, rightful succession and divine favour enjoyed by Henry VII; finally, the speaker identifies Henry Tudor as the fulfilment of prophecy: Meagher, 'First Progress', p. 61. For further discussion of the Janitor pageant see Anglo, *Spectacle*, pp. 30–1 and McGee, thesis, pp. 159–64.

[116] Followed by the cancellation of –f.

Whiche in the felde great Goly did prosterne
And al his enemyes overcome in fight
God being guyde that yave hym strength and myght.

Welcome Scipio the whiche toked Hanyball
Welcome Arture the very Britan kyng
Welcome defence to England as a walle
Cadwaladers blodde lynyally descending
Longe hath bee towlde of suche a prince commyng
Wherfor frendez if that I shalnot lye
This same is the fulfiller of the profecye.

Whiche he is this mor pleynely to expresse
Henry the vij chosen by grace and chaunce
For singuler beautie and for high prowesse
Now to be king of England and of Fraunce
And prince of Wales with al thappurtenances
Lord of Irelande moost famous of renome
Withal the titill perteynyng to the coroune.

And now welcome our noble souveraigne lorde
Better welcome was never prince to us
We have desirede long God to recorde
To see your moost noble persone graciouse
Welcome myghty pereles and moost famous
Welcome commyng byding gooing and alweys knowen
In token whereof I yelde to you the keyes
[f. 17] Now al this citie seith welcome to your oune.

And on Wittsonday[117] [the king] went in procession and hard his dyvyne service in the cathedrall chirche of the saide citie, having no roobez of estate upon hym but a gowne of cloth of golde of tissue lynede with blake satene.[118] The bisshop of that see did the dyvyne service in pontificalibus; and in the processyon commynge toward the quere ayene the bisshop went into the pulpitt and made a bref and a fructifull sermonde, in conclusion of the whiche declarede the popez bulles[119]

[117] (Pentecost Sunday). Sun. 14 May 1486.
[118] Possibly made from the fabrics ordered from Doncaster on 30 Apr., as the king made his way from York to Worcester: *Materials*, i, p. 419.
[119] The bishop of Imola granted the required dispensation for the union to proceed on 16 Jan. 1485/6, and the marriage took place on 18 Jan. The papal dispensation was granted on 2 Mar. 1485/6 and confirmed on 27 Mar. See *Calendar of Entries in the Papal Registers*, xiv, pp. 1–2, 14–28; 'Bull of Pope Innocent VIII on the Marriage of Henry VII with Elizabeth of York', *Camden Miscellany*, i (1847), pp. 3–7; Chrimes, *Henry VII*, Appendix D, pp. 330–1; Anglo, *Spectacle*, p. 19; McGee, thesis, App. D, pp. 257–60.

touching the kinges and the quenes right and the confirmacion[120] of the same. Present ther: the bisshop of Ely and of Excester, the duc of Bedeforde, the marques of Dorset, therle of Lyncolln, therle of Oxinforde, the vicount Welles, the lorde fitz Water, Sir William Stanley (called lorde chambrelayn), the lorde Husey (chieff jugge of the kinges benche), and great nombre of knyghtes and esquiers and of other people; and by for dyner, in his chambre, Sir Thomas Towneshende (justice knyght). And at the tyme accustumed on that day he had his largez cried by his officers of armes, &c.

On the Monday[121] the king remevede and roode to Herforde, wher a myle and moore oute of the town and over Long Brigge[122] the meire[123] of the towne, with on vj^{xx} horse and above, mette the king and receyved hym; and further nere the towne[124] the frerez[125] of the saide citie yave ther attendaunce in the procession after the parishe chirches[126] as accustomed, with great multitude of people of the countrey,[127] whiche in rejoysing of the kinges commyng cried "King Henry! King Henry!", and holding up ther handez blessed and prayde God to preserve our king. And when he entred the gate[128] ther was ordeyned a pageaunt of Seint George, with a speche as ensueth:

[f. 17v] S. George[129]
Moost cristen prince, and frende unto the feith
Supporter of truth confounder of wikkednesse

---

[120] Final –o obscured by an inkblot.
[121] 15 May 1486.
[122] Probably Lug Bridge, crossing the Lug River on the route of the Roman road running from Kenchester to Worcester: McGee, thesis, p. 169. Lugg Bridge appears on the 1757 map of Hereford printed inside the back cover of J. and M. Tonkin, *The Book of Hereford* (Chesham, 1975). A possible route taken by the royal procession at this stage of the journey, not described by the herald, is set out in McGee, thesis, pp. 170–1.
[123] Thomas Mey.
[124] Preceded by the cancellation of 'towne', with –n interlineated above.
[125] Dominicans, Franciscans, Knights Templar, Knights of St John, the priory of St Guthlac, and the chapel of St. Martin in the castle: Tonkin, *The Book of Hereford*, p. 36.
[126] St Peter's, All Saints, St Nicholas's, St. Owen's and St. Martin's: Tonkin, *Book of Hereford*, p. 36.
[127] Followed by a cancellation.
[128] The pageant of St. George may have been located inside the walls and viewed after the king passed through the gate: McGee, thesis, pp. 171–2; Tonkin, *The Book of Hereford*, pp. 27, 29.
[129] Inserted in the left margin. St. George was a common feature of plays, mummings, ridings, disguisings and pageants, both in England and on the Continent, as in the pageantry in London's reception of Henry V in 1415, in Bristol's show for Edward IV in 1461, and in Coventry's reception for Prince Edward in 1474: McGee, thesis, p. 172. He appeared again in Coventry in 1498 when the city welcomed Prince Arthur: *Coventry Leet Book*, iii, p. 591. See also: Chambers, *Medieval Stage*, i, pp. 213, 221–24; R. Withington, *English Pageantry: an Historical Outline*, 2 vols (New York, 1918; repr. 1963),

As people of your realme holy reporteth and saith
Welcome to this citie withoute eny feintenesse
And thinke verely as ye see her in likenesse
That this worme is discomfite by Goddes ayde[130] and myn
So shall I be your helpe unto your lives fine
To withstonde your enemyes with the help of that blessed Virgyn
The whiche loveth you right wele I dar playnly it say
Wherefor ye be right welcome I pray God further you in your way.

Item, at the crosse[131] in the market place was ordeynede a nother pageaunt of a king and ij bisshops (the whiche sensede the king),[132] and the king of that had this speche as ensueth:

Ethelbert Rex[133]

Moost vertuouse prince and gracious in governance
Not rigours but mercifull as David in his juggement
The people of your citie wolde ful fayne your pleasaunce
And prayde me as ther patrone to enforme you of ther entent
My name is king Ethelbert that sumtyme was king of Kent
Whiche in my yong age loost myn erthly liff
And now am protector[134] of this cathedrall and citie present
Wherfor I say welcome both of man child and wiff

---

i, pp. 22–24, 44–6, 57n, 150–1, 161, 196. For similarly emphatic promises of support to Henry VI in 1432 see 'Henry VI's Triumphal Entry into London' in MacCracken (ed.), *Minor Poems*, ii, p. 633; *Coventry Leet Book*, ii, pp. 11–13. For a biography of St. George and discussion of his popularity among the English nobility of the 15th century see S. Riches, 'Seynt George ... on whom alle Englond hath byleve', *History Today*, 50.10 (October, 2000), pp. 26–1.

[130] 'ayde' written above a minor cancellation.
[131] Located in the market place on the High St: Tonkin, *Book of Hereford*, frontispiece.
[132] Presumably King Ethelbert, censed to emphasise his sanctity. See R. Kipling (ed.), *The Receyt of the Ladie Kateryne*, EETS, 296 (London, 1990), p. 13. Censing of pageantic characters regularly took place during the course of a royal entry at the cross in Crosscheaping, Coventry. It was a feature of the receptions of Queen Margaret in 1456, of Edward in 1474, and of Arthur in 1498: *Coventry Leet Book*, ii, pp. 289, 392; iii, p. 590.
[133] Inserted in the left margin. Son and heir of Ethelred I, king of the East Angles; fl. c.794; betrayed and executed by Offa, king of the Mercians; venerated as a martyr; buried at Hereford. The pageantry erroneously states that Ethelbert was King of Kent, raising the possibility that the Hereford pageants were the work of someone from outside the city. Henry's visit occurred about a week before the feast of St. Ethelbert (20 May). Further details of Ethelbert's biography can be found in E. M. Leather, *The Folk-Lore of Herefordshire* (1912; repr. Menston, 1970), pp. 217–19. Like Henry VI in the Worcester pageant, Ethelbert claims to be acting in response to a petition from the city, but the pleas are less urgent than Worcester's.
[134] Preceded by the cancellation of 'pcto'.

And that Blessed Virgin that cessith our mortall striff
Abideth your commyng her what I say you
Wherfor I will not ye tary but I pray God be with you.

Item, at the entre of the minster was the iijde paiaunt of Our Lady **[f. 18]** with many virgins[135] mervealous and richely besen; and Our Lady had her speche as hereafter ensueth:

> Our Lady[136]
> In the best wise welcome myn oune true knyght
> To my chirche and chapelens of our oune foundacion
> Wherfor I thank you and pray you both day and nyght
> For to kepe and defende from al fraudulent imaginacion
> For many thynges I thanke you: the dedes sheweth probacion
> Unto my lande and honour your doth ever atteigne
> Wherfor I thanke you of your good supportacion
> Your rewarde is behinde it shall come certeyne
> That is the blisse of hevyn wherin my sone dooth reigne
> That veraly I promysse you I have graunt a for
> Now goo in and see my chirch: I will tary you nomore.

Item, at the entre within the chirche doore the bisshop[137] in pontificalibus with the dean[138] and the quere receyvede the king as in other cathedrall chirches accustumed. And on the morne,[139] as the king went in procession, the bisshop of that same see made a sermonde declaring the popes bulles touching the kinges and the quenes stile.

Than the Friday next folowing[140] the king roode and remeved to Gloucestre, wher iij myles withoute the towne the mair[141] with his brether and shriffes[142] in

---

[135] Essentially decorative, as was common practice: Meagher, 'First Progress', p. 68. Cf. the pageants of Prudencia and Justicia in Bristol, below (fols 19v–20v), the pageantry prepared by Coventry in 1456 and 1498, and the pageantry prepared for Katherine of Aragon: *Coventry Leet Book*, ii, p. 290; iii, p. 590; *Receyte*, p. 13.

[136] Inserted in the right margin. The key point of Mary's pageant is to usher the king toward the cathedral, but she also thanks Henry for his devotion to her, and promises that her intercession will earn his heavenly reward. See: McGee, thesis, pp. 178–81; Meagher, 'First Progress', p. 68.

[137] Thomas Mylling, bishop of Hereford from 1474–1492. Mylling was often on missions for the Crown, necessitating the appointment of a permanent suffragan, Richard Wycherley, app. 1482: *Extracts from the Cathedral Registers A. D. 1275–1535*, transl. Rev. E. N. Dew (Hereford, 1932), p. 127; *DNB*, xiii, p. 447.

[138] Thomas Chandler, installed 23 Mar. 1482.

[139] Tues. 16 May 1486.

[140] 19 May 1486.

[141] William Francombe.

[142] Robert Rawlins and Philip Predith.

scarlet gownes,[143] and other people in great nombre in rede gownes, and al on horse bakkes, welcomed the king. And without the gate, betwixte both brigges,[144] the procession of the freres, and also the procession of the town of al the pariche chirches,[145] receyvede the king. And in that towne ther was no pageant nor speche ordeynede. Thabbot[146] and his monkes receyvede the king with procession **[f. 18v]** at thabbey chirche doore, wher the king abode Satirday and Sonday al day, whiche was the Trinytie Sonday;[147] and thabbot mitrede sange the highe masse, and in procession. The bisshop of Worcester prechide, shewing the popes bulles touching as afor.

And on the Monday the king remeved to Bristow warde and lay at thabbey of Kinges Woode,[148] and on Tewsday[149] dynyd at Acton with Sir Robert Poynez, shryef of Gloucestreshire; and iij milis oute of Bristow the maire,[150] the shriffes,[151] the bailiffes[152] with ther brethern, and great nombre of othre burgesez al on horsebake, in whos names Treymayle, recorder of the same towne, right connyngly welcomed the king.[153] But the mair of Bristow bar no mase, nor the shrif of that towne bar no rodde unto the tyme they came to a gate of the suburbs[154] wher beginneth ther fraunches. And on a causay wey[155] within that gate the procession of the

---

[143] Costuming to enhance the visual splendour of the event and distinguish rank and authority. Scarlet was the colour of the royal livery and signified the civic officials' status as wardens of the king's city: Wightman, *Royal Entry*, pp. 34–5.

[144] The road beyond the west gate of Gloucester had several bridges. The bridges mentioned in the Memoir are likely to be the first and the last, two of Gloucester's most obvious landmarks: McGee, thesis, p. 183.

[145] The Benedictines of St. Peter's Abbey and St Oswald's Priory; the Augustinian canons of Lanthony Priory; Black Friars; Grey Friars; Carmelites; the Hospitals of Saints Mary Magdalen, Bartholomew and Margaret; St. Ewen's church: *VCH, Gloucester*, ii, pp. 53–61, 84–91, 111–12, 119–22; Leland, *Itinerary*, pp. 171–81.

[146] William Farley, abbot of St Peter's, from 1474 to 1498: *VCH, Gloucester*, ii, p. 53–61.

[147] 21 May 1486.

[148] See *VCH, Gloucester*, ii, pp. 99–101; V. R. Perkins, 'Documents relating to the Cistercian Monastery of St. Mary, Kingswood', *Transactions of the Bristol and Gloucestershire Archaeological Society,* xxii (1899), pp. 179–256.

[149] 23 May 1486.

[150] Henry Vaughan. The authority of the mayor over the Bristol elite is discussed in P. Fleming, 'Telling Tales of Oligarchy in the Late Medieval Town', in *Revolution and Consumption in Late Medieval England*, ed. M. Hicks (Woodbridge, 2001), pp. 177–194.

[151] Richard Sherman and others unknown.

[152] Philip Kingston, Hugh Jones.

[153] Repeated.

[154] Bristol's boundaries began at Lawford's gate, at the east end of the city.

[155] Known as the Old Market on Hunt's map of Bristol *c.*1480. King Henry probably proceeded west along the causeway to the castle moat, before turning right and continuing along Castle Ditch, first north then west to New Gate: McGee, thesis, p. 189. The

frerez[156] receyved the king; and the[n] at the ende of the causey wey the procession of the pariche chirches receyved the king. And in thentre of the towne gate ther was ordeigned a pageaunt[157] with great melode and singing, the whiche cessed [and] ther was a king [that] had the speche as herafter ensuethe:

[King Brennius][158]
Moost dere cosine of England and Fraunce
King Henry the vij noble and victorious
Seint hider by the holsome purviaunce
Of Almyghty God moost mercifull and gracious
To reforme thinges that be contrarious
Unto the comen wele, with a myghty hande
I am right gladde ye be welcome to this lande.

[f. 19] Namely to this towne whiche I Brennyus[159] king
Whilom bildede with her wallez olde
And called it Bristow in the begynnyng
For a memoriall that folke ne wolde
Oute of remembraunce that acte race ne unfolde
And welcome to your subjectes her that with oon accorde
Thankking God highly for such a souveraigne lorde.

This towne lefte I in great prosperitie
Havyng riches and[160] welth many folde
The merchaunt the artyficer everyche in his degre
Had great plentye both of silver and golde

---

causeway was paved under a royal order from the second parliament of the reign: *RP*, iv, pp. 390–1.

[156] Approx. 20 parish churches, 8 chapels, and 6 hospitals, in addition to the houses of the major religious orders: Victorine canons of the abbey of St. Augustine, White Friars, and Augustinians. For brief histories of these see *VCH, Gloucester*, ii, pp. 74–9, 93, 109–11.

[157] For discussion of the possible locations of the pageant at New Gate, see McGee, thesis, pp. 190–1.

[158] Legendary founder of Bristol. Brennius welcomes Henry Tudor as a man sent by God, and as a reformer sent to pull Bristol from the mire of poverty and decay, through support of its principal industries (navy, cloth making, etc). The king is also reminded of the fidelity of the people of Bristol: Meagher, 'First Progress', pp. 69–70. For details of Bennius's biography current in England at the time of Henry VII's first provincial progress see Ricart, *Kalendar*, v, pp. 8–10. For Bristol's economic status during the fifteenth century see esp. C. D. Ross, 'Bristol in the Middle Ages', in *Bristol and its Adjoining Counties*, ed. C. M. MacInnes and W. F. Whittard (Bristol, 1955); E. M. Carus-Wilson, 'The Overseas Trade of Bristol in the Fifteenth Century', in *Medieval Merchant Venturers: Collected Studies*, 2nd edn (London, 1967), pp. 1–97.

[159] Initially written 'Brennnius', before the first –n was expunged.

[160] Proceded by a superfluous 'et'.

And lifed in joye as they desire wolde
At my departing but I have been so longe awey
That Bristow is fallen into decaye.

Irrecuperable withoute that a due remedy
By you ther hertes hope and comfort in this distresse
Provede bee at your leyser convenyently
To your navy and cloth making wherby I gesse
The wele of this towne standeth in sikernesse
Maybe maynteigned as they have bee
In dayes hertofor in prosperitie.

Now farwell dere cosyn my leve I take
At you that wele of bountie bee
To your saide subjectes, for Mariez sake
That bereth you ther fidelitie
In moost loving wise as graunte ye
Some remedye herin and he wille quite your mede
That never unrewarded leveth good dede.

[f. 19v]And from thens the king procedede in to the towne;[161] and at the high crosse ther was a pageaunt ful of maydyn childern richely besene; and Prudencia had the speche as ensueth:

[Prudencia][162]
Mooste noble prynce our souveraigne liege lorde
To this poore towne of Bristow that is youre[s]
Ye be hertely welcome God to recorde
And to your loving subjectes and oratours
That hertely pray for[163] your grace at al houres
The good fame of your renoume so fer dooth sprede
That al your saide subjectes both love you and drede.

For in quiet wise and pesable
Your subjectes ye kepe from devisyon
Ye yef not credence to lightly
Too feyned tales that make myght discencion
And wher peas reigneth is al perfeccion

---

[161] The king probably moved southwest along Winch Street to the intersection of High Street, where the cross stood: McGee, thesis, pp. 195–6.
[162] See Withington, *English Pageantry*, i, pp. 107, 149, 168, 169, 178. Prudence praises the king's success in keeping his subjects in peace and unity, before directing him on his way with a prayer for his guidance.
[163] Preceded by the cancellation of 'you'.

It kepith subjectes as they shulde bee
From al stryves in quyete and unytie.

Crist therfor that on crosse diede
Thoroughe the mediacion of holy seintes all
Save your moost high noblesse and bee your guyde
Confounde your enemyes, make theym to you thrawll
And strenketh with me Prudence in especiall
To withstonde thoo thinges that bee contrarious
And to doo that may please God moost glorious.

And from thens the kyng procedede *ad portam Sancti Johannis*,[164] wher was **[f. 20]** a nother pageaunt of many mayden childern richely besene with girdelles, bedes and ouchez, wher Justicia had the wordes that herafter ensueth, &c:

[Justicia][165]
Welcome moost excellent high and victorious
Welcome delicate rose of this mor Brytaigne
From al mysaventures and thing contrarious
Preserve by dyvyne power certeygne
And so hider sentt I will not fayne
Welcome king of Englande and of Fraunce
To this youre oune towne God sende you right good chaunce.

I am Justicia the kinde and nature
Of God that hath me made and ordeignede
Our realmez and our every creature
By me Justicia is shedding of bloode refreyn[ed][166]
And gilte punysshed whan it is compleynede
I Justice defende possessions
And kepe people from oppressions.

This is welle considerde by your noble grace
For ye have had alway an ye therunto
Minisshing justice duly in every place
Thorough this region wher ye ride or goo

---

[164] Henry VII probably turned right at the high cross and proceeded northwest up Broad St. to St. John's Gate in the inner wall of the city: McGee, thesis, p. 200.

[165] This abstract morality character often appeared in entertainments, political poetry, and religious verse in the company of the other cardinal virtues: Withington, *English Pageantry*, i, pp. 104, 186–7, 200, 212. Here Justice primarily welcomes Henry to the town, describes her own relationship to God, and praises Henry for his administration of justice, praying that he persevere: Meagher, 'First Progress', pp. 70–1.

[166] Written 'refreynyng', although this does not fit the rhyme scheme.

Indifferently both to frende and foo
God sende you therin good perseveraunce
As may bee to His grace most singuler pleasaunce.

I have oftyme rede in bokes olde
That *omnia parent virtuti*
[f. 20v] The whiche maketh me more bolde
To eschewe you this prossesse by and by
Praying Almyghty God whiche is on high
That from vertue to vertue ye may procede
And in all your journeys sende you right good spede.

And then the king proceded towarde thabbey of Seint Austeyns;[167] and by the way the[r] was a bakers wiff cast oute of a wyndow a great quantitie of whete[168] crying "Welcome and good look!" And a litill furthermor ther was a pageant made, callede 'the shipwrightes pageaunt',[169] with praty conceytes pleyng in the same withoute any speche. And a litill further ther was a nother pageaunte of an olifaunte[170] with a castell on his bakk, curiously wrought [and] the resurreccion of Our Lorde in the highest tower of the same, with certeyne imagerye smyting bellis.[171] And al went by vices merveolously wele done. And within Seint Austeins chirche thabbot and his covent receyved the king with procession as accustumede. And on the morne[172] when the king had dynede he roode on pilgremage[173] to Seint Annes in the wodde.[174]

---

[167] After passing through St. John's Gate, Henry probably proceeded along Christmas or Knifesmith Street to Fromegate. Beyond this gate, he would have turned to the southwest and approached the abbey of St. Augustine via Hore Street and St. Augustine's Back: McGee, thesis, p. 203. The abbey of St. Augustine was the richest and most powerful religious institution in the city of Bristol. See M. H. Fitzgerald, *The Story of Bristol Cathedral* (London, 1936) and P. Fleming, 'Conflict and Urban Government in Later Medieval England: St. Augustine's Abbey and Bristol', *Urban History*, 27.3 (2002), pp. 325–43. Henry VII stayed at the Abbey in September 1491.

[168] See the casting out of obleys and wafers at York above, p. 78.

[169] Appears to have consisted of a mechanical dumb show, as planned by Henry Hudson at York, although none of the city records shed any light either on this show or on the guild. Similar pageants have formed part of civic welcomes in the past: 'Henry VI's Triumphal Entry into London' in McCracken (ed.), *Minor Poems*, ii, pp. 223–271; *Great Chronicle*, pp. 162–3; Bristol's reception of Edward in Ricart, *Kalendar*, p. xviii; London's welcome of Charles V in Withington, *English Pageantry*, i, pp. 176, 177.

[170] See Withington, *English Pageantry*, i, pp. 66–7.

[171] Possibly a mechanical device, such as were popular during the 15th and 16th centuries. Wightman, *Royal Entry*, pp. 86–92 reveals evidence for the use of mechanical devices as far back as 1377.

[172] Wed. 24 May.

[173] –r unclear.

And on the Thursday nexte folowing, whiche was Corpus Christi day,[175] the king went in procession[176] aboute the great grene ther, callede 'the sentuary',[177] whether came all the processions of the towne[178] also; and the bisshop of Worcestre prechide in the pulpit[179] in the middes of the forsaide grene in a great audience of the meyre and the substance of al the burgesse of the towne and ther wiffes, with muche other people of the countery also. And after evensonge the king sent for the mayre and shrife and parte of the best burges of the towne, and demaunded theym the cause of ther povertie; and they shewde his grace for the great losse of shippes and goodes that they had loost within v yeres. The king comfortede theym that they shulde sett on **[f. 21]** and make newe shippes,[180] and to exercise ther marchaundise as they wer wonte for to doon; and his grace shulde so helpe theym by dyvers means[181] like as he shewde unto theym, that the meyre of the towne towlde me they harde not this hundred yeres of noo king so good a comfort. Wherfor they thankede Almighty God that hath sent theym soo good and gra-

---

[174] Situated in Brislington Wood, the chapel of St. Anne belonged to the Augustinians of Keynsham Abbey. See F. W. Weaver, *Keynsham Abbey* (1907), pp. 29–30.

[175] Thur. 25 May.

[176] See the religious procession in the precincts of York Minster, as described by D. Cowling, 'The Liturgical Celebration of Corpus Christi in Medieval York', Records of Early English Drama, *Newsletter*, 2 (1976), pp. 5–9.

[177] Probably St Augustine's Green, commonly known as 'the Sanctuary' by contemporaries. Strictly speaking the privileged lands of the abbey included the Green – the area of open land lying to its east and serving as the abbey's cemetery – as well as the churchyard, church and church precincts: Fleming, 'Conflict and Urban Government', pp. 329, 331; J. Bitton, *The History and Antiquities of the Abbey, and Cathedral Church of Bristol* (Bristol, 1836), p. 17. For discussion of ecclesiastical sanctuary during the reign of Henry VII see P. I. Kaufman, 'Henry VII and Sanctuary', *Church History*, 53 (1984), pp. 465–576.

[178] The parishes of St James, St. Mary Redcliffe, St. John the Baptist, All Saints, and St. Ewen's. The account books of the proctor of St Ewen's church for 1486–7 record payment for 'beryng the beste Crosse' and for the 'berynge of iiij torches': B. R. Masters and E. Ralph (eds), *The Church Book of St Ewen's Bristol 1454–1584*, Bristol and Gloucestershire Arch. Soc., Records Section, vol. vi (1967), p. 120. Various other payments are also recorded in relation to food, labour, cleaning, the breakfasting of participants, and the purchase of candles and frankincense.

[179] See the statements on open-air preaching and the construction of pulpits in G. R. Owst, *Preaching in Medieval England: an Introduction to Sermon Manuscripts of the Period c. 1350–1450* (1926; repr. New York, 1965), pp. 196, 199, 202, 214.

[180] 'and make newe shippes' are given as catchwords at the bottom of fol. 20v.

[181] Henry Tudor's contribution to English shipping is discussed by W. Busch, *England under the Tudors*, transl. A. M. Todd (London. 1895), i, pp. 70–3. 80–1, 155–6 and also Chrimes, *Henry VII*, pp. 226–8, who plays down the extent to which Henry Tudor's policies fostered the prosperity of this industry in the latter decades of the fifteenth century. Cf. the alternative statement that Henry VII's economic policy was directly responsible for the prosperity of merchant shipping, especially 1495–1505: D. Bur-

ciouse a souveraigne lorde. And on the morne[182] the king departede to London warde.

Item, it is to bee remembred that in every shire that the king our souveraigne lorde rode the shriffes of the same shire yave ther attendaunce and bar ther white roddes, and in like wise the nobles of that countre visitede the kinges grace as he passed by. As touching the giftes and presents whiche citiez, townes or abbeyes gave the kinges grace I am not certeynede, but I undrestande ther wer dyvers both of golde, silver, wyne, bedes and metenz.[183]

And on the vth day of June, whiche was upon a Monday, the king came by water from Shene[184] and landede at Westminster Brigge. The mayre[185] of London with al his brether and al the craftes in London in great multitude of barges[186] garnysshede with baners, penonncez, standers and penselles mett with his grace as far as Putname[187] and hertely welcommede hym home, and then went aboute ther barges and landede byfor the king. And every craft[188] stode by theym silf a longe in a rowe from the brygge ende thorough the paloys to Seint Margarettes[189] chirche yerde, wher thabbot and procession of Westminster receyvede the king and yave hym his septre;[190] and the procession of Sent Stevens chapell,[191] whiche hade receyvede hym in the paloys byfor, departede. And then when the king had offrede in the abbey, and *Te Deum* songen, the king went to his paloys.

---

     wash, *English Merchant Shipping 1460–1540* (Toronto, 1947), pp. 155–6.

[182]   Fri. 26 May.

[183]   Probably bracelets, necklaces, or ornaments to adorn a gown, together with other precious metals, wine, foodstuffs and the like. Food items were often given as gifts to visiting noblemen and sovereigns, although the meaning of the word 'metenz' is unclear; it may refer to mittens.

[184]   The manor of Sheen, several miles up the Thames from London, was destroyed by fire in 1498 and subsequently replaced by Richmond Palace on the same site.

[185]   'mayre' interlineated above.

[186]   Seemingly the earliest record of a water procession as part of a royal entry: Wightman, *Royal Entry*, p. 22. *Records of the Worshipful Company of Carpenters*, eds B. Marsh and A. M. Millard, 7 vols (1913–68), ii, p. 72 notes payments for barge-hire for this event, and for bread, ale and copes for the journey itself. Cf. the procession of Elizabeth of York going to her coronation above, pp. 129–30, and that of Anne Boleyn in *The Antiquarian Repertory*, ii, pp. 233–4.

[187]   –m partly obscured by two inkblots.

[188]   The members of the crafts, attired in red gowns and distinguished from one another by devices embroidered on the sleeves of their gowns, usually lined the route of entry: Wightman, *Royal Entry*, pp. 34–40.

[189]   This parish church still stands where it did when Henry returned, just south east of Westminster Abbey.

[190]   Presumably Eastney presented Henry with the sceptre of St. Edward, which was kept among the relics of Westminster.

[191]   This was a royal chapel within Westminster Palace. The canons did not come under the authority of Eastney.

THE EDITION

And on the morne[192] the maire of London[193] with **[f. 21v]**[194] his brether came efsones and visitede the kinges grace. Sir [Thomas][195] fitz William, recorder of London, in al ther names made to the king a noble proposicion in the rejoycing of the kinges good spede. And after that the king receyved in his great chambre a great ambassat[196] from the king of Skottes lettres: the lorde Boythvayle, thabbot of Holy Roode House, lorde Kenedy,[197] Maister Archeball (secretary to the king of Scottes), John Roosse (esquier and counceller of the saide king) [and] Lyon King of Armes;[198] and also Roos Heralde[199] [and][200] Unycorne Purservant gave their attendaunce and came with the saide ambassad, with dyvers other gentilmen and servantes to the nombre of iiij^{xx} hors. And the saide secretary made a longe proposicion in Laten, &c. And they wer loggede at Seint Johns at the kinges coost and after, at ther departure, had great giftes and rewardes.

And sone after, the king departed from Westminster towarde the west parties[201] and huntede; so to Wynchestre, where on Seint Eustas day[202] the prince

---

[192] Tues. 6 June.
[193] Sir Henry Colet.
[194] At the top of fol. 21v in a 17th-century hand: 'The Christening of Prince Arthur Hen .7. sonn and the Cerimonys then and … ' (the final word is illegible).
[195] No name given. On f. 45 (below, p. 150) he is mistakenly called William Fitzwilliam.
[196] For the diplomacy of the period see especially John M. Currin, 'England's International Relations, 1485–1509: Continuities amidst Change', in S. Doran and G. Richardson (eds), *Tudor England and its Neighbours* (Hants., 2005), pp. 14–43.
[197] Preceded by the cancellation of 'lo'.
[198] In the left margin in red ink in a 17th-century hand: 'Lyon King of Armes of Scotland & Unicorne pursuivant'.
[199] Final –e obscured by an inkblot.
[200] Written 'et'.
[201] The municipal records of Salisbury contain the following entry: '1486, 30 August – Every person being of the number of the xxiiij to ride at the first coming of the King to the City in one suit of livery, and they that are of the number of the xlviij in such clothing as they have honestly ready. The king is to be presented with the sum of 20*l*. of which 12*l*. is to be furnished by the xxiiij. 2. Hen. VII, Wednesday next after the feast of St. Bartholomew the Apostle': 'Muniments of the Corporation of the City of Salisbury', in *HMC. Report on Manuscripts in Various Collections*, vol. iv (1907), p. 210. See also *Paston Letters and Papers*, ii, pp. 446–7 for the king's letter to John Paston III from Sheen on 12 August, 1486.
[202] Wed. 20 Sept. 1486. Although secondary sources differ over the exact date of Arthur's birth (cf. Chrimes, *Henry VII*, pp. 66–7, 342, *York Chamberlains' Account Rolls*, p. 187n, K. Staniland, 'Royal Entry into the World' in D. Williams (ed.), *England in the Fifteenth Century. Proceedings of the 1986 Harlaxton Symposium* (Woodbridge, 1987), p. 298 and Anglo, *Spectacle*, p. 46), the Memoir assigns it to the feast of St. Eustachius, a Roman military officer martyred in 118 A.D and whose feast day was 20 September. *The Book of Remembrance of Southampton*, ed. H. W. Gidden, Southampton Record Soc., 3 vols (Southampton, 1927–30), iii, p. 53 states that the birth occurred before daybreak on 20 September (although the editor has incorrectly assigned it to 1496). The

Arture was borne[203] and cristenede (in maner and forme as ensueth),[204] whiche was the furste begoten sone of our saide souveraigne lorde King Henry the vijth, whiche was in the yere of Oure Lorde m^i iiij^C lxxxvj,[205] the dominicall lettre A, and the ijde yere of the reigne of our saide souveraigne, whiche was not cristen[206] unto the Soneday then next folowing by cause therle of Oxinforde was at that tyme at Lanam in Suffolk,[207] whiche shulde have ben on of the godfaders at the font. And

---

suggestion that the prince was born in the early hours of the morning is corroborated by an independent heraldic narrative of Prince Arthur's christening: 'Christenynge' in John Stowe, *Three Fifteenth Century Chronicles*, ed. J. Gairdner, Camden Soc., n.s., 28 (1880), pp. 104–5.

[203] The political significance of the birth of a son and heir was immense, while the choice of the name Arthur and the birthplace at Winchester represented an appeal to the themes of the *British History*. See Anglo, *Spectacle*, p. 46; idem, '*British History*'; Bernard André, 'Vita Henrici' in *Memorials*, pp. 38–9. It is curious that the Memoir makes no mention of the connection, and the description of the christening that follows suggests that the full propagandist potential of the event was never realized.

[204] In the left margin in red ink and the same hand as above, n. 198: 'Prince Arthur borne and the Ceremonyes of the Chrystening'. Cf. derivative accounts in BL, MSS. Add. 6113, fol. 75 (1st half of 16th century) and Stowe 583, fol. 8 (end of 16th century; printed in *Antiquarian Repertory*, iv, pp. 193–7); Coll. Arms, MSS. I.7, fols 10v–12v (mid 16th century) and M6, fols 28–30 (mid 16th century); and the materials found in Alnwick MS. 467, fols 94v–96 (*temp*. Mary I) and Lambeth Library, MS. 306, fol. 53 (late 16th-century transcription in the hand of John Stowe; printed in Gairdner (ed.), *Three Fifteenth Century Chronicles*, pp. 104–5). See above, chapter 1, for discussion of the transmission of the christening narrative in Julius B. XII, fols 21v–24 (also printed in *Somers Tracts*, pp. 22–24). Staniland, 'Royal Entry' offers the best discussion of Arthur's christening and the associated ritual and symbolism. The ceremonial of baptism is fully described from the point of view of the dean of the chapel royal in the *LRC*, pp. 67–72, while more brief descriptions are given in the extracts of the *Ryalle Book* printed in *Antiquarian Repertory*, i, pp. 304–6, 333–8. The procedures for baptism were set down in 1493 in the 'Articles ordained by Henry VII for the Regulation of his Household' in *PO*, pp. 125–8 (although incorrectly dated to 1494), and a pictorial depiction, produced *c*. 1485, of the birth and baptism of Richard Beauchamp, earl of Warwick (d. 1439) may be found in BL, MS. Cotton Julius E. IV and printed editions such as Alexandra Sinclair (ed.), *The Beauchamp Pageant* (Donington, 2003). See also: H. D. Fisher, *Christian Initiation: Baptism in the Medieval West*, Alcuin Club Collections, xlvii (1965), pp. 111–16; C. S. Cobb, *The Rationale of Ceremonial 1540–1543*, Alcuin Club Collections, xviii (1910), pp. 7–12. Further insight into the ritual of christening, if principally of a slightly later date, may be gleaned from D. Cressy, *Birth, Marriage, and Death: Ritual, Religion, and the Life-Cycle in Tudor and Stewart England* (Oxford, 1997), esp. chapter 1.

[205] In the left margin, possibly in the hand of Scribe B: 'm^i iiij^C lxxxvj' (1486). Arthur's birth is incorrectly assigned to 1487 in *Great Chronicle*, p. 241, J. G. Nichols (ed.), *Chronicle of the Grey Friars of London*, Camden Soc., o.s., 53 (1852), p. 24 and Fabyan, *New Chronicles*, p. 683, presumably due to the practice of dating by mayoral years.

[206] In the left margin in the hand of Scribe B: 'Cristenyng'.

[207] Sun. Sept. 24 1486. The ceremony was postponed for four days due largely to the

also that season was al rayny.

Incontynent after the birth *Te Deum* with procession[208] was songe in the cathedrall chirche and in al the chyrches of that citie, and great and many fiers made[209] in the stretes, and messengers sent to al the astatez and cities[210] of the realme with that comfortable and good tydynges, to whom[211] **[f. 22]** were geven great giftes. And over al *Te Deum Laudamus* songen with ringging of belles, and in the moost parties fiers made in the presing of God and the rejoysing of every true Englisshe man.

The body of al the cathedrall chyrche[212] of Wynchestre was hangede with clothes of arras, and in the medell beside the font of the saide chirche was ordeigned and preparede a solempne fonte[213] in maner and forme as ensueth:

---

      absence of the earl of Oxford, who was staying at his capital manor in Lavenham, Suffolk. Arthur was born in the thirty-fifth week of queen's pregnancy, which may account for the failure of Oxford to be ready and lodged near the queen's chamber with the other 'gossips', as was required: *LRC*, p. 67.

[208] Seemingly the standard means of proclaiming the birth of a royal child: Staniland, 'Royal Entry', p. 303. See also Anglo, *Spectacle*, p. 47.

[209] Repeated.

[210] Southampton's *Book of Remembrance*, iii, p. 53 records the receipt of the news on the afternoon of the birth: see Armstrong, 'Some Examples of the Distribution and Speed of News in England at the time of the Wars of the Roses', in idem, *England, France and Burgundy*, pp. 97–122.

[211] At the bottom of fol. 21v appears the following addition in the hand of Scribe B: 'Dieu, par sa grace, doint bonne vie et long au treshault, puissant et excellent prince, fils du roy, Arthur, par la grace de Dieu prince dEngletter, duc de Cornewall, duce de Chestre & as moche in Inglishe'.

[212] The porch and doorway were traditionally hung with cloths or tapestries, and carpets laid on the ground. Inside more cloths and tapestries were hung, with cloth of gold draped around the high altar and chancel: Staniland, 'Royal Entry', p. 303. Cloths and other materials used for the decoration of the church on this occasion are in *Materials*, ii, p. 34. Other purchases associated with the confinement of the queen, the birth and the preparation for the christening may be found in *Materials*, ii, pp. 38–9, 52, 168–9, 176–9; TNA, E404/79/46(201), E404/79/300, E404/79/303. A more comprehensive picture of provisions appears in a group of entries added to the *Ryalle Book* soon after Arthur's birth: BL, MS. Add. 38174; *Antiquarian Repertory*, i, pp. 333–8. 16th-century copies of the same include BL, MS. Harley 6079, printed in Leland, *Collectanea*, iv, pp. 179–84 and erroneously attributed to Margaret Beaufort by Thomas Hearne.

[213] During the 15th century the silver font from Christ Church Canterbury, purchased in 1447, was often used for royal baptisms; it may have been used for the baptism of Edward IV's ten children: Staniland, 'Royal Entry', pp. 303–4, n. 33; C. E. Woodruff, 'Notes on the Inner Life and Domestic Economy of Christ Church, Canterbury, in the Fifteenth Century', *Achaeologia Cantiana*, liii (1940), pp. 11–16. The font was usually adorned with fine cloth of 'reyns' (linen made in Rheims), cloth-of-gold drapes and precious and semi-precious stones: *LRC*, p. 68. It was placed in a prominent position beside the cathedral's own font, between the capitals of the north aisle, and raised on an iron post above several steps covered with red cloth and secured with gilt nails:

furst ther was ordeignede in maner of a stage of vij steppes, square or rounde like an high crosse coverde with rede worstede; and up in the myddes a poost with a [pin][214] made of iron to bere the fonnt of silver over gilte, whiche within fourth was wele dressede with fyne lynen clothe; and nere the same, on the west side, a steppe like a blokk for the bisshop to stonde on, coverede also with rede say; and over the font of a good height a riche canape[215] with a great gilte bolle celid[216] and fringede without curteyns. And on the north side[217] was ordeignede a travers hanged with cloth of arras; and uppon the on side therof withinfourth a nother travers of redde sarsenet, wherof James Hide and Robert Brent had the charge. And ther was fyer with fumygacions[218] redy ayenste the prince commyng. And without, the grese of the sayde fonnt was raylede with good tymbre and coverede as the gresis wer, havyng ij entres: on over the este and a nother in the weste, whiche were kept by v yomen of the coroune, that is to say [Richard] Rake, [John] Burle, Robert Walker, William Vaughan and John Hoo. And after the lorde John Alkok, bisshop of Worcestre, had halowed the fonnt it was kepte by Sir David Owen and Sir Hugh Persall, knyghtes for the body, and Richarde Wodevile, Thomas Poyntz, John Crokker and Thomas Brandon,[219] esquiers for the body.

On the Sunday when the chapell was come into **[f. 22v]** the priours great hall, whiche was the quenes great chambre,[220] the tresourer[221] of [the] householde toke the say of salt to the sargeaunt of the pantery and delyverde it to therle of

---

Staniland, 'Royal Entry', p. 306. The area around the font was carpeted, and above was suspended a large, ornate canopy. See also *Antiquarian Repertory*, i, pp. 334–5.

[214] The missing word is supplied in BL, MS. Add. 6113, fol. 76.
[215] *LRC*, p. 68 describes the canopy as made of satin or damask with a valance embroidered with flowers and trees of gold. See also *Antiquarian Repertory*, i, p. 334.
[216] Followed by a cancellation, possibly of –e.
[217] A clear space was created around the font by the erection of a tapestry or cloth-covered barrier, and two guarded entrances gave access to the participants chosen by the king. An illustration of this structure may be found in the 16th-century sketches accompanying the narratives of Prince Arthur's baptism in BL, MS. Stowe 583, fols 4–7v and Coll. Arms, MS. 6, fols 77v–82v. Before the baptism the dean of the chapel royal filled the font with warmed holy water, sealing it with cloth of gold, before the water was hallowed (here, by Bishop John Alcock of Worcester). See *LRC*, pp. 68–9 and J. G. Davies, *The Architectural Setting of Baptism* (London, 1962), p. 74.
[218] Between the choir and the font a closet was constructed with carpets, cushions, fire and heated water, gold and silver bowls, and towels: *LRC*, pp. 68–9; *Antiquarian Repertory*, i, p. 334.
[219] Superfluous minium on the final –n cancelled.
[220] The place of the queen's confinement, the prior's great hall, lay adjacent to the baptismal church; here the procession toward the church commenced. The main items for use in the baptism were ceremoniously delivered to the courtiers in the procession by the appropriate household officers: *LRC*, p. 69; *Antiquarian Repertory*, i, p. 334. A more detailed description of these items is given below, p. 105.
[221] Preceded by a cancellation.

THE EDITION

Essex and a towell withall, whiche the saide yerle caste aboute his nek. In like wise the sergeant of the chaunderye [bore] a taper garnisshede with iiij wrethen bowtes and bowles and with banerolles[222] and penssell with praty imagery and scripture, the whiche the lorde Nevell, sone and heire of therle of Westmerlande, bare. Item, the sergeaunt of the eury delyverde to the saide trezorer a pere of gilt basons with a towell fowlden upon theym, whiche were delyverde to the lorde Straunge. And as followeth they preceeded towarde the chirche:[223] furst ther were vj^{xx} torches borne unlight ij and ij togeders by henxmen, squiers, gentilmen and yomen of the coroune, the governance[224] of whom had [Nicholas] Knyfton, ... Gedding, Pers of Wreyton, and John Amyas; after theym the chapell; after the chapell ther wer withoute order certen knyghtes and esquiers; after them kinges of armes, herauldes and pursurvantes, having ther cotes on ther armes,[225] and sergeauntes of armes as been accustumede; and therle of Derbye and the lord Maltravers; after them the basonns, the taper, then the salte of golde covered; and then a riche cresome, whiche was pinnyde on the right brest of my lady Anna, sister of the quene, hanging over her left arme; Sir Richarde Gilforde, knyght constable, over on the right hand and Sir John Turburvill, knyght mershall, on the lefte hande bering ther staves of office; and after theym my lady Cecill, the quenes eldest sister, bare the prince wrappede in a mantell of cremesyn clothe of golde furred with ermyn with a trayne whiche was borne by my lady the marquesse of Dorset; and Sir John Cheyny supportede the medell of the **[f. 23]** same; and the lorde Edwarde Widevill, the lorde la Warre, the sonne and heire of the lorde Audeley and Sir John of Aroundell bare the canapie; the marques of Dorcett and therle of Lincolln yave assistence to my lady Cecill.

And at this cristenyng was my lady Margaret of Clarence, my ladye Gray Rithyn, my lady Straunge the elder, my ladye la Warre, Maistres Fenys, my lady Vaux, my lady Darcy (ladye maistresse), my lady Bray, my lady Dame Kateryn Grey, my lady Dame Elynonour Haut [and] my lady Wodell, with dyvers othre gentilwomen.

---

[222] –r cancelled between –a and –n.

[223] Usually led by 200 squires or men-at-arms with unlit torches, although here and at Princess Margaret's christening (below, pp. 179–81) only 120 torches appeared. The torches were the followed by the chapel royal, other knights and esquires, the officers of arms and serjeants at arms, dignitaries, the christening regalia, the chrismal cloth, the godparents (although on this occasion the earl of Oxford and Elizabeth Woodville were both absent from the procession), the royal baby carried beneath a canopy, and so on: *LRC*, p. 69 and *Antiquarian Repertory*, i, pp. 354–5. Cf. the brief notes on the christening of Princess Bridget in 1480, printed in P. Routh, 'Princess Bridget', *The Ricardian*, 3.49 (1975), pp. 13–14, where only 100 torches were used.

[224] A superior –a is written over an erroneous contraction intended to signal the omission of –er.

[225] In the left margin in red ink and the same hand as above, p. 99, n. 198: 'The heralds going to church hold there Coates upon theyre Armes'.

And thus [they] procedede thorough the cloister of thabbey unto a litill doore beside the weest ende of the chirche[226] in the south parte of the saide chirche, wher was ordeynede a riche and a large clothe of estate, for the wether was to cowlde and to fowlle to have been at the west ende of the chirche. And the queen Elizabeth[227] was in the chirche abyding the commyng of the prince, at whiche tyme tydinges came that therle of Oxinforde was within a myle. And there was the bisshop of Worcestre, lorde John Alkok, whiche cristende the prince in pontificalibus; and the bisshop of Excestre, lorde Pers Courtnay; and the bisshop of Saresbury, Lorde Thomas Langton; thabbot of Hide and the prior of the same place, in like wise accompanyede with many noble doctours in riche copes and grey amys (Mayster Robert Morton, the maister of the rowles; the deane of Welles, Maister John Gonthorp; Doctor Fox, the kinges secretary, with many moo).

Howbeit they taried[228] iij oures largely and more after the saide erle of Oxinforde, and after that, by the kinges commaundement, procedede; and therle of Derbye and the lorde Maltravers weren godfaders at the fonnt, and quene Elizabeth godmoder. And incontinent after the prince was put into the fonnt the officers of armes put on ther cootes[229] and all the torches weren light; and then

[226] The inclement weather, also mentioned on p. 101, prevented the baptismal procession from entering the cathedral at the large door on the west end of the nave, as was usual practice. The herald's statement has confused modern commentators, such as Staniland, who assume the second 'west' to have been a scribal error for 'east', and thus that the baptismal font was usually set up at the east end and only relegated to the west in 1486. In fact the christening font was usually set up at the west end of the church: J. C. Dickinson, *The Later Middle Ages: from the Norman Conquest to the Eve of the Reformation* (London, 1979), p. 450. The herald's statement signals no more than a change from the great door on the west end of the nave to a smaller entrance around the corner on the nave's south wall, out of the prevailing north winds. For a basic description of a cathedral interior see Dickinson, *Later Middle Ages*, esp. pp. 444–53.

[227] The herald refers to the dowager queen Elizabeth Woodville, one of the godmothers, not, as Sydney Anglo mistakenly believed, to Elizabeth of York: Anglo, *Spectacle*, p. 47. The predominance of the Woodvilles, Yorks and their kin on this occasion is remarkable, suggesting a desire on the part of Henry VII to integrate the queen's family into court life and publicly display their loyalty to his kingship: J. L. Laynesmith, *The Last Medieval Queens. English Queenship 1445–1503* (Oxford, 2004), pp. 205–6.

[228] Delay in proceedings caused by the absence of the earl of Oxford, who should have been one of the godfathers at the font. The king and queen probably waited in the queen's outer chamber during this time, whence the king could order the christening to begin: Staniland, 'Royal Entry', p. 307. Francis Sandford, *A Genealogical History of the Kings and Queens of England, and Monarchs of Great Britain*, ed. S. Stebbing (London, 1707), p. 479 states that Oxford also stood godfather to Prince Henry in 1491. No other evidence exists in support of this notion, and it is possible that Sandford simply confused the princes.

[229] In the right margin in red ink and the same hand as above, p. 99, n. 198: 'After the Prince was put into ye the font the heraldes put on theyre Coates'; the –t of 'font' has been cropped.

entrede therle of Oxinford.[230] And from the font the prince was had to his **[f. 23v]**[231] travers (and above his cremesyn clothede as by fore), and from thens in faire order was borne to the high auter and leide therupon by hys godmoder. After certeyn ceremony, whan the goospell was doon, *Veni Creator Spiritus* was begon and solempnely songen by the kinges chapell with orgons and *Te Deum* also, during whiche season therle of Oxinforde toke the prince in his right arme; and the bisshop of Excestre confermed hym and the bisshop of Saresbury knytt the bande of lynene aboue his nek. And then the marquisse of Dorcet, therle of Lyncolln and the lorde Straunge servede quene Elyzabeth of towell and water,[232] and Sir Roger Coton and Maister West servede the other gossepes.[233] And byseide the saide high auter was ordeynede a travers for the prince, where quene Elizabeth yave a riche cuppe of golde coverde,[234] whiche was borne by Sir Davy Owen; and therle of Oxinforde yave a pere of gilte basonns with a sayer, whiche were borne by Sir William Stoner; and therle of Derbye yave a riche salt of golde coverede, whiche was borne by Sir Raynolde Bray; and the lorde Maltravers yave a cofer of golde, whiche was borne by Sir Charles of Somersett; from thens procedede to Seint Swythens shryne[235] and ther offrede, wher was a nother travers. Then *Iste Confes-*

[230] Entering late, Oxford accompanied the baby to the high altar for presentation and confirmation. Lambeth Library, MS. 306 (printed in Gairdner (ed.), *Three Fifteenth Century Chronicles*, p. 105) states that the Lord Neville carried the baby's lit taper to the altar. This detail is not recorded in the Memoir christening narrative or its derivative accounts.

[231] At the top of the folio in a 17th-century hand, but cancelled: 'The Cristining of Princ Arthu [sic] An° Hen. 7'; to the right of this, in a late 15th-century secretary hand (poss. Scribe B), is 'Prince arthur cristinyng'.

[232] Re-commencement of the secular ceremonial after baptism. The infant was redressed in the closet and the godparents washed to remove surplus holy water and chrism: Staniland, 'Royal Entry', p. 306.

[233] The queen's familiar companions, or 'gossips', taking part in the ceremony: the Ladies Anne and Cecily, sisters of the queen, and others listed on p. 103.

[234] At this point in proceedings provision could be made for the ceremonial presentation to the infant of the godparents' gifts, in the form of gold cups, gilt basins, salts and coffers of coins; the gifts would then be included in the procession which returned from the church to the queen's chambers: Staniland, 'Royal Entry', p. 307. The 'Articles' of 1493 state that it was for the king to decide whether the gifts were carried back 'privily or openly': *OHR*, p. 126.

[235] The place of offering of the godparents' gifts. The shrine was located in the retrochoir, behind the high altar, and stood over the place where Swithun's remains are reputed to have been re-interred some time after their exhumation from the old Saxon church in 971. The present shrine was constructed in 1969. For discussion of the medieval shrine see 'The Thirteenth-Century Shrine and Screen of St Swithun at Winchester', *JBAA*, 138 (1985), pp. 125–31; P. Tudor-Craig and L. Keen, 'A Recently Discovered Purbeck Marble Scupltured Screen of the Thirteenth Century and the Shrine of St Swithun' in *Medieval Art and Architecture at Winchester Cathedral* (Leeds, 1983 for 1980), pp. 62–73; J. D. Le Couteur, D. H. M. Carter, 'Notes on the Shrine of St. Swithun

sor with an antyme of Seint Swythyne[236] was songen, and spices and ipocras with other swete wynys[237] great pleyntye; whiche doon the prince retournede[238] and was borne home by my ladye Cecill, accompanyede as byfore (saving the salt, the basons, and the taper and all the torches brennyng); and in the entering of the norserye wer the kinges trumpettes and mynstrelles pleying on ther instrumentes; and then was he borne to the king and the quene and had the blessing of Almyghty God, Our Lady and Seint George, and of his **[f. 24]** fader and moder. And in the chirche yerde wer sett ij pipes of wyne that every man myght drynke ynow.[239] Memorandum: that the bisshop wesshede at the font with coverde basons.[240]

And after that the quene was purified[241] and hole of an agu[242] that she had the

---

formerly in Winchester Cathedral', *Antiquaries Journal*, 4 (1924), pp. 360–70.

[236] Named bishop of Winchester in 852; chaplain and counsellor to King Egbert of the West Saxons and tutor to his son Ethelwulf (d. 2 July 863). He was known for his humility and aid to the poor and needy. See M. Lapidge, *The Cult of St Swithun* (Oxford, 2003), esp. chs. 2 and 3, pp. 9–24, 25–64.

[237] Wines and spices were served for the principal participants. The spices were probably administered in powdered form, and possibly added to the wine on the spot according to personal taste: Staniland, 'Royal Entry, p. 306n.

[238] The baptised infant was taken into the queen's inner chamber by her ladies, and offered first to the queen and then to the king. The infant was presumably then returned to the care of its governess, nurses and rockers in its nursery, and celebrations ensued: *LCR*, p. 72; *OHR*, pp. 126–7; *Antiquarian Repertory*, i, 306.

[239] This was followed by the deletion of 'and the king gave great largesse'. In the left margin alongside the deletion, in the hand of Scribe C, is written: 'no'. In the right margin is written: 'only but xx li for lake of advertiseme[nt] but ther ben presidency [sic] ynow to be shewede of a C li or a C marces'. The final –nt of 'advertisement' has been cropped.

[240] A line is left blank, probably to signify the commencement of new material.

[241] The purification ritual, or 'churching', is not described by the herald. Following the birth and baptism the queen was usually isolated from court for a period of approximately 40 days. Although *LRC*, p. 72 specifies 60 days in accordance with church teaching (Leviticus, xii), normal practice seems to have entailed shorter confinement. The problem is discussed in K. Staniland, 'The Birth of Thomas of Brotherton', *Costume* 19 (1985), pp. 1–13, esp. pp. 12–13. The queen's emergence for churching was also an integral part of royal birth celebrations: *LRC*, pp. 72–3; Staniland, 'Royal Entry', p. 308; Cressy, *Birth, Marriage, and Death,* chapter 2; Laynesmith, *Last Medieval Queens*, pp. 115–19. See the eye-witness account of the churching of Elizabeth Woodville after the birth of Elizabeth of York in 1465 in M. Letts (ed. and trans), *Travels of Leo of Rozmital*, Hakluyt Soc., 2nd ser., cviii (1957), pp. 46–8. Cf. the herald's statement below, p. 181, where Elizabeth of York had a private churching after the birth of Princess Margaret because of an outbreak of measles. An idea of the socio-political import of the churching ritual for the royal court of the mid 14th century may be gleaned from C. Shenton, 'Philippa of Hainault's Churchings: the Politics of Motherhood at the Court of Edward III', in Richard Eales and Shaun Tyas (eds), *Family and Dynasty in Late Medieval England*, Harlaxton Medieval Studies, ix (Donington, 2003), pp. 105–21.

[242] Illness unknown, perhaps related to childbirth generally or the premature birth of the

king and the quene, my lady the kinges moder and al the court remeved to Grenewiche,²⁴³ and ther they kepte the solempne fest of Al Halowes,²⁴⁴ greatly accompanyed with estates and noble people as folowing: furst the marquis of Dorcet, therle of Lyncolln, therle of Oxinforde, therle of Derbye, therle of Notingham, the viscount Lisley, the lorde Maltravers, the lorde Straunge, the lorde Dodeley and many moo great lordes, knyghtes and esquiers in great nombre. And that day the king went in a goune of clothe of golde furred and in no robes of estate. And also the king yave his larges to his officers of armes as accustumed, and they did ther devoir therfor.

And like wise the king kept his Cristemas at the same place aforsaide, howbeit he was not accompanyede with lordes, as he was at Alhaloutyde;²⁴⁵ nor the king kept ther non astate in the halle, but his grace gave to his officers of armes on the iij dayes as of olde he have and other kinges accustumede.

And on newyeres day²⁴⁶ Thomas Lovell delyverde the kinges larges in boke,²⁴⁷ but that and al other lordez [and]²⁴⁸ ladies yeftes ben in our regestre, as the rewarde of my lady the kinges moder, the marquis of Dorcett, therle of Derbye.

[f. 24v]And after Cristemas the mooste reverende fader in God, the lorde John Morten, aforesaide was on a Sonday the [vij]²⁴⁹ day of Janyver intrononysed at Ca[n]terbury,²⁵⁰ greatly accompanyed with lordes both espiritueles and

---

baby on this occasion. Queen Elizabeth died after giving birth in 1503 and so perhaps suffered some weakness associated with childbirth.
²⁴³ *Plumpton Letters and Papers*, p. 67 records that the king and queen were in Greenwich by November 29. They might even have been there by November 18: T. Stapleton (ed.), *The Plumpton Correspondence. A Series of Letters, Chiefly Domestick, Written in the Reigns of Edward IV, Richard III, Henry VII and Henry VIII* (1839), pp. 52n.
²⁴⁴ Wed. 1 Nov. 1487.
²⁴⁵ Preceded by the cancellation of –h.
²⁴⁶ Mon. 1 Jan. 1487.
²⁴⁷ The complete sentence intially read: 'And on Newyeres day Thomas Lovell delyverde the kinges and the quenes larges, but for the quene so little a largesse wer any was yeven was ther non in our dayes sene, wherfor I passe over to sett the service in boke'. This curious cancellation seems to suggest that the heralds were dissatisfied with the queen's largess on this occasion. For the heralds' New Year customs, and their receipt of gifts, see Wagner, *Heralds*, pp. 95–6.
²⁴⁸ Written 'et'.
²⁴⁹ The scribe does not give a date, but it was perhaps Sun. 7 Jan. 1487. Morton was made Chancellor on 6 Mar. 1486 and archbishop before the end of the year: *CPR*, p. 360; Chrimes, *Henry VII*, pp. 57, 105. The herald-recorder of this event was clearly not present for Morton's progress toward Canterbury, but probably joined the party in the cathedral city. His information is thereafter detailed and accurate, and his favourable opinion of the feast probably based on eye-witness experience. Cf. the preparations for the installation of Archbishop Nevill and the account of the installation of Archbishop Warham in Leland, *Collectanea*, vi, pp. 2–14, 16–35.
²⁵⁰ Written 'Carterbury'.

temp[er]eles, as it aperethe more at large in a book made of the same fest. And as I undrestande he by his journay towardes his trononyzacion after his licence of the king at Lambeth, and gretely accompanyed, roode furst to Croydon, and from thens to Knowle, from thens to Maydeston, from thens to Charring, and from thens to Chartham, wher he lay the Satirday at nyght. And on the Soneday when he entrede Cauntrebury and al the belles of the citie were rong, he alight and went on his fete. And at the great gate within fourthe met hym the procession of Criste chirche and sensede hym. And whan he was entrede a litill within the west doore ther was ordeignede a stole with a riche clothe of silke and cousthyns, wher he knelede a tracte of while or tyme and lete falle many a tere of his yene, and after proceded to the high auter. And then *Te Deum* was songe; and then he and al the prelates did on theym riche coopes and with procession went and recountrede the pall sent from our holy fader the pope, whiche was borne by the bisshop of Rochestre. And then they retourned by fore the high auter, wher the bisshop of Worcestre red and declared the popez bullez and made a great proposicion of the same and eshewing the vertue and the betokenyng of the pall, whiche so delyverde to the saide lorde of Canterbury sat in a cheire; and all the[251] prelates that wer ther kyste the saide relique or palle and after the cheke of the saide archebisshop, and in like wyse after theym al the religiouse people of that house.

This [f. 25] doon, tharchebisshop and al other prelates went into the vestory. The bisshop of Ely was deken and redde the gospell; the bisshop of Rochester bar the crosse and redde the pistell; the bisshop of Saresbury was chaunter and byganne the office of the masse. As for al the solempnytie of that masse and in that fest, it is written in the other boke, wherfor I passe over her. But it was the best orderde and served fest that ever[252] I sawe that myght be comparede to. And the kinges servantes and officers of armes that wer ther, on the morne when they toke ther leve, were wele and worshipfully rewardede. Also ther was the marquis of Dorcet with viij or ix other barons,[253] besides knyghtes and esquiers, whiche were in marvelous great nombre and al in his lyverey of mustredeveles.

And after candell masse[254] the king being at Shene had a great counsell[255] of his lordes both spiritueles and tempereles, at whiche tyme ther was a great ambas-

[251] Followed by the cancellation of 'people'.
[252] Minor cancellation after –r.
[253] –o interlineated above, and –e cancelled after –n.
[254] Thur. 2 Feb. 1487.
[255] Held at Sheen and probably concluded on 3 March: *Paston Letters and Papers*, i, p. 653. The council involved discussion of measures to combat the Simnel plot, then unfolding, and the decision to deprive Elizabeth Woodville of her widow's jointure and confine her to a nunnery: *Materials*, ii, pp. 148–9. Chrimes, *Henry VII*, p. 76n. 3 refutes the notion that the king suspected the dowager queen's involvement in the plot. It might also have been resolved at this time to parade the earl of Warwick in London, as suggested in the following chronicle sources: Molinet, *Chroniques*, i, pp. 562–3; André, *Vita*, pp. 49–50; Vergil, *Anglica Historia*, p. 17; Hall, *Union*, 'Henry the vii', fol. 7v;

sad of Fraunce.[256] And at that counseill was therle of Lincolln, whiche incontynently after the[257] saide counseil departede the land and went into Flaunders to the lorde Lovell and accompanyed hym silf with the kinges rebelles and enemyes, noysing in that countrey that therle of Warwike[258] shulde bee in Irelande, whiche him selffe[259] knew and dayly spake with him at[260] Shene afor his departing. And in the begynnyng of Lenton,[261] after his arryvyng in thoos parties, ther they dayly preparede[262] them to the see; and in conclusion so departed into Ireland,[263] al thorough the narow see.[264]

The king departede the ijde weke of Lente[265] and roode into Essex, and so into Suffolk to Bery,[266] and from thens kept his Ester[267] at Norwiche in the bisshops

---

Holinshed, *Chronicles*, p. 486. Evidence of conspiracy dated back to end of 1486 and the beginning of 1487: *Plumpton Letters and Papers*, p. 67, p. 54; *Paston Letters and Papers*, ii, pp. 448–9 and i, p. 653; *CPR*, 1485–1494, pp. 158, 172, 179; *Materials*, ii, p. 118; TNA, E404/79/109(263); *RP*, vi, pp. 436–7. The best discussion of the earliest days of the conspiracy is in Bennett, *Lambert Simnel*, esp. pp. 41–68.

[256] For mention of other embassies to and from England, see pp. 99, 156, 162, 163–4, 165, 173, 175, 182–5.

[257] Written 'they' before –y was cancelled.

[258] Refers to the impostor, 'Lambert Simnel', then in Ireland and touted as Edward earl of Warwick, son of the late duke of Clarence, nephew to Richard III and Edward IV, and Yorkist heir to the English throne. The real Warwick had been committed to the Tower at the beginning of the reign, and remained there until his execution on 21 Nov. 1499: Chrimes, *Henry VII*, pp. 336, 51, 72, 70, 92, 284, 337, 88, 92, 307, 337.

[259] 'selffe' inserted above in the hand of Scribe C.

[260] Preceded by the cancellation of 'in Irland'.

[261] Lent commenced on Wed. 7 Mar., 1487.

[262] –rep cancelled between 'daly' and 'preparede'.

[263] The king probably did not learn of Lincoln's departure for Ireland until the time that he was drawing near to Coventry, *c*.20 Apr.

[264] The English Channel.

[265] The royal entourage left Sheen no earlier than Wednesday March 7, when a courtier wrote 'in haste' of the projected itinerary: *Paston Letters and Papers*, i, pp. 653–4. The 2nd week of Lent commenced on Sun. 11 Mar., the 3rd week on Sun. 18. Edwards, *Itineraries*, p. 41 favours 13 or 14 Mar. as the departure date. The nature of the journey at its outset is uncertain, although the ride through East Anglia carried the royal entourage into the heartland of de la Pole territory and coincided with security measures and recruitment in the area: *Materials*, ii, pp. 106–7, 135, 136–7; TNA, E404/79/178, E404/79/109(263); J. P. Collier (ed.), *Household Books of John duke of Norfolk, and Thomas Earl of Surrey, 1481–1490*, Roxburghe Club (London, 1844), p. 493. Nevertheless, a relaxed outlook was still possible in early March: *Paston Letters and Papers*, i, p. 654. *Materials*, ii, p. 122 indicates that the king ordered two new doublets of black satin for this leg of the journey.

[266] Bury St. Edmunds, Suffolk.

[267] Thurs. 12 to Mon. 16 Apr. 1487. Holinshed, *Chronicles*, p. 486 refers erroneously to Christmas Day in Norwich, although the rest of his timing for the battle of Stoke is accurate.

palois; and al the dyvyne servyce was al that season doon ther by the moost reverende fader in God the archebisshop of Canterbury. And on the Thursday the king did his halmes and the observance of the maundye in the hall of **[f. 25v]** the paloys. And also ther wer with the king at the fest the reverende fader in God the lorde Richard[268] Fox, bisshop of Excestre. Item, the duc of Suffolk, therle of Oxinforde, therle of Derbye, the lorde fitz Water (stewarde of the kinges howse), Sir Robert Willoughby, and a great nombre of knyghtes and esquiers, and in substance al the nobles of that parties; for in that tyme they had dayly tydinges of the preparing of his rebelles and enemyes, whiche then wer in Selande and Flawndres to the see warde and, as was reportede, [were] to lande in this realme, in what parte it was no certeynte. Wherfor the king, on the Monday in Estre weke, rode to Walsingham, and ther with good devocion did his offering;[269] and from thens fourth towardes the middes of his realme – that is to say to Coventrye, whether dayly his true servantes and subjectes drewe towardes his grace[270] – and rode by Caumbrige, Huntyngdon[271] and Northampton, and on Sent Georges even came to Conventrye,[272] wher he [kept][273] his fest of Seint George.

And ther tharchebisshop of Canterbury, the bisshop of Wynchester, the bisshop of Ely, the bisshop of Lincoln, the bisshop of Worcester, the bisshop of Excester and the priour of Coventrye, al in pontificalibus,[274] redde and declarede the popes bulles[275] touching the kinges and the quenes right, and ther in the quere in the bisshops see, by the auctoritie of the same bulles, cursed with boke, bell and candell al thoo that dyd any thyng contrary to ther right, and approving ther tytles good.

And that yere [the king] ordeyned the duc of Suffolk to bee his depute at Wyn-

[268] Written above the cancellation of 'John'.
[269] The shrine of Our Lady of Walsingham. See C. King, 'Shrines and Pilgrimages before the Reformation', *History Today*, 29.10 (1979), pp. 664, 669. The king's devotion at the shrine is mentioned by Vergil, *Anglica Historia*, p. 21.
[270] –h cancelled between 'his' and 'grace'.
[271] Even here, on 20 Apr., the king seems to have believed in the continued possibility of invasion along the east coast of England: *YHB*, ii, pp. 550–1.
[272] A mark of suspension signalling the omission of –er was placed against –v, but subsequently cancelled. Coventry formed the focus for the rallying of the king's supporters who had joined him during the Easter week. On 30 Apr. the king ordered the delivery of ordnance from Scarborough to York, but by 4 May he was able to write to the city of York that the rebels had left the Low Countries and gone westward: *YHB*, ii, pp. 556, 557–8.
[273] Written 'kelpt'.
[274] -p appears to have been written over an error.
[275] The pronouncement of the papal bulls at Coventry was the result of excursions to the pope in February that year and earlier: TNA, E404/79/58(213), E404/79/162. The papal bulls were also promulgated at Furness and nearby Cartmel in the north west: *YHB*, ii, pp. 557–8. For discussion of the papal dispensation regarding the king's marriage, see Chrimes, *Henry VII*, App. D, pp. 330–1.

desore[276] for the fest there, whiche was accompanyed with the lorde Maltravers, the lorde Dodely and other.

And when the king had very worde that his enemyes and rebelles wer landed in Irelande, and the great party of the nobles of the south parties, to ther great and importunat charges, wer whith his grace at his citie of Coventrye, **[f. 26]** [he] lycenced dyvers of theym to goo to ther countreys and prepare[277] theym silf [so that][278] they myght upon a day sygned retourne[279] unto his grace for aide and strengeth of theym silf and of the hole realme. And some nobles wolde not departe from his grace, but sent parte of ther people into ther countreis for ther releve, upon warnyng as above is saide. And [the king] hym silf roode to Kenelworth[280] to the qwen[281] and to my lady the kinges moder,[282] whether within a shorte whyle after came tydynges that his enemyes were londede in the north parties besidesse Furnesse Fellez.[283] Incontynent the king assemblede his counseill[284] for the order-

---

[276] The Garter feast, under the duke of Suffolk as the king's deputy, was postponed until Sun. 13 May after the king neglected to instruct the treasurer to make funds available for 23 April: TNA, E404/79/183; *Materials*, ii, pp. 152–3. See also Beltz, *Garter Memorials*, p. lxxvii.

[277] Written 'prepared'.

[278] The scribe has written 'and', but this does not fit the sentence structure.

[279] Preceded by 'to', but this does not fit the sentence structure.

[280] Kenilworth, Warwicks. Whitsuntide, 1487. The instructions for the celebration of the Garter feast were dispatched from Kenilworth on 8 May, and on 15 May the king wrote to the city of York from Kenilworth: *Materials*, ii, pp. 152–3; *YHB*, ii, p. 562.

[281] 'to the qwen' interlineated above by Scribe C.

[282] Around 13 May, from Kenilworth Castle, Henry Tudor made arrangements for his wife and mother to join him: BL, MS. Titus, B. XI, fol. 24; J. O. Halliwell (ed.), *Letters of the Kings of England*, 2 vols (London, 1848), i, p. 171; H. Ellis (ed.), *Original Letters Illustrative of English History*, 1st ser., i (1825), p. 18 (although the latter volume erroneously dates the letter of summons to the 1495 Perkin Warbeck conspiracy). See also C. H. C Cooper, *Memoir of Margaret Countess of Richmond and Derby* (Cambridge, 1874), pp. 37–9 and E. M. G. Routh, *A Memoir of Lady Margaret Beaufort, Countess of Richmond and Derby, Mother of Henry VII* (Oxford, 1924), pp. 67–8.

[283] Vergil, *Anglica Historia*, p. 23 suggests that Henry VII had his almoner Christopher Urswick stationed in the area at the time the rebels landed.

[284] The mobilisation of the vanguard and cavalry wings was probably attended by the heralds on campaign, as their formation is described in detail in the Memoir. Cf. the similar description, albeit attributed to the reargard, in Molinet, *Chroniques*, i, p. 564. Historians generally assume, by reference to a later amendment to Vergil (*Anglica Historia*, pp. 22–3n), that the main battalion was commanded by the duke of Bedford; yet the herald-recorder says nothing of the main battalion, which was probably then stationed in Coventry. Molinet and other early chronicle sources also say little or nothing about the main battalion: Molinet, *Chroniques*, i, p. 564; Vergil, *Anglica Historia*, pp. 20–1; *Great Chronicle of London*, p. 241. Logistical reasons for the separation of the main battalion and vanguard doubtless rested upon the small size of Coventry and Kenilworth; the former town had a population of *c*.6000, and Kenilworth was smaller still: M. Keen, *English Society in the Later Middle Ages* (Harmondsworth, 1990), p. 87.

ing of his hooste; and the noble and corayiouse knyght therle of Oxinforde desired and besaught the king to have the conduyt of the fowarde, whiche the king grauntede, and accompanyede hym with[285] many great coragious and lusty knyghtes – that is to say therle of Shrewesbury, the vicount Lisley, the lorde Gray Rythyn, the lorde Gray, the lorde Hastinges, the lorde Ferres of Charteley, with great nombre of other banerettes, bachelers and esquiers. The lorde Powes, Sir Edwarde Wydvyle (whos sole God pardon),[286] Sir Charles of Somersett, Sir Richard Haut, with many oothre galantes of the kinges howse, wer the for riders and also [the] wyng of the right hande[287] of the fowarde; and Sir Richard Pole and other of the lefte hande.[288] And when the king had thus preparat and ordeynede his fowarde, [he] ordeynede for his proclamacions and goode rule of his hooste, by the advise of the reverende fader in God the archebisshop of Canterbury, the bysshop of Wynchestre, the bisshop of Excestre, and of al othre tempereles lordez ther present and of othre his councellers, in maner as ensuethe:[289]

[f. 26v]The king our souveraigne lorde straytly charge and commaunde that nomaner of man of what so ever state, degre or condicion he bee robe ne spoyle any chyrche; ne take oute of the same any ornament therunto belonging; nor touche ne sett hande on the pixe wherin the blessed sacrament is conteynede; nor yet robbe ne spoyle any maner man or woman, upon peyne of deth. Also, that nomaner of persone ne persones, what so ever they bee, make no quarell to any man, nor sease, nor vex, ne troble any man, by body or goodes, for any offence, or by coloure of any offence heretofor doon or comyttede ayenst the roial magestie of the king our saide souveraigne lorde, withoute his auctoritie and especiall commaundement yeven unto hym or theym that so doon in that behalf, upon peyne of deth. Also, that no maner of persone ne personez, what soever they bee, ravisshe no relygios woman, nor mannes wif, doughter, maydyn, ne no mannes ne womans servant, nor take ne presume to take any maner of vytayll, horsemet, nor mannes mete, withoute paying ther for the resonable pryce therof assisede by the clerke of the market or other the kinges officers therfor ordeynede, upon peyne

[285] Superfluous initial minum cancelled on –w.
[286] –g cancelled between 'sole' and 'God'.
[287] Molinet, *Chroniques*, i, p. 564 suggests that the right and left cavalry wings comprised 2,000 and 12,000 horses respectively. The leadership of the right cavalry wing was probably granted to Sir Edward Woodville: Bennett, *Lambert Simnel*, p. 75.
[288] The leadership of the left cavalry wing was probably granted to Sir John Savage: Molinet, *Chroniques*, i, p. 564.
[289] The disciplinary regulations proclaimed over the army and town, tantamount to a declaration of martial law, were probably copied verbatim by the herald from a document prepared at the council of war. The regulations were subsequently put into effect in Leicester and Loughborough, with a special emphasis upon the expulsion of prostitutes and other camp-followers: see below, p. 114. See Hughes and Larkin, *Tudor Royal Proclamations*, p. 17. For a discussion of the use of proclamations by Henry VII, see R. W. Heinze (ed.), *The Proclamations of the Tudor Kings* (Cambridge, 1976), pp. 65–84.

of deth. Also, that nomaner of persone ne persones, what so ever they bee, take uppon theym to logge theymsilf, nor take nomaner of logging ne harbygage, but suche as shalbe assignede unto hym or theym by the kinges herbygeours; nor disloge no man, nor chaunge no[290] logging after that he be assignede, without advyse and assente of the said harbygeours, upon peyne of imprisonment and to be punysshede at the wille of our saide souveraigne lorde. Also, that no maner of man, what so ever he bee, **[f. 27]** make no quarell with any other man, what soo ever he bee, for nomaner of cause, olde ne newe; ne make no maner of fray within the hooste ne withoute, upon peyne of imprisonament and to bee punysshede according to ther trespas and defautes. And if ther happen any suche quarell or affray to be made by any evyll disposede personnes, that then nomaner of man, for any acquentaunce or feliship that they bee of, take noo parte with no suche mysdooers in any suche affrayes or quarelles, upon peyne of imprysonament and to be punysshede at the kinges wille; but that every man endevour hym silf to take al suche mysdoers, and brynge theym to the mershalles warde, to be punysshed according to ther desertes. Also, that nomaner of personne, what so ever he bee, hurte, trobel, bete ne lette nomaner of personne – man, woman or childe – brynging any vytayle unto the kinges hooste, upon payne of imprisonament and his bodye to bee at the kinges wille. And over this, that every man being of the reteyne of our saide souveraigne lorde, at the furste sounde or blaste of the trumpet to sadill hys hors; at the ij^{de} doo brydell; and at the iij^{de} be redy on horsebake to wayte upon his highnesse, upon peyne of imprisonament. Also, that nomaner of persone, what so ever he bee, make no skryes, showtinges, or blowing of hornesse in the kinges hooste after the wache bee sett, upon peyne of imprisonament and his bodye to bee at the kinges wille. Also, that no vagabounde, nor other folowe the kinges hoste, but suche as bee reteynede or have maisters within the same, upon peyne of imprisonament and to be punysshede in exemple for other; and that no coman woman folow the kinges hooste, upon payne of imprisonament and openly to be punysshede in exemple of al othre. Also, whan soever it shall please the king our souveraigne lorde to commaunde any of[291] hys officers of armes to charge **[f. 27v]** any thing in his name, by hys high comaundement, or by the comaundement of his counstable or marshall, that it be observede and kept upon payne of imprisonament and his body to be punysshede at the kinges pleasur.

And from thens the king procedede[292] to Conventrye,[293] wher the bisshop of[294] Wynchestre toke his leve and went to the quene and the prince;[295] and the sub-

[290] Interlineated above.
[291] Repeated.
[292] Mark of suspension signalling omission of –re cancelled above –p.
[293] This is probably the point at which the main battalion re-grouped with the vanguard and cavalry wings in preparation for the march northward.
[294] Repeated.
[295] It is doubtful whether the eight-month-old prince was actually summoned to Kenil-

stance of his companye waytede upon the king under the standerde of his nevew therle of Devonshire. And from Coventrie the king remevid unto Leycestre, wherby the commaundement of the moost reverende fader in God, tharchbisshop of Canterbury, then chanceller of England, the kinges proclamacions were put in execusion, and in especiall voydyng commen women and vagaboundes – for ther wer imprisonede great nombre of both – wherfor ther was more reste in the kinges hooste and the better rule. And on the morow,[296] whiche was on the Monday, the king lefte ther the forsaide reverende fader in God and roode to Loughborough; and the saide lorde chaunscellers folkes were commyttede by his nevew Robert Morton unto the stander of therle of Oxinforde in the fowarde. And at Loughbourgh the stokkes and prisounes wer reasonabley fyllede with harlattes and vagaboundes. And after that were but fewe in the hoste unto[297] the tyme the felde was doon.

And on Tewsday[298] the king remevede and lay al nyght in the felde under a wode callede Bonley Ryce.[299] And on the Wedensday[300] the kinges mershalles and herbigers[301] of his hoste did not so welle ther diligence that way the king remevede: ther was no propre grounde appoyntede wher the kinges hooste shulde logge that nyght then folowing. But it was a roiall **[f. 28]** and a merveolouse fayre and a wele temperat day, and the king with his hooste wandrede her and ther a great espace of tyme, and so came to a fayre longe hille wher the king sett his folkes in array of batell[302] – that is to say a bow and a bill at his bak, and al the

---

worth with his mother and grandmother; p. 111, above bears a reference to the queen and king's mother only, while the letter of summons itself, dispatched from Kenilworth Castle *c.* May 13 (see above, p. 111, n. 282), makes no mention of the baby.

[296] Mon. 11 June 1487. Evidence suggests that Lord Clifford was routed at Bramham moor on the night of 10 June, and the advance party near Doncaster around the same time: *YHB*, ii, pp. 571–3; Molinet, *Chroniques*, i, pp. 563–4; Pollard, *Contemporary Sources*, i, p. 54.

[297] Minor ink smudges lie behind the words 'host' and 'unto'.

[298] 12 June 1487.

[299] Possibly Bunny, Notts.: Bennett, *Lambert Simnel*, p. 81. Vergil, *Anglica Historia*, p. 23 states the town was called 'Banrys' in the vernacular; Hall, *Union*, 'Henry the vii', fol. 9v and Holinshed, *Chronicles*, p. 487 have 'Bowres' [Bonres?].

[300] 13 June 1487.

[301] The harbingers and marshals were in charge of arranging accommodation for the king and his company. Although the Memoir contains other references to procedural problems (below, pp. 134, 136–7), this is the only case where blame is explicitly apportioned. For information on the function of the king's harbingers and marshals, principally under Edward IV, see Myers, *Black Book*, pp. 225–6.

[302] Probably the vanguard, facing southward to Nottingham with lines of archers and billmen to the rear. The army appears to have advanced as far north of Nottingham as Redhill – perhaps to secure a Derbyshire and north-western following and provide support for the advance party under Woodville – although the household accounts record a stop at Redhill for the night of Tuesday 12 June: TNA, E101/412/19. Bennett, *Lambert Simnel*, pp. 81–4, 94–5 provides the best reconstruction of the king's movements lead-

fowarde were wele and warely loggede under the hille to[303] Notyngham warde. And when the king hade sene his people in this fayr array [he] roode to a village iij myle a this side Notingham, on the high way syde, wher in a gentilmannes place his grace logede; and in that village, and in a benefelde to Notingham warde, lougede al his batell, whiche evenyng wer taken certeyn espies[304] whiche noysede in the contrey that the king had ben fledde. And summe wer hangede on the ashe at Notyngham brygge ende.

And on the morowe, whiche was Corpus Christi day,[305] after the king had harde the dyvyne servyce in the pariche chirche and the trumpettes hadde blowne to horse, the king, not letting his hoste to understand his entente, rode bakewarde[306] to see and also welcome the lorde Straunge, whiche brought with hym a great hoste I now to have beten al the kinges enemyes[307] (only of my lorde his faders – therle of Derbye – folkes and his), and all wer fayre embaytailled, whiche unknowne turnyng to the hooste causede many folkes for to mervaille. Also the kinges standerde and muche cariage folowde after the king unto the tyme the king was advertysede by Garter Kyng of Armes,[308] whom the king commaunded to turne theym al ageyn, whiche so dide and [had] theym al in bataile on the heder side of the great hille a this side Notingham[309] unto the tyme the king came.

---

ing up to the battle.

[303] Written above the cancellation of the word 'of'.

[304] Yorkist agents spread the news that the king had been put to flight, with the result that reinforcements turned back and other allies fled to sanctuary. Bennett suggests that the panic might have been encouraged by accurate report of the rout of the advance party to the north and the fact that the king had retired to undisclosed lodgings for the night: Bennett, *Lambert Simnel*, p. 82. See also the false reports of the king's flight in Molinet, *Chroniques*, i, pp. 563–4; *Great Chronicle*, p. 241; *Letters and Papers*, i, p. 94 (although not necessarily in reference to this occasion), and two similar incidents at Lenton and Radcliffe, below, p. 116.

[305] Thurs. 14 June 1487. The York civic muniments suggest that, having returned to the city to deal with a minor assault on Bootham Bar led by Lords Scrope of Bolton and Masham, the earl of Northumberland rode northward: *YHB*, ii, p. 572.

[306] Cf. Henry Tudor's reputed actions at the battle of Bosworth in Ellis, *Vergil's English History*, pp. 217–18.

[307] The herald's statement suggests that the combined armies of George, Lord Strange and his father the earl of Derby were enough to tip the balance either way. Strange's host possibly made up the rearguard: Molinet, *Chroniques*, i, p. 564. Vergil, *Anglica Historia*, pp. 22–3, and esp. the editorial amendment in n. 15, point to the arrival of a great number of lords, captains and knights at this point, although there were perhaps only six peers in the royal army. John Viscount Welles may not yet have arrived with men of London and the home counties: M. J. Bennett, 'Henry VII and the Northern Rising of 1489', *EHR* 105 (1990), p. 52; Molinet, *Chroniques*, i, p. 563; Bennett, *Lambert Simnel*, p. 77.

[308] John Writhe, Garter King of Arms from 1478 until his death in 1504. For biographical details see W. H. Godfrey et al., *The College of Arms* (London, 1963), pp. 41–5.

[309] As the Memoir was probably produced in the vicinity of London, the king must have

And that nyght the kinges hooste lay undre the ende of al that hille towarde Notingham to Lenton[310] warde, and his foward byfor **[f. 28v]** hym to Notynham[311] Brige warde, and therle of Derbyes host on the kinges lifte hande to the medowes besides Lenton. And that evenyng ther was a great skrye,[312] at whiche skrye ther flede many men, but it was great joy to see how sone the king was redye and his trwe men in array. And from thens on the Friday[313] the king, undrestanding that his enemyes and rebelles drew towardes Newarke warde, passing by Southwelle and the furside of Trente, the king with his hoste remevede thedarwardes and logged that nyght beside a village callede Ratcliff,[314] ix myle oute of Newark. And that evening ther was a great skrye,[315] whiche causede many cowardes to flee, but therle of Oxinforde and al the nobles in the fowarde with hym wer sone[316] in a good array and in a fayre bataile, and so was the king and al the very men that ther wer. And in this estrye I harde of noman of worship that fledde but raskelles.

And on the morne, whiche was Satirday,[317] [the king] erly arros and harde ij masses,[318] wherof the lorde John[319] Fox, bisshop of Excester, sange the ton. And the king had v good and true men of the village of Ratecliff, whiche shewde his grace the beste way for to conduyt his hoost to Newark, whiche knew welle the countrey and shewde wher wer marres, and wher was the ryver of Trent, and wher wer vilages or grovys for busshementes or strayt weyes, that the king myght conduyt his hoost[320] the better.[321] Of whiche guydes the king yave ij to therle of Oxinforde to conduit the fowarde,[322] and the remenant reteynede at his pleasur. And

---

      passed the night south of Nottingham.

[310] The royal army occupied a series of encampments around Nottingham, the battalion positioned toward Lenton, the earl of Derby's following to the left, and the vanguard by Nottingham Bridge: Bennett, *Lambert Simnel*, p. 82.

[311] Sic.

[312] The desertions on this occasion may have been caused by the return of the royal advance party, which had been routed near Doncaster: Molinet, *Chroniques*, i, p. 563. See the report of panic above, pp. 115, 116.

[313] 15 June 1487. The royal army moved out from its encampments, 'in the direction of the morning sun', in three columns with cavalry wings: Bennett, *Lambert Simnel*, p. 83; Molinet, *Chroniques*, i, p. 564. For a breakdown of the royal host at this point, and an idea of its movements, see Bennett, *Lambert Simnel*, pp. 83–4.

[314] Radcliffe on Trent, Notts. Cf. Vergil, *Anglia Historia*, pp. 22–5 who suggests that the royal army pushed further eastward beyond Newark. See also A. H. Burne, *More Battlefields of England* (London, 1952), pp. 151–6 and Bennett, *Lambert Simnel*, p. 84.

[315] See also reports of panic and flight above, pp. 115, 116.

[316] Followed by the cancellation of 'agane'.

[317] 16 June 1487.

[318] Probably held in the local church at Radcliffe.

[319] An error for 'Richard'.

[320] Followed by the cancellation of –b.

[321] The royal host appears to have followed the course of the River Trent, at least as far as East Bridgford: Bennett, *Lambert Simnel*, p. 94.

so in good order and array before ix of the clok, beside a village called Stook,[323] a large myle oute[324] of Newarke, his fowarde recountrede his enemyes and rebelles, wher by the helpe of Almyghty God he hade the victorye.[325] And ther was taken **[f. 29]** the lade[326] that his rebelles callede King Edwarde (whoos name was in dede John)[327] – by a vaylent and a gentil esquier of the kinges howse called Robert Bellingham – whiche also that same day [rallied][328] to the stander of a manly man of warre callede Martyn Swerte.[329] And ther was slayne therle of Lincoln, John,[330]

[322] *YHB*, p. 573 indicates that the vanguard (which included the retinues of the earl of Shrewsbury and Viscount Lisle) contained 10,000 men; Bennett, *Lambert Simnel*, p. 95 suggests *c.*6,000. The figures in Molinet, *Chroniques*, i, p. 564 imply a total army size of at least 40,000.

[323] East Stoke, Notts., four miles from the market town of Newark. The report suggests that the vanguard, and probably the main battalion, were in place by 9 o'clock in the morning.

[324] Repeated.

[325] The earliest descriptive account of the battle is found in Vergil, *Anglica Historia*, pp. 24–5. He is followed by the likes of Holinshed, *Chronicles*, p. 489; and Hall, *Union*, 'Henry the vii', fol. 10. See also the names of the principal battle-dead in the *Great Chronicle*, p. 241; Molinet, *Chroniques*, i, p. 564; *Greyfriars Chronicle*, p. 24; Fabyan, *New Chronicles*, p. 683; Vergil, *Anglica Historia*, p. 25; Holinshed, *Chronicles*, p. 488. The list compiled by Vergil and copied by Holinshed and Hall, and the names given by the *Greyfriars Chronicle*, derive from intelligence gathered before it was known that Lovel was not among the bodies on the field. See below, p. 118, n. 331, for the subject of Lovel's fate. A blow-by-blow reconstruction of the battle itself is given in Bennett, *Lambert Simnel*, pp. 97–9. News of the victory reached York around 3 o'clock on Sunday morning: *YHB*, p. 573; Armstrong, 'Speed and Distribution', pp. 119–20.

[326] 'The lad' given as catchwords at the bottom of fol. 28v.

[327] This is the earliest independent reference to the name of the boy-pretender known to posterity as Lambert Simnel. The other English source most closely related to the battle, the civic muniments of York, offers no clue to the boy's identity: *YHB*, ii, p. 573. The name Lambert Simnel first appears in the Act of Attainder of November 1487: *RP*, vi, p. 397. Cf. the version of the Memoir in Leland, *Collectanea*, iv, p. 214, where the herald's sentence has been altered to read 'whos Name was indede Lambert'. Any number of explanations for the boy's name (or nickname) may be postulated, but the mystery surrounding his identity is discussed in detail in Bennett, *Lambert Simnel*, esp. chapter 4 'The Lambert Simnel Mystery', pp. 41–56. See also the statement in *Chroniques de Adrien de But*, pp. 674–5 where the young 'Warwick' is said to have been removed from the field to the safety of Guines once the odds against the rebels became apparent.

[328] Verb omitted.

[329] Martin Zwart or Schwartz, the son of an Augsburg shoemaker, was the leader of the German mercenaries in the rebel contingent. He had risen from small-time troop-master to military entrepreneur with a Europe-wide reputation for arrogance and flamboyance. He had been among the mercenaries recruited by the Emperor Maximilian the previous year for the suppression of the rebellious Flemish cities and to drive the French from Flanders: Bennett, *Lambert Simnel*, pp. 60–1, 64. The battle of Stoke was Schwartz's last campaign, as he perished on the field.

[330] The earl of Lincoln forfeited his estates, but the de la Pole patrimony remained safe at

and dyvers other gentilmen, and the vicount Lovell[331] put to flight; and ther wer slayne of Englisshe, Duche and Irisshe iiij^{ml};[332] and that day the king made xiij banerettes and lij knyghtes whos names ensueth:[333]

---

that time: Bennett, *Lambert Simnel*, p. 108. Vergil, *Anglica Historia*, pp. 26–7 suggests that Henry VII was angered to find Lincoln dead, having wished him to be brought in for questioning. The fate of Lincoln's corpse is unknown, although legend has it that he was buried where he fell, a willow stave driven through his heart and a clump of willow trees marking his grave: Molinet, *Chroniques*, i, pp. 564–5. Bennett, *Lambert Simnel*, p. 101 suggests the king may have wished to display Lincoln's body to prevent rumours of his escape.

[331] Preceded by the cancellation of 'lover'. This was Francis Lovel, the ninth and last baron Lovel, and a close friend of Richard III. Lovel disappeared after the battle of Stoke and his fate remains a mystery. His wife was still searching for him in early 1488: *Paston Letters and Papers*, ii, pp. 455–6. Unlike the Memoir, *YHB*, p. 573 and a closely contemporary note in Coll. Arms, MS. 2M6 (printed in R. F. Green, 'Historical Notes of a London Citizen', *EHR*, 96 (1981), p. 589) which mention Lovel's flight, Richard Arnold's *Chronicle*, the *Greyfriars Chronicle* and Vergil, *Anglica Historia* (and thus Holinshed and Hall) suggest that Lovel was found dead on the field. The *Great Chronicle*, p. 238 states that Lovel met his death at the battle of Bosworth in 1485, a story that is easily disavowed but which may have originated with Henry VII himself: a few days after Bosworth Henry VII issued a proclamation to the city of York in which a number of prominent Yorkists who survived the conflict, including Lovel, were said to have perished: *YHB*, ii, p. 736. The alleged discovery of a skeleton in an underground vault at Minster Lovell Castle, Oxon., in the eighteenth century gave rise to a renewed speculation: *Peerage*, viii, p. 255n; *VCH Lancaster*, viii, p. 403. See also Bacon's reference to the 'cave or vault' which may have concealed Lovel: Bacon, *History*, p. 56. A list of men slain in battle in England between 1447 and c.1490, which does *not* give Lovel's name among the Stoke casualties, may be found in Kingsford, *Chronicles of London*, pp. 276–9. The Lovel mystery is discussed in detail in D. Baldwin, 'What Happened to Lord Lovel?', *The Ricardian*, 89 (June, 1985), pp. 56–65.

[332] Denotes the mercenary soldiers hired by the rebel leaders and includes levies from the Low Countries (principally Dutch and Flemish), and from the forests and high valleys of upper Germany and Switzerland, as well as renegade English soldiers removed from the garrisons at Calais and the Channel Islands because of Yorkist sympathies, gaelic Irish billmen, archers, horsemen and footsoldiers, and the formidable Scots-Irish galloglasses: Bennett, *Lambert Simnel*, pp. 60, 61, 63, 68. Contracts between agents of Margaret of York, dowager duchess of Burgundy, and German troop-leaders were drawn up at the end of 1486 or beginning of 1487: Molinet, *Chroniques*, i, pp. 562–3. In July 1487, c. 15,000 men were sent to Brittany under the command of Baldwin of Burgundy: B. A. Pocquet du Haut-Jussé, *François II, Duc de Bretagne et L'Angleterre (1458–1488)* (Paris, 1929), p. 278. For illustrations of fifteenth-century German mercenaries and early sixteenth-century Irish warriors see Bennett, *Lambert Simnel*, pp. 62, 67.

[333] Cf. the names of the knights and bannerets created at the battle in *Paston Intro and Supp*, p. 157, and those recorded by Garter Writhe in BL, MS. Add. 46354, fols 16v–18. All three sources are closely related.

Theis bee the names of the banerettes:

    Sir Gilbert Talbot   (theis iij wer
    Sir John Cheyny   made byfor the
    Sir William Stoner   batell).[334]

And after the batell wer made the same day:

    Sir John of Aroundell
    Sir Thomas Cokesay
    Sir John Fortscu
    Sir Edmund Benyngfelde
    Sir James Blount
    Sir Richarde Crofte
    Sir Humfrey Stanley
    Sir Richarde de Laver
    Sir John Mortymer
    Sir William Trouthbek

The names of the knyghtes made at the same bataill:

    Sir James Audeley
    Sir Edwarde Norres
    Sir Robert Clifforde
    Sir George Opton
    Sir Robert Abroughton
    Sir John Paston
    Sir Henry Willoughby
    Sir Richard Pole
    Sir Richard fitz Lewes
    Sir Edwarde Abrough
    Sir George Lovell
    Sir John Longvile

Theies noble knyghtes welle and liberally payde the hole fees and thies that folowen have payde as yet but parte:

[f. 29v]

    Syr Thomas Terell
    Sir Roger Bellyngam
    Sir William Carew
    Sir William Trouthbek
    Sir Thomas Pooll
    Sir William Vampage

Theys that folow hath promysede to pay al sone:

    Sir James Haryngton (whiche is not willing never to doo as a gentilman shulde doo as he saith as yet. I pray God lerne hym better)
    Syr John Devenysshe

    Syr Edwarde Darell
    Sir Edwarde Pykerynge
    Sir Thomas of Wolton
    Syr William Sander
    Syr Robert Brandon
    Syr Mores Barkley
    Sir John Dygby
    Syr Raf Shirley
    Sir William Litilton
    Sir William Norres
    Sir Thomas Hanserde
    Sir Christofor Wroughton
    Syr Thomas Lyn
    Sir Mores Aborough

---

[334] The creation of three bannerets on the field before the battle probably betokened the rewards and honours that would follow a victory: Bennett, *Lambert Simnel*, p. 95. Among the creations following the combat, Sir Edmund Bedingfield was a knight of the king's body granted several manors formerly held by Viscount Lovel: *Materials*, ii, p. 203. Sir [William] Todd and Sir Richard York were rewarded with knighthood and annuities of £20 each for life: *CPR 1485–94*, pp. 256–7, 303; Palliser, *Tudor York*, p. 44. Other rewards may be found in TNA, 5404/79/151. Henry VII made similar creations before and after the battle of Bosworth in 1485: BL, MS. Harley 78, fol. 31; Chrimes, *Henry VII*, p. 42n.

Sir John Sabarottes	Syr Thomas Manyngton
Sir Thomas Lovell	And that same somer at Coventrye
Sir Humfrey Savage	the kinges baner was splayde.
Sir Antony Browne	Item, at Yorke: Sir [William][335] Tod,
Sir Thomas Grey	mayre of the same. Sir Richarde York,
Sir Nicholas Vaux	mayre of the Staple.
Sir William Tyrwytt	Item, at Deram Sir Richard Salkilde
Sir Amyas Pallet	(payde half his fees).
Sir Rauff Langforth	Item, at Crofft on Seynt Laurence even:[336]
Sir Henry Bould	Sir Richard Clervaux
Sir William Redmyll	Item, at Repon on Seynt Bartholowes
Sir Thomas Blount (hath	day:[337] Syr John Waren; Sir Thomas
truly payde)	Hasheton[338]
Sir Robert Cheyny	And in the kinges retournyng to
Sir John Wyndam	London, in Harnesey Park, he dubbed
Sir John a Musgrove	Sir William Horne, meire of London
Sir George Nevell the baster[d]	And the same day, Sir John Persevall
Sir James Parker	marchaunt of London.[339]

[340][f. 30]The kyng our souveraigne lorde, the thirde yere of his moost noble reigne at Warwik, the monethe of Septembre last passede, determynede the coronacion of Elizabeth[341] his der wiff, eldeste doughter and heire of the famous prince

[335] The scribe wrote 'Richard'.
[336] Thurs. 9 Aug. 1487.
[337] Fri. 24 Aug. 1487.
[338] –H interlineated above.
[339] Immediately after the battle, the royal entourage rode back to Coventry and Kenilworth, toured Warwickshire, and then returned to London. The king's re-entry was perhaps delayed to heighten the drama of the occasion: Bennett, *Lambert Simnel*, p. 106; Edwards, *Itineraries*, p. 41. See also the collection of funds in the aftermath of the battle in TNA, E101/413/2, part 1, fols 1–28.
[340] At the top of fol. 30 in the same hand as above, n. 231: 'Coronation of the Lady Eliz: king Hen. 7 wife in the .3. year of his raigne'.
[341] Henry VII probably delayed his wife's coronation for political reasons, although preparations had been underway since 1485. Purchases included ermines, wood-work, thread, candles and much labour at the wardrobe, as well as eight coursers brought from France to carry the litters or 'chairs' used in conveying the queen and her ladies in procession: *Materials*, i, p. 253; TNA, E404/79/98(375). Also extant is a mandate for payment toward jousts and tourneys in honour of this event: *Materials*, ii, p. 198. For comparative heraldic narratives of queens' coronations see: G. Smith (ed.), *The Coronation of Elizabeth Wydeville* (London, 1935) and Sutton and Hammond, *Richard III*, pp. 270–82, where in the latter case the queen was crowned with her husband. Chronicle accounts of the coronation of Margaret of Anjou, queen to Henry VI, may be found in the following sources: F. W. D. Brie (ed.), *The Brut; or, The Chronicles of England*,

[of] excellent memorye of King Edwarde the iiijth, to be solempnysede at Westminster the day of Seynt Kateryn[342] then next ensuyng; and therupon directe[d] his moost honourable lettres unto the nobles of this his realme to geve ther due attendaunce upon the same; and directe[d] also othre lettres unto dyvers nobles to prepare and arredy theym silf to be with his grace at London at a certeyne day to theym appoyntede ther to, to be made knyghtes of the bath and so to reseve the honourable order of knyghthode in worshiping the saide coronacion, whoos names bee expressede in order herafter folowing.

And a vj dayes byfore[343] the sayde coronacion ther was a commyssyon made oute of the chauncery to the high and myghty prynce [the] duc of Bedeforde, great stuwarde of Englande for that feste, and to dyvers other estates like as sheweth by the copy folowyng:

HENRYCUS et cetera carissimo avunculo suo Jaspari duci Bedefordie ac carissimis consanguinijs suis Johanni c[o]miti[344] Oxonie, magno[345] camerario nostro Anglie, Thome comiti Derbye et Willemo comiti Notingham, nec non dilectis et fidelibus suis Johanni Radeclyff de Fitzwater militi, Johanni Suliarde, militi, uni justiciariorum nostrorum ad placita coram nobis tenenda et Johanni Hawes, uni justiciariorum nostrorum de communi banco[346] salutem. Sciatis quod nos de[347] industria et circumspectione vestris plenius confidentes assignavimus vos conjuntim et divisim ad omnia et singula que ad officium senescalli Anglie ad coronatione[m][348]

EETS, orig. ser., 131, 136 (1906–8), ii, pp. 488–9; R. Flenley (ed.), *Six Town Chronicles of England* (Oxford, 1911), p. 119; C. L. Kingsford (ed.), *Chronicles of London* (Oxford, 1905), p. 156; J. Gairdner (ed.), *The Historical Collections of the City of London in the Fifteenth Century*, Camden Soc., n.s., 17 (1874), p. 186; and *Great Chronicle*, p. 178. A 16th-century copy of the Memoir account of Elizabeth of York's coronation is in BL, MS. Eg. 985, fols 10v–25v. See also Legg, *Coronation Records*, pp. lvii–lxiii. The best recent discussion of the coronation of English queens in the second half of the 15th century is provided by Laynesmith, *Last Medieval Queens*, pp. 82–110.

[342] Sun. 25 Nov. 1487. Certain chronicle sources, following mayoral years, mistakenly attribute the coronation to the year 1488: *Great Chronicle*, p. 241; Fabyan's, *Chronicle*, p. 68. The coronation may have been timed to coincide with the feast of St. Katherine, and may have served to reinforce Henry VII's own position: Fabyan, *New Chronicles*, p. 683; Laynesmith, *Last Medieval Queens*, p. 89; K. A. Winstead, 'Capgrave's Saint Katherine and the Perils of Gynecocracy', *Viator*, 26 (1995), pp. 361–75).

[343] Mon. 19 Nov. 1487.

[344] Written 'camiti'.

[345] Written 'magnno'.

[346] Written 'bancho' before the –h was cancelled.

[347] Preceded by the cancellation of –d.

[348] Written 'coronatione'.

preclarissie consorte Elizabeth Regine Anglie pertinet hac vice tantum facienda et exercenda et ideo vobis mandamus quod circa premissa diligenter intendatis et ea faciatis et **[f. 30v]** exequamini modo et forma debitis et antiquitus usitatis. Damus autem universis et singulis, quor[um] interest in hac parte, tenore presentium firmiter in mandatis quod vobis in executione officii predicti intendentes sive auxiliantes, consulentes et obedientes in omnibus pro ut decet. In cujus rei, et cetera. Teste me ipso apud Westminsterium IX° die Novembris anno regni nostri tercio.

Whiche duc with other, by force of the saide commission, satt the saide day in the white hall at Westminster and lete make a proclamacion by an officer of armez that al maner of men, what estate or degre they wer of,[349] that helde any lande by servyce royall (that is to say to do any servyce at the coronacion of the quene) shulde comme in and eschew ther clayme,[350] and they shulde ther upon bee answerede and have that [which] right and law requirede; werupon therle of Oxinforde put in his clayme by bylle too bee[351] chaumbrelayn as ensueth:

A treshonourable seigneur Jasper, frere et uncle dez roys, duc de Bedford et counte de Penbrok, senescall dEngleter,

Supple le vostre John de Ver, counte de Oxinforde, que cum il tient lez maners de Fringrith [en][352] la countie dEssex et Hormede en la countye de Hertforde de nostre dit seigneur le roy par serjauntie destre chambrelayne nostre treshonourable dame la reigne et sa chamber et de huys de tell le jour de sa coronement de garder preignant comme sone droit le lite nostre dit dame la reigne lez basynz et tous autre chosys al chambrelayn apperteignantes et auxi du une clerk en le chequer nostre dit seigneur le roy pour demaunder et receyver lore nostre dit dame la reygne que pour se fair p'adra chesun jour del dit ore pur sey lyner vj d. et dit que toutz sees auncestrez que heire il est seisez de lez ditz maners ount este chaumberleynes les reignes dEngleter de tempe dount memorie ne

---

[349] Followed by a cancellation.
[350] During the 15th century a Court of Claims was held in advance of a coronation for peers to register and defend their hereditary claims to perform specific services at the event. The genesis of the Court of Claims and the individual claims of noblemen are discussed in Sutton and Hammond, *Richard III*, pp. 245–53; Legg, *Coronation Records*, pp. lxvii–lxxxi; and Schramm, *History*, pp. 61–71. The earliest known minutes of proceedings of the Court of Claims, those for Richard II, are printed in Legg, *Coronation Records*, pp. 131–168 and summarised in Schramm, *History*, p. 86. Several petitions survive, some endorsed with the decisions, for the coronation of Henry V: T. A. Sandquist, 'English Coronations, 1399–1483' (unpub. Ph.D thesis, Toronto, 1962), pp. 204–5, 365–6. See also J. H. Round, *King's Serjeants and Officers of State* (London, 1911).
[351] Preceded by the cancellation of 'the'.
[352] Written 'in'.

courte et par mesure le tous les jours dez coronementes **[f. 31]** de ditz reignes[353] dEngleter de temps dount memorye ne court ont gardes les chambres et les huys dycels et ount ewe lez litz, basins et toutz autre choses que a lez ditz chambrelayns apperteignier le dit jour come lore droyt par reason del tenure dez maners avante ditz come en leschequer nostre dit seigneur le roy appiert de recorde pluis au pleyne que il please[354] a vostre hautesse[355] de luye accept a son dit office fair a ceste coronement.

Also therles of Derbye and Notingham and Sir John Wynkfelde made[356] ther cleyme as ensueth:

> A le tresnoble prince Jaspar duc de Bedeforde,[357]
>
> Come William counte de Notingham, Thomas counte de Derbye, et John Wynkfelde chevalier esteant seisez del countye de Warene le quel countie et tennez par la service de estre pantelers cheson jour du coronacion de roy ou reigne. Please vostre grace de eux admitter de occupie le office avauntdit le jour du coronacion du reigne si comme ils et lure auncestres, segnours de counte susidit,[358] ount use de occupier de temps dount memory ne court avesque le fees et custumes avaunt dit office annexez et coteux trenchanz et la salar et coverpagne.

The duc of Suffolk made his clayme as ensueth:

> To the right high and myghty prince Jasper duc of Bedeforde, stuarde of Englande,
>
> Besecheth humbly John duc of Suffolk, sonne and[359] heire to William late duc of Suffolk, that wher as the moost blessed prince King Henry the vj, late king of England, was seased of the maner of Nedthinger with thappurtenances in the countie of Suffolk in his demeane as of fee and so therof seased by his lettres patenz gave and grauntede the saide maner with thapurtenantes to the saide William late duc of Suffolk and to **[f. 31v]** his heires by the servyce that he and his heyres shulde bere a rodde, septre of ivery with a dove of golde of the hight of the same befor the quene of England the day of her coronacion, of whiche service the same John hath ben alowede at festes of coronacion of Dame Elyzabeth and of Dame Anna, late quenes of Englande.

[353] Superfluous mark of suspension attached to –g.
[354] 'il' and 'please' initially joined, before a separation marker was inserted.
[355] Preceded by the cancellation of 'al'.
[356] –y cancelled between –a and –d.
[357] In the right margin, probably in the same hand as above, p. 105, n. 231: 'Pro Com' Warwick'.
[358] Ie. 'suisdit'.
[359] Followed by the cancellation of –e.

Therle of Notyngham and the lorde Latymer made ther clayme as hereafter ensueth:

> A treshonourable seigneur Jaspar duc de Bedforde et counte de Penbrok, senescall dEngleter,
>
> Come William counte de Notingham et Richard Seigneur de Latymer esteant seises del barony del [B]edeforde[360] in lour done come de fee lesquel ut ilz teignent par servicer de estre avineour chesun jour du coronacion le roy ou reygne. Please vostre grace de eux admitter de occupier le office avant dit le jour de coronacion le reygne sicone ilz et lours auncestres, seigneurs de la dit barony, ount use de occupier [dount][361] memory ne court preignant pur le exercise de le dit office le almes dysshe devant luye servyce.

The barons of the v portes claymede by bylle as ensueth:

> A treshault et trespuissaunt prince le duc de Bedeforde, seneschall dEngleter,
>
> Supleaunt humlement lez humbles et feialx lyeges du roy nostre souveraigne seigneur lez barons de cink portes que come le ditz suplyauntes aient tyel lybertye dount memory ne court que quaunt ascun roy dEngleter ou reygne serount corones soloient lez ditz barons par semence de bref de roy a ceulx direct par xl jours devant **[f. 32]** la dit coronement estre garniz pur venir a faire lore custumble services et honours duez, cest assaviour le jour de coronement due roy nostre ditz seigneur ou del reigne quant il ou elle [v]eigne[362] destre corones et quant nostre dit seigneur le roy ou la reigne reviendra de son coronement soloient et duissent lez barons dez ditz cink portz porter aultre et desiues le roy ou reigne une drap' de soy eu dore en lieux accustumables par xvj barons dez portez avant ditz, issunt que nul eutre soit par entre eux, et soloient lez avant ditz xvj barons out les plus nobles et vaillauntes de ceux de mesme le v portes illoquez venir en suete honestement vestues et apparalez, et quant ils ferount loffice portant le suis ditz drap sur quart launces de sius argentees chesun launce avrent une champ[er]nel dergent[363] desuis erres del purveaunce du tresorour nostre dit souveraigne seigneur le roy, et a chesun launce devoient aler quartre barons issuit que le dit drap[364] seroit[365] porte par xvj barons et soloient yoeux xvj barons ensemblement

---

[360] Written 'Sedeford' and preceeded by the cancellation of –d.
[361] The scribe appears to have written 'domyt' or something similar.
[362] The scribe has written 'reigne'.
[363] Followed by a cancellation, possibly –z.
[364] Preceded by the cancellation of 'souveraigne seigneur'.
[365] Superfluous –i cancelled between ser– and –oit.

out teutz autres barons dez cink portez que illeoquez estre vendre soloient, avoir et seer a la chef table pur manger en la graunt sale du roy ou de reigne sur [d]e mayne dextere de mesme le roy [ou roigne de droit et dauncien temps use et accustume, et quaunt ils sunt licence ou conuge de roi]³⁶⁶ nostre seigneur ou de nostre dame le reigne de retourner ou departier ils averount le suisdit drap ovesque lez launcez champerneylx et toutz autres ceus appertenances come ils ont de tout temps uses et ont estre seises devant cestes hoeures. Please a vostre tresnoble seigneur de considerer³⁶⁷ les liberties et usage suisdit et sur ces par vostre tresage advis et discrecion que lez ditz supliauntes puissent et present et de tout temps en apres avoire et enjoier mesmes les liberties et usages solonque ceo quils les ount uses et ajuries du temps dount memory ne court come droit et reason demand[ent].

The clayme of Humphrey Tyrrell of Kent as ensueth:

[f. 32v] Sheweth unto your good and gracyous lordeship Humphrey Tyrell, sonne and heyre of Henry Terell, by John Bradfelde, Richard Higham and Thomas Marowe, his gardens, that wher the saide Henry was seasede of an C of londe, xx acres of medow, xl acres of pasture, lxvj s. viij d. ob. of rent of assise with thappertenances in Chaddewell and littil Turrok in the countye of Essex in his demeane as of fee and soo seasede and helde the same lande, medow, pasture and rent of King Edwarde the iiijth, late king of England, by the service of graunt serjaunt, to be gardein of the napery of our souveraigne lorde the king and of suche astate died seasede, after whos deth the same landes and tenementes descendid to your said supliant as sone and heire to the saide Henry Terell your said supliaunt then, and yet being within age and for that cause seasede warde to the saide late king. Please it your lordeshipe to consider the premyssez and that your said suppliant may bee admitted to the said service by suche a depute as it shall please your lordship to provide, and to have suche fee as to the saide servyce belongeth, for the love of God and in the way of charytie.

Here is shewde the clayme of theyre of Alyngton:

To the right high and myghty prince Jaspar duc of Bedeforde, steward of England,

    Sheweth unto your good lordeship Gylys of Alyngton, by Richard Garden, hys gardien, that wher he holde the maner of Wymondeley with the appertenances in the countie of Hertford³⁶⁸ of our souveraigne lorde the

---

³⁶⁶ The scribe has omitted a portion of the text.
³⁶⁷ 'jour' incorrectly inserted between 'seigneur' and 'considerer'.
³⁶⁸ –t interlineated above.

king by graunt serjaunte, that is to sey to serve the king or the quene ther day of ther coronacion at the furste cuppe for his fee. Pleasith your good lordeship to admytte and receyve the sayde Gylys by his saide garden or his depute **[f. 33]** to doo the service above saide at the coronacion in lik wise as it was alowed to the saide suppliant at the coronacion of our souveraigne lorde the kinge.

The clayme of my lorde of Burgaveny:

Suple a vostre tresnoble seigneur je George Nevell seigneur de Burgaveny, que come ill est seise de le maner de Skulton avec les appertenances en le counte de Norffolk autrement appelle le maner de Bordeles en Skulton en le dit counte le quel[369] maner il tient de nostre seigneur le roy que ore est par les services de estre lardonar al roy et al reigne le jour de loure coronement que please i[l] a vostre dist tresnoble seigneur les premissez considerer[370] et de admitter et suffrer vostre dist suppliant pur faire de ditz service et de aver toutz lez feez et regardes a le ditz officez devez et appendauntez.

The clayme of the lorde fitz Water:

Suple vostre tresnoble seigneur je John seigneur fitz Water, chyvaler, senescall dell hostell nostre seigneur le roy, que cume il[371] et toutz sez auncetres, seigneurs fitz Water, qil heire il est, ount use de temps[372] dount memory ne court de sewer devant le roy et lay reygne al temps de loure coronement et de eux server en[373] mesire loffice que il[374] poet estre admitte a la dist office et service daunt temps duez et accustumes et lez toutz esquellz dount nostre dame la reigne serra servy a le pri[m]ier[375] cours la jour de [sa][376] coronacion.

The clayme of therle of Warwik [is] in the kynges handes.

The clayme of the wafers:

A le tresnoble prince Jaspar duc de Bedeforde,

Supple a vostre tresnobles seigneur je Thomas Say, que cum il est seise de le maner de Liston Overhall en la counte dEssex et le dist maner il tyent de nostre seigneur de roy que ore est par lez servicez de luy wafers

---

[369] Preceded by the cancellation of –l.
[370] Followed by a cancellation.
[371] Initially written 'ille' before the final –le was cancelled.
[372] Preceded by the cancellation of –d.
[373] Followed by the cancellation of –se.
[374] Initially written 'illes' before the final –les was cancelled.
[375] Written 'prinier' and followed by a cancellation.
[376] The word written by the scribe here is not clear.

et dein server al dit roy [f. 33v] et al reigne le jour de lour coronement que please a vostre dist seigneur lez premissez a conciderer de admitter[377] et sufferer vostre dist suppliant pur faire lez ditz services et de avere touz lez fees et regardes al dist office denez et appendaunces &c.

The clayme of therle of Aroundell:

Suple Thomas counte dAroundell de luy receyavoire a fair sone office de chief boteler que luy appertient de droyt pur le counte dAroundell en temps de jour coronacion de reigne receyvant lez fees out dues.

The clayme made by the gardens for John Aspelond:

A treshonourable seigneur Jaspur duc de Bedeforde et count de Penbrok, senescall dEngleter,

Suple a vostre bonne grace Bryon Roucliff, un de les barons del eschequer nostre seigneur le roy, et Robert Castell, gardeyns de un John Aspland, deinez age, fitz et heire de John Aspelonde, trespasse que cume lavant dist John Asplande, le fitz, tenet certeing tenementes [en][378] Heydon en la countie dEssex quel sount la moite del maner de Heydon avant dit de nostre seigneur le roy par serjauntie, cest asavoir de tenez un towell quant nostre seigneur le roy lavera sez mayns deunt memmery le jour de sa[379] coronement del roy et ensemblament de[va]nte la reigne la jour de sa coronement, pur quell service il devoit au lavaunt dit towell et quel mute del maner de Heydon avant dit jades fust en la season John Wilshire citezin de Londours que ceo tenoit de Richard [l]e ijde nedgarres roy dEngleter par la service suisdites come piert par la recorde et entaunt que lavaunt ditz John Asplond est deinz age en garde de les avantditz suppliauntes ils priount que lavaunt dit John Aspland puist estre acceptez de faire la dit service de sergeauntie in tiel maner [et][380] forme come il apperteint a luy est [ouit] deinz age la fayre ensy que ils ne soit prejudicall a son [f. 34] droyt ne a sees heires enfaunt lez ditz servicez pur son dit tenure autrefoyes quant il ou sez heires sereunt de playne age.

The clayme to make potage appered not at that fest.

The kinges highnesse for the determynacion and good accomplisshement of the saide coronacion by hym as above determyned, the Satirday nexte byfore the feste of Alhalowes[381] begane his journey;[382] and both he and the quene remevede

[377] Followed by a cancellation.
[378] Written 'in'.
[379] Written 'say' before the final –y was cancelled.
[380] Written 'and'.
[381] 28 Oct. 1487.
[382] This was the king's first return to London since the battle of Stoke, possibly delayed to heighten the moment; it was watched from a secret vantage point by the queen and

from Warwik towardes London, and in[383] his way at Seint Albons kepte the fest of Alhalowes. And on Alsolne day[384] the morne after, when he had harde dyvyne service and dynede, his grace removede from thens to Barnet and ther lay al nyght. And on the morne[385] as he was commyng towardes London, in Harnesses Park, the mayre, shryffes and aldremen, and dyvers comens of London therto chosen oute of every craft,[386] met his grace al on horsebak, ful wele and honourably[387] besene in on lyverey, to attende upon his highnesse, wher Sir William Horne, maire, was dubbede knyght; and bytwene Iseldon and London Sir John Percyvale was also dubbed knyght.

And ayenste the comyng of the king into his citie of London al the streytes that his grace shulde ride thorough with his roiall company were clensede, and of both sides the strete the citezins of every crafte that roode not wer sett in row, every craft in due order in ther lyveres welbesene, from Bisshops Gate unto Powles. And so at afternone the king, as a comely and roiall prince, apparailled accordingly, entred into his citie wele and honourabley accompanyed as was fitting to his estate with many great lordez and other clenly horsed and richely besene; and so came riding thorough the citie to the weste doore of Powles, wher his grace a lightyde. And to receyve hym into the chyrche was[388] the quere of Powles **[f. 34v]** in ther habites and copes. Ther was present the bisshop of Canterbury and many other bisshops and prelates of the chyrche to geve ther attendance upon his hyghnesse. And at his entre into the chirche his grace was sensende with the grate senser of Powles by an angell commyng oute of the roof, during whiche tyme the quere sange a solempne antyme and after *Te Deum Laudamus* for joy of his late victory and prosperouse commyng to his saide citie.

And in his so commyng thorough the citie al the howsez, windowes and stretes as he passed by wer hogely replenysshede with people in passing great nombre that made great joye and exaltacion to be holde his most royal persone soo prosperously and princely commyng into his citie after his late tryumphe and victory ayenste his enemyes; and so to be holde the faire and goodly sight of his so commyng the quenes grace and my lady the kinges moder, with other dyvers ladies and great astates in ther companye, were secretly in an hous besides Seint

---

Margaret Beaufort, and became the context for the knighting of several loyal adherents. See Bodl., MS. Rawlinson 146, fol. 158.

[383] 'in' interlineated above.
[384] Fri. 2 Nov. 1487.
[385] Sat. 3 Nov. 1487.
[386] Preceded by the cancellation of 'park'; 'craft' and 'met' joined and then separated. This was a grand civic reception in the traditional manner, and the reaction of the Londoners may have even more effusive than that which greeted the king after Bosworth: Anglo, *Spectacle*, p. 49.
[387] Preceded by the cancellation of 'hol'.
[388] The scribe has actually used the abreviation for 'with'.

Mary Spetell withoute Bisshops Gate. And when the sight was passede theyme they went from theyns to Grenewiche to ther beddes.[389] And after the kinges highnesse was thus receyvede in Powles, and had offred at places accustumed ther, he went in to the bisshops paloys of London and ther restede al nyght. And on the morne, whiche was Sonday,[390] he went [in] a procession in Powles and harde the sarmond ther.

And the Fryday next byfor Seint Kateryns day[391] the quenys good grace, royally apparelled and accompanyede with my lady the kynges moder and many other great estates, both lordez and ladyes richely besene, came forwarde to the coronacion. And at ther commyng fourth from Grenewiche by water[392] ther was **[f. 35]** attendyng upon her ther the maire, shriffes and aldremen of the citie, and dyvers and many worshipfull comeners chosene oute of every crafte[393] in ther lyveres, in barges fresshely furnysshede with baners and stremers of silk, richely besen with the armes and bagges of ther craftes; and in especiall a barge called the 'bachelers barge', garnysshed and apparielede passing alother, wherin was[394] ordeynede a great red dragon spowting flamys of fyer[395] into Temmys; and many other gentil-

[389] Preceded by the cancellation of –a.
[390] 4 Nov. 1487.
[391] 23 Nov. 1487.
[392] In contrast to her predecessors, Elizabeth of York made the traditional journey to the Tower of London by barge along the Thames in the company of vessels manned by civic dignitaries and representatives of the London guilds. This is one of the earliest known records of pageantry on the Thames, although no information survives as to the devices used. These journeys varied in length and provided the occasion 'for shaping images of ideal queenship appropriate to the individual woman': Laynesmith, *Last Medieval Queens*, pp. 82, 90. Cf. the description of Margaret of Anjou's journey to the Tower in Kingsford, *Chronicles*, p. 156; Flenley, *Six Town Chronicles*, p. 119; Brie,*The Brut*, ii, pp. 488–9. The departure from tradition in 1487 may have been intended to emphasise Elizabeth of York's part in a new dynasty and to distance her from the old dynasty, in which lay her claim to be queen regnant; the presence of the king's mother reinforced this process: Laynesmith, *Last Medieval Queens*, p. 89. Some idea of the immense organisation required for this event may be seen in Anglo, *Spectacle*, p. 10; E. W. Ives, *Anne Boleyn* (Oxford, 1986), p. 215; Wickham, *Early English Stages*, i, pp. 285–8.
[393] Representatives of the London guilds on specially furnished barges. On the topic of the guilds of London and river pageantry, see G. Unwin, *The Guilds and Companies of London*, 4th edn (London, 1963), esp. 267–92. See also W. C. Hazlitt, *The Livery Companies of the City of London: Their Origin, Character, Development, and Social and Political Importance* (1892; repr. New York, 1969).
[394] –s unclear and seemingly accompanied by a superfluous mark of suspension.
[395] The mechanical fire-breathing red dragon on the bachelors' barge was unprecedented in England and probably like that used for Anne Boleyn's coronation in 1533: *Antiquarian Repertory*, ii, pp. 233–43; Hall, *Union*, 'Henry the viii', fols, 212–217; Anglo, *Spectacle*, pp. 246–61. The reference is to ancient Britain, and could have celebrated Elizabeth of York's genealogy as much as Henry Tudor's: Anglo, *Images*, pp. 41–71; Laynesmith, *Last Medieval Queens*, p. 90.

manly pajantes wele and curiously devysed to do her highnesse sport and pleasur with. And her grace thus roially apparellede and accompanyed, and also furnysshed on every behalf with trumpettes,[396] clarions and other mynstrellyes[397] as apperteignyng and was fitting to her estate royall, comme from Grenewyche afor saide and londed at Towre warff; and so entred[398] into the Towre, wher the kinges hyghnesse welcommede her[399] in suche maner and forme as was to al thastates and other ther being present a very good sight and right joyous and comfortable to be holde. And ther the gentilmen called by the kinges moost honourable lettres to receyve the order[400] of knyghthod were created knyghtes of the bath[401] in maner and fourme as the picture therof made shewethe,[402] whos names with the[403] names [of][404] the esquiers (governours by the kinges appoyntement to attende upon the tyme of ther saide creasocion) bee her after written:

The sone and heir of therle of Devonshir:		{ John Crokker { his brother	
The lord Dudley:	{ Edward Blount { Edward Bensted	Edward Barkley:	{ William Wodall { Thomas Troys
William Gasixyne:	{ Thomas Totost { Jamys Flemmyng	Wylliam Lucy:	{ W. Trevrye { John Bell

[396] 'with trumpettes' was initially joined and then separated.
[397] Error, perhaps a cancellation, between the final –l and –y.
[398] –m cancelled between 'so' and 'entred'.
[399] Possibly a politically-suggestive enactment of an English sovereign welcoming his foreign queen to his kingdom: Laynesmith, *Last Medieval Queens*, p. 90.
[400] 'And ... orders' underlined, possibly in the hand of the scribe or editor.
[401] The creation of knights of the Bath was an integral part of the coronation of both kings and queens. For brief descriptions of the knights' creation, see Sutton and Hammond, *Richard III*, pp. 28–9 and Laynesmith, *Last Medieval Queens*, p. 91. Here, fourteen knights were created, and at the joint coronation of Richard III and Anne Neville, the number was seventeen: Sutton and Hammond, *Richard III*, p. 28. Cf. the 40 and 38 knights created at the coronations of Margaret of Anjou and Elizabeth Woodville respectively: John Benet, *Chronicle for the Years 1400 to 1462*, eds G. L. Harriss and M. A. Harriss, *Camden Miscellany*, 24, Camden Soc., 4th ser., 9 (1972), p. 191; J. Stevenson (ed.), *Letters and Papers Illustrative of the Wars of the English in France during the Reign of Henry the Sixth*, 2 vols, RS, 22 (London, 1861–4), ii, pp. 783–4.
[402] *Writhe's Garter Book* (MS in the possession of the duke of Buccleuch) contains a pictorial record of the form of creating KBs. Wagner, *Heralds of England*, p. 138, suggests the document was created for John Writhe, Garter King of Arms, in connection with either the 1487 creations, described here, or those on the occasion of the knighting of Edward Prince of Wales in 1475. Heraldic notes for the creation of KBs may be found in 'The maner of makynge Knyghtes after ye custome of England in tyme of peace, and at the coronacion, that is to say Knyghtes of the Bathe' in Gairdner (ed.), *Three Fifteenth Century Chronicles*, pp. 106–13
[403] 'whos names with the' underlined, possibly in the hand of the scribe or editor.
[404] Written 'with'.

THE EDITION

Thomas Butteler: { Thomas Laurence Thomas Hungreforde: { Robert Knowles
                 { John Langforth   { ... Karleton

[f. 35v] Guydo Wolstan: { [Nicholas] Audeby
                              { Alexander Oxton

Richard Pemery: { John Fortson
                              { William Watesley

John Shelton: { John Wharff
                              { Pyers Brent

Hugh Loterell: { the[405] serjeunt porter
                              { Thomas Penyngton

Thomas Pultney: { William Trussell
                              { Henry Lisley

Hugh Conwey: { ...[406]
                              { Otewell Butteler

Nicholas Lisley: { William Burges
                              { Robert Gethyn

The Satirday[407] next befor the day of the quenes coronacion her grace being at the Tower of London after dyner was rially apparelde, having about her a kyrtill[408] of white[409] cloth of golde damask[410] and a mantell of the same suete furrede with ermyns, fastened by for her brest with a great lase curiously wrought of golde and silk and riche knoppes of golde at the ende taselled, and her faire yelow her hanging downe[411] pleyne by hynde her bak with a calle of pipes over it. She had a

[405] Followed by a cancellation.
[406] A space is left for the insertion of a name, but no name is given.
[407] 24 Nov. 1487.
[408] Preceded by the cancellation of 'kir'.
[409] –h cancelled between –t and –e.
[410] Cf. the descriptions of the apparel of Queens Margaret of Anjou, Elizabeth Woodville and Anne Neville on the day of the Vigil of their coronations: Brie, *The Brut*, ii, p. 489; Smith, *Elizabeth Wydeville*, p. 17; Sutton and Hammond, *Richard III*, p. 28. White clothing betokened virginity and heavenliness, while its combination with gold, worn only by the high nobility, signified the wealth of the occasion: *The Statues of the Realm*, 2 vols (London, 1810–28), ii, p. 399.
[411] It was customary for queens to wear their hair down in the procession on the eve of the coronation; loose hair was also a symbol of virginity. For discussion of the idea of queens as virgins, an ideal that generally superceded physical reality, see Laynesmith, *Last Medieval Queens*, pp. 93–4; J. L. Chamberlayne, 'Crowns and Virgins: Queen-making during the Wars of the Roses' in K. J. Lewis, N. James Menuge, and K. M. Philips (eds), *Young Medieval Women* (Stroud, 1999), pp. 54–7, 60–3. This is perhaps the only surviving contemporary information for Elizabeth of York's appearance, namely her fair colouring, although she was described by the Venetian ambassador as a very handsome woman: *CSP Venetian*, i, p. 754. Her funeral effigy appears in Chrimes, *Henry VII*, plate 16b.

serkelet of golde⁴¹² richely garnysshed with precious stonys upon her hede; and so emparelede departed from her chambre of astate unto her litter, my lady Cecille, her sister, beryng her trayne and many great astates,⁴¹³ both lordes and ladies, with othre nobles in great nombre, gevyng also ther attendaunce uppon her highnes. And when she was dressed in her saide **[f. 36]** litter, the tymbre werke therof coverde with cloth of golde of damaske and large pelowes of downe covered with lik clothe of golde laide aboute her most roiall persone to susteyne the same, her grace so proceded from the Towre throwgh the citie of London to Westminster, al the stretes ther she shulde passe by clenly dressed and besene with clothes of tappestrye and arras, and some stretes, as Cheepe, hanggede with riche clothes of golde vellvettes and silkes.

And a longe the stretes from the Tower to Powles stode in order al the craftes of London⁴¹⁴ in ther lyvereyes. And also ther was a merveolous sight of people, some in howses and wyndowes and other in stretes, to be holde the sight of the quenes passing thorowgh in her royall apparell, accompanyed and orderde as herafter is shewde. And in dyvers pa[r]tes of the citie were ordeynede wele singing childerne, some arrayde like angelles and other like virgyns, to sing swete songes as her grace passed by. And ther rode nexte byfor the lytter⁴¹⁵ the right high and myghty prince the duc of Bedeforde (great stuarde of England for the tyme being of this feste) and therle of Oxinforde (great chambrelayn), and byfor theym⁴¹⁶ therle of Derby (lorde Stanley, constable of Englande) and therle of Notingham (mershall of Englande), and next byfor theym Garter.⁴¹⁷ And the maire of London and the ij esquiers of honour, that is to say Nicholas Gaynysforde and Verney, welle horsede in gownes of cremesyne velwett, having mantelles of ermyne, roode next byfor theym with ij latkins, bawdrik wise, and on ther hedes hattes of rede clothe of golde ermyns, the bekes **[f. 36v]** forwarde. And then byfor theym roode the duc of Suffolk and other great astates; and byfor theym kynges of armes, heraulds and poursevantes, whiche rode nexte by hynde the newe made knyghtes of the bathe, riding in a suett in ther blewe bacheler gownes in order after ther baynnes. And next byfor the newe⁴¹⁸ made knyghtes roode al oother banerettes, knyghtes and esquiers, wele horsede and richely besene, and some of theyme on merve-

---

⁴¹² See the description of Elizabeth Woodville's jewelled coronet, said to be part of 'thatyre of virgins': Smith, *Elizabeth Wydeville*, p. 17.
⁴¹³ The large number of noble persons in the procession implied their approval and hence affirmation of her husband's sovereignty: Laynesmith, *Last Medieval Queens*, p. 94.
⁴¹⁴ The guild members lining the streets likewise affirmed the compliance of the commonality: Laynesmith, *Last Medieval Queens*, p. 94.
⁴¹⁵ –l written over another letter.
⁴¹⁶ Repeated.
⁴¹⁷ Followed by the cancellation of –b.
⁴¹⁸ Followed by a cancellation.

olous dooing[419] horses. And on every side to make the way for the presse of people thofficers of the mershall, many[420] in nombre, al in rede gownez of a lyverey with tippede staves in ther handes, went on foote.

And over the quenes grace sitting in the litter was borne a cele, a canapye or a palle of clothe of golde with valaunces of the same, richely fringede, upon[421] iiij gilte stavys, alweys susteyned by iiij knyghtes of the body, wherunto were assigned xij suche knyghtes (every to ease other by the way) in forme and place as ensuethe:

Syr Richarde Pole Sir Edwarde Burgh Sir John Saynlowe Sir James Parkar	assignede to bere the canapie fro the Tower to the begynnyng of Mark Lane.
Sir Edwarde Ponynges Sir Antony Browne Sir William Stoner Sir Robert Clifforde	from the begynnyng of Mark Lane unto thende thereof.
Sir Davyd Owen Sir James Blont Sir Richard Hault Sir Nicholus Vaux	to bere from Marke Lane to Grasshechirche.

[f. 37]The forsaide[422] Sir Richard Pole with his iij felowes to ber ayene the saide canapie from Grasshechirche to Seint Peters in Cornylle.
The forsaide Sir Edwarde Ponnynges and his feliship: from Seint Peters in Cornhill to the standerde in the same.
The forsaide Sir David Owen and his felyship: from the standerd in Cornhill to the stokkes.
And then the forsaide Sir Richard Pole, &c: to ber from the stokkes to the great coundite in Chepe.
Sir Edward Ponynges, &c: from the great condit in Chep to the standerde in Chepe.
Sir David Owen, &c: from the standerde in Chepe to the coundit in the same.
Sir Richard Pole, &c: from thens to Powlles chirche yerde.
Sir Edwarde Ponynges, &c: from thens to Ludgate.
Sir David Owen, &c: from[423] thens to the coundit in Flete Strete.

[419] Followed by the cancellation of 'do'.
[420] A superfluous mark of suspension signalling the omission of –er and attached to –n has been cancelled.
[421] Repeated, and then the first 'upon' cancelled.
[422] 'the forsaid' given as catchwords at the foot of fol. 36v.
[423] –o cancelled between –f and –r.

And then Sir Richarde Poole, &c: from thens to Temple Barre.
Sir Edwarde Ponynges, &c: from thens to the Stronde Crosse.
Sir David Owen, &c: from thens to the bishop of Chesters place.
Sir Richard[424] Poole &c: from thens to Charing Crosse.
Sir Edward Ponynges &c: from thens to the mewes.
Sir David Owen[425] &c: from thens to Westminster.

And next folowing the litter by fore the henchemen was led by Sir Roger Cooton, knyght, maister of the quenes horse, the **[f. 37v]** hors of astate sadeld with a womanys sadell of rede clothe of golde tissue (wiche after the opynyon of dyvers herauldes shulde have folowed next after the henxmen); and then vj henxmen riding in sadelles of the sute of the sadell of astate upon faire white palfreys harneshed with cloth of golde garnysshed with white roses and sonnes[426] richely embroderde. And nexte theym folowed ij chares coverde with riche cloth of golde, wele and clenly horsede: in the furst chare satt my lady of Bedeforde and my lady Cecill; in the ijde chare satt the duches of Suffolk, the duches of Norfolk and the countes of Oxinforde. And then folowed vj baronesse – the lady Straunge, lady Gray, lady Lawar, lady Ferres of Chartley, lady Dudley, lady Powes – upon faire palfereys in gownes of cremesyn velwett al in a sute, ther horseharnesse and the sadelles of the same sute that the henxmens horse wer of. And after theym came ij other chares, richely coverede and wele horsede, with the remenant of the quenes ladies and gentil women; and after those chares, the gentilwomen of my lady Bedfordes in a sute; and next theym the gentil women of my lady Cecilles in a nother sute. And so folowing iche other, the gentilwomen of every astate that waytede upon the quene come riding upon goodly palferees wele and richely besene with great beddes and cheynes of golde aboute ther nekes in merveolous great nombre. And the quene thus riolly commyng to Westminster had her voyde, &c.[427]

And on the morne, the day of the coronacion, she was apparelde **[f. 38]** in a kirtil and a mantell[428] of purple velwet furred with ermyns,[429] with a lace afor the

[424] Written over the cancellation of 'Edwarde'.
[425] Preceded by the cancellation of –o.
[426] The white rose and the sun were dynastic emblems of the House of York: the sun had been a favoured device of Edward IV. See Anglo, *Images*, p. 77; *Privy Purse Expenses*, esp. pp. 117, 118, 119, 136, 137, 143, 144, 152. The presence of these emblems on the trappers of the squires' palfreys was not only a symbol of the individuality of Elizabeth of York, but also testament to the growing security and credibility of the new regime in the aftermath of the birth of a prince and the victory at Stoke: Laynesmith, *Last Medieval Queens*, p. 94. See also the marginal note in the *Great Chronicle*, p. 178, suggesting that the trappings which accompanied Margaret of Anjou in procession were embroidered with her name flower.
[427] Refreshments at Westminster Hall, probably in the form of a supper of fish, as appropriate to the vigil of any major liturgical feast: Laynesmith, *Last Medieval Queens*, p. 94; Sutton and Hammond, *Richard III*, p. 34.
[428] –t written over –d.

mantell in her her and a serkelett of golde richely garnysshede with perle and precious stonys. And so apparellede, my lady Cecill bering her trayne, she reme[vede] furthe of Westminster hal and [th]er[430] stode under a cloth of astate unto the tyme the procession[431] was orderde, from the[432] whiche place to the pulpit in Westminster chirche she wentt upon[433] new ray clothe. And al the day from thens forth the bar[o]ns[434] of the v portes[435] bare the canapie according to ther privileges. And the order of the procession was as ensueth: furst esquiers proceded and knyghtes folowing theym; and after theym went the new made knyghtes wele besene in dyvers silkes, every man as hym best likede after his degre; and after theym the barons and other estates in order as they wer, the heraldes on every side the procession and sergeauntes of armes to make rome; then folowed abbottes; and next theym bisshops in pontificalibus to the nombre of xv bisshops (besyde abbottes), wherof the bisshop of ... bare Seint Edwardes chales, the bisshop of Norwiche bare the patent; byfor whiche prelates went the monkes of Westminster al in albes, and the kinges chapell folowing theym; and next the queue of all the bisshops went tharchebissop of York, except the bisshop of Wynchester and the bisshop of Ely, whiche went on ether hande the quene undre the canapie to susteyne her grace; and after tharchebissop of Yorke was Garter King of Armes and the maire of London next byfor the counstable and mershall, befor **[f. 38v]** rehersede; and next

---

[429] Cf. the descriptions of the purple apparel of Queens Elizabeth Woodville and Anne Neville on the day of their coronations: Smith, *Elizabeth Wydeville*, p. 14; Sutton and Hammond, *Richard III*, p. 276. Under the richly garnished circlet, the queen would have worn her hair down once again.

[430] Written 'ster'.

[431] Regardless of whether a queen was crowned alone or with the king, the initial stages of the ceremony remained the same: from Westminster Hall she was escorted to the Abbey by a procession of clerics bearing the coronation regalia; she walked in stockinged feet along a carpet rolled out for the occasion. See Laynesmith, *Last Medieval Queens*, p. 98. On this occasion Elizabeth's younger sister Cecily, third daughter of Edward IV and wife of John Viscount Welles, bore the queen's train.

[432] Joined and then separated.

[433] Actually written 'uupon'.

[434] The scribe evidently started to write 'banerets'.

[435] See the petition of the barons of the Cinque Ports to carry the canopy over the queen on the way to the Abbey, above, pp. 124–5; cf. their petition to Richard III in 1483 in Sutton and Hammond, *Richard III*, p. 195. A history of the Cinque Ports and the coronation service, and a note on the importance of their corporate records, may be found in the same, pp. 190–1 and in F. Hull (ed.), *A Calendar of the White and Black Books of the Cinque Ports 1432–1955*, HMSO (1966), introd., esp. sections ii–iii, vii, xiii, xv. For an idea of their maritime activities see N. A. M. Rodger, 'The Naval Service of the Cinque Ports', *EHR*, 111 (1996), pp. 636–51. See also Round, *King's Serjeants*, pp. 328–37 and K. M. E. Murray, *Constitutional History of the Cinque Ports* (Manchester, 1935), pp. 19–21, 91, 140–3.

unto theym therle of Aroundell bering[436] the virge of iverye with a dove in the tope; and after hym the duc of Suffolk bering the septre;[437] then therle of Oxinforde, great chambrelayn,[438] in his parliament roobees, having in his hand the staff of his office;[439] and the duc of Bedforde barhedede in the roobes of astate bering a riche corowne of golde;[440] then folowed the quene apparelde as is afor rehersede; and next her my lady Cecill, whiche bar her trayne; and next her folowing the duchesse of Bedeforde and other duchesse and comttesse apparelled in mantelles and sircootes of scarlet, furred and powderde,[441] the duchesse having on [t]her hedes coronalles of golde richely garnysshed with perle and precious stones, and the countesse on [t]her hede[s] had serkelettes of golde in like wise garnysshed, as dooth apper in the bok of picture therof made. But the more pitie ther was so hoge a people inordynatly presing to cut the ray cloth that the quenes grace yode upon, that in the prece certeyne persones wer slayne[442] and the order of the ladies folowing the quene was broken and disterbled.

---

[436] Preceded by the cancellation of 'byfor the counstable'. See the earl of Arundel's petition to perform the office of chief butler, above, p. 127, for which office he carried the 'virge of iverye with a dove in the tope'. Arundel had been chief butler at the coronations of Elizabeth Woodville and Henry VII, and perhaps also at that of Richard III: Round, *King's Serjeants*, pp. 146–65; Smith, *Elizabeth Wydeville*, p. 14; S. Anglo, 'The Foundation of the Tudor Dynasty: The Coronation and Marriage of Henry VII', *Guildhall Miscellany*, 2 (1960), p. 9; Sutton and Hammond, *Richard III*, p. 250. For further notes on the chief butler and his duties see Sutton and Hammond, *Richard III*, pp. 27, 44, 45, 447.

[437] See the duke of Suffolk's petition to carry the sceptre of ivory, as he had at Elizabeth Woodville's coronation, above, p. 123. Cf. the statement by the author of the account of Elizabeth Woodville's coronation that the duke of Suffolk carried the 'septor of ye Reaume', probably an error based on the confusion of the ceremonies for king and queen: Smith, *Elizabeth Wydeville*, p. 15; Laynesmith, *Last Medieval Queens*, p. 105.

[438] A hand marker in the left margin points to 'great camberlayn'.

[439] See the earl of Oxford's petition to be 'queen's chamberlain' on the day of her coronation, above, pp. 122–3. For the coronation duties of the Lord Great Chamberlain, an office filled at the coronation of Richard III by the duke of Buckingham, see Sutton and Hammond, *Richard III*, esp. pp. 246–7.

[440] See the commission issued to the duke of Bedford, above, pp. 121–2. As well as presiding over the court of claims, the high steward had coronation duties that included carrying the crown before the king or queen in the procession to the abbey and nominal supervision over the table service at the banquet. Bedford also fulfilled these duties at the coronation of Henry VII: A. Taylor, *The Glory of Regality* (London, 1820), p. 108; Round, *King's Serjeants*, p. 74; *CPR*, 1476–85, p. 360; Legg, *Coronation Records*, p. 227.

[441] 'et' cancelled before 'and'.

[442] See Bodl., MS. Rawlinson 146, fol. 161, and also the account of the collapse of a scaffold laden with spectators inside the church at the coronation of Henry VII in BL, MS. Eg. 985, fols 1–10.

And the quenes grace thus comyng forth, when she came to the entre of the west dore of the chirche of Westminster[443] ther was saide by the ... this orison:[444] *Omnipotens sempiterne Deus*.[445] And that doon she precedede thorough the quer into the pulpit, wherin was a sege royall dressed with[446] cloth of golde and cusshins accordingly. And tharchebisshop of Canterbury, ther being present and revested as apperteyneth to the selebracion of the masse, receyved the quene commyng from her royall sege with the lordez bering her corowne, septer and rodde, and the bisshops susteynyng her as is above saide. And the greces byfor the high auter wer honourably dressed and arrayed with carpettes and cusshins of astate, where-upon the quene lay prostrate[447] afor the arche bisshop whiles he saide over her this orison: *Deus qui solus habes*,[448] &c. And that doon **[f. 39]** she aros and kneled, and my lady ... toke her kerchef from her hede and tharchebysshop opond her brest and anoyntede her[449] ij tymys: furst in the former parte of her hede, and sec-

---

[443] What follows is a reasonably full account of the religious service. Although the ritual was not under the heralds' jurisdiction, the description is perhaps derived from a combination of eye-witness experience and the records of the chapel royal. A synoptical table of coronation service, as performed at the double coronation of Richard III and Anne Neville in 1483, is included in Sutton and Hammond, *Richard III*, pp. 207–12; see esp. pp. 209–10 for the queen's anointing and crowning.

[444] No identity is given for the prelate who said the *Omnipotens sempiterne Deus*.

[445] 'Omnipotens sempiterne Deus' underlined, possibly in the hand of the scribe or editor. This orison, commencing 'Almighty and eternal God' was uttered on the queen's arrival at the church door, and contains the only reference to childbearing in the ceremony; but it was as a woman and not as an anointed queen that her fertility was prayed for. This contrasts with the explicit connection between right of the king's children to rule and the king's anointing: Laynesmith, *Last Medieval Queens*, p. 99; Legg, *Coronation Records*, p. 109. See also J. C. Parsons, 'Ritual and Symbol in the English Medieval Queenship to 1500', in L. O. Fradenburg (ed.), *Women and Sovereignty* (Edinburgh, 1992), p. 62 and Laynesmith, *Last Medieval Queens*, p. 104.

[446] Followed by a cancellation.

[447] A gesture of humility, as the archbishop recites the prayer beginning *Deus qui solus habes immortalitatem* ('God who alone has immortality'), exalting the humble and meek and comparing the queen with the Old Testament heroine Queen Esther, whose humility enabled her to save the Israelites: Legg, *Coronation Records*, pp. 87, 110; Laynesmith, *Last Medieval* Queens, p. 104. Cf. the 'grovelynge' and other gestures of humility performed by Richard III and Anne Neville at their joint coronation in 1483: Sutton and Hammond, *Richard III*, pp. 219, 221, 256.

[448] 'Deus ... habes' underlined, possibly in the hand of the scribe or editor.

[449] The anointing placed the queen in a quasi-sacerdotal role: Laynesmith, *Last Medieval Queens*, p. 99. She was anointed on the forehead rather than the crown of the head like kings and priests, but like them wore a coif to protect the holy oil; she was also anointed on the breast, for which she wore a special laced dress: Sutton and Hammond, *Richard III*, pp. 224, 229; Laynesmith, *Last Medieval Queens*, p. 99. Cf. the anointing of kings in Sutton and Hammond, *Richard III*, pp. 221–2. See the statement

ondly in her breste afor, sayng thies wordes: *In nomine patris et filii, &c. prosit tibi hec unctio*, with this orison: *Omnipotens sempiterne Deus*.[450] And that doon the said lady closed her brest, and folowingly the saide archebisshop blessed her ring, seing this orison: *Creator*,[451] and cast holy water upon it and then put this same ring on [the][452] iiij° finger of the quenes right hande, saing theyes wordes: *Accipe annulum*,[453] and then seid *Dominus vobiscum*[454] with this collet: *Deus cuius*, &c.[455] And then after the said archebisshop blessed the quenes corone, seing: *Oremus Deus tuorum*.[456] And that doon he sett the corowne[457] uppon her hede, wherupon was a coyff[458] put by my seid lady for the conservacion of the holy uncion[459] (whiche is afterwarde to be delyverde unto the saide archebisshop), seing theys wordes: *Officium nostrum*,[460] &c. And then he delyverde unto the quene a septer in her right hande and a rodde[461] in her left hande, saing this ori-

---

in the *Ryalle Book* that a queen should also be anointed on the back: *Antiquarian Repertory*, i, p. 303. Laynesmith, *Last Medieval Queens*, p. 100, n. 127, believes this is an error based on the king's anointing.

[450] 'Omnipotens sempiterne Deus' underlined, possibly in the hand of the scribe or editor.

[451] 'Creator' underlined, possibly in the hand of the scribe or editor.

[452] Written 'her'.

[453] 'Accipe annulum' underlined, possibly in the hand of the scribe or editor. Commencing, 'Receive the ring (of faith)', this orison denotes the pact or covenant between the queen and God that she might eschew all infection of heresy and bring barbarous nations to the truth: Legg, *Coronation Records*, p. 110. The exhortation to convert barbarians had originated in the early days of Christianity, when Christian queens had been integral to the spreading of the faith among their husbands' subjects: Laynesmith, *Last Medieval Queens*, p. 103.

[454] 'Dominus vobiscum' underlined, possibly in the hand of the scribe or editor.

[455] 'Deus cuius &c.' underlined, possibly in the hand of the scribe or editor.

[456] 'Oremus Deus tuorum' underlined, possibly in the hand of the scribe or editor.

[457] The receipt of the crown was accompanied by an injunction to seek wisdom and virtue and, ultimately, a godly death: Laynesmith, *Last Medieval Queens*, p. 103.

[458] For the protection of the unction, as also worn by kings at their coronations.

[459] The herald does not specify whether holy oil or chrism (oil and balsam) were used. See the *Liber Regalis* in Legg, *Coronation Records*, p. lviii, where it is stated that the king should be anointed by chrism and the queen by 'holy oil' at joint coronations, but chrism when crowned alone; the chrism appears to have confirmed the king's authority. The form of the holy unction used for queens is discussed in Laynesmith, *Last Medieval Queens*, pp. 100–2.

[460] 'Officium nostrum' underlined, possibly in the hand of the scribe or editor.

[461] The coronation regalia are described in Legg, *Coronation Records*, introduction, and in Sutton and Hammond, *Richard III*, pp. 228–44, although not all items are relevant to the coronation of a queen. Possibly an ivory rod and gilt sceptre, each topped with a dove, accompanied by a prayer that the queen make good the dignity she has been obtained and establish the glories granted to her by God: Legg, *Coronation Records*,

son: *Omnipotens Domine*. The quene thus corownede was lede by the above saide bisshops up into the sege of her estate, and al the ladies folowing her. And whiles the offratory was in playing at organs, she was ledde corownede from her sege royall by the saide ij bisshops unto the high auter, her septer and roode of golde borne byfor her as is afor saide. And then tharchebisshop turned his face to the quer warde; and after this the quene was as byfor, brought up ageyn to her sege roiall of astate, wher she satt stille. Th[u]s[462] *Agnus Dei*[463] was begone, and after *Per omnia secula seculorum*[464] turned hym to the qwene,[465] blessyng [her] with this orison: *Omnipotens Deus* **[f. 39v]** *carismatum*,[466] &c, wherunto the quene answerde *Amen*.

And in the tyme of singing of *Agnus Dei*[467] pax[468] was brought to the qwene by the bisshop of Worcester, whiche brought; and when the quene had kissed it she descendid and came to the high auter and had a towell holden byfor her by ij bisshops. And ther she lowly inclynyng her self to the grounde seide her *Confiteor*,[469] the prelates seing *Misereatur*, and tharchebisshop the absolucion; and then the quene, sumwhat areysyng hersilf, receyved the blessed sacrament. And thies thinges reverently accomplisshede, the quene retournede to her sette roiall and ther abode til the masse was ended. And the masse doon her grace, accompanyed with prelates and nobles, descended from her sege roiall of astate and went to the high auter, wher the saide archebisshop, arrayde in pontificalibus as he saide masse, with all the mynisters[470] of the auter[471] byfore hym, went byfor the auter of

---

p. 268. However, there is also evidence that when Anne Neville was crowned with Richard III she carried only one septre or rod with a dove and another without; the inference is that the queen's regalia increasingly resembled that attributed to the king in the *Liber Regalis*, viz. a rod with a dove and a sceptre with a cross (although his were both gold): Sutton and Hammond, *Richard III*, pp. 276, 278–9; Laynesmith, *Last Medieval Queens*, p. 106; Legg, *Coronation Records*, p. 121. Cf. the *Liber Regalis* which specifies a dove on both of the queen's rods. Further discussion of the rods and sceptres used for 15th-century kings and queens, and contemporary confusion over the same, may be found in Laynesmith, *Last Medieval Queens*, pp. 106–7.

[462] Written 'this'.
[463] 'Agnus Dei' underlined, possibly in the hand of the scribe or editor.
[464] 'Per omnia secula seculorum' underlined, possibly in the hand of the scribe or editor.
[465] –w cancelled between 'the' and 'quene'.
[466] 'Omnipotens Deus carismate' underlined, possibly in the hand of the scribe or editor.
[467] 'Agnus Dei' underlined, possibly in the hand of the scribe or editor.
[468] A tablet decorated with a sacred image, such as the Crucifixion, and ceremonially kissed by participants at mass. See below, p. 156, where the king and queen are the only two to perform this devotion at matins on St George's Day, 1488.
[469] 'Confiteor' underlined, possibly in the hand of the scribe or editor.
[470] Preceded by the cancellation of 'mynstrell'.
[471] Preceded by the cancellation of 'same'.

the shryne of Seint Edwarde the king; and after hym folowed al other prelates and lordes. And [at] the quenes grace commyng byfor the saide auter of the shryne, the said archebisshop toke the corowne from her hede and sett [it] upon the same auter.

And in the forsaide chirche, on the right side betwixt the pulpit and the high auter, was ordeynede a goodlye stage coverde and welebesene with clothes of arras and wele latizede, wherin was the kinges grace,[472] my lady his moder and a goodly sight of ladies and gentilwomen attending upon her, as my lady Margaret Pole, doughter to the duc of Claraunce, and many othre.

And when the dyvyne service was thus solemply ended and al doon, the retourne of the quene to her paloys with all her goodly and royall company was after the maner as ensueth: **[f. 40]** furst esquiers, knyghtes, and then the barons of the eschequer and jugges, officers of armes, and then al thabbottes and bis-shops in the cappis or robes of parliament al on the right side; and the barons in ther roobes and therles in ther roobes of astate, saving the great chambrelayn whiche was in his parliament robees,[473] went al on the lefte side; and after theym went ner the presence the duces and Garter, and the maire of London next byfor the constable and mershall. And when the quene was come into the hall, she went into the white hall, and so to her chambre.[474] And in the meane tyme:[475] the high and myghty prince duc of Bedforde, in a gowne of clothe of golde richely furrede, on a goodly courser richely trapped with a trapper embroderde with red roses [and] a border of golde smythes werk[476] enraumpisshede with rede dragons,[477] a

---

[472] The presence of the king is unusual and in this case remained discreet; contemporary records of the coronations of Catherine de Valois, Margaret of Anjou and Elizabeth Woodville make no reference to the king. Drawing on Kantorowicz's discussion of the royal funeral and the role of the funeral effigy, Laynesmith suggests that the 15th-century queen, at the moment of her anointing with the chrism that confirmed the king' authority, was the sole representative of the king's public body; the king could therefore not be present as the person of royal dignity: E. H. Kantorowicz, *The King's Two Bodies: A Study in Medieval Politcial Theology* (Princeton, 1957), p. 240; Laynesmith, *Last Medieval Queens*, p. 102.

[473] A hand marker in the right margin points to 'robees'.

[474] Preceded by the cancellation of a majascule –S.

[475] In the absence of the queen before the commencement of the coronation banquet, lords on richly dressed horses rode about Westminster Hall, the principal banquet setting, to push back the crowds. See the description of the coronation of Richard III and Anne Neville in Sutton and Hammond, *Richard III*, p. 279. This also reinforced the chivalric atmosphere of the secular celebrations. Here the duke of Bedford was principal among the lords, who also included the king's step-father, the earl of Derby, and the earl of Nottingham. Each carried staves symbolic of the offices they performed at the coronation.

[476] 'border' and 'of' intially joined and then separated with a marker.

[477] The red rose and dragon were emblems of the House of Tudor, the latter being symbolic of the red dragon prophecy: Anglo, *Images*, p. 80. The red rose was also relevant

longe white rodde in his hande, a riche cheyne aboute his nek; and therle of Derbye,[478] lorde Standeley and constable of England, also in a riche gowne furred with sables, a merveolus riche cheyne of golde many fowldes aboute his neke, also his courser richely trappede and enarmede (that is to say qarterly golde: in the furst quarter a lyon gowles, having a mannes hede in a bycokett of silver; and in the ijde a lyon of sable. And this trapper was right curiously wrought with the nedell, for the mannes visage in the bicokett shewde veryly wel favrourede),[479] and he had his staff of office in his hande. And therle of Notingham roode also on a nothre cowreser richely trapped in a trapper of cloth of golde bordered with …[480] and his gilte staff of his offices in his hand. Thus theys iij great estates roode aboute the hall. And in especiall therle marshall had great plenty of his servantes with tipped staves to voyde the people, for the preyse was so great.

And after that[481] **[f. 40v]** the quene was retourned and had wasshede,[482] tharchebisshop[483] of Canterbury saide grace. Dame Kateryn Gray and Maystres Dittoun wente undre the table, wher the satt on ether side the quenes fetee al the dyner tyme. Tharchebisshop of Canterbury satt at the tables ende on the right hande. The duches of Bedeforde and my lady Cecill, the quenes sister, satt at the other ende of the lifte hande. And the countesse off Oxinforde and the countesse of Ryvers knelede on ether side the quene, and at certeyne tymys helde a kerchaef byfor her grace. And in the ende of the hall, on high byfor the wyndow, the[r] was made a stage for the trumpettes and mynstrelles (whiche when the furste course was sett forwarde by gan to blowe), the sergeauntes of armes byfor theym, the controller and tresorer, and then the iij estates on horsbak afor rehersede. And the lorde fitz Water, sewer,[484] in his surcott with tabarde sleves and a hode aboughte his nek, and his towell above all, sewde the masses[485] as ensueth, al borne by

---

to the queen, who was now very much a part of the Tudor dynasty. See also below, p. 174, where the red roses were used to adorn a canopy in the queen's lying-in chamber in 1489.

[478] Followed by a cancellation.
[479] Sic.
[480] The scribe has left the space blank.
[481] 'after that' repeated.
[482] After the long anointing and crowning, the queen returned to her own chambers to wash, change her clothes and, presumably, to rest before the great feast; it was during this interval that Bedford, Derby and Nottingham cleared the hall.
[483] –p lost in the binding.
[484] Preceded by the cancellation of –w.
[485] The feast itself was a heavily-spiced spread of game meats, poultry, wildfowl, fish and eel, each stewed, mashed, roasted, broiled or baked: an extravagant profusion of 48 dishes in two courses. Numerous works, some of them very old indeed, are of value for fifteenth-century recipes, glossaries, etc: F. J. Funrivall (ed.), *Early English Meals and Manners* EETS, o.s. 32 (London, 1868); T. Austin (ed.), *Two Fifteenth-Century Cookery Books*, EETS, o.s., 91 (London, 1888); M. J. Webb (ed.), *Early English Recipes*

knyghtes:[486]

Furst a warner[487] byfor the course	Conys of high grece
Sheldes of brawne in armour	Moten roiall richely garnysshed
Frumetye with veneson	Valance bake
Bruet riche	Custarde royall
Hart powderd graunt chare	Tarte poleyn
Fesaunt in traind royall	Leyse damask
Swan with chawdron	Fruter synaper
Capons of high grece	Fruter formage
Lamprey in[488] galantyne	A soteltie with writing of balades,
Crane with cretney	whiche as yet I have not
Pik in latymer sawce	
Herounsew with his signe	
Carpe in fowle	
Kid reversed	
Perche in jeloy deperte	

And in like forme as many disshes also coverde was servede to the archebisshop of Canterbury, savyng **[f. 41]** they were bore by esquyers, or shulde have ben and in substance wer. Also at[489] the table on the right hande of the hall next to the walle begane the barons of the v portes, and byneith theym the benchers of the

---

(Cambridge, 1937); R. Napier, *A Noble Boke of Cookry* (London, 1882); Samuel Pegge, *The Forme of Cury* (London, 1780); R. Warner, *Antiquitates Culinariae: Tracts on Culinary Affairs of the Old English* (London, 1791). Secondary sources include W. E. Mead, *The English Medieval Feast* (London, 1931); A. Sim, *Food and Feast in Medieval England* (Stroud, 1997); A. Sim, *Food and Feast in Tudor England* (Stroud, 1997); Schramm, *History*, pp. 9, 90–1. The importance of the coronation banquet as a means of display and political expression is discussed in Sutton and Hammond, *Richard III*, pp. 282–88 and J. Burden, 'The Practice of Power: Rituals of Royal Succession in Late Medieval England, c.1327 to c.1485' (unpublished D.Phil thesis, York, 1999), 'Ritual Banqueting'. It is possible that as many as 3000 people were fed at Westminster that day. Cf. the descriptions of coronation feasts, number of courses and dishes, and the subtleties (see below, n. 487) in Sutton and Hammond, *Richard III*, pp. 283–9. Here the banquet reinforced the widespread acceptance of the queen's role: Laynesmith, *Last Medieval Queens*, p. 109.

[486] The newly made KBs were expected to carry the dishes served by specially appointed nobles.

[487] Subtleties were elaborate confections of sugar, pastry, wax, paint and paper, usually symbolic or emblematic; the 'warner' was the subtlety that preceded the banquet. Unfortunately the subjects of the subtleties for Elizabeth of York's coronation are not known. Cf. subtleties for coronations of Henry V and Henry VI in Sutton and Hammond, *Richard III*, pp. 283–4.

[488] Followed by the cancellation of lo–.

[489] Interlineated above.

THE EDITION

chauncery.[490] And at the table next the walle on the lefte hande next the cupborde satt the[491] mare of London and his brethern, and by neith theym satt other merchauntes and citezins.[492] And at the table on the right side the hall in the myddes satt the bisshops and abbottes al on oon side, and on the other side sat the lordes temperall, and byneith theym the jugges, barons of the eschequer, knyghtes and great nombre of noble people. And at the table on the lifte side satt the duchesse, countesse, baronesse, banerettes wiffes and bachelers wyffes, and other noble gentilwomen, al on oon side to the nombre ner hand of iiij^{xx}. Also ther was made a goodly stage[493] oute of a wyndow on the lift side of the hall, richely besene with clothes of arras and wele latysede, for the king and the high and myghty princesse his moder might prively at ther pleasur see that noble feste and service. And at the right ende of the table ther was ordeynede a stage for kinges of armes, heraulde[s] and purservantes, whiche kinges of armes stode corownede and behelde the noble service the wise that they cowde, having dyvers straungers with theym.[494] And when the hall was honourably servede thorow, the trumpettes blew to the ijde course, whiche was accompanyede as the furste course:

A warner byfor the course	Bittowre[495]
Joly ipocras	Fesawnte
Mamene with lozenges of golde	Browes
Pekok in hakell	Egretes in beowetye
[fol. 41v] Cokkes	Venesone in past royall
Partricche	Quince baked
Sturgyn fresshe fenell	Marche payne[496] royall
Plovers	A colde bake mete florisshede
Rabett sowker	Leche ciprus
Seyle in fenyn enterly served richely armes	Leche ruby
Red Shankkes	Fruter augeo
Snytes	Fruter mounteyne
Quayles	Castelles of jely in

[490] A minor error precedes –y, perhaps a superfluous letter.
[491] A minor cancellation adjoins –e.
[492] Apart from the members of the nobility, carefully arranged according to rank and gender, citizens of London were also included in the coronation feasts; they typically received fewer courses and different dishes from the nobility.
[493] The king was again not publicly present for the celebrations in honour of his queen. See explanation above, p. 140, n. 472.
[494] The sentence actually reads: 'ther was ordeynede a stage for kinges of armes *stoode corownede*, herauld[s] and purservantes, whiche kinges of armes stode corownede ...' (my italics). The insertion of 'stoode corownede', between 'armes' and 'heraulds' is almost certainly an error of transcription, probably caused by eyeskip.
[495] Preceded by a cancellation.
[496] A second –y in payne has been cancelled.

Larkes ingraylede	temple wise made
Creves de eu deuce	A soteltie

And as the high borde was servede,[497] Garter King of Armes with othre kinges of armes, herauldes and purservantes did ther obeysaunce, and at the presence in the name of al the officers yave the quene[498] thankinges as foloweth, seiyng: "Right high and myghty prince, moost noble and excellent princesse, moost christen quene,[499] and al our most drad and souveraigne liege ladye, we the officers of armes and servantes to al nobles beseche almyghty Gode to thank you for the great and habundaunt largesse whiche your grace hathe geven us in the honour of your most honourable and right wise coronacion, and to send your grace to liff in honour and vertue." And that doon she was criede as ensuethe in v places of the hall, by the saide Garter, largesses iij tymes: "de la treshault, trespuissaunt, tresexcellent princes, la tres noble reigne dEngleter et de Fraunce et dame dIrland, largesse." And at every ijde crye as ensueth, largesse as a for: "de la treshault,[500] trespuissant, tresexcellent princesse, [la tres][501] crestien roigne de Fraunce et dEngleter et dame dIrland." That doon, the officers went to the cupborde to therle of Aroundell, the **[f. 42]** great botteler, and drank. Then playde divers mynstrelles both of the kinges and[502] the quenes mynstrelles, and after theym the mynstrelles of other astates.

Then the quene was served of frute and wafers. And then Sir John Turburvile, knyght mershall, drew the surnap. And then the torches hanging in the hall [were] lightede. And when the quene was up and had wasshed, and grace seide, came in the voyde. The[n] blew the trumpettes, and the maire of London, Sir William Horne, servede the quene[503] of ypocras after the spices and toke the coppe of golde coverde for his fee. And then the qwene departede with Goddes blessyng, and to the rejoysing of many a trwe Englisshemannes hert.

And on the morow[504] the king harde masse in Seint Stephins chapell, and the quene [and] my lady the kinges moder, also greatly and nobly accompanyede with

[497] Followed by the cancellation of 'the kynges mynstrelles playde a songe by for the quene'.
[498] Preceded by the cancellation of 'quew'.
[499] Preceded by the cancellation of 'king'. This statement emphasises the queen's generosity and her role as a good 'lord'. The address used here was probably closely based on that for a king: Laynesmith, *Last Medieval Queens*, p. 109.
[500] Preceded by a cancellation.
[501] The scribe has actually written 'de late hault ...', an error presumably resulting from rapid copying.
[502] 'divers ... and' interlineated above.
[503] The lord mayor served the queen (or king) with wine in a golden cup at the end of the banquet in a gesture which Laynsmith suggests mimicked the culmination of the abbey ritual in the mass: Laynesmith, *Last Medieval Queens*, p. 109.
[504] A tournament in Westminster sanctuary usually followed the coronation and, according to the *Ryalle Book*, should have lasted for three days: *Antiquarian Repertory*, i, p.

THE EDITION

duchesse, countesse, vicountesse, baronesse and other ladies and gentelwomen to the nombre of iiij^{xx} largly. And that [day] the quene kepte her astate in the parlyament chambre, and my lady the kinges moder satt on her right hande,[505] and my lady of Bedeforde and my lady Cecill satt at the bordez ende on the left hande. And at the side table in the same chambre satt the duchesse of Suffolk, the duchesse of Norfolk, the countesse of Oxinforde, the countesse of Wiltshir, the countesse of Ryvers, the countesse of Notingham, my lady Margaret Pole, my lady Straunge, my lady Gray, my lady La Warre, my lady Dudeley, my lady Mountjoy, and many other ladies whos names I have in order as: Dame Kateryn Grey,[506] Dame Kateryn Vaux, Dame El[i]zabeth Gilforde, Dame Elizabeth Wynkfylde and Dame Elysabeth Longvyll. And at the other side table satt the lady Ferres of Chartley, **[f. 42v]** my lady Bray, and dyvers other ladyes and gentilwomen. And Geynsford drue the surnap and made the quene the hole astate, and my lady the kinges moder half astate, and terss[507] also.

And after dyner the quene and the ladyes dawnsede; and on the morne she remevede to Grenewiche for the great besynesse of the parlyament, elles the fest[508] had dured lenger. Amen.

Thies bee the names[509] of the astates, lordes, lad[i]es and knyghtes that wer at the coronacion of quene Elizabeth, eldest dowghter of the full noble memoury of king Edwarde the iiijth:

tharchebisshop of Canterbury	Thabbottes:[510]
(then chaunceller of England)	thabbot of Westminster
tharchebisshop of York	thabbot of Seint Austeyns
the bisshop of Wynchester	of Canterbury
the bisshop of London	thabbot of Abenden
the bisshop of Norwiche	thabbot of Seynt Albens

304; Brie, *The Brut*, ii, p. 489. Elizabeth Woodville's was probably only for one day and Elizabeth of York's may have been postponed. Accounts of expenditure in *Materials*, ii, p. 223, indicate tournaments were held in 1487. See also Sutton and Hammond, *Richard III*, p. 46.

[505] A notable example of the semi-regal honours accorded Lady Margaret Beaufort, of which there are many examples throughout the text. See discussion above, pp. 41–2, and Jones and Underwood, *The King's Mother*, pp. 69–70.

[506] –b cancelled between 'Kateryn' and 'Grey'.

[507] It is difficult to be certain what is meant by this word, but it perhaps refers to Terce, the third of the canonical hours, although the context is odd. The word appears originally to have been written 'tersso' before –o was cancelled. The Leland-Hearne version gives 'Tersse' in italics.

[508] Followed by the cancellation of –a.

[509] The herald presents an extended catalogue of all principal persons present at the coronation, under categories of rank and gender. The list contains some three hundred important names from both sides of the old political divide.

[510] Underlined, possibly in the hand of the scribe or editor.

the bysshop of Chechestre
the bisshop of Ely
the bisshop of Rochester
the bisshop of Seyntas
the bisshop of Harforde
the bisshop of Lyncoln[511]
the bisshop of Worcestre
the bisshop of Seynt Davys
the bisshop of Saresbury
the bisshop of Landaff

[f. 43]

thabbot of Reding
thabbot of Glowcestre
thabbot of Peterborough
thabbot of Cisteter
thabbot of Colchestre
thabbot of Malmesbury
thabbot of Wynchecombe
thabbot of Selby
thabbot of Evesham
thabbot of Waltham
thabbot of Holme or of Seint Benet
thabbot of Thorney
thabbot of Barmesey was mytred (thowgh he wer no lorde of the parliament)

Lordes temperell:[512]
the duc of Bedeforde
the duc of Suffolk
therle of Aroundell
therle of Oxinforde
therle of Northumbreland
therle of Shrewesbury
therle of[513] Essex
therle of Wi[l]tshyre
therle of Ryvers
therle of Huntyngdon
therle of Derby
therle of Notingham
therle of Devonshir
therle of Urmonde
the lorde Edmonde of Suffolk
the vicounte Wellys
the vicounte Lisley
the lorde Straunge
therle of Devonshyrse sone and heire

the lorde Gray
the lorde Burgaveny
the lorde Dudeley
the lord la Warre
the lord Audeley
the lorde fitz Water
the lorde Powes
the lorde Hastinges
the lorde Dynham, trezorer[514]
the lorde Dawbeney
the lorde Storton
the lorde Cobham
the lorde Beauchampe of Powyk
the lorde Grey of Wilton
the lord Dacre of the north
Sir William Stanley, (the lorde chambrelayne)
the lorde fitz Waren
the lorde Morley
the lorde Beauchamp of Seyamant
the lorde Barnes

---

[511] –k cancelled between –n and –c.
[512] Underlined, possibly in the hand of the scribe or editor.
[513] Repeated.
[514] –o is unclear and may equally be –e.

The names of the ladies:
my lady the kinges moder
the duchesse of Bedeforde
the quenes sister, my lady Cecill
the duches of Suffolk
the duchesse of Norfolk
the countesse of Oxinforde
the countesse of Wiltshire
the countesse of Ryvers
the countesse of Notingham

The names of the baronesse:
the lady Straunge
the lady Grey
the lady la Warre

[f. 43v]
the lady Dudeley
the lady Hastynges
the [lady] Ferres
the lady Mountjoy

And at that tyme the substance of al therles of the realme wer wedowers or bachelers, that is to say:

therle of Aroundell, wedower
therle of Notingham, wetower
therle of Westmerlonde, wedower
therle of Essex, bacheler
therle of Wiltshire, bacheler
therle of Huntingdon, wedower
therle of Urmonde, wedower
the vicount Lysley, wedower

The names of the banerettes:

Sir John Cheyny	Sir James Terell
Sir Thomas Abrough	Sir Hugh Hastinges
Sir Richard Tunstall	Sir Thomas Malyvery[515]
Sir Thomas Mongomery	Sir John Savage
Syr Gilbert Talbott	Sir William Evers
Sir John Aroundell	Sir John Everingham
Sir Edwarde Stanley	Sir James Harington
Sir William Stoner	Sir John Grey of Wilton
Syr Thomas Cokesey	Sir James Strangnes

[515] The majascule –M is unclear, perhaps written over an error.

Sir John Fortscue
Sir Edmonde Benyngfelde
Sir James Blount
Sir Richard Crofte
Sir Richard de la Ver
Syr John Mortymer
Sir Walter Harbert

Sir Thomas Grey
Sir Rauff Hastinges
Sir Edmounde Mauntforde
Sir John Counstable of Holdreness
Sir John Melton
Syr John Savell

The names of the knyghtes bachelers:[516]
Sir Robert Willoughby
Sir Christofor Willoughby
Sir William Willoughby
Sir Henry Willoughby
Sir Richard up Thomas
Sir John Morgon
Syr Davy Owen
Sir Charles of Somersett
Sir Edward Ponynges
Sir John Clifforde[517]
Sir Walter Hungerforde
Sir John Turburvyle
Sir Edwarde Aborough

[f. 44] Syr Hugh Persall
Sir Richard Egecombe
Sir Richard Clifforde
Syr John Fogge
Sir William Haut
Sir Thomas Milbourne
Sir William Norres
Sir John Risley
Sir John Alwyn
Sir Robert Poyntes
Sir Roger Lukenore
Syr Henry Heydon
Sir Raynolde Braye
Sir John Verney
Sir James Audeley
Sir George Nevell
Sir Robert Clyfforde

Syr Humfrey Savage
Sir John Beron
Syr Thomas Bourser[518] of Ledes
Sir John Bourser
Sir Thomas Bourser of Barnesse
Syr Roger Dymmoke
Sir William Tyrwitt
Sir Antony Browne
Sir John Wynkfelde
Sir Gilbert Debynham
Sir Richard Haut
Sir Thomas Grey
Sir Nicholas Vaux
Sir Henry Roose
Sir Amyas Pawlett
Sir William Redmyll
Sir Thomas Blount

[516] –s lost in the margin.
[517] Appears to have been written 'Clyifford' or 'Chifford'.
[518] –r written above the cancellation of –gh.

Sir George Opton
Sir Robert of Browghton
Sir John Paston
Sir[519] Richard Pole
Sir Richard fitz Lowys
Syr Gregory Lovell
Sir John Longvyll
Sir Thomas Terell
Sir Roger Bellingham
Sir William Carew
Sir William Vampage
Syr John Devenysshe
Sir John Sabacotes
Syr Thomas Lovell
[f. 44v] Sir John Doon
Sir William Sandys
Syr John Deveres
Syr John Seynlow
Sir William Brandon
Sir Thomas Cornuall
Sir Roger Corbett
Sir John Harley
Sir William Knevett
Sir Richard …
Sir Henry Wentworth
Sir William Sayy
Sir Robert Medelton
Sir John Nevell of Lyversage
Sir Marmaduc Counstable
Sir William Malory
Sir Robert Plompton
Sir John Manyngham
Sir Olyver Manyngham
Sir Robert …
Sir James Lawrence
Sir Randolph Pygott

Sir Robert Cheyny
Sir James Parker
Sir Edwarde Derell
Sir Thomas …
Sir Morres Barkley
Syr John Digby
Syr Thomas …
Sir John Wroughton
Sir Thomas Lynne
Sir Mores Abarow
Sir Thomas Barow
Sir Richard Sakkylde
Sir Henry Ferres

Syr William Lucy
Sir Thomas Hungreforde
Sir Guydo Wolston[520]
Syr Thomas Pomery
Syr Roger Knyfton
Sir John Norbery
Sir Davy William ap[521] Morgon
Sir Thomas Vaughan[522] up Roger
Syr James Rateclyff
Sir Raff Shelton
Sir Hugh Loterell
Sir Thomas Poulteney
Syr Hugh Conway
Syr Nicholas Lissley
Sir William Pyrton
Sir James Lawrence
Sir Thomas fitz William
Sir Robert Walton
Sir Richard …
Sir Edmonde Mountforde[523]
Syr William of Hylton
Sir John Slyveld

---

[519] –ir obscured by an inkblot.
[520] Preceded by the cancellation of 'Wof'.
[521] Written 'vap'.
[522] Preceded by the cancellation of –v.
[523] –de smudged.

Sir Roger Coton
Sir Thomas Bowles
Sir Alexander Baynam
Sir Gervys of Clifton
Syr Edmounde Cornuall
Sir Thomas Manyngton
Syr William Gascon
Syr Thomas Butteler
Syr Edwarde Barkley

Syr Bartholomew de Ryvers
Syr Robert Rateclyff
Syr Henry Boulde
Syr William Yonge
Syr William, cheff jugge
Sir Thomas Bryan
Syr William Hody
Syr Guy Fayrefax

[f. 45] Sir John …
Sir Roger Towneshende
Sir Thomas Twhaytes
Sir William Horne, maire of London
Sir [Thomas] fitz William, recorder of London
Syr Hugh Bryce
Sir Edmond Shawe
Sir Nicholas Bilsdon
Sir Henry Collett
Sir Thomas Brown
Sir William Capell
Sir John Senkell
Sir John Persevall
Syr William Parker
Syr Richard Yorke

Ladyes:
Dame Gascon
Dame Kateryn Grey
Dame Kateryn Vaux
Dame Anne Wynkfelde
Dame Johanna Gilforde
Dame Elizabeth Lovell
Dame Elyzabeth Brandon
Dame El[iz]abethe Longvillde
Dame Margaret Cotton
Dame … Blount
Dame … Blount[524]
Dame Clifforde
Dame Lysley

Gentilwomen:[525]
Mastres Fenys
Maistres Seint John
Maistres Verney
Mastres Zouche
Maystres Denton
Maystresse Geynsforde
Maistresse Crowmer
Maistresse Margery …
Maistres Crofte
Maistres Breton
Maistres Scrope
Maystresse Ovedale

[524] The Scribe has listed two Blount ladies, but does not give the Christian name of either.
[525] Underlined, possibly in the hand of the scribe or editor.

THE EDITION

[526][f. 45v] The kyng oure souveraygne lorde, the same yere of his noble reigne, incontynently after the parliament[527] removed from Westminster unto the maner of Grenewiche, wher he kepte his Cristemesse[528] ful honourably as ensueth: furst on Cristemasse even our saide souveraigne lorde the king went to masse of the vygill[529] in a riche gowne of purple velwett furred with sables, nobly accompanyed with dyvers great estates, as shalbe shewde hereafter; and in like wise to evenson[g]e, savyng he had his officers of armes byfor hym. The reverende fader in God the lorde John[530] Fox did the dyvyne servyce that evensong, and on the morow also. The king sat at dyner also on Cristemesseday in the great chambre nexte the galary,[531] and the quene and my lady the kinges moder with the ladies in the quenes chambre.

And on Neweyeres day[532] the king, being in a riche gowne, dynede in his chambre and yave to his officers[533] of armes vj li. of his largesse, wher he was cryed in his style accustumede. Also the quene yave to the same officers xl s. and she was cried in her style. Item, my lady the kynges moder yave xx s. She was criede largesse iiij tymes: "de hault, puissaunt et excellent princesse, la mer du roy notre seigneur, countesse de Richemonde et de Derbye, largesse." Item, the duc of Bedforde yave xl s. [and][534] he was cryede largesse: "de hault et puyssaunt prince, frere et uncle des roys, duc de Bedeforde et counte de Penbroke, [largesse]." Item, my lady his [wife] gave xiij s. iiij d. and she was criede larges: "de hault et puissaunt

---

[526] At the top of fol. 45v in the same 17th-century hand as above, p. 105, n. 231: 'The feast of Christmas in the third year of Hen. 7.'.

[527] The second parliament, which opened on 9 Nov. 1487 and dissolved on 23 Feb. 1488. It commenced with a discourse from the Chancellor, Archbishop Morton, on the evils of discord, and proceeded through the attainder of the earl of Lincoln, the punishment of men from both sides (including many of the king's own supporters), and the introduction of two fifteenths and tenths, partly in lieu of the uncollected balance of the fifteenth and tenth granted to Richard III in 1484: Bennett, *Lambert Simnel*, p. 109; Chrimes, *Henry VII*, p. 197; *RP*, vi, pp. 400–1. It was this taxation which indirectly contributed to the rising of 1489.

[528] Cf. the descriptions of Christmas 1486, 1488 and 1489 on pp. 107, 164–5 and 182–3. Although the coronation of Elizabeth of York was followed by a hiatus in state ceremonials and public or semi-public spectacles, the annual festivites and weekly routine of ceremony at court, governed by the liturgical calendar, continued apace: see for example Fiona Kisby, '"When the King Goeth a Procession": Chapel Ceremonies and Services, the Ritual Year, and Religious Reforms at the Early Tudor Court, 1485–1437', *JBS*, 40.1 (January, 2001), pp. 44–75 and below, pp. 151–60, 164–5.

[529] 'the' interlineated above, in the form of þe.

[530] An error for 'Richard'.

[531] Preceded by the cancellation of –l.

[532] See Wagner, *Heralds*, p. 94 for a description of the heralds' observance of New Year customs.

[533] –rs rendered unclear by an inkblot.

[534] Written 'et'.

princesse, duchesse de Bedeforde et de Bokingham, countesse de Penbrok, Stafford, Harford et de Northampton, et dame de Breknok, largesse."[535] **[f. 46]** Item, the reverende fader in God[536] the lorde John[537] Fox, bisshop of Excester, pryvy seale, yave xx s.[538] Item, therle of Aroundell gave x s., and he was criede largesse: "de noble et puissaunt seigneur le counte dAroundell et seigneur de Maltravers, [largess]" Item, therle of Oxinforde yave xx s., and he was cryede largesse: "de noble et puissaunt le counte dOxinforde, marquis de Devlyn, vicount de Bulbik, et seigneur de Scales, graunde chaumbrelayn et admirall dAngleter, largesse." Item, my lady his wyff, xx s., and she[539] was cried largesse: "de noble et puissaunt dame la countesse dOxinforde, marquise de Develyn, vicountesse de Bulbik, et dame de Scales, [largesse]." Item, therle of Derbye yave xx s., and he was cried largesse: "de noble et puissaunt seigneur le beauper de roy notre seigneur, counte de Derbye, seigneur de Stanley et de Man, counstable dEngleter, largesse." Item, therle of Devonshire yave xiij s. and iiij d., and he was cried largesse: "de noble et puissaunt seigneur le counte de Devonshire et seigneur de Couton, largesse." Item, my lorde Welles yave for him and his lady his wiff xx s., and he was cryede largesse: "de noble et puissaunt seigneur, uncle de roy notre seigneur, le[540] vecounte de Wellys, largesse.[541]" Item, Sir William Stanley,[542] the king[es] chambrelayn, yave x s., and he was cryed largesse: "de noble seigneur le chambrelayn de roy notre seigneur, largesse." Item, therle of Urmond gave xx s., and he was cried largesse: "de noble et puissaunt seigneur le counte de Urmonde, seigneur de Rocheforde, chambrelayne de la royne notre souveraigne dame, largesse." Item, the lorde Straunge yave x s. Item, the tresorowre yave vj s. viij d. and the countroller yav[e][543] a corone, wherfor they wer cryede largesse: "dez **[f. 46v]** nobles officers le trezouror et le countroller de tres noble lestell de roy notre seigneur, largesse." Item, the secretary yave vj s. viij d., and he was not criede, for it is not the custume to crye noman of the chirche, nor no lower degre than a vicount withoute it bee the stewarde or the chambrelayn. And al other barons, banerettes, knyghtes and esquieres with ther wiffes wer wont to bee cryede in generall. And that was left this yer, savyng my lorde Straunge, that yave any largesse.

[535] In the left margin in a 17th-century hand: 'Fees given to the officers of Arms at Neweyres [sic] tide'.
[536] 'in God' initially joined and then separated.
[537] An error for 'Richard'.
[538] The statement 'Item, the reverende fader in God ... xx s.' is actually accompanied by the following style: 'Item, largesse de noble princesse la seur de la reigne notre souveraigne dame et vicountesse de Welles'. This is clearly the style of the lady Cecily, sister to the queen. See p. 47 for discussion.
[539] Followed by cancellation of –s.
[540] Inserted above.
[541] Preceded by the cancellation of We–.
[542] A flourish on –n, probably a mark of abreviation, has been cancelled.
[543] Written 'yava'.

Thys Cristemasse ther wer many lordes moo in the courte, some comyng and some goyng, whiche yave no rewardes to the officers of armes, whoo shalbe shewde in the[544] great nombre of the xij day. And on New[ye]res day at nyght ther was a goodly disgysyng, and also this Cristmasse ther wer many and dyvers playes.

On the xijth even[545] the king went to the evensong in his surcott overte with tabert sleves, the cappe of astate on[546] his hede and the hode aboute his showlders in docter wise. And that nyght ther was no lorde in roobes saving the kyng. That feste lorde John Morton, archebisshop of Canterbury, dide the dyvyne servyce.[547] And on the morowe at matens tyme al other astates and barons had ther sircotes overtes with ther hodys, and in the procession tyme they were all in ther roobes of astate; and the king and the quene wer corouned;[548] and my lady the kinges moder had on a riche corounall. The duc of Bedeforde bare the cappe of astate next byfor the king, and therle of Oxinforde, great chambrelayn of England, bar the kinges trayne; therle of Derbye and therle of Notingham went next byfor the cappe of astate, whiche wer on the right hand a litille byfor the swerde; and next byfor the counstable, **[f. 47]** Garter King of Armes; and on his lift hande the kinges secretary and the tresowrer of Englande byfore theyme; and byfor hym the tresowrer and countroller of the kinges house; byfor theym all other officers of armes, herauldes and pourservauntes; and byfor theym carvers and cupeberes in [t]her roobes. And the gentilmen usshers yave ther attendaunce on the chambrelayn, or shulde have[549] doon. The duc of Suffolk folowed next unto the king and accompanyed the lorde Dawbeney embassatours of Fraunce; and the bisshop of Excester accompanyed the prothonatory of Sandovill, and all other erlys and vicountes folowede theym; and then the quene corouned; and my lady the kinges moder, in like mantell and surcott as the quene with a riche corownall on her hede, went aside the quenes half trayne;[550] and Fowler bar on his right arme, cast over his shulder, the trayne of my lady the kinges moder. And then folowde the countes of Oxinforde and the countesse of Ryvers with riche circulettes on ther hedes; and soo al other ladyes and gentilwomen folowed theym; and then the barons, banarettes and gentylwomen folowed theym.

[544] 'shewde in the' repeated.
[545] The celebration of Epiphany by the court stretched over two days; the herald's description is of interest chiefly for its portrayal of a royal crown-wearing, a means of identifying with the reputed unchanging nature of the Crown and linking the new regime with England's past: Armstrong, 'Inauguration Ceremonies', pp. 92–4.
[546] Preceded by cancellation of 'of'.
[547] Appears actually to have been written 'serviyce'.
[548] This is the only mention in the text of the queen's appearing crowned, although Henry VII enacted a crown-wearing in York during his progress. See above, p. 80.
[549] Repeated.
[550] This sentence actually reads: '... and my lady the kinges moder in like mantell and surcott as the quene, with a riche corownall on her hede, went aside *half the ~~quenes~~ quenes half trayne*' (my italics).

And when the high masse was doon the king went to his chambre, and from thens to the hall, and ther keptt his estate in maner as ensueth: corownede with a riche corowne of golde sett with ful many riche precious stonys, and under a merveolous riche cloth of astate; and tharchebisshop of Canterbury on his right hande; and the quene also corowned under a clothe of estate hanging sumwhat lower[551] than the kinges, on his lift hande; whiche al iij estates wer servede coverde. And the erle of Oxinforde, great chambrelayn of Englande, waytede on the kinges coroune, and therle of Urmonde, the quenes chaumbrelayn, **[f. 47v]** knelede betwene the quene and my lady the kinges moder, wayting on the quenes coroune. Sir David Owen was kerver that day; Sir Charles [of Somersett] cupeberer (and they wer in ther robes); Sir William Vampage, sewer (and whiche was in no roobes but in a gownne of rosset damask);[552] Sir John Fortscu waytede upon the cupborde in a gowne of cremesyn velwett with a riche coler aboute his nek.

And after the secunde cours, when the mynstrelles hade pleyde, thofficers of armes descendede from ther stage, and Garter yave the king thankinges for his largesse and besought the kinges highnesse to owe thankinges to the quene for her largesse. And that doon, the largesse bothe of the king and of the quene was cryede and Edwarde Beauchampe, on of the kinges mershalles, drwe the surnape and made the king and the quene both hole astates; and to my lady the kinges moder half astate; and the same to tharchebisshop of Canterbury.

At the table in the medell of the hall[553] sat the deane ande thoo of the kinges chapell, whiche incontynently after the kinges furst course sange a carall. The duc of Bedeforde beganne the table on the right side of the hall; and next unto hym the lorde Dawbeney, an ambassator of the Frenche kinges; and next unto hym the duc of Suffolk; and then the protonathory of Sandevill, also an ambassatour of the Frenche kinges, [and] therle of Aroundell; and ayenst hym satt therle of Notingham; and ayenst hym satt therle of Huntingdon, then the vicounte Welles and the vicount Lisley with al other barons and knyghtes ensuyng in order at that table to thende thereof. And at the table on the lifte side of the hall beganne my **[f. 48]**[554] lady Cecill, the quenes sister, and next unto her the[555] countesse of Oxinforde, the countesse of Ryvers, the lady Straunge and so forth al that table, with ladyes and gentilwomen al on oon side, &c.

---

[551] The queen's canopy was traditionally suspended at a lesser height than the king's as a sign of role differentiation and of her unequal dignity. Their appearance together was nevertheless a potent symbol of unity.

[552] Preceded by the cancellation of 'velwett'.

[553] Another occasion for royal display and largess, and another potent symbol of unity; the great men and women of the realm attended and were again seated according to rank and gender.

[554] A the top of fol. 48 in the same 17th-century hand as above, p. 105, n. 231: 'The feasts of Easter and St Georg. 4 Hen. 7.'

[555] 'her' and 'the' initially joined, before a separation marker was inserted.

THE EDITION

And that in the iijde yere of the kinges reigne he solempnysed the fest of Ester[556] at Wyndesore (and the quene and my lady the kinges moder, companyede with therle of Derbye, therle of Essex, the lorde Edmonde of Suffolk, the lorde Nevell, the lorde Morley, the lorde Latymer and the lorde Barnesse) and yave[557] his largesse to his officers of armes. And the reverende fader in God the bisshop of Excester did the dyvyne servyce, and as touching his maundye and other almesse as of olde tyme accustumed.[558] And after in the same wek the king roode unto Hampton to see the vj galyes[559] that wer ther at ons; and ther the king fested the patrons and the capitayns and they presented his grace with swetewynys, sugurys, spyces and many other godly thynges.

And hys grace kept his dyvyne servyce the day of Sent George[560] in his oune chapell above the castell, by cause he had differrede the feste [to][561] the Sondey then next folowing. At the furst evensonge of Seint Georges even the king, not non other lorde of [the] garter ther beyng present, ware no gowne[562] of the lyverey but other gownes of silke under ther mantellys,[563] &c. And ther was upon the right side of the king therle of Oxinforde and the lorde Dawbeney; and on the lifte side, therle of Derby and the lorde Dynham; and thus the king kepte the quere, and on the morne was at matens; and the quene [and] my lady the kinges moder wer in gownys of the garter[564] of the same as the kyng and **[f. 48v]** the lordes wer in, and

[556] This was the first Easter of the reign celebrated at home, viz. Windsor Castle.
[557] Inserted in the left margin in the hand of Scribe A.
[558] –as cancelled between tyme and accustomed.
[559] A galley was a long, narrow warship, propelled primarily by oar and decked at the bow and stern. See N. A. M. Rodger, *The Safeguard of the Sea. A Naval History of Britain. Volume One, 600–1649* (London, 1997), pp. 64–9 for the development and characteristics of the galley. The six galleys inspected by Henry VII in 1488 were perhaps built to protect the ports to windward of England's south coast from the expanding power of France. Sources for English naval activity under Henry VII and his fifteenth-century predecessors include Rodger, *Safeguard*, chapter 12, pp. 153–163 and C. F. Richmond, 'English Naval Power in the Fifteenth Century', *History*, 52 (1967), pp. 1–15.
[560] The king deferred the traditional ceremonials of St George's Day until Sun. 27 April, perhaps because St. George's day fell mid-week in 1488: *Materials*, ii, p. 290. As the king was not attended by the Garter knights at the first evensong of St George's Day, he forbore to wear his Garter robes at evensong on St George's Eve, opting instead for a suitably sumptuous silk gown beneath his mantle.
[561] Written 'of'.
[562] –n interlineated above.
[563] Followed by a contraction, possibly 'ge', for which no meaning is apparent.
[564] The Garter robes were brought out for matins the following day. It is noteworthy that on this occasion the queen and king's mother were also issued with livery of the Garter, a further indication of the semi-regal status which Margaret Beaufort was accorded at her son's court: Jones and Underwood, *The King's Mother*, p. 69. See also above, p. 145, and the verse composed to celebrate the wearing of the Garter robes together by king, queen and king's mother on pp. 159–60.

at *Te Deum*[565] and *Benedictus*[566] [were] sensede next after the king and byfor the knyghtes; but noon kissede the gospell nor pax, save the king and the quene. Therle of Oxinforde bare the trayne of the kinges mantell that season, &c. The king and the quene and my lady the kinges moder also went [in] a procession aboute the cloystre; and the king both dynede and sowped in his oune corner glasid chaumbre; and the forsaide iiij lordes satt at his borde. And on the morne the kyng and the lordes harde ther masse of requiem in his oune chapell, and offerd, &c.; and so did the quene and my lady the kinges moder.

On the Sonday next folowing, the king kept a great and a noble feste[567] at Wyndesore aforsaide, in maner and fourme as ensuethe: furst on Seint Georges even[568] ther wer assembled great nombre of estates of this realme, and in especiall of the kinges counseill, as tharchebisshop of Canterbury, thar[ch]bisshop[569] of York, the bisshop of Lincoln, the bisshop of Excester, the chieff jugge of the kinges benche; for that season arryved many ambassatours of dyvers countreys,[570] as of the king of Romayns and his sonne the duc; also from the king of Scottes and from the duc of Bretayne; for whiche great maters the king differred the chapiter[571] unto after-

---

[565] 'Te Deum' underlined, possibly in the hand of the scribe or editor.

[566] 'Benedictus' underlined, possibly in the hand of the scribe or editor.

[567] This year the feast of St George was celebrated in notably lavish style, perhaps in recompense for the problems of the previous year. The ceremonials were attended by the Garter brethren, the king's council, ambassadors from the king of Scots and several continental rulers, and on this occasion George Talbot, the 4th earl of Shrewsbury, was installed as KG. The bishop of Winchester conducted the mass. An early printed 'guide' to the celebration of the feast of St. George and the investiture of knights elect, issued under the command of King Charles II, is *The Order of the Ceremonies used at the Celebration of St. George's Feast at Windsor, when the Sovereign of the Most Noble Order of the Garter is Present*, compiled by Sir Edward Walker, Garter (London, 1674); the copy held by the Bodleian Library, Oxford, has been annotated by the aptly-named Thomas St George (Somerset 1660–80; Norroy, 1680–1686; Garter, 1686–1703), who took part in the feast in 1674.

[568] Sat. 26 Apr. 1488. The participants were expected to assemble in the guard and presence chambers by three o'clock in the afternoon, in carefully designated order and appropriately dressed (the poor knights in their own habits, the heralds in the royal coats of arms, and the knight companions in the habit of the order of the Garter), before the procession to chapel began: *Order of Ceremonies*, pp. 1–11.

[569] Written 'tharbisshop'.

[570] See above, p. 99, n. 196.

[571] The usual manner of holding chapter is described in *Order of Ceremonies*, pp. 5–6. The choice of place and time for the chapter appears to reside with the king: *Order of Ceremonies* notes that a chapter is to be held on St George's Eve, 'unless it hath been kept before in the Privy Chamber, by agreement of the Sovereign and Companions'. On this occasion it appears that the entire procession made its way direct to chapel, without the usual hiatus for chapter attended only by the king and the knights and officers of the order (Cf. *Order of Ceremonies*, pp. 6–7). Chapter seems to have been held in three separate sittings, *viz.* on the consecutive afternoons of St George's Eve (Saturday) and

noone and commaunde the lorde Dynham and Sir Thomas of Breugh to enstalle in his name therle of Shrewsbury, the reverende fader in God the bisshop of Wynchester (prelate of the order, present at his charge) and also the lord Woodvile (whose soule God pardon). And this was a solempne masse of Our Ladye songon by theym of the college, wherfor[572] the saide erle[573] yave to the singers of the quere a great rewarde.

And at after noone the king, accompanyed with his brether of the garter in ther mantelles and in the gownes of ther lyvery of the last yer, roode from the quadraunt on hakneyes to the college and went to ther chapiter and helde ther chapiter a great tract of tyme. And from thens went to evensonge the quene and my lady the **[f. 49]** kinges moder, being in like gowne of the lyverye riding in a riche chare coverde with riche cloth of golde, vj coursers in that same chare harnest with that same clothe of golde; also xxj ladyes and gentilwomen folowing the quene, cledde al in cremesyne velwett gownes and riding upon white palfereys, ther sadelles of cloth of golde, the harnesse of golde smythes werk with white roses[574] demy trapper wise; item, Sir Roger Cooton, maister of the quenes hors, riding upon a courser trapped with golde smythes werk, leding the quenes hors of astate in his[575] hande with a sadill of cloth of golde and therupon iij corounes of silver gilt with sambres of that same cloth of golde hanging unto the knees of the hors of bothe sides, the horse harnest in golde smythes werke demy trapper wise.

And at that evensonge the king and the knyghtes of the garter wer sensede, and nother the quene nor my lady the kinges moder. That [day] the king fastede,[576] and therfor the voyde was incontynent after he came into the great chambre. And after that the knyghtes sowped[577] al on oon side and satt after ther estates.

On the morne[578] all the knyghtes of the garter reasemblede in the lyverey of the newe yer – that is to say of white clothe with garters – al on horsbak with riche horse harnesse, and the kinges courser trapped with a trapper of Seint George of white clothe of golde; and the lorde Barnesse bar the kinges swerde, his courser trappede with a riche trapper of Seint Edwardes armys; and thus in order and as ner after ther stalles as they myght, roode downe to the chapell and so straite to the chapter, and then to matens. The quene and my lady the kinges moder, in lik

---

St George's Day (Sunday) and on the Monday morning. See pp. 155–9.
572 Preceded by a cancellation.
573 Initially written 'yerle' before the –y was cancelled.
574 A favoured Yorkist emblem.
575 'her' cancelled and 'his' written in the left margin in a contemporary hand (poss. Scribe B).
576 The clause actually reads 'That that the king fastede'.
577 See *Order of Ceremonies*, pp. 19–21.
578 The knights were expected to be assembled in the presence chamber by eight o'clock in the morning, fully dressed in the Garter livery in preparation for the procession to matins: *Order of Ceremonies*, p. 22.

astate as byfor, came to matens and bode the masse; but they had nother sensing nor pax, nor they offrede nott. (And also the[y] came to the ijde evensonge). And when matens wer doon therles and the lordes went the next way to the denes place to brekfast; and from thens to the chapiter ayene; and after to procession and to the high masse; and after to dyner. And the king kep[t] his astate in the hall in maner[579] and fourme as ensueth:

[f. 49v]The day of the feste[580] the king kepte his estate in the hall, the bisshop of Winchester on his right hande. And that day nonother estate sat [at] the kinges table. Item, ther was in the hall iij tables. At the table on the right hande satt all the knyghtes of the garter that wer present, al on oon side and after ther estates, that is to say furst the duc of Suffolk, therle of Aroundell, therle of Oxinforde, therle of Derbye, therle of Shrewesbury, the lorde Dynham, the lorde Wodevile, the lorde Dawbeney and Sir Thomas Borough. And alitill byneith theym satt, on both sides the table, the dean, the chanoignes and the por knyghtes of the college in ther mantelles; and by neith[581] theym the residew of that quere. Item, at the borde in the medell of the hall satt the lorde Boithvaile, embassatour of the king of Scottes, and the lorde Edmonde of Suffolk, lorde Gray, the lorde Morley, the lorde Latymer, the lorde Delawarre and the lorde Barnesse; and a litill byneith theym satt the kinges chapell. Item, at the table on the lifte side of the hall satt the president of Kusshemborough with other ambassatours of the king of Romayns, and his sonnes the yonge duc; also afor yenste theyme the lorde Malparteus, ambassatour of the duc of Bretayne, and the lorde Hausey, chiff justice of the kinges benche; and al that side satt furnysshede with knyghtes and esquiers. And that day the hall was merveously orderde and servede: knyghtes of the garter servede[582] the king of water, Sir Davy Owen kerved, Sir Charles of Somersett was cupberer, Sir William Vampage sewer, and Edwarde Beau[cham]pe, marshall, drew the surnape. And also incontynent after the king hath wasshede the knyghtes of the garter served the king of the voyde, and other gentillmen the prelate; and then wer served knyghtes of the garter.

And from theyns the king and the lordes[583] went to the kinges chaumbre, and after a tract of tyme toke ther horse and roode to the college; and after theym the quene and my lady the kinges moder with ladies and gentilmen richely besene, as afor rehersede. And the king and his brether of the garter entrede the chapiter [f. 50] hous, and with theym the prelate of the order, the dean and Mayster Olyver Kyng, then regestre, and[584] Garter King of Armes and noo moo. And the black rode kept the door withoute fourth. And [when] the king with the other of the order

[579] Damage to the paper obscures –a.
[580] See *Order of Ceremonies*, pp. 34–7.
[581] Initially written 'byneith' before a separation marker was inserted.
[582] Repeated.
[583] Initially written 'lordies' before –i was cancelled.
[584] Followed by cancellation of –l.

of the garter had helde ther chapyter, they went unto evensong, and after evensonge[585] roode up ageyne; the quene and my lady the kinges moder folowede as afor. And then the king souped in his great chambre, the prelate at his borde, and the[586] remenant[587] at a side table in the presence.

After souper was had the iijde voyde was brought in by knyghtes and othre the kinges servantes and delyverde to the knyghtes of the garter; and then the king went to his chambre. And al this fest was accomplisshede by daylight, the ordynances wer so well kept.

The names of parte of the ladies and gentilwomen that awaytede on the quene and my lady the kinges moder at this fest: my lady Anne (sister unto the quenes grace), the countesse of Ryvers, the lady Margaret of Clarens (wiff of Sir Richard Poole), Dame Kateryn Grey, my lady Bray, my lady Longevile, Mastres Paston, Mastresse …, Maistres Seynt John, Maistres Nafant, Maistres Blount, Maistres Crofte, Maistres Scrope, Maistres Lacy and Maistres …

On the morne [of] the Monday the king and the knightes of the garter toke avene in the quadraunt [on] [t]her hakneyes, some in gounes of blak cloth and some in gounes of velwet; and so roode to the college doore wher they did on ther mantelles; and so procedede to the chapter; and after that to the masse of requiem.[588] And byfor the offering of mony the duc of Suffolk and the erle of Aroundell offerde the swerde of the lorde William, late erle of Aroundell; therle of Oxinforde and therle of Derbye, his helme and creste; therle of Shrewsbury and the lorde Dynham, the swerde of the lorde Dodeley;[589] the lorde Dawbeney and the lorde Wodvyle, his helme and creste; whiche swerdes and helmys wer delyverde to the forsaide[590] lordes by Garter King of Armes. And then[591] the **[f. 50v]** king offerde and after him every knyght after his estate; and whan masse was doon and *De profundis* saide, the fest was accomplisshede.

> [592]England now rejoysse, for joyous may thou bee,
> To see thy king so flowring in dignytie!
> O moost noble king, thy fame doth spring and sprede!

585   Written 'evengone'.
586   –e obscured by an ink-smudge.
587   –re interlineated above.
588   The scribe appears to have inserted a superfluous superior –i above –ie. The requiem mass was conducted in similar manner to the presentation of the knight's armour at a noble funeral. See Wagner, *Heralds of England*, pp. 106–9 for the manner of conducting funeral ceremonials in the late 15th century, *Order of Ceremonies*, pp. 41–4.
589   Repeated.
590   –e partially obscured by damage to the paper.
591   Repeated.
592   This poem appears to have been written specifically for the occasion, and was perhaps recited at the Garter feast. It it is notable *inter alia* for its mention of the wearing of matching livery of the Garter by the king, queen and king's mother, Margaret Beaufort. See above, p. 155, n. 564.

Henry the vij, our souveraigne, in yche region
Al Englande hath cause thy grace to love and drede:
Seing ambassates seche for proteccion,
For aide, helpe, socour, whiche lieth in thyn eleccion.
Englond now rejoysse, for joyous may thou bee,
To see thy kyng so flowring in dignitie!
This realme, a season stode in great jeopardie
When that noble prince disceasede, king Edwarde,
Which in his dayes gate honour ful noblye.
After his disceasse nygh hand al was marred.
Eche region this londe[593]
dispised myschief when they harde.
Wherfor now rejoyse, for joyouse may thou bee,
To se thy king so flowring in dignytie!
Fraunce, Spayne, Scotlande, and Bretayne, Flawnders also,
Thre of theym present keping thy noble feste
Of Seynt George in Wyndesor, ambassates comyng moo,
Yche of theym in honour, bothe the mor and the leste,[594]
Seching thy grace to have thy noble beheste.
Wherfor now rejoysse, for joyous may thou bee,
To see thy king so flouring in dignitie!
O knyghtly order, clothed in robes with garter:
The quenes grace, thy moder in the same;
The nobles of thy realme, riche in aray, after;
lordes, knyghtes and ladies unto thy great fame.
Now shall all ambassates knowe thy noble name
By thy fest royall. Now joyous may thou bee,
To see thy king so flowring in dignitie!
[f. 51][595]Here this day Seint George, the patrone of this place,
Honowrede with the garter, chief of chevalrye.
Chaplayns, chapell singing, procession keping space,
With archebisshops and bisshops, besene noble;
Muche people present to see thee, King Henry.
Wherfor, now Seint George, all we pray to thee,
To kepe our souveraigne in his dignytie!

---

[593] Followed by the deletion of 'this'.
[594] 'lesse' cancelled between 'the' and 'leste'.
[595] At the top of fol. 51 in the same hand as above, p. 105, n. 231: 'The Feast of Witsontid. Ano–3 Hen .7.'.

[596]And that the iijde yer of his regne his grace, the quene [and] my lady the kinges mouder kept the feste of Whitsontid at Windesore,[597] accompanied with the erle of Derby. The reverent fadir in Gode, the bishopp of Excestre, privey seall, did the divyn service. Also ther was the lorde Broke (stuarde of the kinges house), the lord Daubeney, Sir Richard Egecombe (conttrouller of the kinges house), Sir Raynold Bray, Sir Thomas Lovell, Sir Gilbert Talbot, with many mor ouder knightis and esquiers.

And after that, all the sommer following, [the king] huntid and sportid[598] hym merely, and slew his gresse in the parke of Wodstok and in the foreste of Whichewod. And that somer was the king of Scottes slaine by his sone and outher his adherentis[599] by sidis Sterlyn, and divers Scottes came to the king for releve. And also that yer Sir Edduart Wideville, a noble and a coragious knight, was slaine in Bretaigne[600] by Frenshemen. And incontinent aftir that same tyme deide the duke of Britayne,[601] for whos dethe that contre hade grete losse.

---

[596] Commencement of the hand of Scribe B. The title 'Lord Broke' was only created in 1491 for Sir Robert Willoughby (d. 1502). This scribal interpolation offers a further clue to the dating of the text. See above, p. 56.

[597] Itineraries of this period reveal little movement by the king, suggesting that the realm was comparatively peaceful at this time.

[598] June–September was the season for red deer stag hunting, and was known as 'greasetime' or the 'fat-season': Richard Almond, *Medieval Hunting* (Stroud, 2003), pp. 86–8.

[599] James III of Scotland was defeated on 11 June at the battle of Sauchieburn, against his brother, Alexander duke of Albany, and various noblemen. See Virgil, *Anglica Historia*, pp. 41 and Chrimes, *Henry VII*, pp. 86–7. The herald's statement that James III was murdered by his son is not entirely correct: hoping to force the old king's abdication in favour of his son, Albany's faction made the king's 15-year-old son James (IV) their leader, probably with minimal consent; James sen. fell from his horse fleeing from the battlefield and was allegedly stabbed to death by a stranger posing as a priest.

[600] Edward Woodville, uncle to the queen and governor of the Isle of Wight, was killed at the battle of St. Aubin du Cormier fighting in support of Breton independence from France. His expedition is discussed in Adelstan, marquis de Beauchesne, 'Expédition d'Edouard Wydeville', *Revue de Bretagne, de Vendée et d'Anjou*, xlvi (1911), pp. 185–214. Vergil, *Anglica Historia*, p. 37, Holinshed, *Chronicles*, p. 91 and Francis Bacon, *A History of the Reign of King Henry the Seventh*, ed. J. Weinberger, new edn (Ithaca and London, 1996), pp. 66–8, 74 mention Woodville's expedition and death, at times with doubtful accuracy (eg. Bacon, *History*, p. 68n). Commissions were granted at the end of 1488 for the muster of archers toward the 'relief of Brittany' (*Materials*, ii, pp. 384–7), although English enthusiasm for war with France over Britany was probably waning: John M. Currin, 'Persuasions to Peace: The Luxembourg-Marigny-Gaguin Embassy and the State of Anglo-French Relations, 1489–90', *EHR*, 113 (1998), p. 891. See also *idem*, '"The King's Army into the partes of Bretaigne": Henry VII and the Breton Wars, 1489–1491', *War in History*, 7 (2000), pp. 379–412.

[601] Francis II; died three weeks after unwillingly acknowledging himself the vassal of Charles VIII of France: Chrimes, *Henry VII*, p. 280.

And the king, the quene [and] the kinges moudre, well accompaynyed with many oudir knightes and esquiers and noble companye, kept his All Hallowtide[602] at Windesore, that is to say with the lorde Richard[603] Fox, bishope of Excetre and prive seall (whiche dide the divin service), therlle of Oxonforde, therlle of Shrewsbury, therle of Essex, therle of Urmonde (the quenys chamberlayn),[604] the lorde Edmond of Suthfolk, the lorde filtz Waren, the lord Latymer, the lord Dacre of the northe, the lorde filtz Waultier, the lorde Saye, the lorde Barneis, the lorde Broke (stiwarde of the kingis house), the lorde Bothville (a Scotisheman), Sir Gilbert Talbot, Sir Edduard **[f. 51v]** Bourgh, Sir Davy Owen, Sir Richard Gilforde, (vichamberlain), Sir Thomas Louvell, Sir Reynolde Bray, Sir James Parker, Sir Edduard Darell, Sir Richard Haulte, Sir William Sondis, Sir Rogier Cotton, Sir Thomas Leighton, Sir John Fortescu, Sir George Nevyll the baster.

And[605] from Windesor the king, the quene and the housholde remevid to Westmynster to the gretest conseille[606] that was many yers withoute the name of parlement. And also ther wer at that season many enbassatours,[607] that is for to say from Fraunce the lorde Charbonell and the prothonotoire of Sandevill, and frome the king of Romanis the lorde Malpertus (a Breton) and Maister Piers le Puissant; also enbassatours frome the king of Spaine.

Also[608] at the breking up of the conseille ther entrid into this reaulme a cubiculer of the popes, whic[h]e broght to the kyng a suerde and a cappe,[609]

---

[602] Cf. the brief notices of All Hallowtide in 1487 and 1489 on pp. 128 and 173. The latter coincided with the queen's confinement before the birth of Princess Margaret.

[603] Written above the cancellation of 'John'.

[604] –er unclear.

[605] Preceded by a paragraph marker in red ink and probably inserted by the individual responsible for the red marginalia, as above, p. 99, n. 198.

[606] This meeting, held in Nov. 1488, discussed the state of affairs regarding Brittany, and apparently authorised the levy of a subsidy of a tenth, ratified by parliament three months later: Chrimes, *Henry VII*, p. 144. The 'great council' denoted the non-parliamentary assembly of lords without the commons, and was summoned five or six times during the reign of Henry VII. A definitive account of the great council is given in Peter Holmes, 'The Great Council in the Reign of Henry VII', *EHR*, 101 (1986), pp. 840–62. See also Chrimes, *Henry VII*, ch. 7 and esp. pp. 141–4 and J. Guy, *Tudor England* (Oxford, 1988), pp. 59, 322.

[607] This was the first of a series of embassies to arrive from the continent around this time. Negotiations with Spain resulted in the treaty of Medina del Campo, a detailed account of which is provided, along with descriptions of the embassy to Spain and Portugal by Roger Machado, in *Memorials*, pp. 157–99, 328–68. See also M. Jones, 'Les ambassades de Roger Machado, le héraut Richmond en Bretagne (1490)', in *La Bretagne, terre d'Europe*, ed. J. Kervéhé and T. Daniel (Brest and Quimper, 1992), pp. 147–60.

[608] Preceded by a paragraph marker in red ink and probably inserted by the individual responsible for the red marginalia, as above, p. 99, n. 198.

[609] In in the left margin in red ink and the same hand as above, p. 99, n. 198: 'The receyving of a cap and sword sent from the Pope to the King'. The gift of sword and cap of

whiche for hounour of the pope was hounourably receipvid by the kinges comaundement in maner as ensieweth: firste the king sente an officer of armes to the see side, also to cause thos religious places of Caunterbury and outher townes by the way to make hym goode chiere and well to entret theamme; after that his highnes sent certaine knightis to met hym as fer as Rochester; and after them the reverentz faders in Gode the bishoppe of Durame, the bishope of Exceter, the bishope of Rochester, therle of Shrewsbury, therle of Wilshire, the lorde Morley, the lorde Hastingis and the prior of Lantony, with many mor lordis and knightis (whos names I have not) receipved hym at Blakheth; and after theme the bishope of Winchestre and therle of Arundell met hym at Saint Georges in Southwerke, wher the cappe was sette upon the pointe of the suerde. And so the saide cubiculer, riding bitwen the bishope of Winchester and therle off Arundell, openly bar the said swerde thorowt Southwerke and on London brigge, wher he was also recepved and wellcomed by the maire of London and his brethern; and so as he procedet thorow the cite to Poulles stode all the craftes in ther clothinges, and at the west ende of Poulles he was recepvid by the metropolitan and divers[610] outher bishopes in pontificalibus and[611] with the procession; and so proceded to the high autar; and from thens[612] it was borne in to the **[f. 52]**[613] revestry.

In to the morne that same Saterday, the king remevid from Westminster to the bishopes pales (and the quene and my lady the kinges mouder). And ther was so grete a miste upon times that ther was no man cowde telle of a grete season in what place in Temys the king was. And [o]n[614] the morne whan the king was comen into his travers, the cape was brought oute of the revestry to bifore the high auter by the said cubiculer, acompagnied with the bishope of Winchester and therle of Arundell and many outher nobles bothe espirituel and temporell. And the king come forth of his travers, wher the saide cubiculer presentit the king a l[ettr]e frome the pope, closit with corde and lede, that was rede by the reverent fader in God the lord John Morton, archebishope of Canterbury, then chaunceler[615] of England. That doon the said cubiculer holding the said suerde and cape made a noble proposicion, to the whiche the saide lord chaunceler ansuerde

---

    maintenance by Pope Innocent VIII (1484–92) denoted papal favour, and the public display of these items did much to enhance the king's prestige at home and abroad. See J. W. Legg, 'The Gift of the Papal Cap and Sword to Henry VII', *Archaeological Journal*, 57 (1900), pp. 183–203. Henry VII had a particularly good relationship with the pope until 1489, and thereafter relations 'remained smooth with isolated exceptions': Guy, *Tudor England*, p. 71.

[610] A stain partially obscures –ve.
[611] A stain partially obscures –nd.
[612] Followed by a small stain.
[613] At the top of fol. 52 in the hand of Scribe B: 'A° iiijth H7'.
[614] Written 'an'.
[615] –l (possibly –ll) entirely obscured by an inkblot.

full clerely and nobly. Present: the ambassatours of Fraunce, also ambassatours of the kinges of Romanis, and of the kinges of Castille, and of Bretaigne, and of Flandres, with divers outher straungiers, as Scottis, Esterlingis and outher.

And that finishid[616] the king and all those estates went [in] a procession, and the cape was borne on[617] the pomel of the suerde by the saide cubiculer. And whan [the] procession was done, during al the masse hit was set on the high auter. The messe doone the archebishope song certain orisons over the king, whic[h]e come from his travers bifore the high auter to the highest stepe nexte the auter; whiche oroisons and benediccions done the archebishope, in ordre after the booke whiche was brought frome Rome, gerdit the suerde aboute the king and set the cape on his hede. And so the king so turned to his travers whilles *Te Deum* was a singing and the colet rede; and it was taken of again and as bifore borne by the said cubiculer to the bishopis palles, and thier delivert to the chamberlain.

That day the king made a grete feste and kepte open housholde, and by cause the palais was so littil for suche a feste the said cubiculer dynnyt in the doiens palace,[618] acompagnied[619] with divers bishopis and lordis, as the lorde of Saint Johns and outhre. And incontinent aftir the king sente his ambassatours in to divers parties,[620] that is to saie Maister Christofer Urswike, doian of Yorke, and Sir John Don, knight, in to Fraunce, and with them Yorke the heraulde; Doctor **[f. 52v]** Sauvage, Sir Richart Nanfant and Richemond King of Armes in to Portingal, also with the garter for the king of Portingal; Doctor Wanswort[h][621] and Sir John Riseley, knight, and Carlill herauld to the king of Romains; Sir Richart Eggecombe, knight, and Faulcon the pourservant into Bretaigne.[622]

And that yer he kepte his Cristmas at Shene, and the quene also, accompagnied with miladi the kinges mouder, the Ladi Anne (the quenes sister),[623] Elisabeth[624] of Boukingham, the Ladi Margaret of Clarence, the lady Rivieres, the lady Bray, the lady Eggremonde, the lady Gilfort, the Ladi Longville, the lady Nanfant, Mastres Verney, Mastres Saint John, Mastres Ferres, Mastres Paston, Mastres Blount, Mastres Scrope, Mastres Turbeville and ouder mor. Also the reverent fader in God the lorde Richard[625] Fox, bishope of Excester, dide the divin service, bothe Cristmas day and

[616] Ink partially obscures –in.
[617] Written above a cancellation.
[618] A smudged letter –a interlineated above.
[619] Initial –a partially obscured by ink.
[620] In the right margin in red ink and the same hand as above, p. 99, n. 198: 'Most of the heraldes employed in buisinese [*sic*] beyond the seas with embassadors to diverse princes.'
[621] –h lost in the binding.
[622] Followed by the cancellation of 'and after Clarenceux King of Arms and Master John Lacy, clerk of the prive seall to the king of Daunemark'.
[623] 'kinn' cancelled between 'qwenes' and 'sister'.
[624] Preceded by the cancellation of 'the'.
[625] Written over an erasure, probably 'John'.

the xijth day. Item, the king was acompagnied with therle of Derby, therle of Essex, therle of Urmond, the lord Daubeney, the lorde Latimer, the lorde Edmund of Suffolke, the lord Powis, the lord chamberlain, the lorde Saie, Sir John Sauvage, Sir Davi Owen, Sir Richart Polle, Sir Richart Hault, Sir Reignolde Bray, Sir Thomas Louvell, Sir George Nevvill, Sir Edward Stanley, Sir Richart Gilfort, Sir Edward Darell, Sir James Parker and Sir Richart Croftis. All thise were continuelly ...[626]

Here folowen the names of the lordes, ladies, and knightes and esquiers the whiche acompanied the king at Shene at Cristemas the iiijth yer of his regne:[627]
the quene
my lady the kinges mouder
the lorde Richard[628] Foxe, bishope of Excestre
therle of Derby.

[f. 53][629] The king kept his Ester[630] at Hertford, whier at that season the reverent fadir in God the lord Richard[631] Foxe dide the divine service, and on Saint Georges day also. And on the morne he songe the mas of requiem. And of the brethern of the gartier ther was therll of[632] Derby, the lord Scrope and Sir Richart Tunstall.

This season thier came in to this londe a greate ambassade frome the king of Romains, that is to say Don Ladron de Guavera, the vicounte of Piversalle, a doctor called Mestir Lewys, and Mestir Piers le Puissant; and also a noder ambassade in thair compagnye that came frome the king of Portyngall. Wherfore the king sent for the lorde John Morton, then archebishope of Canterbury and chauncelier of Englonde, for to have his counseill and advis. And also ther had ben an ambassatour of the king of Naples[633] as long as the king had leyn at Hertford. And at that season thier was the quene, the lady the kinges modir, therle of Derby, therle of Essex, therle of Ormond, Sir Richart Gilford, Sir Raynold Bray, Sir Thomas Lovell, Sir Charles Somersett, Sir Richart Haulte, Sir John Ryseley, the kingis aumener, the kingis secretary and the lorde Bothewell, a Scotisheman. And also this same Estir, the king of Denmarckis oncle, called Yonker Garrard, was sworne the kingis servaunt.

[626] Nothing more is written for this paragraph.
[627] Despite the promise of an extensive list, only four names appear at the bottom of fol. 52v. No spaces or blank leaves were left, and the scribe simply commences discussion of Easter 1489 on the subsequent fol.
[628] Written over an erasure beginning with –J, presumably 'John'.
[629] At the top of fol. 53 in a late 15th-century hand (prob. Scribe B): 'The A° iiij^{to}'. Beneath that note, in the same 17th-century hand as above, p. 105, n. 231: 'The feast of Easter An° 4 Hen. 7'.
[630] Thurs. 16 to Mon. 20 Apr. 1489.
[631] Written over an erasure.
[632] Repeated as 'off' followed by 'of'.
[633] In right margin in hand of Scribe B: 'A° iiij^{to} R h v ...'; the final –ij on what should read 'vij' has been cropped.

And on Saint Vitalles day, the xxviijth day of Apprill, was slayne therle of Northumberlonde⁶³⁴ besidis Thurske, besidys Blackamor Egge. Tydingis heroff had the king sone ansuerde all the abovesaide ambassatours, and on the xxijth⁶³⁵ day of May departed fromme Hertforde towardes the northe and lay that nyght at Dunstable, acompagnyed with the bishop **[f. 53v]** off Excestir, privey seall, and outher, as is rehersid in the booke off the kinges gystys.

This bene the names of part of the nobles whiche atended on the kinges grace into the northe parties the iiijth yer of his reigne:⁶³⁶

The xijth day of May⁶³⁷ his grace remeved fromme Hertford to Dunstable acompaynyed with the lorde Richard⁶³⁸ Fox, bishop off Excestir and privey seall, therle off Derby, therle of Essex, therle off Surrey, the lorde Edmund off Suffolke, the lord Barnesse, the lorde Bothwell, Mestir Christofer Urswicke (the kingis aumener), Mestir Ollivier king (the kingis secretary), Sir Thomas Lovell, Sir Edward Darell, Sir Henry Wenworthe, Sir John Ryseley, Sir Edward Wingfeld, Sir Rogier Cotton (whiche was knight herbergier), the kingis coffrier, with all the substans of oudir

---

⁶³⁴ Killed at Cocklodge on 28 Apr. 1489. News reached the court at Hertford within days: *YHB*, ii, pp. 646, 647–8; anon., 'The Yorkshire Rebellion', p. 464; Bennett, 'Northern Rising'; TNA, KB 9/381; *Great Chronicle*, p. 242; Vergil, *Anglica Historia*, pp. 38–9; Hicks, 'Yorkshire Rising Reconsidered', pp. 43–4; *Paston Letters and Papers*, ii, p. 659; J. Scattergood (ed.), *John Skelton: The Complete English Poems* (Harmondsworth, 1983), p. 31. The rising was in origin a tax revolt encouraged by the levy of onerous subsidies in the parliaments of 1487 and 1489, and doubtless encouraged by Northumberland's personal unpopularity: Chrimes, *Henry VII*, p. 80. Northumberland had made his intentions of facing the rebels clear four days earlier in a letter to Sir Robert Plumpton: *Plumpton Letters and Papers*, p. 84.

⁶³⁵ An error for 'xijth'.

⁶³⁶ The report of 1489 is a bland and orderly composition, apparently compiled some time after the conclusion of campaign; yet it still bears hallmarks of eyewitness experience. The best analysis of the herald's report is by Michael Bennett, who was the first to point out the omission of several crucial folios from the Leland-Hearne edition of the Memoir: Bennett, 'Northern Rising'.

⁶³⁷ Tues. 12 May 1489. News of the disturbance appears to have reached the king within days. On 30 April he ordered funds for weapons and ammunition: *Materials*, ii, pp. 444–5. Letters were dispatched to magnates and castles across England, and the earl of Oxford prepared to hold a council at Castle Hedingham in the first few days of May: *Paston Letter and Papers*, ii, pp. 459–60; *Materials*, ii, pp. 444–5. On 6 May, Oxford also requested that Sir John Paston meet him at Cambridge six days later with as many armed men as he could muster: *Paston Letters and Papers*, ii, p. 460; *Annals of Cambridge*, pp. 234–5. Among those involved in the rising were one John Egremont, a cadet of the house of Percy, the governors of Beverley, Thomas Bullock and Eli Cass, and Thomas Wrangwysh, Alderman of York: Hicks, 'Dynastic Change', p. 78. See also *CSP Venice*, p. 181; Vergil, *Anglica Historia*, pp. 38–9; *Paston Letters and Papers*, i, pp. 349–40; *YHB*, ii, pp. 648, 649–50; *Tudor Royal Proclamations*, i, 20–1.

⁶³⁸ Written above the cancellation of 'John'.

THE EDITION

officiers of the kingis hounourable housholde,[639] Sir Adam Forman, Sir … Turnbull, Thomas Brandon (whiche bare the kingis estandard), John Crokker, Thomas Morton, Edward Bensted.

The xiijth day frome Dunistable to Stonystratford: the reverent fadir in God the lord John Morton, archebishop of Canterbury and chauncelier off Englonde, Sir Thomas Bourghshier off Barnesse, Sir John Fortescu, the lorde Zouche, Sir Rogier Lewkenor, Sir John Devenyshe, Sir Richart Gilford, William Scotte off Kent, Nicholas Cromer, Edmund Hampden.

Item, on the xiiijth day frome Stonystratford to Northehampton: John Saintjohn, Mathew Browne, Sir Thomas Grene, Sir Nicholas Vaux, Sir Richart **[f. 54]** Hault (whiche after was made knight marshall at Leyrcestir, and Wellis undir hym), the lorde Laware, Sir John Donne, Sir William Willougby.

Item, on the xvth day frome Northehampton to Herborow, thier and by the way: therle of Oxenford. And in his compagnye: Sir John Wingfeld, Sir Robert[640] Brougton, Sir Thomas Terell, Sir Richart Fitzlowis, Sir William of Carow, Philip Lewis, Simond Wisman, Rogier Hastinges, John Raynsford, John Colt, John Peke,[641] Robert Terell

Sir Robert Cheyne	Thomas of Brereton[642]
… Lawder	Thomas Totoste
James Isaack	John Whytyng (with
William Denton	the compeynye of the
John Darell of Kente	marquis of Barkeley)
therle of Arundell	therle of Shrewsbury
the lord Gray Ruthyn	the lord Hastinges
the lord Cobham	Sir Edward Rauley
Sir George Nevell	Sir James Harington
Sir Henry Roos	of Northampton shir
John Dudeley	Sir John Sauvage
Thomas Yden	John Gyse
William Crokker	Robert Throgmarton
Edward Blount	Robert Harington

[639] The contribution of the royal household to military expeditions, such as exhibited here, was a notable feature of the reign, although in this case the time required to raise county levies and the danger of their sympathising with the rebels made it sensible for the king to turn first to his own retinue and the companies of trusted lords and knights: M. Condon, 'Ruling Elites in the Reign of Henry VII', in *Patronage Pedigree and Power in Later Medieval England*, ed. Charles Ross (Gloucester, 1979), p. 127; Bennett, 'Northern Rising', pp. 40, 51; *Tudor Royal Proclamations*, i, pp. 20–1.

[640] Followed by the cancellation of –b.

[641] After John Peke, the scribe places the names of those attendant upon the king in columns.

[642] –er obscured by a stain.

Item, on the xvjth day frome Herborow to Leircestir, thier and be the way:

Piers Courtois
the Viscounte Lisle
the lord Straunge
  (and in his compeyney
  siche as her after shalbe
  shewid of Lancashire)
the lord Latymyer
the lord Dudeley
[f. 54v]Sir Simon Montford
Sir Richart Crofte
Sir Richart Cornualle
Sir Richart Corbet

therle of Wiltshir
the lord chamberlain
  (and with hym many noble
  man whos names I have not)
Sir Ris up Thomas
Sir John Mortemier
Sir Thomas Cookesey
Sir Thomas Blount
Sir Thomas of Manyngton
Sir Moris of Barkeley
Sir Humfrey Sauvage
James Hyde

And on the morow at the moustres off Lancashir with the lorde Straunge:

Sir Thomas Bottler,
  baron of Warington[643]
Sir John of Langton,
  baron of Walton
Sir John Waren,
  baron of Stockport
Sir Thomas of Pooll
Sir Piers of Legh
Sir Thomas Talbot
Sir Alixandre Hoghton
Sir Richart Sherburne
Sir William Trowtbeck
Sir William Stanley
  of Howton
Sir John of Bouthe
  of Barton
Sir Alixandre Standishe
Sir Henry Boulde
Sir William Norreis
Sir Thomas Striklond
Sir Thomas Maulevrier
Sir Christofer Standishe
Sir John Talbot
Sir John off Legh
Sir Rauff Longford

Raff of Brereton
Andreu of Brereton
Gerard of Ynshe
John of Ravenscrofte
Rauff of Egleston
Richart of Asheton
John of Irlonde
Thomas Hyde
Thurston of Anderton
Henry of Farington
Thomas of Legh[644] of Adlyngton
John Legh of Legh
Thomas of Legh of Bouthe
Nicholas Beron
Richart Medilton
John Flemmyng
Clement Skelton
Rogier Hilton
Elis of Prestwiche
James Bottler of Rawcleff
William Skillicorne
William Hesketh
Thomas of Rigmaiden
William Kirkby

[643] –r smudged.
[644] Cancellation conjoined to –h.

Sir Geffroy Mascy	Richart[645] Dalton
John of Stanley	Hamond Massy
Piers of Stanley	Radclef of Urdishall
Thomas Laurens	Radclef of the Tour
Edmund Trafford	Elis Entwesell
Thomas Cotton	Thomas Lancaster
Piers Gerard	Hugh of Aghton
Thomas Doucunfeld	Rouland Scarsbrek
Thomas Mainwaring	… Halsall
John Mainwaring	Robert Worsley
William Damport	Rauff of Orell of Tourton
[f. 55]Rogier Lever	James of Clifton
Rogier Bothe	Richart Heton
Richart Radcliff	Robert Langley
Henry Banester	Richart Molynneaulx

The xvijth day frome Leircester to Notingham, and by the way in a medow besides Montsorell, ther the king tooke the vew of therle of Derbys folkes:

Sir Rogier Tokettis	Robert Harrecourt
Sir William Stoner	John Donham
Sir John Babington	Sir Nicholas Styrlay
Sir Edward Norreis	Sir George Hopton

The xviijth day at Notingham al day:

the lord Saintamond	Sir Hugh Conway
the lord Powis	Sir Henry Perpoint
Sir John Saint Low	Sir George Nevell the Bastard
Sir Thomas of Borough	Henry Vernon
Sir Thomas Geiseley	Robert Strette
Sir Charles Sommerset	… Walshe, coustumer of Bremstow

The xix[th] day to Wourshop: … Pudsey, esquier for the body.

The xxth day frome Worshop to Pontfret the archebishop of York met the king beside Tykhill: Sir John Everyngham and other.

The xxijth day at Pontfret all day wher war put vj of the rebellis to execucion, that is to say ij ware bihedid in the market place besides the high cros (and one of their heddis set on the pillory, anoder on the barriers nexte the priory); and ij hangid in their jackes and cheyned on Saint Thomas hille to Yorck ward; anodir hongid at Ferybrigge townes ende; another hangid at Wentbrigg.

Item, the same day certain lordes and ouder nobles whiche had bene in the chase of the kinges rebelles came to Pontfret to see the king, that is to say:

the lord Welles	Sir Gervais of Clifton
the lord Grey Codnar	Sir Robert Cliffton

---

[645] Followed by the cancellation of 'Tunstall'.

[f. 55v]Sir Thomas Tempeste				Sir Thomas Mylburne,
John Howsey					whiche came frome Salesbury
Sir James Blount, whiche			Sir James Audeley
  came frome Calais

Item, on the xxijth day frome Pontfret to Yorck:[646]

Sir Richart Yorck				Sir William Tyrwhyt
Sir Richart Tode				Sir John of Musgrave
David Philipe					Richart Musgrave
Bryan Sandford					Sir John of Melton
Henry Scroppe					Ollivier Saint John
the baron of Graystok				the abbot of Saint Marye Abbeye

And all the residew of the said moneth the king lay stille in the bishoppes palais. And thier was one named Bladis drawen and quarterd[647] in the pavement of Yorck; and divers ouder war hanged in divers parties of the towne; and one called Warton was hanged in the posterne whier the rebelles entred. And in this season the king pardont some day iij^c knelyng on their knees, and some day ij^c – some day mor and some day lasse – so that season his grace pardont upon a xv^c.

Also the king being at Yorck ther entred divers nobles, wherof some had bene in the chase and some came frome therle of Northumberlonde:

George Percy
Sir John of Medilton				the lord Dacre of the northe
Sir Humfrey Stanley				the lord Clifford
Richart Clifford				Sir Richart Tunstall
James Metcalff					Sir Robert Ryder
Sir Rauff Bygod					Sir Christofer Warde
Sir John Pykeryng				Sir William Malory
Sir Martin of the see				Sir Christofer Moresby

---

[646] By the time he neared York, the king was probably aware that a number of knights of Yorkshire and the Midlands had independently taken action north of the Trent, and that the rebels had begun to pull back: *YHB*, ii, pp. 650–1; TNA KB 9/381; Bennett, 'Northern Rising', pp. 45–6; Palliser, 'Richard III and York', p. 65; *Great Chronicle of London*, p. 242; Vergil, *Anglica Historia*, pp. 38–9; Pollard, *Contemporary Sources*, i, p. 80. Despite the creditable line-up of lords and knights, a number of important figures were absent at this point: Edward Woodville was dead (see above, p. 161); Sir Richard Edgecombe, Lords Cheney, Daubeney and Willoughby, and other veterans of Bosworth and Stoke, were engaged in battle on the continent; Richard Nanfan and his company were on embassy in Spain: *Materials*, ii, pp. 384, 419; *Memorials*, pp. 328–78; Bennett, 'Northern Rising', pp. 39–40.

[647] For details of the city of York's attempts to appease the king, see *YHB*, ii, pp. 651, 652, 653. Holinshed, *Chronicles*, p. 492–3 and *Great Chronicle of London*, p. 242 give divergent descriptions of the hanging of 'John of Chamber' and others at York, and there is some uncertainty as to the number executed. See also Bennett, 'Northern Rising', pp. 47–8 for the possible identities of several put to death.

Sir James Danby
Sir Marmenduc Conestable
[f. 56]Sir William Bekewith
Sir Thomas fitz William
Sir Randolffe Pygot
Sir James Strangweys
Sir John Nevell
Sir John of Waterton
Sir Piers Medilton
Sir John Sayvell
Sir William Stapilton
Sir Robert Denmocke
Sir Thomas Markenfeld
Sir William Yvers
Sir John Pudsey
James Pykering

Sir William Gascon
William Cognyers
John Hastinges, sone and
　heire of Sir Hugh
Geffroy Franc
James Roos
the lord Lumley
the baron of Hylton
Sir Robert Hylyerd
Sir John Conestable of
　Holdernes
John Radcleff
Rouland Plays
Sir Rogier Belingam
Miles of Wilsthorppe
and other mor.

And at the kinges returne he established in the northe parties therle of Surrey, Sir Richard Tunstall and Sir Henry Wentworthe.

The same yer the king kept his Whytsontid at Notingham, acompaynyed with therle of Oxonford and therle of Northumberlonde; and frome thens remeved to Windesore and their hontid and sportid hym.

On this season the Flemmyngis holding the Frenshe partie, and on especial thoos of Brugges with the asistence of the lord Quardis, had beseged Dixemue[648] on Flaunders. The lord Dawbeney, the kinges lieutenant of Calais, and the lord Morley, with divers oudir noble knightes and esquiers of the garuyson and of the crew of Calais and of the Englishe marche in thoos parties, rescued Dixemue [f. 56v] and brake the sege. And thier ware slayne the substance of all thoos whiche had beseged it, as well the lord Guardes servauntis, as the garuyson of Scottes, whiche lay at Ostenguen with the substance of the Bruggelingis. And of the Englishe partie ther was slayne that gentill yong knight the lorde Morley, and many noble man hurt, as Sir James Tyrell (sore wounded in the legge with a quarell), and a gentill and a couragieus esquier called Robert Bellyngam, the whiche foughte in his cotte of armes fast gerdid with his swerd upon his harnois. And thier was wonnen moche artillerye, wherof moche was brente with the gowne pouldre.

And also it is not to be forgoten, but to by had in ramenbrance, the goode courage of an Englyshe yoman called John Person, whiche was somtymes a baker off Coventre; whiche John Person, after that a gowne had borne away his foote by

---

[648] In the right margin in the hand of Scribe B: 'A° iiij^{to} R h vij Dixemew'. For discussion of the events at the Flemish town of Dixmude, see J. D. Mackie, *The Earlier Tudors: 1485–1558* (Oxford, 1957), pp. 98–9. The siege of Dixmude is described in Bacon, *Reign of King Henry the Seventh*, pp. 88–90.

the small of the legge yet that notwithstonding, what setting and what kneling, shotte affter many of his arows. And when the Frenshe men fledde and his[649] felowes ware in the chase, he cried to one off his fellowes and saide: "Have thow thise vj arawes that I have lefte and folow thow the chase, for I may not", the whiche John Person died within few dayes aftir, on whose saulle Gode have mercy.

And from thens the saide lorde Daubeney by apointement toke hostenges, and so with moche honnour turned to Calais to refresche the hurt peple. The lorde Querdes, hering of this rescusse, assembled a greate power and recouverd hostenges; and frome thens leid the sege to Newport, whier he lay well viij dayes **[f. 57]** and which ordounance bette parte of the walles. And on mydsomer day he made a gret assault in ij or iij places, but he was rebouted and loste many of his peuple, as it was saide mor then xiiij^c. And thenne the saide lorde Guerdes departed to Brugges ward, and thier was slayn a bastard off Bourbon and the lord Pyennes, a lord of Pyguardye.

The names off the nobles being with the lorde Daubeney at Dixemue: *in primis* Sir Humfrey Talbot (marshall of Calais), Sir Gilbert Talbot, Sir James Terell (leutenaunt off Gysnes), Sir Waultier Hungerford, Sir Gilbert Debnam (baneret), Sir Henry Wilougby, Sir Edward of Bourowgh, Sir Edward Ponynges, Sir Anthony Browne, Nycholas Tempeste, Robert off Bellyngam, ... Danet, ... Loveles ...[650]

This yer the feste of Saint George[651] was deferred unto the xixth day off Jully, and thenne it was hounourably kept b[y][652] the erle of Arundell, then lieutenant.[653] Also at that same tyme, on the Saterday evene of the feste, ther was enstalled by the lord Scrop and by the lord Dynham, the vicounte Wellis, **[f. 57v]** John, and Sir John Sauvage, baneret, the whiche v knightes kept fulwell and hounourably in all thinges apperteynyng [to] the said noble feste. And on the morne after the feste, at the mas of requiem, ther ware offred the swerdes, helmes and crestis of therle off Northumberlond, and off Sir Edward Wideville. During this season the king went an hunting in Envillchase.[654] And a littell before Oure Lady day the latter[655]

---

[649] Preceded by a cancellation.

[650] Followed by approximately a third of a page of blank space, probably intended to include further names of nobles present at Dixmude with the lord Daubeney, but never filled.

[651] In the right margin in the hand of Scribe B: 'Festu' st'i Georg ...'; the final –e has been cropped. The feast was again deferred, as it had been in 1488, this time to 29 July. St George's Day also fell mid-week in 1489, but the deferment on this occasion was presumably due to pressing domestic concerns. See *Materials*, ii, pp. 497–500 for purchases of cloths etc. for this celebration.

[652] Written 'be'.

[653] Written above the cancellation of 'president'.

[654] For Henry VII's attention to the condition of game parks in the duchy of Lancaster, including Enfield Chase, see Somerville, *Duchy of Lancaster*, p. 269.

[655] Tues. 8 Sept. 1489 (nativity of B.V. Mary).

thier came ambassatours oute off Fraunce, that is to say the abbot off Saint Mattelyns, Sir William Zaintes (lord of Mareny and baylly off Senlys) and Montjoie King off Armes off Frenshemen, whiche ware sone ansuerde; and Sir John Ryseley and Mest[er] Estephene Fryon ware sent with theym into Fraunce[656] in ambassade.

And thenne the kinge roode into Wiltshir an hunting and slew his gres in iij places in that shire (and also he was at Ramsbury with the bishoppe off Salesbury): furst was in the forest of Savernacke; the ijd in the goode parke off Fastarn; the iijd in Blackamor forest; and so retournede to Windesore, and soo remeved to Westmynster. And then sone aftir thier came ambassatours off the king off Romains, and also oute of Flourens, and also ambassatours out of Bretaygne.

The parlement[657] was countynued in to the xvjth day of Octobre, and that day the lordes entred the parlement house withoute any mas or oudir solempnitie, but as it had bene still, at the whiche season the king kepit a chappitre off the gartier[658] at Westmynster, whier the king off Romains was choysen knight of the gartier. The king ramenbring on his **[f. 58]**[659] furst begoten sone was not yet creatid prince ne yet doubyd knight, wherfore he determynned on Saint Andrews evene then nexte folowing bothe to dobe hym knyght and alsoo to his creacion, and thier upon directid his lettres myssyves for the sonnes and heires of divers of the greate estates off this royaulme. And the oudir nobles that had their londes in their hondes, they had pryve sealles also to geve their atendaunce.

Item, upon All Halow even[660] the quene tooke [to] her chambre[661] at West-

[656] 'into Fraunce' repeated.
[657] The third parliament opened on Tues. 13 Jan. 1489 and involved the ratification of a subsidy, proposed at the great council of November 1488, to help finance the military expedition to aid Brittany: Chrimes, *Henry VII*, pp. 144, 198.
[658] In the left margin in the hand of Scribe B: 'chapit''. Chapters of the order usually oversaw the election of new members to replace deceased KGs, and on this occasion the king of Romans took the place of the slain earl of Northumberland: Beltz, *Memorials*, p. clxviii. See also Collins, *Order of the Garter*, pp. 19–24, 36–9.
[659] At the top of fol. 58 in the same 17th-century hand as above, p. 105, n. 231: 'The maner of the Queens taking of hir Chamber An° .5.to Hen. 7. when she was with Child'.
[660] Fri. 31 Oct. 1489.
[661] In the right margin in red ink and the same hand as above, p. 99, n. 198: 'The Queene taketh her chamber wth the ceremonyes thereof' and in the hand of Scribe B: 'Regina capt cubiculu A° v^{to} Reg h. vij'. Late 15th-century accounts of court ceremonials do not stipulate a time for withdrawal (*Antiquarian Repertory*, i, p. 304), but a 16th-century document suggest four to six weeks was normal (BL, MS. Eg. 985, fol. 32). See also Staniland, 'Royal Entry', p. 301. In contrast to the coronation, the rituals of childbirth were witnessed by only a small elite at court but similarly followed a highly ritualised set of proceedings. Sixteenth-century notes on the preparations for confinement, probably derived from a document penned in connection with the pregnancies of Elizabeth of York, are found in 'How the Queenes chambre shalbe apparelled, when she shall take her rightes, and hath received them; which shalbe vj weekes, or a moneth, at the lest, before she be delivered, by estimacion' in BL, MS. Eg. 985, fols 32r–32v.

mynster, gretly acompagnyed with ladyes and gentilwomen[662] – that is to say the lady the kinges modir, the duchesse off Northfolk and many oudir – havyng before hir the greate parte off the nobles of this royalme being present at this parlement. And she was ledde by therle off Oxenford and therle of Derby. And the reverent fader in God the bishop off Excestir song the mas[663] in pontificalibus, and aftir *Agnus Dei* and that the bishop had used, the quene was led as before. And therles off Shrewsbury and of Kente hylde the towelle when the quene toke hir rightes, and the torches ware holden by knyghtes (and aftir mas, accompanyed as before) and when she was comen into hir greate chambre[664] she stode undir hir clothe of estate. Then their was ordeyned a voide off espices and swetwyn. That doone, my lorde the quenes chamberlain in very goode wordes desired, in the quenes name, the peuple thier present to pray God to sende hir the goode oure.

And so she departed to her inner chambre,[665] whiche was hanged and steyled with riche clothe of arras of blew with flourdelissis off golde,[666] without any oudir clothe off arras of ymagerye, which is not convenient aboute [f. 58v][667] wymen in suche cas. And in that chambre was a riche bedde and a palliet,[668] the whiche pal-

[662] Women played a more prominent role in these proceedings than in marriages or coronations. See *The Travels of Leo of Rozmital*, Hakluyt Soc., 2nd ser., 108 (1957), p. 46. See other examples of the roles played by senior women of the royal family during childbirth and churching in Laynesmith, *Last Medieval Queens*, p. 112, and the case of Jacquetta de Luxemburg, in P. Eames, *Furniture in England, France and the Netherlands from the Twelfth to the Fifteenth Century* (London, 1977), p. 263.

[663] Before her withdrawal into seclusion, the queen attended mass in a suitably decorated chapel.

[664] The queen was then accompanied into her great chamber, which was furnished with a cloth of estate, denoting status, and where she would receive a 'void' of wine and spices similar to that which had completed her coronation banquet; the king was again absent on this occasion, as befitted any 'celebration of the female aspects of the king's public body': Laynesmith, *Last Medieval Queens*, pp. 113–14.

[665] The lords and ladies who attended mass usually processed with the queen into her inner chamber for the final stages of the ritual: Laynesmith, *Last Medieval Queens*, p. 114.

[666] The golden fleur-de-lys was an emblem appropriate to both kingship and the Virgin Mary: Laynesmith, *Last Medieval Queens*, p. 112. They were evidently considered more appropriate for women in labour than more decorative and colourful images.

[667] At the top of fol. 58v in a late 15th-century hand (prob. Scribe B): 'A° v^{to} R h vij. Novembre'; below this note, in the same 17th-century hand as above, p. 105, n. 231: 'The Creation of Arthur Princ [*sic*] of Wales An° 5to Hen. 7.'

[668] The precise details of colouring and quality of furnishings for the bed and pallet are given in the *Ryalle Book*, and correspond closely to both the details given by the herald and the list of furnishings ordered for Margaret of Anjou's lying-in: *Antiquarian Repertory*, i, pp. 333, 336; TNA, E101/410/12. The pallet, at the foot of the bed, was probably used for the day and may therefore have been a couch or 'half throne, half bed': Laynesmith, *Last Medieval Queens*, p. 113. See also Percival Willughby, *Observations in Midwifery*, ed. H. Blenkinsop (1863; repr. 1972), p. 19, where the pallet may be used for delivery, and Staniland, 'Royal Entry', pp. 301–2.

THE EDITION

liet had a merveillous riche canope of clothe of gold with velvet paly of divers coulleurs, garneshed with rede roses, enbrodured with ij riche pannes of ermyns, couverd with raynes of lande. Also ther was a riche autar[669] well furnyshed with reliques, and a riche cupborde well and richely garnished. And then she recomanded hir to the goode praiers of the lordes; and then my lorde hir chamberlain drew the travers.[670] And frome thens forthe no maner off officier came within the chambre but ladies and gentilwomen after the olde coustume.

Within alittell season aftir thier came a great ambassade oute of Fraunce – among the whiche ther was a kynsman of the quenes called Francois monsieur de Luxenburg, the prior of Saint Mattelyns, and Sir William[671] de Zaintes (bailly of Senlis), and Monjoie King of Armes of Frenshemen – whiche desired to se the quene, and so they dide and in her awne chambre.[672] Ther was with hir hir modir, Quene Elisabeth, and my lady the kinges modir, but ther entred no mor then ben affore reherced, savyng my lord the quenes chamberlain and Garter King of Armes.[673]

Item, on the xxjth day of Novenbre[674] was my lorde prince receipvid in maner

[669] Among the principal items of furniture in the room, the altar and its relics functioned like a good luck charm. The relics on the altar may have included the girdle of Our Lady, evidently worn by Elizabeth of York at the birth of her last child in 1503: N. H. Nicolas (ed.), *Privy Purse Expenses of Elizabeth of York: Wardrobe Accounts of Edward IV* (London 1830; repr. 1972), p. 78. See also Eamon Duffy, *The Stripping of the Altars: Traditional Religion in England, 1400–1580*, 2nd edn (London and New Haven, 2005), p. 384.

[670] Men were barred, while women took on the roles of butlers, servers, and the like. The presence of physicians was believed to cause great anxiety to the woman in labour, so childbirth usually took place in the company of female relatives and friends or, in the case of queens, a professional midwife: Laynesmith, *Last Medieval Queens*, p. 114; L. Howarth, 'The Practice of Midwifery in Late Medieval England' (unpub. MA thesis, York, 1995), pp. 15–18; Staniland, 'Royal Entry', p. 302; M. Greilsammer, 'The Midwife, the Priest, and the Physician: The Subjugation of Midwives in the Low Countries at the End of the Middle Ages', *JMRS*, 21 (1991), p. 290. The earliest printed midwifery book, *The Birth of Mankynde, otherwyse named The Woman's Boke*, first published in 1540 by Thomas Raynalde, reveals the various treatments administered for the relief of discomfort in late pregnancy. See also, Nicolas, *Privy Purse Expenses*, p. 102 for a reference to Alice Massy, midwife to Elizabeth of York during her last confinement.

[671] An error for Waleran. For discussion of this embassay and the French peace overtures of 1489–90, see especially Currin, 'Persuasions to Peace', pp. 882–904 and also *idem.*, 'Henry VII and the Treaty of Redon (1489): Plantagenet Ambitions and Early Tudor Foreign Policy', *History*, 81 (1996), pp. 343–58.

[672] The admittance of four men of the French embassy went against custom, as explicated by the herald on p. 175. See *Paston Intro and Supp*, pp. 158–9 for difficulties in obtaining an audience with Elizabeth Woodville during her confinement.

[673] In left margin in red ink and same hand as above, p. 99, n. 198: 'Garter admitted wth the Ambassadors to Come into the Queenes chamber'. In text, in a 17th-century hand, 'Principal' has been inserted into 'Garter King of Arms'.

[674] Inserted above 'day of Novenbre' in red ink and the same hand as above, p. 99, n. 198: 'Creatio: Principis Arthuri'.

as ensueth, by watter, when he came to his creacion:[675] furst frome **[f. 59]**[676] Ashehurst to Shene, whier he lay and on the W[e]nsday the xxvjth day of Novenbre, the yer of Oure Lord a thousand foure hondreth[677] iiij^{xx} and ix, and the vth yer of the reigne of King Henry the vijth as ensueth: furst the kinges barge was ryally prepared; and at Shene in the mornyng after mas and brekfaste thier, he entred the saide barge; and by the way, betwene Murtelake and Chelseth, ware ordeyned certain barges[678] bothe of lordes espirituell and temporell, whiche lordes in their owne parsons entred the princes barge (and none of thair servauntes with theyme),[679] that is to say the bishoppe of Winchester, the bishoppe of Ely, the bishoppe of Salesbury, the bishopp of Duresme, with othir; therle of Aroundell,[680] therle of Oxonforde, therle of Derby, therle off Shrewsbury, therle off Essex, therle of Kente, therle of Huntingdon, with divers other lordes, knightes and esquiers, kinges of armes, herauldes and poursuivauntes,[681] trompettes and mynstrelles within the saide barge. And at Chelchethe mette with his grace the maire of London with all the croftes in their barges, empareilled with banyeres [and] penons royally besene. And when he came before Lambeth, ther met hym the ambassatours of Spayne;[682] and with theyme many marchauntes of their nacion in shipbottes, shutting gownnes in nombre and after casting apples – as it had bene in fighting on the see with targes – **[f. 59v]** all in rejoishyng of the princes comyng.

[675] In the left margin in red ink and the same hand as above, p. 99, n. 198: 'The Creation of Arthur Prince of Wales'. Created Prince of Wales, earl of Chester, and KB: *Materials*, ii, pp. 541–2. The order of proceedings for the creation ceremony set down in the Memoir corresponds exactly to a preparatory list or plan compiled by Garter Writhe less than a week before the event and entitled 'the Articles concernyng the Creacion of my Lord Prince': Coll. Arms, MS. L8, fols 17v–19. For an heraldic account of the creation of Arthur's younger brother Henry (later King Henry VIII) as duke of York in 1494, see Julius B. XII, fols 91–110 or 'The Creation of Henry Duke of York, Seconde Sone to King Henry the seventh, 1494', in *Somers Tracts*, pp. 24–6 (printed from Cotton MS. Claudius A. VIII, which was subsequently destroyed by fire).

[676] At the top of fol. 59 in hand of Scribe B: 'm^i iiij^C iiij^{xx} ix; A° v^{to} R h vij'.

[677] Followed by the cancellation of 'xx'.

[678] A further example of pageantry on the Thames during the reign of Henry VII. Cf. the descriptions of the barges ordained for the procession to the Tower of London before Elizabeth's coronation, above, pp. 129–30. *Records of the Worshipful Company of Carpenters*, ed. B. Marsh, 4 vols (Oxford, 1913) ii, pp. 78–81 gives payments for the year 1489, including some for barge hire which may or may not have related to this event, pp. 78, 80.

[679] In the right margin in hand of Scribe B: 'A° v^{to} R h 7'.

[680] –A written over the top of two letters, possibly –er; the emendation appears to be in a later hand.

[681] In the right margin in red ink and the same hand as above, p. 99, n. 198: 'The Kings of Armes & heralds in the Princes barge'; a hand marker points to the annotation.

[682] Spanish interest in Prince Arthur was encouraged by Henry VII, who saw possibility of a marriage alliance with Ferdinand and Isabella of Spain through their youngest daughter, Katherine: Anglo, *Spectacle*, pp. 52–3.

And when he landed at the kinges brigge, all the wourshipfulist craftes of London stode in ordre on bothe sides frome the brigge to the kinges benche in Westmynster halle, wher abode the maire and the aldermen and so forth. The prince proceded to the kinges presence, whiche was in the great chambre of the briketoure.

And on the xxixth day of Novenbre, when the king went to dinar, my lord prince hild the towelle; the lord Stourton bar the watter; therle of Northumberlond toke the say; the lord Mautravers and the lorde Gray Ruthyn hilde the bassyn; and the remenant waited on the sewer and bare dishes, that is to say Thomas West (son and heire to the lord Lawar), John Saint John, Henry Vernon, John Hastinges, William Griffith, William Tyndalle, Nicholas Mongomery, William Uvedall, Mathew Browne, Thomas Darcy, Thomas Cheyney, Edmund Gorges, Waultier Denis, William Scotte, and John Gyse; and then their esquiers (gouvernours that war apointed by my lorde the kinges chamberlain), that is to say to awaite opon the prince:[683] Thomas Brandon and Thomas of Brereton.

On therle of Northumberlond:	James Hide John Parker (whiche John emploied the money otherwise that he had receipvid of the sectours for that cause and not to his wourship)
[f. 60] On the lord Mautravers:	John Baret Henry Uvedall
On the lord Gray Ruthyn:	John Griffith John Stanshow
On the lord Stourton:	David Baupie (male for by hym thoffice of armes lost moche of hir dowrie)[684]
On Sir Thomas West:	Edward Benstede Richart Fisher Thomas Mortemer
On Sir John Saint John:	Nicholas Awdeby Thomas Digby
On Sir Henry Vernon:	John Fortescu Christofer Longdale

---

[683] The esquires chosen to attend the prince and nineteen knights of the of the realm are set out in an extensive list, which also mentions the financial misdemeanours, presumably at a loss to the heralds, of two of the esquires.

[684] 'male ... dowrie' inserted in the right margin alongside 'Davide Baupie', The meaning of this statement is not entirely clear, but it is possibly that 'male', French for 'wicked', denotes Baupie's falling out of favour with the heralds for failure to pay his dues.

On Sir John Hastinges:	{ Richart Wrotesley Thomas Thorp
On Sir William Griffith:	{ John Leighton Stephen[685] Dyngley
On Sir William Tyndalle:	{ John Carleton Thomas Ferres
On Sir Nicholas Mongomery:	{ James Cayle William Mendam
On Sir William Uvedall:	{ John Knolles John Almer
On Sir Mathew Browne:	{ John Lakyn John Nell
On Sir Thomas Darcy:	{ William Paris Thomas Gardener
On Sir Thomas Cheyney:	{ James Metcalff John Warffe
On Sir Edmund Gorges:	{ Robert Githyn Alexandre Oxton
On Sir Waultier Denis:	{ James Conyers Hugh Denis
On Sir William Scotte:	{ John Sigesmont Thomas Winter
On Sir John Gyse:	{ Henry Hamps John Wistow

[f. 60v]And when it was night, the princes bayne was prepared in the kinges closet. And in the entre betwene the parlement chambre and the chappelle ware the baynes off therle off Northumberlond and the lord Mautravers and the lord Gray Ruthyn. And all the remenant ware in the parlement chambre in ordre as above written. [686]And the king in his parson gave them the advertisment of thordre of knyg[t]hode.

And that same season wer al thos[687] of the kinges chapell redyng the sauter for the good spede of the quen, wiche then traveled. And a non, upon ix of the cloke that same nyght, she was delivered of a princess,[688] wiche[689] was cristened on Seint

[685] Written 'Sthephen'.
[686] Commencement of the hand of Scribe C.
[687] Followed by the cancellation of –th.
[688] Margaret was born at nine o'clock in the evening on Sun. 29 Nov. 1489. Unlike Prince

Andreus day⁶⁹⁰ in Westmynster cherche.

And on the morn when the prince had herd his mass he was, with al his forsaid compeny, princely conveid thorought Seynt Stephens chappell to the netherend of the steiers toward the vicars logyng, wher he tooke his hors; an[d] the remenant in the paless at the sterchambre steir foot toke ther hors; and therle of Essex bere the princes swerd and spores. And soo thei roode aboute the standard in the pales in to Westmynster hall, the prince formest and the oder folowyng in ordre after ther baynes. And before the kinges benche thei alighted of ther horses, and so proceded in to the Whitt hall and stode along bi the side table. In tyme the kyng came. And when the king was comyn the marquis of Barkeley and therll of Arundell led the prince to the **[f. 61]**⁶⁹¹ presence; and therll of Oxonford, great chamberleyn of⁶⁹² Englond, toke of therl of Essex the swerd and the spores and then presented the right spore to the king. The kyng commaunded the marques of Barkeley to sett hit on the princes ryght hele, and lykewyse did therll of Arundell on the lyfft hele the toder spore. And then the kyng gard on his swerde and dubbed hym knyght, and after al his compenye in ordre, commaundyng oder lordis and knyghtis to present them and to sett on ther spores.

And when the kyng had dubbed al thos knyghtys he create[d] a pursuvaunt for the prynce and named hym Walyngford. And when the prince had offred his swerd and forgon his spores, he went efft[sonez] to the kyngis closett and put apon hym his robes of astate, and fro thens was led in to the parlement chambre to the kyngis presence by the marques of Barkeley and therll of Arundell; and therll of Derby bere his cape and cornall apon the golden rode, and the ryng of gold; and therll of Shrewesbury bere the swerd the pomell upward; and ther he was creat as acustumed. And thos lordes that led hym or bere any of the appartenans to his creacion⁶⁹³ wer in ther robes, and oder nott, havyng officers of armes next **[f. 61v]** before them.

Then the kyng departed, and the prince that day kept his astate under the clothe of astate in the same parlement chambre. And at the bordes ende satte the marques of Barkeley [and] therlles of Arundell, of Derby, and of Schrewesbury. And all the oder new mad knyghtis sat along the on side the chambre. And the prince licensed them to ett ther mett. And affter the mynstrelles had pleyd, the

---

    Arthur's birth, Margaret's may have come slightly later than anticipated for it coincided with both a session of parliament and the ceremony of Arthur's creation as Prince of Wales.

⁶⁸⁹ Repeated.

⁶⁹⁰ Mon. 30 Nov. 1489. The christening probably took place right after the last of her brother's ceremonials.

⁶⁹¹ In the right margin in red ink and the same hand as above, p. 99, n. 198: 'The King created Wallingford Pursuivant to yᵉ Prince'; a hand marker points to the annotation.

⁶⁹² Repeated.

⁶⁹³ –e obscured by an inkblot.

officers of armez came to the presence of the prynce, and Garter Kyng of Armez gave hym thankynges in the name of al the office for his largess, wyche was xxii li. delyvered by the handes of Sir Thomas Lovell, knyght and trezorer of the kynges chambre. And after that the princes largess was cryed, the largess[694] of the oder new made knyghtys was also cryed. And after dyner Sir William Uvedall was chosyn and gave the kyng thankynges in the name of al his compeny.

[695]And on the morn [of] Seynt Andreas day the fo[r]seid new born princess was cristened[696] in maner as ensewith: the riche font of Canterbury[697] and Westmynster cherche wer **[f. 62]** prepayred as of old tyme ben accustumed for kynges chyldren, wythe a riche rounde canepe with a grett gilt boll. This forsaid pryncess was brought from the qwens chambre in to the Whitthall,[698] born by my ladie marquise of Barkeley;[699] and to her gave assistence therlles of Arundell and of Schreuesbury; and my ladie Anne the qwenes sister bere next by fore here the crysome[700] with a mervelous riche crosslace; and byfore her the vicount Wellis bere a riche salt of gold[701] garnyshed wythe precyous stones; and before hym therll of Essex bere a taper[702] with certeyn boughtes floreshed and on lyght to the

[694] Repeated.
[695] In left margin in red ink and same hand as above, p. 99, n. 198: 'The Christening of the Princesse'.
[696] Cf. the account of Prince Arthur's christening on pp. 100–6. Margaret's christening is described in less detail, and in a less organised fashion, but it appears to have experienced no hitches like those at her brother's. The presence of the king at Arthur's creation the same day, and the fact that the queen had only given birth the night before, further suggests that the sovereign parents did not typically attend a baptism.
[697] See above, p. 101, n. 213, for the use of the silver font of Christ Church, Canterbury at the baptism of royal children. The herald's statement confirms that this was the font used for the baptism of Princess Margaret, if not also for Prince Arthur.
[698] See Prince Arthur's birth, above, p. 102, where the queen's outer chamber was the prior's great hall at Winchester.
[699] The infant was typically carried beneath an ornate canopy by a princess or high-ranking noblewoman, who were in turn accompanied by high-ranking men. Cf. above, p. 103.
[700] The chrismal cloth, borne in procession by a duchess, was by this date a richly jewelled and embroidered cloth pinned to the right breast: *LRC*, p. 69. It was originally a linen strip or square given by the godparents to the priest to be bound around the anointed head of the infant. Cf. the statement above, p. 105, where the bishop of Salisbury 'knytt the bande of lynene about [Prince Arthur's] nek' after confirmation. The description of Arthur's baptism above describes the chrismal cloth pinned to the right breast of the bearer; in 1480 it was pinned to the left: Routh, 'Princess Bridget', p. 13. The sixteenth-century pen-and-ink sketches in BL, MS. 583, fols 4–7b and Coll. Arms MS. 6, fols 77v–82 show the cloth being carried.
[701] Hallowed salt was used at baptisms to represent the word of God, and was placed on the tongue of the infant: Cobb, *Rationale of Ceremonial*, p. 7.
[702] This was probably the lit taper which, at the end of the church ritual, was placed in the right hand of the baptised infant that he might represent a guiding light and godly

cherche ward; and before hym therll of Kent, wiche bere a peyre of gilt basyns;[703] and before hym the constable and mareshall of England with the staves of ther offices; and by fore them the officers of armez on every side the chappell, savyng Garter, wiche went next[704] bifore the grett constable;[705] and before the chappell wer vj^{xx} torchess[706] on lyght, borne by knyghtes, esquiers and oder gentilmen and yemen of the crowne. And when the said princess was brought to the porche of Westmynster cherche – wich porche **[f. 62v]** was rialy besen and [had] a riche celyng of brodrywerke – the lord John Alcoke, bishoppe of Ely, was the[r] redie in pontificalibus, wiche cristened the princess. Alsoo ther was in his abite of bishoppe the lord John Morton, archebishopp of Canterbury and chaunceler of England, wiche was godfader, and the high and excellent princess my ladye the kynges moder, and the duchess of Norffolk, doughter of the good Talbot, erl of Schreuesbury, wiche wer godmoders; and soo she was named Margaret[707] after my ladie the kinges moder. And my ladie [Elizabeth] of Bokyngham bere the trayne and the lord Strange gave her assistence, holdyng the mydys of the trayne; and the canepe was borne bi iiij noble knyghtis banerettes, that ys to sey Sir John Savage, Sir Gilbert Talbot, Sir Edward Stanley, Sir James Blount; and after folowyd a great numbre of ladyes and gentilwemen.

And after that she was cristened and brought bifore the high auter, the lord Thomas Roderam, archebishopp of Yeorke, beyng in pontificalibus, confermed her; and the ladie marquese of Barkeley was ther a[s][708] godmoder.[709] Then weshe[d] the gossibpes and went to the closett or **[f. 63]** canves, and ther they had spices and wyn (and alsoo all oder nobles, ladies and gentyllwemen, and oder alsoo). And as son as she was put in to the font[710] all the torchess wer light and the

---

example to all men: Cobb, *Rationale of Ceremonial*, p. 12.

[703] It was customary for godparents who held the infant during anointing to wash, after which the water very carefully disposed of: Davies, *Architectural Setting*, p. 74. See also Cobb, *Rationale of Ceremonial*, pp. 7–12.

[704] 'nexevery side' cancelled between 'went' and 'next'.

[705] In the right margin in red ink and the same hand as above, p. 99, n. 198: 'Garter went next before the consta[ble]'; the final portion of 'constable' has been cropped.

[706] Preceded by a cancellation. Cf. the requisite 200 torches in *LRC*, and the account of Princess Bridget's baptism, where only 100 were used: Routh, 'Bridget', p. 13.

[707] The most explicit statement in the Memoir of the great esteem in which Margaret Beaufort was held at her son's court. See esp. Jones and Underwood, *The King's Mother*, p. 69.

[708] Written 'at'.

[709] The number, sex, identity and specific function of the godparents were probably a matter of choice for the royal parents, and variations are apparent: cf. Routh, 'Bridget', p. 13; above, pp. 100, 104.

[710] This portion of the account appears to backtrack. The lighting of the torches and the donning of the heralds' coats of arms typically took place at the point of the baptism at the font, which itself occurred before the baby was carried to the high altar and confirmed: see above, p. 104; Staniland. 'Royal Entry', p. 306; Routh, 'Bridget', p. 13.

taper also, and the officers of armes put on ther cotys of armes; and this with al thes lightes, turnyng to the kinges pales ageyne; and therll of Kent ber styll the basyns; and therll of Essex the taper brennyng; and next after them the vicount Lisle ber ij flagons gilt and a holywater stoke wythe a spryngell of gold garnyshid with precyous stones, wyche her godfader gave her; and the lord Lawarre ber a salt of gold garnyshed with presious stonys, wyche the ladye marquise gave her; and the ... ber a cope of ...[711] wyche the duchess of Norfolk gave her; and the Vicont Welles bere a chest[712] of silver and gilt full of gold, wiche my ladie the kinges moder gave her. And this in ordre, wythe nois of trompettis, she returned with Crystis blessyng. Amen.

And the kyng, the qwen [and] my ladie the kinges moder by ganne Crismass at Westmynster. And at that season ther wer the meazellis[713] soo strong, and in especiall amongis the ladies and the gentilwemen, that sum deid of that sikeness, as the ladie Nevill, doughter of William Paston; wherfor on Seint Johns day the qwen **[f. 63v]** was prively[714] cherched or purified.[715]

And on Seynt Thomas day the king, the qwen, with the court, by water remeved to Grenwich. On Cristmasday the bishoppe of Excester did the dyvynne servyce, and was accompeyned with therll of Northehumberland, therll of Derby, therll of Essex, therll of Urmond and therll of Angwyshe, wiche that day sat at the bord end with the bishoppe and ij oder erlles. Item, ther was the lord Edmonde of Suffolke, the vicount Lisle, the lord Zouche, the [lord] Latymer, the lord Dynham (trezorer of England), the lord Dawbeney (lieutenant of Caless), Sir William Stanley (the kynges chamberleyn). Alsoo the wer a great ambassad of Fraunce, that ys to sey Franchois monsieur de Luxembourgh, vicount of Geneve [and] the generall of thordre of the Trenite of Fraunce, wiche on Seynt Johns day dyned at the kinges boorde. Item, to the numbre of a xlij knyghtis or ther a bout, as Sir Thomas Bourser, Sir Davy Owen, Sir Richard Corbet, Sir John Riseley, Sir Reynold Bray, Sir Thomas Lovell, Sir John Don, Sir William Knyvett, Sir William Vampage, Sir Richart Haut, Sir Edward Wyngfeld, Sir William Hosey, Sir John Savage, Sir John Fortescu, Sir Water Hungerford, Sir Water Herbert, Sir George Nevyll, Sir Thomas Cokesey, Sir Edward Darell, Sir Richard Gilford, Sir Richard Nanfant, Sir Gilbert Debenham, Sir Roger Coton, Sir John Musgrave, Sir William Parker, **[f. 64]**[716] and oder; and esquiers for the bodie Edward Blont, Davy Philipp, Harry Pudsey, John Croker and Nycholas Ruysston. The king[717] in al this fest wer noo robes of astate but oder

---

[711] Details omitted from the text.
[712] Followed by a cancellation. In the right margin in the hand of Scribe C: 'A° v^{to} R h 7'.
[713] This is the second of two references to deadly contagion, the first being above, p. 70, where the herald records deaths in Newark in March 1486.
[714] –iv obscured by ink.
[715] See above, p. 106, n. 241.
[716] In the right margin in the hand of Scribe C: 'A° v^{to} R h 7', xijth day'.
[717] Preceded by the cancellation of –g.

THE EDITION

gownes of riche clothis of gold, and in especiall i gowne wiche was wrought by the ladyes in the stoolle and richely furred wythe sabuls.

On Newyers day the kyng rewarded his officers of armez as he ys yerly accustumed. Item, the qwen gave them forty shillinges.[718] Item, my ladye the kinges moder twenty s. Item, the reverent fader in God the bishoppe of Excester twenty s. Item, therll of Derby twenty shillings. Item, therll of Essex i noble. Item, therll of Urmond ij nobles. Item, the kinges chamberleyn three s. Item, the lord Danby xl.s. And as of old accustumed Garter King of Armez desired and besaut the king to ow them thankynges and affter cryed ther largess. On the[719] xij[th] day the ambassatours of Spayne dyned at the kinges borde, and the officers of armes had ther largess as the[y] wer acc[ust]umed. This Cristmass I saw no disgysynges and but right few pleys,[720] but ther was an abbot of misrule[721] that **[f. 64v]** made muche sport and did right well his office.

And on the morn the king rode to Waltham forest a huntyng; and soon affter with his court came to Westmynster, a[nd] ther had his consell ordeynd for suche maters and tethynges as he had by officers of armez out of Fraunce, of Bretayngne[722] and Scottland, and oder his maters ageynst the parlement;[723] and soon aughter returned the baylu of Seyn Lys out of Fraunce.

And on Candell mass day[724] the king, the qwen, my ladye the kinges moder,

---

[718] This and subsequent sums are as given by Hearne. The actual words are scarcely legible.

[719] Repeated.

[720] Christmas was a season of merry-making as well as religious devotion, when the court became the setting for further pageantry, display and the fancy dress of 'disguisings': Chambers, *Medieval Stage*, i, pp. 390–419. Account books of the reign of Henry VII reveal elaborate court revels: see especially *Materials*; Nicolas, *Privy Purse Expenses*; *Excerpta Historica, or Illustrations of English History*, ed. S. Bentley (London, 1831), pp. 85–133. The only full account of a disguising during the reign of Henry VII, that following the wedding of Prince Arthur and Katherine of Aragon in 1501, may be found in BL, MS. Harley 69 (printed in J. P. Collier, *The History of English Dramatic Poetry*, n.e., 3 vols (London, 1879), i, pp. 58–61, n. 2). See also W. R. Streitberger, *Court Revels, 1485–1559* (Toronto, 1994).

[721] The abbot or lord of misrule was a special officer in charge of the revels and entertainments of the Christmas season; an abbot of misrule was recorded for nearly every Christmas during the reign of Henry VII: Chambers, *Medieval Stage*, i, p. 403; Collier, *English Dramatic Poetry*, i, pp. 48–55; Bentley (ed.), *Excerpta Historica*, pp. 90, 92.

[722] On Breton heralds see M. Jones, 'Servir le duc: remarques sur le rôle des herauts à la court de Bretagne à la fin du Moyen Age' in *A l'ombre du pouvoir: les entourages princiers au Moyen Age*, ed. A. Marchandisse and J. L. Kupper (Geneva, 2003).

[723] Probably refers to a session of the third parliament of the reign, which opened on 13 Jan. 1489 and dissolved on 27 Feb. 1490, and may have involved extension of business discussed in the council also mentioned by the herald.

[724] In left margin in late 15th-century hand (prob. Scribe B): 'purific' A° v^{to}'.

with the subtance of al the lordes temporell present at the parlement,⁷²⁵ and grett part alsoo of the espirituell lordis, wenten a precessicion from the chappell in to the hall, and soo in to Westmynster hall, wiche hallis and alsoo al the kyng[es] chambres wer that day as richely beseen and hanged as ever I saw them.⁷²⁶ And the riche bed called 'hewdykes bede'⁷²⁷ was hanged in the kynges chambre. Therll of Oxonford, grett chamberleyn of Englond, ber the kynges taper; and therll of Urmond, the qwenys chamberleyn, ber the qwenys taper; and Sir William Knevett bere my ladye the kinges modres taper; the lord Lisle bere the kynges swerd; **[f. 65]** the lordes constable and mareshall ber ther staves of offices in gownys of clothe of gold; Garter and Lion of Scotland Kynges of Armes, in ther cootys, we[n]ten next before them; and the archebishoppe of Yeorc accompeyned the popes cubiculer; therll of Shreuesbury and the popes collectour the ambassatours of Fraunce; the byshoppe of Ely ...⁷²⁸ and Sir Richard Nanfant the ambassatours of Castyll; and byfore them oder bishoppe[s] (as the bishoppe of Norwiche), the lord trezorer and the lord st[e]ward of the kynges hous; and before them the officers of armes, as heraudys, sergenttys at armes⁷²⁹ and pursuvantes on every syde the precession.

The kyng was that day in a riche gowne of purple pirled wythe gold furred wythe sabuls. And the bishoppe of Excester, prive seall, dyd the dyvyne servyce in pontyficalibus. Al thes strangers dyned yn the court that day, but nott in presence. At nyght the kyng, the qwene and my ladye the kynges moder came in to the Whit hall, and ther had a pley and after a voyde, great acompened wythe therlles of Oxonford, Northumberland, of Derby, and many oder lordes, knyghtes and esquiers, but no strayngers. **[f. 65v]** And a non affter the bayly of Sayn Lyss returned; and the ambassatours of Fraunce had soon ther answer, and wer ryght greatly and largely rewarded and well conduyt to the see syde by the kynges amoner and Sir John Ryseley, knyght.

Son after the Kyng sent a grett ambassad in to Fraunce, that ys to sey the lord prive seall, bishoppe of Excetur,⁷³⁰ therll of Urmond (the qwenys chamberleyn) [and] the prior of Crystischerche of Canterbery. And on them wayted Yeorc the herauld. Alsoo the abbott of Abyndon⁷³¹ and Harry Swan and oder wer attaynt of treson in that parlement; and Edward Franke, Harry Davy, taileur of London, and ... wer beheded at the Tourhill.⁷³²

---

⁷²⁵ 'And on candell mass day ... parlement': several of the words of this clause have been smudged, as though by running something across the wet ink.
⁷²⁶ –th obscured by an inkblot.
⁷²⁷ Possibly an ornament or jewel (i.e. a bead) of some sort hung in the chamber, as would certainly be in keeping with Henry VII's attention to display and finery.
⁷²⁸ Details omitted from the text.
⁷²⁹ 'at armes' interlineated above.
⁷³⁰ Followed by a cancellation.
⁷³¹ Interlineated above.

And after mydlent ensewyng ther came to the kyng dyvers and many ambassatours, that ys to say a legatt from the pope; also ambassatours from the kyng of Romayns; also a grett and a solempne ambassad from the duchess of Bretayngne, this ys to sey the chaunceler of Bretayngne, the capiteyn of ...,[733] Gwilliam Gwillemett, the seneschall of Gyngham, with oder. Item, anoder ambassad from the mareshall **[f. 66]** of Bretayngne.[734] Item, oder ambassatours from the towne of Bruges. Item, and officers of armes from the kyng of Scottys. And al the above seyd ambassatours the kyng herd and alsoo delyvered at Westmynster in the pashecyon weke, and retourned to Shen a geyne wher his houshold lay.

---

[732] The names of two of those executed with the abbot of Abingdon may have been John Mayne and *Christopher* Swan: *RP*, vi, pp. 346–7; Kirby, *Plumpton Letters and Papers*, p. 88. Luckett, 'Patronage and Violence', pp. 151–2 (gives Davy's Christian name as Christopher). Plumpton suggests the felons were executed by hanging, the herald by beheading; but it may have been a case of execution by hanging, drawing and quartering, a punishment typically reserved for non-noble traitors.

[733] Details omitted from the text.

[734] Second –n partially obscured by an inkblot.

GLOSSARY

This glossary is intended to explain unfamiliar words and meanings, elucidate contextual sense, and identify words which seem orthographically disguised.

affiance *n.* faith, trust.
agu *n.* ague, sickness.
albes *n. pl.* albs; white vestments reaching to the feet, worn here by the monks of Westminster.
almesse *n. pl.* alms.
ambassat *n.* embassy; **ambassates** *n. pl.*
amys *n. pl.* amices; fur lined hoods or hooded caps.
aproprede *pp.* assigned or attributed (as proper to something).
arras *n.* hanging screen of rich tapestry, usually on the walls of a room.
artyficer *n.* craftsman.
assisede *pp.* measured.
assuffrayn *n.* sovereign(?)[1]

bachelor *n.* young knight who followed the banner of another.
bake mete *n.* dish baked in a shell of pastry, such as a meat pie, tart, or custard.
bandes *n. pl.* shackles, fetters, bonds.
banekolles *n. pl.* long, narrow flags or streamers.
baner *n.* banner, **banyeres** *n. pl.*
bawdrik *n.* baldric; belt for sword hung from shoulder across body to opposite hip.
baylu, bay(l)ly, bailly *n.* bailiff.
baynnes *n. pl.* baths.
bayting *pr. p.* abating, stopping, pausing.
bekes *n. pl.* peaks or points; here, the pointed forward peaks on the hats worn by esquires of honour.
beneson *n.* benison; blessing.
benynge *n.* magnanimity.
besene, besen *pp.* arrayed, dressed.

[1] Although 'sufferayn' was a common form of 'sovereign' in the fifteenth and sixteenth centuries, there is no precedent for the spelling 'assufferayn'. It is possible that the original poet intended 'theas sufferayn' (this sovereign) or 'the as sufferayn' (thee as sovereign) but that Memoir Scribe A copied it incorrectly.

GLOSSARY

bicokett *n.* bycocket; men's hat, pointed and pulled down at the front, with turned-up brim at the back.
bittowre *n. pl.* bitterns.
borde *n.* table laid out for a feast.
boughtes *n. pl.* coils.
brennyng *pr. p.* burning; **brente** *pp.* burned.
Bretayne, Bretaigne, Brytaigne *n.* Brittany; Britain.
brodrywerk *n.* embroidery.
Bruggelingis *n. pl.* inhabitants of Bruges.
busshementes *n. pl.* (location from which to launch) military ambushes.

calle *n.* caul; woman's close-fitting indoor headdress, especially the plain back part.
cele *n.* cover, canopy, awning.
celid *pp.* adorned with a cover or canopy.
cesterne *n.* cistern.
chales *n.* chalice.
chanoignes *n. pl.* canons.
chare *n.* chair, meat; *graunt* ~ ground meat.
chaunderye *n.* chandlery; department of the chandler or dealer in candles, oil, soap, paint and groceries.
chaunter *n.* chanter, singer, poet, minstrel.
chawdron *n.* sauce for fowl or fish containing chopped entrails.
Chelchethe, Chelseth *n.* Chelsea, London.
circulettes *n. pl.* circlets or coronets, ornamental bands for the head.
clarions *n. pl.* shrill, narrow-tubed war trumpets.
clenly *adv.* splendidly, elegantly, handsomely; ~ *horsed* elegantly mounted.
coffrier *n.* cofferer; household official in charge of the coffers.
comfettes *n. pl.* comfits; sweets containing a nut, seed, etc. encased in sugar.
conding, condigne *adj.* condign; equal in worth or dignity.
conduit, conduyt, coundite, condit *v.t.* conduct, escort; *n.* conduit.
copes *n. pl.* ecclesiastical vestments, long cloaks worn by Catholic priests on special occasions.
corounall, corownall, cornall, *n.* coronal, coronet, ornamental bands for the head.
courser, cowreser *n.* courser; swift horse, charger.
cousthyns, cusshins *n. pl.* cushions.
coyff *n.* coif; close cap covering top, back and sides of head.
cremesyn, cremesyne *adj.* crimson.
cresome, crysome *n.* chrism; here, denoting the chrismal cloth or child's white robe at baptism.
cristene *adj.* Christian; **cristenly** *adv.* in Christian manner.

croyser *n.* bearer of the crosier, or hooked staff symbolising the pastoral office of the bishop.
cubiculer *n.* chamber servant.

deken *n.* deacon.
demeane *n.* demesne.
demy trapper *n.* horse's caparison of half-length.
deperte *pp.* dipped.
devince *v.t.* defeat, overcome; **devincede** *pp.*
devoir *n.* endeavour.
disperclede *pp.* dispersed.
dissaveaunce *n.* deceit, deception.
distorbled *pp.* stirred or broken up.
Dixemue *n.* Dixmude in modern-day Belgium.
doian *n.* dean; **doiens** *n. poss.*; *the ~ palace* the dean's palace.
dooing *adj.* (?)working; *~ horses* (?)work-horses.
dynnyt *pp.* dined.

efsones, -z, efftsonez *adv.* soon after.
egretes *n.* lesser egret (fowl).
embaytailled *pp.* stationed and arrayed for battle.
emparelede *pp.* apparelled, arrayed.
enarmed, enarmede *pp.* adorned with coats of arms.
enbrace *v.t.* inflame with passion.
enduede *pp.* endowed, invested (with power, quality, spiritual gift, etc.).
enraumpisshede *pp.* decorated, adorned.
ensence *v.t.* enlighten, instruct, inform.
eschew(e) *v.t.* show, demonstrate, reveal; **eschewing** *pr. p.*
espace *n.* period, duration.
eury *n.* ewery; household office responsible for the crockery.

filede *pp.* defiled, polluted, corrupted.
flourdelissis *n. pl.* fleurs-de-lis.
forwarde *n.* vanguard.
for ryders *n. pl.* foreriders, scouts; men who rode ahead of an army or as part of the vanguard.
fraunches *n. pl.* franchises.
freres, frerez *n. pl.* friars.
frumetye *n.* frumenty; potage made of boiled hulled grain mixed with milk and sweetened.
fruter *n.* fritter
fumygacions *n. pl.* perfuming with aromatic herbs, usually to ward off disease or evil.

GLOSSARY

galantes *n. pl.* gallant knights.
galyes *n. pl.* galleys.
gardein, gardien *n.* guardian; **gardens** *n. pl.*
garuyson, garryson *n.* garrison.
gerdit, gerdid *pp.* girded, encircled, fastened about the waist.
glasid *adj.* made of glass; here, (?)adorned with windows.
Goly *bibl.* Goliath.
gosseps, gossibpes *n. pl.* gossips or familiar acquaintances; here, the queen's female companions.
gowles *n. pl.* jowls.
gownne, gowne, gounne *n.* gown; gun; **gounes, gownys, gownes, gownnes** *n. pl.*
grese, grece, gres, gresse *n.* red deer stag; rendered cooking-fat; step, stair, flight of stairs; **greces** *n. pl.*
grotes *n. pl.* **groats**; small silver coins worth about 4p.
gystys *n. pl.* lodgings, resting places (us. on progress or journey).

hakneyes *n. pl.* hackneys; horses for ordinary riding.
harbygage *n.* lodge.
heder *adv.* hither, to here.
henshemen, henxmen, henchemen *n. pl.* henchmen; trusty followers (usually squires or pages of honour).
herbigers, herbygeours, herbergier *n. pl.* harbingers; those sent as purveyors of lodgings for the royal party or camping ground for an army.
Herborow *n.* Market Harborough, Leicestershire.
hider *adj. comp.* higher; *adv.* hither.
hode *n.* hood; **hodys** *n. pl.*
hostengis, -es *n. pl.* hostages.

incontynent(ly) *adv.* immediately, forthwith.
ingraylede *pp.* dyed purple.
inordynatly *adv.* excessively and in a disorderly manner.

jackes *n. pl.* jacks; reinforced tunics worn by men-at-arms, akin to the modern flak jacket.
Jude *bibl.* Judaea.

kerved(e) *pp.* served as carver at the royal banquet
knoppes *n. pl.* the ornamental studs, knobs or knots on the end of the laces or cord used to fasten the queen's mantle.
kynnerede *n.* kindred.

lase *n.* lace.
lazares howsez *n. pl.* 'Lazarus houses'; hostels for poor and/or diseased people, esp. lepers.
legeaunce, liegence *n.* sway, jurisdiction.
leyn *pp.* stayed, dwelt briefly.
logge *v.i.* lodge; **loggede** *pp.* lodged.
look *n.* luck.
lynene *n.* linen.

manerly *adv.* in the manner of.
marche payne *n.* marzipan.
marres *n. pl.* marshes.
mase *n.* mace; staff of office.
meane *n.* mediator.
messe *n.* mass.
metenz *n. pl.* (?)meats; (?)mittens.
moten *n. pl.* (?)meats.
minisshing *pr. p.* ministering, supplying, handing out.
moustres *n. pl.* musters, marshalling of troops.
mustredeveles *n.* musterdevillers; mixed grey woollen cloth of the fourteenth and fifteenth centuries.
mysdooers *n. pl.* miscreants.

napery *n.* household linen; the office that deals with this.
ne *conj.* nor.
Noe *bibl.* Noah.
norserye *n.* nursery.
noysing *pr. p.* noising, spreading gossip, hearsay or slander
nygh *adv.* nigh; ~ *hand* near at hand, nearby.

obles *n. pl.* obleys; thin pastry cakes or wafers.
ouchez *n. pl.* a buckle or broach worn as an ornament, often set with precious stones.
overt(e) *adj.* open.

palferees, palfereys *n. pl.* palfreys; saddle-horses for ordinary riding, especially for ladies.
palliet *n.* pallet, straw bed or mattress.
paly *n. (heraldic)* a divided pattern of equal vertical stripes.
pannes *n. pl.* panes, panels.
pashecyon *n.* Passion; ~ *week* the week between Passion Sunday and Palm Sunday.

patenz *adj.* letters, letters patent.
pax *n.* plaque decorated with an image of Christ's passion or similar, passed among congregation after the priest has given it the kiss of peace.
pennoncez, penons *n. pl.* pennants.
penssell *n.* small pennant or streamer; **penselles** *n. pl.*.
pistell, pistill *n.* epistle.
pixe *n.* pyx; the vessel in which the consecrated bread is kept.
Pomfreyte, Pomfret, Pontfret *n.* Pontefract, Yorkshire.
pontificalibus, –z *n. pl.* bishop's official robes; *in* ~ in pontificals, in the vestments appropriate to the ecclesiastical dignity of the wearer.
Portyngall *n.* Portugal.
pouldre *n.* powder
powderde *pp.* 'powdered'; decorated all over with a small, usually embroidered, designs.
Powles *n.* St Paul's Cathedral, London.
preordynaunce *n.* a previously established ordinance.
prepotent *adj.* pre-eminent, most excellent.
prosterne *v.i.* lie flat, prostrate.
prothonatory, prothonotoire *n.* the principal notary of a court; the chief clerk in the Court of Chancery.
purede *adj.* wholesome.
purified *pp.* churched; taken through the ritual of thanksgiving and purification after the birth of a child.
Putname *n.* Putney, in modern-day Greater London.
Pyguardye *n.* Picardy.

quadraunt *n.* courtyard or quadrangle.
quarrell *n.* short heavy arrow or bolt used in a crossbow or arbalest; **quarelles** *n. pl.* skirmishes, affrays.
quarterd *pp. drawen and* ~ put to death through hanging, disembowelling and cutting into quarters; **quarterly** *adv. (heraldic)* the manner of dividing coats of arms arranged on one shield to denote alliances of families, etc.; **quarter** *n.* one part of this division.

race *n.* story, narrative.
ray *adj.* ~ *clothe* decorative striped or streaked cloth.
raylede *pp.* striped.
raynes *n. pl.* fine linen, possibly of Rheims or Rennes.
rebouted *pp.* routed.
recountrede *pp.* met in battle.
redoubtede *pp.* feared, respected, venerated.
refresche *v.t.* provide relief for, rescue from siege.

regesly *adv.* with rage; in fury or anger.
regestre *n.* registrar; register.
remytting *pr. p.* resigning, surrendering, giving up.
rescusse *v.t.* rescue.
residencers *n. pl.* residents.
revested *pp.* re-robed, dressed again in the appropriate vestments.
revestry *n.* vestry.
rigours *adj.* rigorous.

sad *adj.* serious, earnest.
Salamon *bibl.* Solomon.
sambres *n. pl.* saddle cloths.
sapience *n.* wisdom.
sarsenet *n.* fine soft silk material, often used for linings.
say *n.* cloth of fine texture resembling serge, sometimes partly of silk.
seche *v.i. (pr. 3 pl.)* search for.
sege *n.* chair, seat; seige.
sewed *pp.* performed the duty of sewer at a banquet.
sewer *n.* the person superintending the arrangements of the table, esp. the high table, and the tasting and serving of dishes.
seyle *n.* seal.
Sherethursday *n.* Maundy Thursday
shipbottes *n. pl.* small vessels used for sailing into shallow waterways or canals
sith *conj.* since, because.
skrye *n.* panic, pandemonium; **skryes** *n. pl.*
snytes *n. pl.* common snipes.
sobre *adj.* serious, dignified.
soke *pp.* suckled.
soteltie *n.* subtlety, a sugar confection modelled in an elaborate motif.
sothfastness *n.* constancy, steadfastness, fidelity.
sothly *adv.* truly.
soyson *n.* season, given period of time.
splayde *pp.* displayed.
Staunford *n.* Stamford, Lincolnshire.
stole, stoolle *n.* stool; *ladyes in the* ~ the queen's female attendants.
Stook *n.* Stoke-on-Trent, Staffordshire.
striff *n.* dissension, discord, conflict; **stryves** *n. pl.*
sturgyn *n.* sturgeon, large fish resembling a shark and esteemed as food.
suete, suett, sute *n.* suit, matching garb or livery or material.
sugurys *n. pl.* sugars.
supporacion *n.* help, assistance, aid, backing.
surnap *n.* a towel or napkin provided at the table for use when washing the hands.

GLOSSARY

tabarde, tabert *n.* tabard; knight's short emblazoned garment worn over armour or herald's official coat emblazoned with arms of the sovereign.
Temmys, Temys *n.* River Thames.
tethynges *n. pl.* tidings, news.
thedawards *prep.* toward it/this/that.
thwarte *prep.* toward(s).
tracte, tract *n.* period (of time).
trainde *pp.* (?) placed in a line (?).
trapper *n.* horse's caparison, or ornamental covering; **trapped** *pp.* dressed with a trapper or adorned with trappings.
traveled *pp.* travailed, suffered the pains of childbirth.
travers *n* screen, partition, curtain.
trononyzacion *n.* enthronisation, installation; ceremony of installing primate upon the archiepiscopal throne; **intrononysed** *pp.*

uncion *n.* unction; anointing with oil or unguent.
undeseverable *adj.* cannot be disunited.[2]

valance *n.* short curtain, made from cloth of gold, around the canopy of the queen's litter
vew *n.* view; *took the ~ of* surveyed, looked over, assessed.
vices *n. pl.* mechanical devices.
void(e), voyd(e) *n.* parting meal, usually with wine and spices; *v.t.* to part.
vytayll *n.* victual(s).

warner *n.* the principal subtlety, or sugar confection, preceding a banquet.
wele, welle, wel *adv.* well; *n.* weal.
Worshop, Wourshop *n.* Worsop, Nottinghamshire.
worstede *n.* worsted; fabric made from twisted yarn spun of long-staple wool, combed to lay the fibres parallel.

ye *n.* eye; **yene** *n. pl.*
yef *v.t. (pr. 2 s.)* give.
yeftes *n. pl.* gifts.
yerle *n.* earl.
yode *pp.* went.

---

[2] Probably derived from the word 'dissever' but constructed for the purpose of the pageantic narrative: McGee, *First Provincial Progress*, p. cxi.

SELECT BIBLIOGRAPHY

I. *Manuscript Sources*

Alnwick Castle
Alnwick 467 — A volume of miscellaneous tracts.

British Library
Additional MS 6113 — *Ceremonies, etc., Edw. III – Eliz. I*: a sixteenth-century volume of heraldic ceremonial proceedings.
Additional MS 46354 — 'Writhe's Book of Knights': vol. 4 of *Wriothesley's Heraldic Collections* and mainly consisting of lists of knights arranged chronologically under the occasion of their creation, and illustrations of their arms.
Cotton Faustina E. V — Miscellaneous tracts on English antiquities.
Cotton Julius B. I — English Chronicle accounts of battles etc, compiled soon after the death of Edward IV, partly copied from earlier hands.
Cotton Julius B. XII — A composite MS. of historical texts, in English, French and Latin, and chiefly of heraldic and genealogical interest.
Cotton Julius C. VI — *John Leland Collections, etc*. Diverse materials largely of antiquarian interest, including tracts in the hands of John Leland.
Egerton 985 — Ceremonial and heraldic proceedings of the late fifteenth and early sixteenth centuries.
Harley 6018 — *Catalogus Librorum Manuscriptorum in Bibliotheca Roberti Cottoni, 1621*.
Harley 6069 — *Heraldic Tracts*. Collection of writings of heraldic interest, including ceremonial accounts and lists of office holders, mostly penned in the sixteenth century.
Harley 7048 — *Baker's Cambridge Collections*. A volume containing diverse materials from Cambridge University particular to heraldic narratives, transcribed in a single eighteenth-century hand.
Stowe 583 — A sixteenth-century volume of royal ceremonial accounts.

College of Arms

I.7   A sixteenth-century collection of ceremonial accounts in various hands.

M6   *Interments of Queens. Tiltings. Tournaments and Ceremonies.* A mid sixteenth-century volume of royal ceremonials and precedents relating to tournaments.

II. Printed Primary Sources

'Account of the Ceremonial of the Marriage of Princess Margaret Sister of King Edward IV to Charles Duke of Burgundy in 1468', ed. Sir Thomas Phillipps, *Archaeologia*, 31 (1846), pp. 326-38.

'An Account of the First Battle of St. Albans from a Contemporary Manuscript', ed. J. Bayley, in *Archaeologia*, 20 (1824), pp. 519–23.

André, Bernard, 'Vita Henrici Septimi' in *Memorials of King Henry the Seventh*, pp. 3–75.

The Anglica Historia of Polydore Vergil, ed. D. Hay, Camden Soc., n.s., 74 (London, 1950).

Bacon, Francis, *The History of the Reign of King Henry the Seventh*, ed. F. J. Levy (New York, 1972).

The Beauchamp Pageant, ed. A. Sinclair (Richard III and Yorkist History Trust, 2003).

'The Beryinge of an Erle', in *Antiquarian Repertory,* comp. F. Grose and T. Astle et al., new edn, ed. E. Jeffrey, 4 vols (London, 1807–9), i, pp. 314–17.

British Library Harleian Manuscript 433, ed. R. Horrox and P. W. Hammond, The Richard III Society, 4 vols (Gloucester, 1979–83).

Calendar of State Papers and Manuscripts, relating to English Affairs, existing in the Archives and Collections of Venice, and in other Libraries of Northern Italy. Vol. 1. Venetian 1202–1509, ed. R. Brown et al. (London, 1864–1947; repr. 1979).

A Calendar of the White and Black Books of the Cinque Ports, 1432–1955, ed. F. Hull (London, 1966).

Cambridge University, *Grace Book A*, ed. S. M. Leathes (Cambridge, 1897).

'The Christenynge of Prince Arthure, Sonne to Kynge Henrie ye VII at Sent Swithins in Winchestar' in Stowe, *Three Fifteenth-Century Chronicles*, pp. 104–05.

A Chronicle of the First Thirteen Years of the Reign of King Edward the Fourth, by John Warkworth, ed. J. O. Halliwell, Camden Soc., 10 (London, 1839).

Chronicle of the Grey Friars of London, ed. J. G. Nichols, Camden Soc., o.s., 53 (London, 1852).

Chronicles of London, ed. C. L. Kingsford (Oxford, 1905).

Chroniques de Jean Molinet (1474–1506), ed. G. Doutrepont and O. Jodogne, 3 vols (Brussels, 1935–7).

A Collection of Ordinances and Regulations for the Government of the Royal

Household made in Divers Reigns from King Edward III to King William and Queen Mary: Also Receipts in Ancient Cookery, printed for the Society of Antiquaries (London, 1790).

The Coronation of Elizabeth Wydeville, Queen Consort of Edward IV, on May 26th, 1465, ed. G. Smith (London, 1935).

'Coronation of Queen Ann, Wife to Henry VIII', in *Antiquarian Repertory*, comp. F. Grose and T. Astle et al., new edn, ed. E. Jeffrey, 4 vols (London, 1807–9), i, pp. 232–7.

The Coronation of Richard III: the Extant Documents, ed. A. F. Sutton and P. W. Hammond (Gloucester, 1983).

English Coronation Records, ed. L. G. W. Legg (Westminster, 1901).

Excerpta Historica, or Illustrations of English History, ed. S. Bentley (London, 1831).

Extracts from the Municipal Records of the City of York during the Reigns of Edward IV, Edward V and Richard III, ed. R. Davies (London, 1843).

Foedera, etc., ed. T. Rymer, 2nd edn, ed. G. Holmes, 17 vols (London, 1727–9).

'From a Chronicle of Tewkesbury Abbey, 1471', in C. L. Kingsford, *English Historical Literature* (New York, 1913), pp. 377–8.

The Great Chronicle of London, ed. A. H. Thomas and I. D. Thornley (London, 1938).

The Great Roll of the Tournament of Westminster. A Collotype Reproduction of the Manuscript, ed. Sydney Anglo, 2 vols (Oxford, 1968).

Hall, E., *The Union of the Two Noble and Illustre Families of Lancastre and York*, ed. H. Ellis (London, 1809).

Holinshed, Raphael, *Chronicles of England, Scotland and Ireland*, ed. V. F. Snow, 6 vols (New York, 1965).

Household Books of John Howard, Duke of Norfolk, 1462–71, 1481–8, ed. Anne Crawford, new edn (Richard III and Yorkist History Trust, 1992).

Household Books of John, duke of Norfolk, and Thomas, earl of Surrey, 1481–90, ed. J. P. Collier, Roxburghe Club (1844).

The Household of Edward IV: the Black Book and the Ordinance of 1478, ed. A. R. Myers (Manchester, 1959).

Illustrations of the Manners and Expenses of Antient Times in England, ed. J. Nichols for the Society of Antiquaries (1797).

Illustrations of State and Chivalry from MSS Preserved in the Ashmolean Museum, ed. W. H. Black (London, 1840).

Ingulph's Chronicle of the Abbey of Croyland, ed. H. T. Riley (London, 1893).

Le Débat des Hérauts d'Armes de France et d'Angleterre, ed. L. C. A. Pannier and M. P. H. Meyer (Paris, 1877).

Leland, John, *De Rebus Britannicis Collectanea*, ed. Thomas Hearne, 6 vols (London, 1774).

Letters and Papers Illustrative of the Reigns of Richard III and Henry VII, ed.

James Gairdner, HMSO, 2 vols (London, 1861–63 ; repr. 1965).
'*Liber Regie Capelle*': *a Manuscript in the Biblioteca Publica, Evora*, ed. W. Ullmann, Henry Bradshaw Soc., 92 (Cambridge, 1961).
Manners and Household Expenses of England in the Thirteenth and Fifteenth Centuries, ed. T. H. Turner, Roxburghe Club (London, 1841).
'Marriage of the Princess Margaret, Sister of Edward IV, A.D. 1468' in Bentley (ed.), *Excerpta Historica*, pp. 223–39.
Materials for a History of the Reign of Henry VII, ed. W. Campbell, RS, 60, 2 vols (London, 1873; repr. 1965).
Memorials of King Henry the Seventh, ed. J. Gairdner, RS, 10, (1858).
Monumenta Franciscana, ed. J. S. Brewer and R. Howlett, HMSO (London, 1858–82; repr. 1965).
'Narrative of the Marriage of Richard Duke of York with Ann of Norfolk, the 'Matrimonial Feast', and the Grand Justing, A.D. 1477' in Black (ed.), *Illustrations of State and Chivalry*, pp. 25–40.
Paston Letters 1422–1509 A.D., ed. J. Gairdner, 6 vols, with introduction and supplement (Westminster 1872–5; repr. 1901).
Paston Letters, A.D. 1422–1509, ed. J. Gairdner, n.c.e., 6 vols (London, 1904).
Paston Letters and Papers of the Fifteenth Century, ed. N. Davis, 2 vols (Oxford, 1971–6).
Plumpton Correspondence: a Series of Letters, Chiefly Domestic, Written in the Reigns of Edward IV, Richard III, Henry VII, and Henry VIII, ed. T. Stapleton. Camden Soc., 4 (London, 1839).
The Plumpton Letters and Papers, Camden 5th ser., 8, ed. J. Kirby (Cambridge, 1996).
The Poetical Works of John Skelton, ed. A. Dyce, 2 vols (New York, 1965).
'Princess Bridget', ed. P. E. Routh, *The Ricardian*, 3.49 (1975), pp. 13–14.
Privy Purse Expenses of Elizabeth of York: Wardrobe Accounts of Edward the Fourth, ed. Sir N. H. Nicolas (London, 1830; repr. 1972).
Proceedings and Ordinances of the Privy Council of England, ed. Sir N. H. Nicolas, 7 vols (London, 1834–7).
The Reburial of Richard Duke of York, 21–30 July 1476, ed. A. F. Sutton and Livia Visser-Fuchs, The Richard III Society (1996).
The Receyt of the Ladie Kateryne, ed. G. Kipling, EETS (Oxford, 1990).
'The Record of Bluemantle Pursuivant, 1471–1472', in C. L. Kingsford, *English Historical Literature* (New York, 1913), pp. 378–88.
Records of the Borough of Leicester, ed. M. Bateson (Cambridge, 1901).
Records of the Borough of Nottingham, being a Series of Extracts from the Archives of the Corporation of Nottingham, ed. W. H. Stevenson, W. T. Baker, et al., 6 vols (London, 1882–1956).
The Red Paper Book of Colchester, ed. W. G. Benham (Colchester, 1902).
The Regulations and Establishment of the Household of Henry Algernon Percy,

the Fifth Earl of Northumberland. Begun A.D. 1512, ed. T. Percy (London, 1770).

The Reign of Henry VII from Contemporary Sources, ed. A. F. Pollard, 3 vols (London, 1913).

Ricart, Robert, *The Maire of Bristowe is Kalendar*, ed. Lucy Toulmin Smith, Camden, n.s., 5 (1872).

Rotuli Parliamentorum, ed. J. Strachey et al., 6 vols (London, 1767–77).

Rutland Papers, ed. W. Jerdan, Camden Soc., 21 (London, 1842).

Select Cases in the Exchequer Chamber before all the Justices of England, ed. M. Hemmant, Seldon Soc., 51 and 64, 2 vols (London, 1933–48).

Smith, Thomas, *Catalogue of the Manuscripts in the Cottonian Library, 1696*, ed. C. G. C. Tite (Cambridge, 1984).

The Travels of Leo von Rozmital, trans. M. Letts, Hakluyt Soc., 2nd ser., 108 (Cambridge, 1957).

Three Books of Polydore Vergil's English History, comprising the Reigns of Henry VI, Edward IV and Richard III, ed. Sir H. Ellis, Camden Soc., o.s., 29 (London, 1844).

Three Fifteenth-Century Chronicles with Historical Memoranda by John Stowe, the Antiquary, ed. J. Gairdner, Camden Soc., n.s., 28 (London, 1880).

Tudor Royal Proclamations, ed. P. L. Hughes and J. F. Larkin, 2 vols (New Haven and London, 1964–69).

A Volume of English Miscellanies Illustrating the History and Language of the Northern Counties of England, ed. J. Raine, Surtees Soc., 85 (1890).

Warkworth's Chronicle of the First Thirteen Years of the Reign of King Edward the Fourth, ed. J. O. Halliwell, Camden Soc., o.s., 10 (1839).

Worcester, William, *Itineraries*, ed. John H. Harvey (Oxford, 1969).

York City Chamberlains' Account Roll, 1396–1500, ed. R. B. Dobson, Surtees Soc., 192 (Gateshead, 1980).

York Civic Records, ed. Angelo Raine, Yorks. Arch. Soc. Records Ser., 98 (Wakefield, 1939).

York House Books, 1461–1490, ed. L. C. Atreed, Richard III and Yorkist History Trust, 2 vols (Stroud, 1991).

'A York Pageant, 1486', ed. A. H. Smith in *London Mediaeval Studies*, 1.3 (1948 for 1939), pp. 382–98.

III. Secondary Sources

Ailes, Adrian, 'Heraldry in Medieval England: Symbols of Politics and Propaganda', in *Heraldry, Pageantry and Social Display in Medieval England,* ed. P. R. Coss and M. H. Keen (Woodbridge, 2002), pp. 83–104.

Alexander, M. van Cleave, *The First of the Tudors: a Study of Henry VII and his Reign* (London, 1981).

Anglo, S., 'The Foundation of the Tudor Dynasty; the Coronation and Marriage of

Henry VII', *The Guildhall Miscellany*, 2.1 (1960), pp. 1–9.

—, 'The Court Festivals of Henry VII: a Study Based upon the Account Books of John Heron, Treasurer of the Chamber', *BJRL*, 43 (Sept. 1960), pp. 12–45.

—, 'The *British History* in early Tudor Propaganda', *BJRL*, 44 (1961), pp. 17–48.

—, 'Financial and Heraldic Records of the English Tournament', *JSA*, 2.5 (1962), pp. 183–95.

—, 'Anglo-Burgundian Feats of Arms: Smithfield, June 1467', *Guildhall Miscellany*, 2.7 (1965), pp. 271–83.

—, *Spectacle, Pageantry and Early Tudor Policy* (Oxford, 1969).

—, *Images of Tudor Kingship* (London, 1992).

—, *The Martial Arts of Renaissance Europe* (New Haven and London, 2000).

anon. 'Yorkshire Rebellion', *Gentleman's Magazine*, 129.2 (1851).

Armstrong, C. A. J., 'Politics and the Battle of St. Albans', in idem, *England, France and Burgundy in the Fifteenth Century* (London, 1983), pp. 1–72.

—, 'The Inauguration Ceremonies of the Yorkist Kings and their Title to the Throne', in idem, *England, France and Burgundy*, pp. 73–96.

—, 'Some Examples of the Distribution and Speed of News at the Time of the Wars of the Roses', in idem, *England, France and Burgundy*, pp. 97–122.

—, 'L'échange culturel entre les cours d'Angleterre et de Bourgogne à l'époque de Charles le Téméraire' in idem, *England, France and Burgundy*, pp. 403–17.

Ayton, A., 'Knights, Esquires and Military Service: The Evidence of the Armorial Cases before the Court of Chivalry', in *The Medieval Military Revolution. State, Society and Military Change in Early Modern Europe*, ed. A. Ayton and J. L. Price (repr. London, 1998), pp. 81–104.

Barker, Juliet R. V., *The Tournament in England, 1100–1400* (Suffolk and New Hampshire, 1986).

Bennett, M. J., *The Battle of Bosworth* (Gloucester, 1985; repr. 2000).

—, *Lambert Simnel and the Battle of Stoke* (Gloucester, 1987).

—, 'Henry VII and the Northern Rising of 1489', *EHR*, 105 (1990), pp. 34–59.

Besant, W., *Medieval London*, 2 vols (London, 1906).

Beltz, G. F., *Memorials of the Most Noble Order of the Garter* (London, 1841).

Brennan, G., *A History of the House of Percy, from the Earliest Times down to the Present Day*, 2 vols (London, 1902).

Briquet, C. M., *Les Filigranes*, 2nd edn, 2 vols (New York, 1966).

Brown, A. L., *The Governance of Late Medieval England, 1272–1461* (California, 1989).

Busch, W., *England Under the Tudors: Vol. 1, King Henry VII*, trans. A. M. Todd (London, 1895).

Calmette, J., *The Golden Age of Burgundy: the Magnificent Dukes and their Courts*, new edn (London, 2001).

Cameron, A., 'The Giving of Livery and Retaining in Henry VII's Reign', *Renais-*

sance and Modern Studies, 18 (1974), pp. 17–35.

Campbell, L., et al., *A Catalogue of Manuscripts in the College of Arms* (London, 1988).

Carpenter, C., *Locality and Polity. A Study of Warwickshire Landed Society, 1401–1499* (Cambridge, 1992).

Cavell, E. 'Henry VII, the North of England, and the First Provincial Progress of 1486, *Northern History*, 39.2 (2002), pp. 189–207.

Chambers, E. K., *The Elizabethan Stage*, 2 vols (Oxford, 1923; repr. 1967).

Chaplais, P., *English Diplomatic Practice in the Middle Ages* (London and New York, 2003).

Chesshyre, H., 'Heralds on Parade', *British Heritage*, 5.6 (1984), pp. 44–51.

Chrimes, S. B., *Henry VII*, new edn (New Haven and London, 1999).

—, *Lancastrians, Yorkists and Henry VII* (London, 1964).

Cripps-Day, F. H., *The History of the Tournament in England and France* (London, 1918).

Collins, Hugh E. L., *The Order of the Garter, 1348–1461: Chivalry and Politics in Late Medieval England* (Oxford, 2000).

Condon, M., 'Ruling Elites in the Reign of Henry VII', in *Patronage, Pedigree and Power*, ed. Charles Ross (Gloucester, 1979), pp. 109–42.

Cooper, C. H. (ed.), *Annals of Cambridge* (Cambridge, 1842), vol. 1.

Crouch, D., *Tournament* (London, 2005).

Cunningham, S., 'Henry VII and the Rebellion in North-Eastern England, 1485–1492. Bonds of Allegiance and the Establishment of Tudor Authority', *Northern History*, 32 (1996), pp. 42–74.

Dawson, G. E. and Kennedy-Skipton, L., *Elizabethan Handwriting, 1500–1650* (Chichester, 1981).

Denholm-Young, N., *History and Heraldry, 1254–1310. A Study of the Historical Value of the Rolls of Arms* (Oxford, 1965).

Dickinson, J. C., *The Later Middle Ages: From the Norman Conquest to the Eve of the Reformation. An Ecclesiastical History of England* (London, 1979).

Doig, J. A., 'Propoganda and Truth: Henry V's Royal Progress in 1421', *Nottingham Medieval Studies*, 40 (1996).

Edwards, R., *The Itinerary of King Richard III, 1483–5* (London, 1983).

Elton, G. R., *The Tudor Revolution in Government. Administrative Changes in the Reign of Henry VIII* (Cambridge, 1953).

—, 'Tudor Government: the Points of Contact. III. The Court', *TRHS*, 5th ser., 26 (1976).

Ferguson, J., *English Diplomacy, 1422–1461* (Oxford, 1972).

Fonblanque, E. B. de, *Annals of the House of Percy*, 2 vols (London, 1887).

Gittings, C., *Death, Burial and the Individual in Early Modern England* (London and Sydney, 1984).

Godfrey, Walter H., et al., *The College of Arms* (London, 1963).

Goodman, A., *The Wars of the Roses. Military Activity and English Society, 1452–97* (London, 1981).
Gransden, A., *Historical Writing in England II, c.1307 to the Early Sixteenth Century* (New York, 1982).
Griffiths, R. A., 'Henry Tudor: the Training of a King', *The Huntington Library Quarterly*, 49 (1986), pp. 197–218.
Green, R. F., *Poets and Princepleasers: Literature and the English Court in the Late Middle Ages* (Toronto, 1980).
—, 'Historical Notes of a London Citizen', *EHR*, 96 (1981), pp. 585–9.
Halsted, C. A., *Richard III as Duke of Gloucester and King of England*, 2 vols (London, 1844).
Hammond, P. W., *Edward of Middleham, Prince of Wales* (Cliftonville, 1973).
—, 'Opposition to Henry Tudor after Bosworth', *The Ricardian*, 4.55 (1976), p. 28.
Hicks, M. A., 'Dynastic Change and Northern Society: the Career of the Fourth Earl of Northumberland, 1470–89', *Northern History*, 14 (1978), pp. 78–107.
—, 'The Yorkshire Rebellion of 1489 reconsidered', *Northern History*, 22 (1986), pp. 39–62.
Horobin, S. and J. J. Smith, *An Introduction to Middle English* (Edinburgh, 2002).
Huizinga, J., *Homo Ludens: a Study of the Play Element in Culture* (London, 1949).
—, *The Waning of the Middle Ages: a Study of the Forms of Life, Thought, and Art in France and the Netherlands in the Fourteenth and Fifteenth Centuries*, transl. F. Hopman (repr. Harmondsworth, 1965).
Jacob, E. F., *The Fifteenth Century, 1399–1485* (Oxford, 1961).
Johnson, C. and Jenkins, H., *English Court Hand, A.D. 1066 to 1500*, 2 vols (repr. New York, 1967).
Jones, C., *An Introduction to Middle English* (New York, 1972).
Jones, M. K., 'Sir William Stanley of Holt: Politics and Family Allegiance in the Late Fifteenth Century', *Welsh History Review*, 14.1 (1988), pp. 1–22.
Keen, M. H., *The Laws of War in the Later Middle Ages* (London, 1965).
—, 'Chivalry, Heralds and History', in *The Writing of History in the Middle Ages: Essays Presented to Richard William Southern*, ed. R. H. C. Davies and J. M. Wallace-Hadrill (Oxford, 1981), pp. 393–414.
—, *English Society in the Later Middle Ages, 1348–1500* (Harmondsworth, 1990).
Kennedy, E. D., *A Manuel of the Writings in Middle English 1050–1500*, 8 vols (New Haven, 1989).
King, C., 'Shrines and Pilgrimages before the Reformation', *History Today*, 29.10 (1979), pp. 46–51.
Kingsford, C. L., *English Historical Literature in the Fifteenth Century. With an Appendix of Chronicles and Historical Pieces Hitherto for the Most Part Unprinted* (New York, 1913).

Kipling, G., *The Triumph of Honour: Burgundian Origins of the Elizabethan Renaissance* (The Hague, 1977).

—, 'Henry VII and the Origins of Tudor Patronage', in *Patronage in the Renaissance*, ed. G. Lytle and S. Orgel (Princeton, 1981).

Laynesmith, J. L., *The Last Medieval Queens: English Queenship 1445–1503* (Oxford, 2004).

Lester, G. A., 'The Literary Activity of the Medieval English Heralds', *English Studies*, 71 (1990), pp. 222–29.

—, 'Fifteenth-Century English Heraldic Narrative', *Yearbook of English Studies*, 22 (1992), pp. 201–12.

London, H. S., *The Life of William Bruges, the First Garter King of Arms* (London, 1970).

Luckett, D., 'Patronage, Violence and Revolt in the Reign of Henry VII', in *Crown, Government and People in the Fifteenth Century*, ed. R. E. Archer (Stroud, 1995), pp. 145–60.

MacCracken, H. N., 'The Earl of Warwick's Virelai', *PMLA*, 22 (1907), pp. 597–607.

McFarlane, K. B., 'The Wars of the Roses', in K. B. McFarlane, *England in the Fifteenth Century. Collected Essays*, ed. G. L. Harriss (London, 1981), pp. 231–61.

Hunt, R. W., F. F. Maden, et al., *A Summary Catalogue of Western Manuscripts in the Bodleian Library at Oxford* (repr. Munich, 1980).

de Maulde, R., 'Les Instructions Diplomatiques au Moyen-Age', *Revue d'Histoire Diplomatique*, 6 (1892).

McGee, C. E., 'A Critical Edition of the First Provincial Progress of Henry VII', unpublished Ph.D. thesis, University of Toronto (1977).

—, 'Politics and Platitudes: Sources of Civic Pageantry, 1486', *Renaissance Studies*, 3.1 (1989), pp. 29–34.

Meagher, J. C., 'The First Progress of Henry VII', *Renaissance Drama,* n.s., 1 (1968), pp. 45–73.

Morgan, D. A. L., 'The House of Policy: the Political Role of the Late Plantagenet Household, 1422–1485', in D. Starkey et al., *The English Court: from the Wars of the Roses to the Civil War* (London and New York, 1987), pp. 25–70.

Olver, P. C., 'Tudor Royal Progress', unpublished MA thesis, University of Swansea (1984).

Palliser, D. M., *Tudor York* (Oxford, 1979).

Parker, J. H., *Some Account of Domestic Architecture in England from Richard II to Henry VIII*, 2 vols (Oxford, 1859).

Payne, A., 'The Salisbury Rolls of Arms, c. 1463', in *England in the Fifteenth Century. Proceedings of the 1986 Harlaxton Symposium*, ed. D. Williams (Woodbridge, 1987), pp. 187–98.

Pilbrow, F. 'The Knights of the Bath: Dubbing to Knighthood in Lancastrian and Yorkist England', in Coss and Keen, *Heraldry, Pageantry*, pp. 195–218.

Pollard, A. J., *North-Eastern England During the Wars of the Roses. Lay Society, War, and Politics, 1450–1500* (Oxford, 1990).

Reid, R., *The King's Council in the North* (London, 1921).

Ross, C. D., *Edward IV* (London, 1974).

—, *Patronage, Pedigree and Power in Later Medieval England* (Gloucester, 1979).

Rowland, D., *An Historical and Genealogical Account of the Noble Family of Neville* (London, 1830).

Samman, N., 'The Progress of Henry VIII, 1509–29', in *The Reign of Henry VIII: Politics, Policy and Piety*, ed. D. MacCulloch (London, 1995), pp. 59–74.

Sandford, F., *Genealogical History of the Kings of England and Monarchs of Great Britain &c. from the Conquest, Anno 1066 to the year 1677* (London, 1683).

Sanquist, T. A., 'English Coronations 1377–1483', unpublished PhD dissertation, University of Toronto (1962).

Schramm, P. E., *A History of the English Coronation,* transl. L. G. W. Legg (Oxford, 1937).

Scofield, C. L., *The Life and Reign of Edward the Fourth, King of England and of France and Lord of Ireland*, 2 vols (London, 1967).

Seyer, S. (ed.), *Memoirs Historical and Topographical of Bristol and its Neighbourhood, from the Earliest Period down to the Present Time*, 3 vols (Bristol, 1823).

Sharpe, K., (ed.), *Sir Robert Cotton, 1586–1631. History and Politics in Early Modern England* (Oxford, 1979).

Shenton, C., 'Philippa of Hainault's Churchings: the Politics of Motherhood at the Court of Edward III', in *Family and Dynasty in Late Medieval England*, eds Richard Eales and Shaun Tyas, Harlaxton Medieval Studies, ix (Donington, 2003), pp. 105–21.

Somerville, R., *History of the Duchy of Lancaster*, 2 vols (London, 1953).

Squibb, G. D. (ed.), *Munimenta Heraldica 1484–1984*, Harleian Soc., 4 (1985).

Staniland, K, 'Welcome Royal Babe! The Birth of Thomas of Brotherton in 1300', *Costume*, 19 (1985), pp. 1–13.

—, 'Royal Entry into the World', in *England in the Fifteenth Century. Proceedings of the 1986 Harlaxton Symposium*, ed. D. Williams (Woodbridge, 1987), pp. 297–313.

Starkey, D., *The English Court: from the Wars of the Roses to the Civil War* (London, 1983).

—, 'Representation through Intimacy. A study in the Symbolism of Monarchy and Court Office in Early Modern England', in *Symbols and Sentiments. Cross-cultural Studies in Symbolism*, ed. I. Lewis (London, 1977), pp. 187–224.

Strong, R. C., *Art and Power. Renaissance Festivals 1450–1650* (Woodbridge, 1984).

Sutton, A. F. and Visser-Fuchs, L., *Richard III's Books: Ideals and Reality in the Life and Library of a Medieval Prince* (Stroud, 1997).

Sutton A. F. and Visser-Fuchs, L. with Griffiths, R. A., *Royal Funerals of the House of York at Windsor* (Richard III Society, 2005).

Temperley, G., *Henry VII* (London, 1917).

Thomson, J. A. F., 'John de la Pole, Duke of Suffolk', *Speculum*, 54 (1979), pp. 528–42.

Tite, C. G. C. ' "Lost or Stolen or Strayed": a Survey of Manuscripts formerly in the Cotton Library', *British Library Journal*, 18.2 (1992), pp. 107–134.

Unwin, G., *The Guilds and Companies of London*, 4th edn (London, 1963).

Vale, M., *War and Chivalry. Warfare and Aristocratic Culture in England, France and Burgundy at the End of the Middle Ages* (Athens, Georgia, 1981).

—, *The Princely Court. Medieval Courts and Culture in North-West Europe, 1270–1380* (Oxford, 2001).

Vaughan, R., *Charles the Bold. The Last Valois Duke of Burgundy*, new edn (Woodbridge, 2002).

—, *Valois Burgundy* (London, 1975).

Virgoe, R., 'The Recovery of the Howards in East Anglia', in *Wealth and Power in Tudor England. Essays Presented to S. T. Bindoff*, ed. E. W. Ives et al. (London, 1978), pp. 1–20.

Wagner, A. R., *Heralds and Heraldry in the Middle Ages: an Inquiry into the Growth of the Armorial Function of Heralds*, 2nd edn (Oxford, 2000).

—, 'Heraldry', in *Medieval England*, ed. A. L. Poole, new edn, 2 vols (Oxford, 1958), i, pp. 338–81.

—, *Heralds of England: A History of the Office and College of Arms* (London, 1967).

—, *The Records and Collections of the College of Arms* (London, 1952).

Walker, C. G., 'An Edition with Introduction and Commentary of John Blount's English Translation of Nicholas Upton's *De Studio Militari*', unpublished D.Phil. thesis, Oxford University (1998).

Williams, C. H., 'The Rebellion of Humphrey Stafford in 1486', *EHR* 43 (1928), pp. 181–9.

Williams, D. (ed.), *Early Tudor England. Proceedings of the 1987 Harlaxton Symposium* (Woodbridge, 1989).

Withington, R., *English Pageantry: an Historical Outline*, 2 vols (New York, 1918; repr. 1963).

Wolffe, B., *Henry VI* (London, 1981; repr. New Haven, 2001).

Wright, C. E., 'The Elizabethan Society of Antiquaries and the Formation of the Cottonian Library', in F. Wormald and C. E. Wright (eds.), *The English Library before 1700* (London, 1958), pp. 176–212.

—, *English Heraldic Manuscripts in the British Museum* (London, 1973).

INDEX

Due to the great number of personal names in the Memoir, this index provides reference only to those men and women who appear independently in the narrative or are referred to in the Introduction. Names which appear only in group format, such as in the extended lists of coronation participants or of campaigners at Stoke, are not indexed separately; however readers are notified of each occasion where a name-list is present. For names appearing both independently and in a list, *every* entry is recorded.

abbeys 98, *and see individual abbeys*
abbots 60, 135, 140, 143, 145–6 (*listed*), *and see individual titles*; of misrule 183, *and see under* Henry VII, court
Abingdon Abbey (Oxfordshire), abbot of 145, 184
Abrough (*Borough, Breugh*), Edward & Sir Thomas, *see* Burgh
accessories & adornments: beads, chains, buckles &c. 95, 98, 131, 134, 141, 154, *and see* Hewdyke's bead; headwear 79, 81, 131–2, 135–6, 137n, 138, 153–4, 169, *and see* cap of estate; surcoats, gowns, mantels &c. 80–1, 103, 131–6 *passim*, 140, 153–8 *passim*, 183, *and see* mantle of estate. *And see* clothing & liveries
Acton (Gloucestershire) 92
Agincourt, battle of (1415) 1
Alcock, John: as bishop of Ely (Oct. 1486–1501) 41, 108, 110, 135, 146, 176, 181, 184; as bishop of Worcester (1476–Oct. 1486) 35, 88, 92, 97,102, 104; as Chancellor of England (1485–Mar. 1487) 68n, 69n, 71, 81
Alington, Giles of, coronation petition 125–6; his guardian (Richard Garden) 125
All Hallows, All Hallowtide 5, 60, 64, 107, 127, 128, 162, 173

All Souls' Day 128
alms, alms-giving 26, 28, 70, 110, 155, 156
Alnwick Castle, MS. 467 64
ambassadors: Continental 41, 131n, 153, 156, 158, 162, 164, 173, 175, 182–5 *passim*; English 9, 156, *and see* Giles Daubeney, embassies; Scottish 156, 158, 162, 183, *and see* John Ramsay, John Kennedy
Amyas, John, yeoman of the Crown 64
Andre, Bernard (d. c.1522), poet laureate 29
Anglica Historia 18, 68n, *and see* Polydore Vergil
Anglo, Sydney 34, 104n
Angus, earl of, *see* Archibald Douglas
Anjou King of Arms 2, 4
Anne of York (d. 1511), queen's sister 35, 41, 103, 105n, 159, 164, 180
Anne, Princess, daughter of Henry VI 14
antiquaries, antiquarian interests 23, 52, 53
Antiquaries, Society of 52
Antoine, Bastard of Burgundy (Count of La Roche) 1, 6, 19
Archibald, Master (?Archibald Campbell, d. 1513), secretary to king of Scots 99
armour, funerary 7, 159, 172

205

arms: coats of 3, 103, 104, 156n, 181n, 182, 184, *and see* heraldry; feats of 11, 15, 16, 19; office of 1–3, 10, *and see* heralds; serjeants at 103, 135, 141, 184
army: rebel 30, 32, 117, 118n; royal 23n, 30–3, 111n, 112–117
Arthur, King & symbolism 19, 35
Arthur, Prince of Wales 89n, 90n, 112n, 113n; birth 34, 35, 36, 63, 80n, 99n, 100, 101n, 134n; christening 21, 34–36, 40, 56, 58–9, 61–3, 100–106, delays & alterations 24, 36, 100–101, 104, 180n, gifts 105, narrative accounts & memoranda of 22, 36, 61, 62, 64, 65n, 100n, 105n, roles of the nobility 64, 103–6 *passim*; creation as Prince of Wales 22, 25, 41, 49, 55, 64, 173, 175–180, *and see* 'Articles concerning the Creacion of my Lord Prince'; death 55, 57; marriage 21, 176n, 183n; putative early health 36
'Articles concernyng the Creacion of my Lord Prince' 22, 49, 176n
Arundel, earl of, *see* FitzAlan
__, Sir John of 103, 147
Ashburnham House 54
Ashurst (Hampshire) 176
Aspland, John, coronation petition 127
Audley, Edmund, bishop of Rochester (1480–93) 108, 163
__, Lord, *see* John Tuchet
__, Sir Humphrey 14
avener 124, *and see* William Berkeley, Richard Neville

bachelors 30, 112, 132, 148–50 (*listed*), their wives 143; 'bachelors' barge' 37, 129, *and see* barges
Bacon, Francis 29
badges, *see* heraldry
Bakers's Cambridge Collection, see British Library, MS Harley 7048
Ballard, William, March King of Arms (1460–1480) 17
Bamburgh Castle & siege (1464) 9, 14

bannerets 30, 32, 39, 112, 132, 147–8 (*listed*), 152, 153, 181, their wives 143; created at Stoke 118n, 119–20 (*listed*)
banquets: at ceremonial events 16, 22, 23, 39, 108, 136n, 142n, 144n, *and see under* Elizabeth of York; on feast days 5n, 39–40, 81–2, 154, 158, 164
baptisms, *see* christenings.
barges 41, 98, 129n, 176n, *and see* 'bachelor's barge'
Barnet (Hertfordshire) 128
Barnsdale (Yorkshire) 72
Bath, knights of the: clothing & liveries 132, 135; creations 8, 20, 37–8, 49, 64, 121, 130–1 (*listed*), 177–8 (*listed*), 179
Bath, Order of the 121, 130, 178
Beauchamp, Edward, king's marshal 154, 158
__, Richard (d. 1439), earl of Warwick 19, 100n
Beaufort, Edmund (d. 1455), duke of Somerset 14
__, Edmund (d. 1471), styled duke of Somerset 14
__, John (d. 1471), 'of Somerset' 14
__, Margaret, countess of Richmond & Derby 37, 42, 107, 111, 114n, 128–9, 140, 143–5, 147, 151, 153–7, 158, 161–5, 174–5, 182–4; as godmother & namesake to Princess Margaret 41, 42, 181; clothing & liveries 40, 42, 153, 155, 157, 159n; prominence in the Memoir 41–2, 145n, 155n, 181n
Bedford, duke & duchess of, *see under* Tudor
Bellingham, Robert, esquire of the king's household 117, 171
bell-ringing 101, 108
Bennett, Michael 29, 31, 33, 65n
Benolt, Thomas (d. 1534), Clarenceux King of Arms 51
Berkeley, Anne (née Fiennes), marchioness of Berkeley 41, 180, 181
__, William (d. 1492), earl of Nottingham & marquess of Berkeley 37, 107, 146,

206

INDEX

153, 154, 179; as Earl Marshal 132, 135, 140n, 141, 181, 184; coronation petitions 123, 124
Berners, Lord, *see* John Bourchier
births, royal 34, 40, *and see* Prince Arthur, Princess Margaret
Bisham (Berkshire) 7
bishops 81, 108, 128, 135–140 *passim*, 143, 145–6 (*listed*), 162–5 *passim*, *and see individual titles*
Black Book of the household of Edward IV 5
Blackheath (Kent) 163
Blackmore Edge (Yorkshire) 166
__ Forest (Wiltshire) 173
Blades (ex. 1489), rebel 33, 170
Bloggs, Joe 31
Blount, Sir James (d. 1492) 32, 119, 148, 170, 181
Bluemantle Pursuivant 15, 25n, *and see* 'The Record of Bluemantle Pursuivant'
Bodleian Library (Oxford) 62
Boleyn, Anne (ex. 1536), queen 37, 60, 82n, 98n, 129n
Bonley Rice (?Bunny, Nottinghamshire) 114
Bosworth, battle of (1485) 19, 28, 31n, 32, 35, 72n, 115n, 118n, 119n, 128n, 170n
Bothwell, Lord, *see* John Ramsay
bouche of court 5, *and see* English heralds: fees, allowances & rewards
Bourbon, Bastard of 172
Bourchier, Henry (d. 1540), earl of Essex 35, 41, 102–3, 146, 155, 162, 165, 166, 176, 179, 182, 183
__, John (d. 1533), Lord Berners 146, 155, 157, 162, 166
__, John (d. 1539), Lord FitzWarin 146, 162
Brandon, Sir Robert 32, 119
__, Sir Thomas, esquire of the body 102, 167, 177
Bray, Sir Reginald (*Raynold, Reynald*, d. 1503) 105, 148, 161, 165

Brennius, King, pageantic figure (Bristol) 28, 93–4
Bridget, Princess, 'of York' (d. 1517), daughter of Edward IV 6, 15, 16n, 103n, 181n
Bristol (Gloucestershire) 26, 28, 89n, 92–7; alleged poverty 97; pageants 79n, 91n, 93–6; recorder, *see* Tremayle
Britain 28, 37, 129n
British Library (London) 49, 50n; MS Additional 6113 61, 62, 63, 64; MS Cotton 394 52, 53; MS Cotton Julius B. XII, *see under* Cotton Julius B. XII; MS Egerton 985 60; MS Harley 7048 (*Bakers's Cambridge Collection*) 64; MS Stowe 583 61, 64
Brittany 21, 56, 118n, 161n, 162n, 173n; chancellor of 185; duchess of 185; duke of 156, 161
Broke, Lord, *see* Sir Robert Willoughby
Browne, Sir Anthony (d. 1506), knight of the body & royal standard-bearer 32, 81, 120, 133, 148, 172
Bruges (Flanders) 6, 15, 17, 171, 172, 185
Bruges, William (d. 1450), Chester Herald, Guyenne & Garter Kings of Arms 1n, 1–3, 5, 10
Buccleuch, duke of 8n, 20, 49n
Buckingham, Elizabeth of, *see* Elizabeth Stafford
Burgh, Sir Edward 32, 119, 133–4, 148, 162
__, Sir Thomas (d. 1496) 72, 81, 147, 157, 158
Burgundy 10, 11; duchess of, *see* Margaret of York; dukes of 11, 15, 18
Burley, John, yeoman of the Crown 62, 63, 102
Bury St Edmunds (Suffolk) 109
butler, chief 127, 136n, 144, *and see* Thomas FitzAlan
Butler, Thomas (d. 1515), earl of Ormond, queen's chamberlain 152, 154, 162, 165, 175, 182, 183, 184

207

Calais (France) 118n, 171–2; lieutenant of, *see* Giles Daubeney; marshal of, *see* Humphrey Talbot
Cambridge 29, 69n, 110, 166n; University of 69
campaigns 2, 9, 24, 25, 161n, 170n, 173n, *and see* Stoke, North Yorkshire rising
Candlemas 108, 183–4
Canterbury (Kent) 15, 107, 108, 163; Cathedral 108
cap of maintenance 26, 80–81n, 162n
captains 115n, 155
Carlisle Herald 25n, 59, 164
carver, carvers 6, 153, *and see* Sir David Owen
Castle, Robert, guardian of John Aspeland 127
Catalogus Librorum Manuscriptorum in Bibliotheca Roberti Cottoni (1621) 52
Cecily of York (d. 1507), viscountess Welles & queen's sister 35, 47, 103, 105n, 106, 132, 134, 135, 136, 141, 145, 147, 152n, 154
censing 90, 108, 128, 156, 157, 158
ceremonial: 15th-century developments 6; and social status 34; and the dukes of Burgundy 11; and the English royal court 4–5, 17, 22, 24, 34, 36, 39, 52, 151n. *And see under* heraldic narratives
chamber: king's 6, 89, 99, 150, 151, 154, 156, 157, 158, 176, 183; parliament 42, 145, 178, 179; queen's 64, 102, 140, 141n, 151, 180, and childbirth 40, 173n, 174n, 175n, *and see under* Elizabeth of York; queen's chamber of estate 132
Chamberlain, Lord Great, coronation duties 136n, *and see* John de Vere
__, Lord 6, *and see* Sir William Stanley
__, the queen's, *see* Thomas Butler
champion, king's 16, *and see under* Henry VII
Chancellor, Lord, *see* John Alcock, John Morton
chancery 121; benchers of 142–3
chandlery, serjeant of 103
chapel, king's (chapel royal) 39, 81, 100n, 102n, 103, 105, 135, 137n, 154, 178, 181, *and see* John Gunthorpe
Charbonnel, Lord, French ambassador 162
Charing (Kent) 108
Chatham (Kent) 108
Chelsea (Kent) 41, 175
Cheney, Sir John (d. 1489) 32, 35, 39n, 72, 81, 103, 119, 147, 170n
Chester Herald 1n, 7, 9, 14, 25n
Chimney, William, mayor of York (1487–8) 73–4, 82
chivalry 10, 11, 19, 24; Court of Chivalry 4
chrismal cloth 41, 62, 103, 105, 180, *and see* regalia
Christ Church (Canterbury): font of 34, 35, 101, 102, 104, 105, 180–1; prior of 184
christenings 5, 7, 15, 16, 34, 36, 63, 101n, 103n, 106 n. 241, 180n, 181n, *and see* Prince Arthur, Princess Margaret
Christmas 4, 5, 15, 22, 34, 42, 58, 60, 64, 69, 107, 109n, 151–2, 164–5, 182–3
Chronicle of Tewkesbury Abbey 14
Cinque Ports, barons of the 135, 142; coronation petition 124–5, 135n
Claims, Court of: commission for office of Steward of England 23, 37, 121–2, 136n; petitions 23, 36, 37, 60, 122–7, *and see individual petitioners*
Clarence, duke of, *see* George Plantagenet, Thomas of Lancaster
Clarenceux King of Arms 3, 7, 19, 25n, 51, 61, *and see* Benolt, Hawley, Holme
Clifford, Henry (d. 1524), Lord Clifford 72, 114n, 170
clothing & liveries 71, 73, 79, 82, 92, 98n, 128, 132, 153; coronation participants 132, 134–6, 140–1. *And see*

INDEX

Order of the Garter, bachelors, bannerets, *and individual dignitaries*
cloth-of-gold 26, 40, 73, 88, 101n, 102n, 131, 132, 133, 134, 137, 140, 157, 175, 183, *and see* cloths & materials
cloths & materials: arras 40, 101, 102, 132, 140, 143; brocade & satin 26, 102n, 109n; canvas 181; carpets & cushions 101n, 102n, 135n, 137; damask 102n, 131, 132, 142, 154; down 132; embroidery work 38n, 40, 98n, 102n, 141, 181; ermine, sables & furs 26, 40, 73, 120n, 131, 132, 134, 136, 140, 141, 151, 175, 182–4 *passim*; gilt, gold & goldsmiths' work 34, 98, 101n, 102, 103, 105, 133 135, 141, 157, 180, 181, 182; iron 34, 102; linen, sarsenet & say 34, 102; musterdevillers 108; pearls & precious stones 101n, 135, 136, 154, 180, 182; rheims 101n, 174; silk 108, 131, 132, 155; silver 34, 98, 102, 182; tapestry 35, 78, 101n, 132; timber 102; tissue 26, 134; velvet 26, 40, 132, 134, 151, 154, 157, 159, 175; worsted 34, 102
Cocklodge (Yorkshire) 56, 166n
Coldharbour House 4, 19, 51
Colet, Henry, mayor of London (1486) 98, 99
Collectanea, De Rebus Britannicis 64, 65
College of Arms (London) 49, 50n, 51, 61; MS. I.7 61, 62, 63; MS. M6 61, 62, 63
comfits (& obleys, &c) 78, 96n
Constable of England 3, 4, 14, 40n, 59, *and see* John Tiptof, Richard III, Thomas Stanley
Conway, Hugh 37, 131, 149, 169
Cony (*Quonyeux*) Street (York) 77n, 78, 79n
Cornwall 53
coronations: and the heralds' duties 4, 5, 7, 15, 16, 20, 21; mishaps 38, 136–7; of queens 16, 34, 37, 39, 60, 120n, 121n, 129n, 130n, 131n, 135n, 136n, 140n, *and see* Elizabeth of York; Richard III & Anne Neville 16, 39, 120n, 130n, 135n, 137n, 139n, 140n, 142n. *And see under* Henry VII, regalia
Corpus Christi Day 97, 115
Cotton Julius B. XII 43–5, 50, 51–5, 65, 66, 67; as Cotton 394 52, 53; constituent parts 43, 52; foliation schemes 43, 50, 53, 54, 55; production process 43, 52–5, 55–7
Cotton, Sir Robert 51–5; hand & signature 53, 54; library & catalogues 52, 53n, 54, 55; treatment of manuscripts 53, 54
__, Sir Roger, king's cofferer & master of the queen's horse 134, 150, 157, 162, 166, 182
__, Sir Thomas 54
council: great 28, 108, 162, 173n, 183; king's 156; of war 14, 30, 111–12
courser, *see under* horses
court, the king's 4, 5, 21, 52; under the Yorkists 12, 17, 18. *And see under* ceremonial, Edward IV, Henry VII
Courtenay, Edward (d. 1509), earl of Devon 32, 114, 146, 152
__, Peter: as bishop of Exeter (until Jan. 1487) 71, 89, 104; as bishop of Winchester (Jan. 1487–1492) 110, 112, 113–114, 135, 145, 156n, 157, 159, 163, 176; as Lord Privy Seal (1485–1487) 71, 81; as prelate of the Order of the Garter 157–9
__, Thomas (d. 1471), earl of Devon 14
Coventry (Warwickshire) 29, 30, 32, 49, 89n, 91n, 110, 111, 113, 114, 120, 171; prior of 110
cramp rings 26, 70
creations 5, 20, 52, 118n, 119n, 128n, *and see under* knights, knights of the Bath, knights of the Garter, Prince Arthur
Croft (Leicestershire) 120
Croft, Sir Richard (d. 1509), treasurer of the household 102, 103, 111n, 141, 148, 152, 153, 164, 168, 184

crown, *see under* England, gentlemen, yeomen, regalia
crown-wearing 81n, *and see under* Henry VII
Croydon (Surrey) 108
cupbearer, cupbearers 6, 153, *and see* Sir Charles of Somerset

Dacre, Thomas (d. 1525), Lord Dacre of Gilsland, of the North 72, 146, 162
Danby, Sir Christopher (d. 1518), Lord Danby 183
Darell, Sir Edward 119, 149, 162, 165, 166, 182
Daubeney, Giles (d. 1508), Lord Daubeney, lieutenant of Calais & ambassador 146, 153, 154,155, 158, 159, 165, 170n,171, 172, 182
David, biblical king, pageantic figure (York) 79
Davy, Harry, rebel 184
Débat des Hérauts 4
Debenham, Sir Gilbert, banneret 148, 172, 182
Derby House (St Paul's Wharf, London) 51, 52
Derby, earl of, *see* Thomas Stanley
Dethick, Sir William (d. 1606), York Herald & Garter King of Arms 51, 52, 53, 68n
Devereux, Cecily (née Bourchier; d. 1493), Lady Ferrers of Chartley 134, 145, 147
__, John (d. 1501), Lord Ferrers of Chartley 30, 112
Devon, earl of, *see* Edward Courtenay, Thomas Courtenay
Digby, Sir John 32, 119, 149
Dinham, John (d. 1501), Lord Dinham & Lord Treasurer 146, 155, 157, 158, 159, 172, 182
disguisings 39, 153, 183
Ditton, Mistress 141
divine service, mass *passim, and see* evensong, matins; coronation mass 137–40, 144n; requiem mass 56, 82, 156, 159, 165, 172
Dixmude (Flanders) 171, 172n
Dodsworth, Roger 52
Don(ne), Sir John (d. 1503) 149, 164, 167, 182
Doncaster (Yorkshire) 26, 27, 69n, 71, 72n, 88n, 114n
Dorset, marquess & marchioness of, *see under* Grey
Douglas, Archibald (d. 1513), earl of Angus 182
Dudley, Lord & Lady, *see under* Sutton
Dunstable (Bedfordshire) 166, 167
Durham 120
__, bishop of, *see* John Sherwood
Dutchmen 118

East Anglia 28, 109n
Easter 4, 5, 26, 27, 28, 29, 58, 60, 64, 155, 165; religious observances 69–70, 109–110
Easterlings 164
Ebrauk (*Ebraucus*), mythical founder of York 28, 75–6
ecclesiastical garments (copes, habits, amices &c) 98n, 104, 108, 128, 135, 181, *and see* pontificals
Edgecombe, Sir Richard (d. 1489), Lord Edgecombe & comptroller of the king's house 72, 141, 148, 152, 153, 161, 164, 170n
Edward I (1272–1307) 8, 9, 10, 11, 12, 14, 17, 24, 38, 53
Edward III (1327–77) 6, 9, 10, 12, 13, 15, 41
Edward IV (1461–70 & 1471–83) 15n, 38n, 50n, 71n, 89n, 90n, 109n, 121, 134n, 145; funeral & burial 16, 17n, 18; household & court 5, 6, 11, 15, 20, 114n; knights & esquires of the body 39
Edward V (April–June 1483) 5n
'Edward VI', pretender king 31, 117, *and see* Lambert Simnel, Joe Bloggs
Edward, Prince of Wales (d. 1471) 14
Edward, Prince of Wales (d. 1553) 60, 61

INDEX

Elizabeth I (1558–1603) 43, 79n

Elizabeth of York (d. 1503), queen 128, 134n, 151, 160, 161, 163, 164, 165, 182, 183, 184; and childbirth 64, 180n, 175n, associated rituals 63, 64, 106–7, 173–5, 181 (*and see* purification), her chambers 40, 59, 101n, 104n, 105n, 106n, 141n, 174–5, in labour 178; chamberlain, s*ee* Thomas Butler; clothing & liveries 38, 40, 42, 129, 130, 131–2, 134–5, 155, 157, 158; coronation 20, 23, 24, 25, 36–39, 42, 56, 60, 98n, 120–21, 129n, 134–45, 151n, 176n (*and see* Court of Claims), anointing and crowning 38, 137–40, 141n, banquet 23n, 24, 38, 39, 42, 140n, 141–4, 174n, creation of knights 49, 130–1 (*listed*), fatal accident 136–7, participants list 39, 145–50, pictorial records of 22, 130,136, roles of the nobility 122n, 132–44 *passim*, Vigil ceremonies 37–8, 131–4; crown-wearing 153, 154; devotional offerings & largess 22, 25, 48, 107n, 151, 154, 156; during the Stoke campaign 111, 113, 114n; henchmen 134; her sisters, *see esp.* Cecily of York, Anne of York, *also* Princess Bridget; illnesses 106; physical appearance 38, 131

Elton, G. R. 20

Ely, bishop of, *see* John Alcock, John Morton

embassies: from Scotland 99, 183; from the continent 28, 40, 108–9, 162n, 165, 173, 175, 182, 183, 185; to the continent 15, 21, 22, 59, 58, 59, 162n, 164, 170n, 173, 175n, 184. *And see* ambassadors

Enfield (*Enville*) Chase (Middlesex) 172

England 1, 3, 4, 6, 11, 15, 19, 37, 65n, 71n, 82, 101, 14; Crown & Throne of 4, 5, 6, 7, 9, 12, 35, 36, 58, 68n, 153n; internecine warfare 9, 13–14; kings of 12, 20, 70, *and see individual kings*; queens of 38, *and see individual queens*; regions of 28, 29, 30, 59, 69, 99, 109n, 110n, 111, 115n, 155n, 166, 170n; relations with France & Burgundy 2, 10, 11, 161n, 175n

English Channel ('Narrow Sea') 11, 30, 109

Englishmen 31, 118, 144

Epiphany 15, 59, 81n, 153–4, 165

Esquires: at Arthur's creation 177–8 (*listed*); at court feast days 41, 89, 107, 110, 152, 158, 161, 162, 165, 184; at royal christenings 103, 181; at the queen's coronation 24, 130–1 (*listed*), 132, 134n, 135, 140, 142; in the company of various noblemen 27, 33, 39, 72–3, 108, 112; in the royal army at Stoke 29, 30, 32, 112, 117; of honour 132; of the body, *see under* Edward IV, Henry VII; Scottish 99

Essex 109

Essex, earl of, *see* Henry Bourchier

estate, cap of 153, 162; cloth of 40, 104, 135, 154, 174, 179; cushions of 137; horse of 24, 134, 157; keeping of 81, 158, 179; queen's chamber of 132; robes of 81, 88, 107, 136, 179; seat of (*sege royall*) 137, 139

Ethelbert, pageantic king (Hereford) 90–1

evensong 26, 70, 71, 80, 82, 151, 153, 155, 157, 159

ewery, serjeant of 103

exchequer, barons of 140, *and see* Brian Roucliffe

executions 30, 33,115, 169, 184

Exeter, bishop of, *see* Richard Foxe, Peter Courtenay

Falcon Pursuivant 25n, 59, 164

feasts, of the calendar year 20, 22, 39, 151n, *and see* St George, Easter &c. *And see also* banquets

Ferrers of Chartley, Lord & Lady, *see under* Devereux

Ferrybridge (Yorkshire) 169

Fiennes, Richard (d. 1501), Lord Saye & Sele 162, 165

FitzAlan, Thomas (d. 1524): as earl of Arundel 41, 147, 152, 154, 158, 159, 163, 167, 176, 179, 180, chief butler 127, 136, 144, coronation petition 127, 136n, lieutenant of the Order of the Garter 80n, 172; as Lord Maltravers 35, 103, 104, 105, 107, 110, 152
__, William (d. 1487), earl of Arundel 159
__, William (d. 1544), Lord Maltravers 177, 178
FitzHugh, Richard (d. 1487), Lord FitzHugh 72
FitzWalter (*fitz Water*), Lord, *see* John Radcliffe
FitzWarin, Lord, *see* John Bourchier
FitzWilliam, Sir Thomas (d. 1497), recorder of London 99, 150
Flanders 109, 110, 117n
Flemings (& 'Bruggelings') 171
fleur-de-lis 174
Fleur-de-Lis Herald 10, *and see* French heralds
foot-washing 26, 70, *and see under* Henry VII
Fortescue, Sir John 119, 148, 154, 162, 167, 182
Fountains Abbey (Yorkshire), abbot of 81, 82
Foxe, Richard (d. 1528), bishop of Exeter 47, 105, 110, 112, 155, 156, 164, 174, 182; as king's secretary 104; as Lord Privy Seal 47, 152, 161, 162, 163, 166, 184; called 'John' 48, 116, 151, 152, 162
France 2, 43n, 59, 75, 79, 82, 83, 88, 93, 95, 120n, 144, 115n, 160, 161n, 183
Franke, Edward (ex. 1489), rebel 184
Frenchmen 161, 171, 172
friars 70, 71, 74, 89, 92, 93
Froissart, Jean 4
Fryon, Stephen (*Estephene*), ambassador 173
funerals 5, 7–8, 16, 159n, *and see* Nevill; effigies 6
Furness Fells (Lancashire) 111

galleys 155
Garrard, Yonker, king of Denmark's uncle 165
Garter King of Arms 1–5, 7, 9, 10, 15, 25n, 40n, 49, 50, 58, 59, 68n, *and see individual officers*; the office 1–3
Garter, knights of the 29, 80n, 81, 82, 155n, 156n, 157–60 *passim*, 165; installations 156n, 157, 172, 173n
Garter, Order of the 1, 3, 42, 110; and English foreign policy 10; chapters 82, 156–9 *passim*, 173; insignia 164; registrar, *see* Oliver King; robes & liveries 26, 40, 42, 80n, 81, 82, 155, 156n, 157, 158, 160; statutes 80n, 81n, 82
Gawain, Sir 19
gentlemen 31, 32, 33, 36, 39, 103, 118, *and see* knights, esquires; Scottish 99; gentlemen ushers, *see under* Henry VII, household
gentlewomen 28n, 103, 181, 182, *and see* noblewomen; at the queen's coronation 39, 134, 140, 150 (*listed*); attendant upon the queen 40, 153, 159 (*listed*),164 (*listed*), 174, 175n
gentry, *see under* gentlemen, gentlewomen.
Gloucester 26, 91–2; Abbey, abbot & monks of 92
__, duke of, *see* Richard III
Gloucestershire, High Sheriff of, *see* Robert Points
godparents: to Prince Arthur 100–5 *passim*; to Princess Margaret 181–2 *passim*
Golden Fleece, Order of the 11
Goldwell, James (d. 1499), bishop of Norwich 109–110, 135, 145, 184
gospel 82, 108, 156
gossips 101n, 105, 181
Great Chronicle of London 29, 33
Green Knight, the 19
Greenwich & Palace 37, 42, 107, 129,

212

INDEX

130, 145, 151, 182

Greenwood, Richard (d. c.1492), Rouge Croix Pursuivant 59

Grete Boke of Sir John Paston 19

Grey, Anne (née Herbert), Lady Grey of Powys 134

__, Anne (née Woodville; d. 1489), Lady Grey de Ruthin 103

__, Cecily (née Bonville; d. 1529), marchioness of Dorset 103

__, Dame Katherine 103, 141, 145, 150, 159

__, Edmund, de Ruthin (d. 1490), earl of Kent 41, 174, 176, 181, 182

__, Edward (d. 1492), Viscount Lisle 30, 32, 107, 112, 117n, 154, 182, 184

__, Eleanor (née St John; d. bef. 1509), Lady Grey, wife of Thomas Lord Grey 134, 147

__, George, de Ruthin (d. 1503), Lord Grey de Ruthin, heir to earl of Kent 30, 71, 112, 17

__, Henry (d. 1496), Lord Grey of Codnor 169

__, John (d. 1494 or 1497), Lord Grey of Powys 30, 32, 72, 112, 165, 169

__, Sir John of Wilton (d. 1499) 72, 147

__, Sir Ralph (ex. 1462) 9, 14

__, Thomas (d. 1501), Lord Ferrers de Groby & marquess of Dorset 49, 89, 103, 105, 107, 108

__, Thomas (d. 1530), Lord Grey, heir to marquess of Dorset 72, 112, 158

groats 70

Gruthuse, Louis de (d. 1492), lord of Gruthuse & earl of Winchester 6, 15

Guevara, Ladrón de, ambassador of the king of Romans 165

Guildford, Sir Richard (d. 1506), knight constable & vice-chamberlain of the household 35, 103, 162, 165

Guilmet, Guillaume (*Gwilm Gwilmet*) 185

Guisnes, lieutenant of, *see* James Tyrell

Gunthorpe, John (d. 1498), dean of Wells & the chapel royal 104, 154, 158

Guyenne King of Arms, *see* William Bruges

Halifax (Yorkshire) 54

Hall, Edward, chronicler 29

hall: the bishop's 81; the king's 5, 154

Hampton 155

harbingers, *see under* Henry VII, household

Hastings, Edward (d. 1506), Lord Hastings 30, 32, 72, 112, 147, 163, 167

Hault, Sir Richard 30, 112, 162, 165, 167

Hawley, Thomas, Norroy & Clarenceux King of Arms 51, 61, 62

Hearne, Thomas 31, 64, 65

Henry IV (1399–1413) 80n

Henry V (1413–22) 1, 2, 3, 89n, 122n, 142n

Henry VI (1422–61 & 1470–1) 8, 9, 10, 12, 14, 69n, 76n, 83n, 89n, 90n, 142n; as a pageantic figure (Worcester) 83–5

Henry VII (1485–509) *passim*; ancestral mythology & symbolism 28, 35; and magnificence & display 20, 34, 37, 39, 50n, 154n, 183n, 184n; and the legacy of Richard III 19, 24, 129n; and the queen's coronation 120–1, 127–8, 129n, 130, 140, 143; banners, standard & symbols of office 26, 115, 120, 167; clothing & liveries 26, 28, 73, 80–1, 82, 88, 107, 109n, 128, 150, 151, 152, 155–8, 182, 184; coronation 19, 20n, 22, 38n, 68, 81n, 136n, 137n; court 20, 28, 34, 40, 41, 58, 59, 107, 151n, 153, 181n, 184, entertainments 39, 153, 183; crown-wearings 20, 22, 26, 39, 41, 80, 81n, 153–4; devotional offerings & Easter observances 26, 28–9, 69–70, 80n, 98, 109–110, 129, 155, 159; entourage 21, 22, 26, 27, 28, 29, 30, 69n, 70n, 109n; gifts to 98, 155, 162, 163n; henchmen 24, 26, 38,

213

73, 103; heraldic style 82, 151; his mother, *see* Margaret Beaufort; household 162, 185, chamberlain 24, 152 (*and see* Sir William Stanley), cofferer (*see* Sir Roger Cotton), comptroller (*see* Sir Richard Edgcombe), cupbearer (*see* Sir Charles of Somerset), esquires & esquires of the body 6, 35, 81, 102 (*listed*), 167n, 169, 182 (*listed*), gentlemen ushers 64, 153, knights marshal (*see* John Turbervill, Richard Hault), knights & gallants 6, 30, 32, 112, 167n, knights of the body 6, 35, 102 (*listed*), 119n, 133–4, marshals and harbingers 30, 114 (*and see* Edward Beauchamp), serjeant chandler 103, serjeant of the pantry 102, steward 24, 152 (*and see* John Radcliffe, Robert Willoughby), treasurer (*see* Richard Croft), treasurer of the chamber (*see* Thomas Lovel), vice-chamberlain (*see* Richard Guildford), yeomen ushers 64; in procession 88, 91, 97, 128–9, 153, 156, 158, 163, 164, 184; keeping estate 81, 158; largess 48, 107, 151, 153; marriage 88n, 110n; military campaigns 24, 25, 29, 34, *and see* Stoke, North Yorkshire rising; on pilgrimage 96; princely qualities 26, 28, 34, 41, 69, 128; progresses, first (1486) 22, 25–28, 29, 43, 46, 51, 52n, 53, 55, 59, 65n, 69–96, 153n, second (1487), *and see* Stoke 28–29, 109–111; recreational pursuits 22, 99, 161, 171, 172, 173, 183; relationship with the heralds 19–21, 24–5, 39, 59; secretary, *see* Richard Foxe, Oliver King; with his wife & mother 107, 111n, 114n, 144, 153, 158, 159n, 160, 161, 163, 164, 181, 183

Henry VIII (1509–1547) 9, 10, 60; as an infant & duke of York 64, 104n, 176n

Henry, Prince (d. 1511), son of Henry VIII & Katherine of Aragon 62, 63

heraldic devices, *see* heraldry

heraldic narratives: and chivalric history 18–19; and court ceremonial 12n, 15, 16–19, 22, 23, 36, 60, 61–4, 65, 153n, ceremonial 'memory' 17, 24, 37; and domestic & foreign affairs 14–15; and feats of arms 11n, 19; and the 'registration' of nobles 17, 18, 24; and twentieth-century scholarship 12–13; and warfare 13–14, 32n; as eye-witness journalism 9, 17, 21, 22, 26, 57; before 1485 12–19; use of external sources & prescriptive texts 17, 18. *And see* Memoir

herald-recorder, *see under* Memoir

heraldry (devices, badges, &c) 4, 12, 16, 26, 38, 40, 98n, 129, 134, 140, 141, 156, 57, 174

heralds, Burgundian & foreign, Breton 11n, 21, 183

__, English: and Arthur's creation 22, 25, 176, 178–9; and Burgundy 11–12; and ceremonial 4, 5, 6, 7, 12, 15–16, 18n, 20, 24, 38, 82n, *and see under* heraldic narratives; and chivalry 8, 10, 18–19; and diplomacy 1, 2, 8, 9–10, 21; and genealogy & heraldry 4, 8, 9, 12, 21; and processions 6, 7, 17n, 40n; and proclamations 21, 122; and royal christenings 7, 15, 103, 104, 181, 182; and the adjudication of coronation claims 36; and the chapel royal 39; and the creation of the Memoir 19–25; and the queen's coronation 20, 22–3, 24, 25, 36, 38, 135, 140, 143; and tournaments & warfare 1, 8, 13, 10, 19; as journalists 17, 21, 22, 26, 58; as a corporation 2–4, 12, 19–20, 51–2; as messengers 9, 10–11; comparison with French heralds 2, 11; crying largess 24, 39, 47, 82, 89, 107, 144, 151–2, 154, 180, 183; earliest functions 8, 9, 10–11, 21; fees, allowances & rewards 3, 5, 7n, 17n, 20, 22, 47, 49, 58, 107n, 108, 119–20, 153, 177, 183; liveries & tabards, etc 19, 20, 103; records & record keeping 3, 12, 24, 3, 4, 17, 32n, 57, 60–65 (*and*

INDEX

see heraldic narratives, Memoir), non-narrative records 8, 20, 21, 22–3, 37, 100n, 102n,107, 130, 136, 180; seigneurial 5, 9, 15, *and see individual seigneurial heralds*; under early Henry VII 19–42; under Edward III 9, 10; under Henry V 1–3, 5; under Henry VIII 9, 10; under the Lancastrians 5, 9, 10, 12; under the Yorkists 3– 8, 5, 9, 12, 18, 24, 17, 20; waiting duties & roster (1487) 5, 20, 23, 25, 53, 58

__, French 2, 11, 183, *and see* Anjou, Fleur-de-Lis, Montjoye, Sicily

__, Scottish 9n, 183, 185, *and see* Carlisle, Lyon, Roos, Unicorn

Herbert, William (d. 1490), earl of Huntingdon 55, 146, 154, 176

Hereford: Cathedral (called minster), dean of 91; pageants 89–91

__, bishop of, *see* Thomas Mylling

Hertford 33,164, 165, 166

Hewdyke's bead 184, *and see* accessories & adornments

hippocras 106, 143, 144

Holinshed, Raphael 29

Holme, Thomas, Clarenceux King of Arms 19, 59

Holt Castle 33

Holy Rood Abbey (Edinburgh), abbot of 99

Holy Trinity Priory (York), prior & brethren of 74

Hoo, John, yeoman of the Crown 102

Horne, Sir William, mayor of London (1487) 120, 128, 129, 132, 135, 140, 143, 144, 150

Hornsey (*Harnessey*) Park (Middlesex) 120, 128

horses 38, 74, 80, 92, 99, 140n, 158, 179l; 'dooing' horses 133; ceremonial trappings 134, 140, 141, 157; coursers 73, 120n, 140, 141, 156, 157; hackneys 157, 159; of estate, *see under* estate; palfreys 134, 157; Prince Arthur's 179; the king's 69; the queen's 134, 157, master of, *see* Sir Roger Cotton.

hospitals, *see* St Leonard's

hostages 172

household, the king's 4–6, 24, 41, *and see under* Henry VII; literature of 5, 27, 80n, 81n.

Howard, Thomas (d. 1524), earl of Surrey 33, 166, 170

__, Thomas (d. 1554), duke of Norfolk 60

hunting 99, 161, 171, 172, 173, 183

Huntingdon 29, 69, 110

__, earl of, *see* William Herbert.

Hussey, John (d. 1537), Lord Hussey, chief justice of the king's bench 72, 89, 158

Hyde Abbey (Winchester) 104

Innocent VIII, pope (1484–92) 64, 88, 91, 108, 110, 162, 163; his collector 184; his cubicular 162, 163–4 *passim*, 184

Inquisitio de Gubernatione Militum Templi in Anglia 43

insignias, *see* heraldry

Ireland 30, 42, 59, 82, 109, 144

Irishmen 31, 118

Isledon (Middlesex) 128

James I [and VI] (1603–1625) 53

James III, King of Scots (1460–88) 156, 158, 161; his councillor, *see* John Roos; his secretary, *see* Master Archibald

James IV, King of Scots (1488–1513) 72n, 161n, 185

James, Richard, Cottonian librarian 54

Janitor, pageantic figure (Worcester) 28, 87–8

Johnston, Dr Nathaniel 54

Jones, Michael 41, 42

jousts 15

judges 82, 140

Justicia, pageantic figure (Bristol) 91n, 95–6

215

Katherine of Aragon (d. 1536), queen 21, 62, 91n, 176n, 183n
Kempe, Thomas (d. 1489), bishop of London 129, 145
Kenilworth (Warwickshire) 30, 42, 111, 114n, 120n
Kennedy, John, Lord Kennedy, Scottish ambassador 99
Kent 53, 90n
Kent, earl of, *see* Edmund Grey de Ruthin
King, Oliver (d. 1503), king's secretary & registrar of the order of the Garter 152, 158, 165, 166
king's bench, chief justice of, *see* John Hussey
King's Wood, Abbey of (Gloucestershire) 92
kings of arms 1, 3, 4, 5, 7, 20, 103, 132, 143, 176, *and see individual kings of arms*, heralds, pursuivants; of Burgundy 11
knights: at ceremonial events 39, 41, 103, 132, 135, 140, 141–2, 143, 176, 181, *and see* knights of the Bath, bannerets, bachelors; at court feast days 81, 89, 107, 110, 152, 154, 158, 161 (*listed*), 162, 165 (*listed*), 182 (*listed*), 184, *and see* knights of the Garter, poor knights of St George; French 19; in the company of various noblemen 27, 33, 39, 72–3 (*listed*), 108, 112; of the royal household, *see under* Henry VII, household; on campaign 29, 31, 32, 49, 59, 115n, 118n, 119–20 (*listed*)
__ bachelor, *see under* bachelors
__ banneret, *see under* bannerets
__ constable 103, *and see* Sir Richard Guildford
__ marshal, *see under* Henry VII
__ of the body, *see under* Edward IV, Henry VII
Knowle (Warwickshire) 108
Knyfton, Nicholas 63, 64

la Roche, count of, *see* Antoine, 'Bastard of Burgundy'
la Ware (de la Warr), Lord & Lady, *see under* West
ladies, *see* noblewomen, gentlewomen
Lambeth & Palace 41, 108, 176
Lambeth Palace, MS 306 64
Lancaster, duchy of 68n, 172n
__, Thomas of (d. 1421), duke of Clarence 3n
Langton, Thomas (d. 1501), bishop of Salisbury 104, 105, 108, 173, 176
lardoner 126, *and see* George Neville
largess, crying of, *see under* English heralds
Lavenham (Suffolk) 36, 62, 100
Laynesmith J.L. 34, 38
lazar houses 70
le Fèvre, Jean, *Toison d'or* King of Arms 18
le Puissant, Piers, ambassador of King of Romans 162, 165
Leicester 19, 30, 32, 112n, 114, 167, 168
Leighton, Sir Thomas 162
Leland, John 31, 64, 65, 71n
Lent 69n, 109, 185
Lenton (Nottinghamshire) 115n, 116
Lesparre Pursuivant 9
Lewis, Mister, ambassador of King of Romans 165
Lincoln & Lincoln Cathedral (called 'Minster') 26, 27, 69, 70, 72n
__, bishop of, *see* John Russell
__, earl of, *see* John de la Pole
Lisle, Viscount, *see* Edward Grey
Llanthony Priory (Gloucestershire), prior of 163
London 4, 15, 26, 33, 69n, 70n, 89n, 115n, 120n, 121, 127n, 128, *and see Great Chronicle of London*; aldermen 128, 177; bishop of, *see* Thomas Kempe; Bishopsgate 128, 129; Bridge 163; Charing Cross 134; Cheapside & Cheap St 132, 133; citizens 143; civic officials 98, 99, 129, 143, 163, *and see* mayor, aldermen; civic reception

INDEX

128; commons 128; Cornhill, Fleet St, Gracechurch, Ludgate, Mark Ln & St Peter's 133; craft guild 4, 37n, 41, 98, 128, 129, 132, 163, 177; houses 128, 132; mayor 41, 60, *and see* Henry Colet, William Horne, Robert Tate, William White; merchants 143; recorder, *see* Sir Thomas FitzWilliam; sheriffs 128, 129; St Margaret's 98; St Mary Spittle 128–9; St Paul's 38, 128, 129, 132, 133, 163; stocks 133; Strand Cross 134; streets, 128, 132; Temple Bar 134; Tower of 37, 38, 42, 109n, 129n, 131, 132, 130, 133, 176n; Tower Hill 184

lords spiritual, *see* abbots, bishops
lords temporal, *see* noblemen
Lords, House of 3
Loughborough (Leicestershire) 30, 32, 112n, 114
Lovel, Francis (d. 1487?), Viscount Lovel 31, 37, 109, 117n, 118, 119n
__, Henry (d. 1489), Lord Morley 146, 155, 158, 163, 171
__, Sir Thomas (d. 1524), treasurer of king's chamber & chancellor of the exchequer 48, 107, 149, 161, 162, 165, 166, 179
Low Countries 29, 43n, 109, 110n, 118n; mercenaries killed at Stoke 31
Lumley, George (d. 1507), Lord Lumley 72
Lutterel, Hugh 37
Luxembourg, Francois de, viscount of Geneva 175, 182
Lyon King of Arms of Scotland 99, 184
Lyston Overall manor (Essex) 126

Machado, Roger (d. 1510), Richmond, Norroy & Clarenceux 20, 21, 58, 103
magnates, *see* noblemen
Maidstone (Kent) 108
Maltravers, Lord, *see* FitzAlan
manuscripts, *see under individual repositories*
March King of Arms 25n, *and see* William Ballard
Margaret of Anjou 14, 120n, 129n, 130n, 131, 134n, 140n, 174n
Margaret of York, duchess & dowager duchess of Burgundy 6, 11, 15, 17, 118n
Margaret, Princess 41, 42; birth & christening 36, 40, 58, 64, 103n, 106n, 162n, 178–181
Margate (Kent) 15
Market Harborough (Leicestershire) 33, 167
marriages 5, 7, 15, 174n, *and see* Arthur, Henry VII
Marshal of England (Earl Marshal) 4, *and see* William Berkeley
marshals, *see under* Henry VII, household
Mary I (1553–8) 61n, 64
mass, *see* divine service
matins 139n, 153, 155, 157, 158
Maundy, Maundy Thursday observances 70, 154, *and see* foot-washing, alms-giving, divine service
Maupertus, Lord, ambassador 158, 162
Maximilian I, King of Romans 58, 117n, 156, 158, 165, 173, 185; his son (Philip) 156, 158
mayors, *see under* London, Staple, York
measles 106n, 182, *and see* pestilence
Memoir: and court ceremonial 17, 22–5 *passim*, 34–41, 49, 55, 64, 107–108, *and see under* heraldic narratives, English heralds; and Henry VII's influence 23–25; and independent sources & prescriptive texts 22, 23, 32, 39, 64; and progresses & campaigns 23, 25, 26–28, 29–33, 70n, 71n, 166n, *and see* North Yorkshire rising, Stoke; architect & authors 51, 57–59; character & subject matter 22–23, 25–42; compilation processes & dates 25, 46–8, 50–1, 55–7, 61, 71n, 161n; draft notes 51, 56, 57, 64; editorial policy 23, 25, 57, 68n; heralds' self-interest & eye-witness observation

217

17n, 22, 26, 57, 58, 82, 83,108, 115, 119, 132, 134, 137n, 151–2, 153, 166n, 176, 177; language 45–6; Leland-Hearne version 31, 33, 65–6, 166n; scribes 43, 44, 45, 46–51, 55, 57, *and see* Scribe A, Scribe B, Scribe C; the herald-recorder/s 26, 27, 29, 30, 31, 32, 34, 35, 36; transmission 49, 60–7

Middleham (Yorkshire) 27, 72, 73

Milford Haven (Wales) 76

minstrels (& trumpeters, clarion players &c) 4, 11, 39, 41, 74, 106, 130, 141, 144, 154, 176, 179, 181

Molinet, Jean 18, 29, 32

More, John, Norroy King of Arms 59, *and see* Norry King of Arms

Morley, Lord, *see* Henry Lovel

Mortlake (Middlesex) 49, 176

Morton, John (d. 1500), archbishop of Canterbury (Oct. 1486–1500) 24, 28, 30, 71n, 110, 112, 128, 137–9 *passim*, 141, 142, 153, 154, 156; as Chancellor of England 114, 151n, 163, 165, 167, 181; as godfather to Princess Margaret 41, 181; clothing & liveries 181; installation & banquet 22–23, 107–8; as bishop of Ely (1479–Oct. 1486) 71, 89

__, Robert, bishop of Worcester (Oct. 1486–97) & Master of the Rolls 104, 108, 110, 114, 139

Mountjoy King of Arms 1, 2, 173, 175, *and see* French heralds

Mountsorrel (Leicestershire) 33

Mowbray Herald 9

__, Anne, duchess of York 16

Multon, Sir Robert, sometime Lord St John 72–3

Mylling, Thomas (d. 1492), bishop of Hereford 91n, 146

Nanfant, Sir Richard 164, 170n, 184

napery, guardian of 125, *and see* Humphrey Tyrell

Narrow Sea, *see* English Channel

Nevill, Mary (née Paston; d. 1489) 182

__ family 27

__, Anne (d. 1485), queen 16, 39, 123, 130n, 131, 135n, 137n, 139n

__, funeral 7–8

__, George (d. 1492), Lord Bergavenny 146; coronation petition 126

__, Ralph (d. 1497), Lord Neville, son & heir of Westmorland 103, 105n

__, Ralph (d. 1499), earl of Westmorland 103, 147

__, Richard (d. 1460), earl of Salisbury 7

__, Richard (d. 1471), earl of Warwick ('the Kingmaker') 11, 14

__, Richard (d. 1530), Lord Latimer 72, 154, 157, 162, 165, 182; coronation petition 124

__, Sir George 'the bastard' 162, 165

__, Thomas (d. 1460) 7

New Year 15, 22, 23, 34, 39, 47, 48, 58, 107, 151–2, 183

Newark-on-Trent (Nottinghamshire) 27, 70,116, 117

Nine Worthies 28, 79n, 87n

noblemen: at Arthur's creation 173, 176–8 (*listed*); at court feast days 81–9, 107, 151–59 *passim*, 161, 162 (*listed*), 164–5 (*listed*), 184; at parliament, great council &c 28, 108, 111–12, 162, 184; at the queen's coronation 36–37, 39, 121–45 *passim*, 146–7 (*listed*); at the royal christenings 35, 103, 104–6 *passim*, 180–2 *passim*; on campaign 24, 29–30, 110–117, 166–71 (*listed*); on progress 27–8, 71–2 (*listed*), 98, 109–10. *And see* knights, esquires

noblewomen: at court feast days 41, 107, 151–4 *passim*, 157–9 *passim*, 161, 162, 164–5 (*listed*), 184; at the queen's coronation 36–37, 39, 41, 121–145 *passim*, 147 (*listed*), 150 (*listed*); at the royal christenings 35, 103, 104–6 *passim*, 180n, 181–2 *passim*; attendant upon the queen 40, 106n, 120n, 128, 139, 159 (*listed*), 173–4, 175; ladies of the stool 182

INDEX

And see gentlewomen
Norfolk, duke & duchess of, *see under* Howard
Norris, Edward & William 32, 119, 148
Norroy King of Arms 3, 21, 51, 59, *and see* John More, Roger Machado, Thomas Hawley
North Yorkshire rising (1489) 23, 32–3, 56, 58, 59, 151n, 166–71
Northampton 29, 110, 167
Northumberland, earl of, *see* Henry Percy
Norwich (Norfolk) 28, 109
__, bishop of, *see* James Goldwell
Nottingham 27, 70–1, 114n, 169; Nottingham Bridge 30, 115, 116
__, earl of, *see* William Berkeley
Nottinghamshire 32
nursery, royal 106

obleys, *see* comfits
organ, organs 80, 139
Ormond, earl of, *see* Thomas Butler
Our Lady: Friary (Doncaster) 71; of Walsingham (shrine) 29, 110; girdle of 175n; pageantic & other representations 77, 78, 83n, 85n, 86, 91, 96
Ouse Bridge (*House* Bridge, York) 76, 77
Owen, Sir David/Davey, knight of the body & carver 81, 102, 105, 134, 148, 154, 158, 162, 165
Oxford, earl & countess of, *see under* Vere

pageantry, civic 23, 28, 75, 94, 95–6, *and see individual towns and cities*; on the Thames 37, 129–30, 176n
pantlers 123, *and see* Thomas Stanley, William Berkeley, Sir John Wingfield
parish churches 71, 74, 89, 92, 93, 101
Parker, Sir James 32, 162, 165
parliament 69, 145, 151, 162n, 166n, 173, 179n, 183, 184; parliament house 173; robes & regalia 140, 158, 184
Parson (*Person*), John 171–2

pas d'armes, *see* feats of arms
Pas de l'Arbre d'Or (tournament) 11
Paston, John (d. 1466) 19
__, Sir John (d. 1504) 119, 149, 166n
__, William (d. 1496) 182
Paulet (*Pallet, Pawlet*), Sir Amyas (d. 1538) 49, 120, 148
Pavement Square (York) 33
pax 139, 156, 158
peers, *see* noblemen
Percival, Sir John (d. 1503), merchant of London 120, 128, 150
Percy, Henry (d. 1455), earl of Northumberland 14
__, Henry (d. 1489), earl of Northumberland 27–8, 39, 72n, 114n, 146, 173n; death 23, 56, 57, 58, 166; funeral achievements 172; his company 27, 72–3 (*listed*)
__, Henry Algernon (d. 1527): as earl of Northumberland 170, 177, 178, 182, 184; as Lord Percy 71
__, Lord, *see* Henry Algernon Percy
Persall, Sir Hugh, knight of the body 72, 102, 148
pestilence 27, 70, *and see* measles
Picardy 172
Piversalle, viscount of, ambassador of King of Romans 165
Planta, Joseph 54, 55
Plantagenet, Edward (ex. 1499), styled earl of Warwick 39, 108n, 109n, 126
__, George (d. 1478), duke of Clarence 5n, 39, 109n, 140
__, Richard (d. 1460), duke of York 14, 16, 18, 82n
Points (*Poyntes, Poynez*), Sir Robert, (high) sheriff of Gloucestershire 92, 148
Pole, Edmund de la (d. 1513), 'of Suffolk' 39, 155, 158, 162, 166, 182
__, Elizabeth 'of York' (née Plantagenet; d. after 1503), duchess of Suffolk 134, 145, 147
__, John de la (d. 1487), earl of Lincoln 24, 27, 30, 31, 35, 71, 81, 89, 103, 105,

107, 117, 118n, 151n; defection 28, 109
__, John de la (d. 1491–2), duke of Suffolk 14, 28, 30, 32, 110, 132, 136, 153, 158, 159; coronation petition 123, 136n
__, Margaret 'of Clarence' (née Plantagenet; ex. 1541), daughter of duke of Clarence & *suo jure* countess of Salisbury 39, 103, 140, 159, 164
__, Sir Richard (d. 1504) 32, 112, 119, 149, 159, 165; his wife, *see* Margaret Pole.
__, William de la (d. 1450), duke of Suffolk 123
Pontefract (Yorkshire) 26–27, 71, 73, 169–70; executions of rebels (1489) 33, 169; Priory 169
pontificals 82, 88, 91, 104, 110, 135, 139, 163, 174, 181, 184, *and see* ecclesiastical garb
pope, *see* Innocent VIII
Portcullis Pursuivant 20n
Portugal, 21, 162n, 164, *and see under* ambassadors, embassies; king of 164, 165
Powys, Lord, *see* John Grey
Privy Seal, Lord, *see* Peter Courtenay, Richard Foxe
processions 89n, 128–9, 163, 164; and the heralds' functions 6–7, 16, 17n; at coronations 16, 20, 24, 37, 38, 98n, 132–4, 135–7, 140–1; baptismal 15, 17n, 24, 35, 36, 40n, 41, 101, 102n, 103, 104n, 105; of religious 89, 91, 92, 93, 96, 97n, 98, 108, 135n, 184; on feast days 88, 97, 153, 155–6, 157n, 159
proclamations 21, 23, 30, 112–113, 122
progresses: of Henry VII, *see under* Henry VII; of various royals 15, 68n, 76n, 80n
prostitutes 30, 112n, 114
Prudencia, pageantic figure (Bristol) 91n, 94–5
purification (after childbirth) 63, 64, 106, 182
pursuivants 5, 132, 144, 153, 176, 184, *and see individual pursuivants*
Putney 98
Pyenne, Lord (d. 1489) of Picardy 172

Queens, Interments of &c, *see* College of Arms, MS. M6
queens, *see under* England *and individual queens*
queenship, ideologies & representations of 36, 129n, 131n, 137n, 138n, 140n, 143n, 144n, 154n, 174n

Radcliffe, John (ex. 1496), Lord FitzWalter 72, 89, 110, 141, 161; as Lord Steward (until 1488) 72, 89, 110, 141, coronation petition 126
Radcliffe-on-Trent (Nottinghamshire) 115n, 116
Rake, (?)Richard, yeoman of the Crown 62, 63, 102
Ramsay, John (d. 1513), Lord Bothwell, Scottish ambassador 99, 158, 162, 165
Ramsbury (Wiltshire) 173
ray cloth 135, 136
rebellion 14, 22, 27, 32–33, 83n, 84n, 108n–109n; *and see* North Yorkshire rising, Stoke
rebels 27, 29–31, 32, 42, 73, 109, 110, 111, 116, 117, 166n, 170n, *and see under* army; punishment & pardon 33, 151n, 169, 184, *and see* Blades, Warton
Record of Bluemantle Pursuivant, the 14, 15
regalia: for christenings 102–3 *passim*, 105–6 *passim*, 180–1, *and see* chrismal cloth, font of Christ Church (Canterbury); for coronations 16, 135–9 *passim*, *and see* Court of Claims; for creations 176, 179; of civic, court & state officials 73, 92, 98, 103, 133, 141, 181, 184; parliament, *see under* parliament

INDEX

Registrum Tractatuum in isto Volumine 54
relics 98n, 108, 175
Resumption, Act of (1485) 20
revels, *see under* Henry VII, court
Richard II (1377–99) 122n
Richard III (1483–5) 4, 5n, 12, 17, 19, 24, 26, 27, 28, 37, 39, 69n, 80n, 81n, 83n, 109n, 151n; as duke of Gloucester & Constable of England 3; coronation 16, 18, 39, 68n, 81n, 135n, 136n, 139n, 142n
Richard of Shrewsbury (d. 1483), duke of York 12n, 15, 17, 41, *and see* Anne Mowbray
Richmond King of Arms 25n, *and see* Roger Machado
Ripon (Yorkshire) 27, 73, 120
Riseley, Sir John 148, 165, 166, 173, 184
Rivers, Earl & Countess, *see under* Woodville.
Robin Hood's Stone (Yorkshire) 72
Rochester (Kent) 163
__, bishop of, *see* Edmund Audley
rod-bearer 123, *and see* John de la Pole
Roland, legendary nephew of Charlemagne 19
Romans, King of, *see* Maximilian I
Rome 164
Roos Herald, of Scotland 99
__, Sir John, esquire & councillor of king of Scots 99
Rotherham, Thomas, archbishop of York (1480–1500) 71, 79, 80, 81, 82, 135, 156, 169, 181, 184
Roucliffe, Brian (d. 1494), baron of the Exchequer & guardian of John Aspeland 127
Rouen (France) 3
Rouge Croix Pursuivant, *see* Richard Greenwood
__ Dragon Pursuivant 20n, 25n
Russell, John, bishop of Lincoln (1480–94) 70, 110, 146, 156

Salisbury (Wiltshire) 170; civic records 99n
__ Roll of Arms 8
__, bishop of, *see* Thomas Langton
__, earl of, *see* Richard Neville
Sandevill, prothonotary of, French ambassador 153, 154, 162
Sandys, Sir William (d. 1496) 149, 162
Savage, Dr Thomas (d. 1507), administrator & churchman 164
__, Sir Humphrey 49, 168
__, Sir John (d. 1492) 55, 111n, 165, 172, 181
Savernake Forest (Wiltshire) 173
Savile family 54
__, John (d. 1504), high sheriff of Yorkshire 72
Say, Thomas, lord of Lyston Overall manor (Essex), coronation petition 126–7
Saye, Lord, *see* Richard Fiennes
Scales, Lord, *see* Anthony Woodville, John de Vere
Schwartz (Zwart), Martin (d. 1487), mercenary leader 117
Scots, King of, *see* James III, James IV
Scots, Scottishmen 161, 164, 171
Scribe A 46–47, 48, 50, 55, 155n
__ B 46, 47–8, 50, 100n, 101n, 161n, 163n, 165n, 171n, 172n, 173n, 174n, 176n, *and see* Thomas Wriothesley
__ C 46, 48–9, 55, 106n, 109n, 178n, 182n, *and see* John Writhe
scribes, scriveners 60–2, 50, 65, *and see under* Memoir
Scrope, John (d. 1498), Lord Scrope of Bolton 27, 72, 81, 115n
__, Thomas (d. 1493), Lord Scrope of Upsall and Masham 72, 115n
Senlis, bailiff of, *see* Waleran de Zaintes
sermons 88, 91, 92, 97, 129
sewer, sewers 6, *and see* Anthony Browne, William Vampage; the queen's 126, *and see* John Radcliffe
Seymour, Jane (d. 1537), queen 61
Sheen 28, 41, 98, 108, 109, 164–5, 176, 185

Shere Thursday, *see* Maundy Thursday
sheriff, sheriffs, *see under individual towns and counties*
Sherwood, John (d. 1493), bishop of Durham 163, 176
Shirley, Sir Ralph 32, 119
Shrewsbury, earl of, *see under* Talbot
shrines, *see under* St Edward, St Swithun, St William
Sicily Herald 2
Simnel, Lambert (d. *after* 1534), pretender, 31, 108n, 109n, 117n, *and see* 'Edward VI'
Sluys (Flanders) 15
Smert, John (d. 1478), Garter King of Arms 1n, 7n, 9, 10, 12
Smithfield tournament (1469) 11, 19, 23
Solomon, pageantic King (York) 76–7
Somerset, duke of, *see* Edmund Beaufort
__, Lord John, *see* John Beaufort
__, Sir Charles of (d. 1526) 30, 72, 105, 112, 148, 165; as cupbearer 81, 154, 158
Southwark (Surrey) 62, 163
Southwell (Nottinghamshire) 116
Spain 21, 162n, 170n, 176n; ambassadors of 41, 162, 176, 183, 185; merchants of 176
spices 106n, 144, 155, 174
St Albans (Hertfordshire) 128
__, first battle of (1455) 14
St Andrew's Day & Eve 173, 179, 180
St Anne in the Wood (Brislington, Gloucestershire) 96, 97n
St Augustine's Abbey (Bristol) 96–7
St Bartholomew's Day 120
St Edward: his army 157; his sceptre 98n; his shrine 140
St Eustachius's Day 99
St George 88n, 106, 157, *and see* Hereford pageants; college of, dean & poor knights 156n, 157, 158; feast of 5, 22, 29, 30, 40, 42, 46, 59, 60, 80, 81–2, 110, 139n, 155–60, 165, 172, celebratory verse (1488) 46, 155n, 159–160

St George's, Southwark 162
St John of Jerusalem (Clerkenwell), prior ('Lord of St Johns') 164, *and see* Sir Robert Multon; priory of 69, 99
St John's Day 182
St Katherine's Day 121, 129
St Lawrence's Eve 120
St Leonard's Hospital (York) 74
St Mary's Abbey (York) 74, 170; abbot of 81, 82
St Matelin's, abbot or prior of, French ambassador 173, 175
St Oswald, *see* Worcester pageants
St Paul's Cathedral, *see under* London
St Stephen's chapel, *see under* Westminster Palace
St Swithun: anthem of 106; shrine of 105; prior of 104, his great hall 102, 180n
St Thomas Hill (Yorkshire) 33, 169
St Thomas's Day 182
St Vitalis's Day 166
St William's shrine (York Minster) 80n
St Wulfstan, pageantic figure (Worcester)
Stafford, Edward (d. 1499), earl of Wiltshire 32, 71, 81, 146, 163, 168
__, Elizabeth, 'of Buckingham' (d. 1530–2), daughter of Henry duke of Buckingham 64, 181
__, John (d. 1473), earl of Wiltshire 14
__, Margaret (née Grey), countess of Wiltshire 145, 147
Stamford (Lincolnshire) 69
Staniland, Kay 34
Stanley family 31, 33, 34; military strength 31, 33–4, 115, 169
__, George (d. 1503), Lord Strange 31, 71, 103, 105, 107, 152; his company 33, 115, 168–9 (*listed*)
__, Joan (née Lestrange; d. 1514), *suo jure* Lady Strange 134, 145, 147, 154
__, Sir Edward (d. 1523), son of Thomas earl of Derby 147, 164, 18
__, Sir Humphrey 32, 72
__, Sir William (ex. 1495), Lord Cham-

berlain 33–4, 71, 89, 152 165, 168, 177, 182
__, Thomas (d. 1504), earl of Derby & Constable of England 28, 32, 39, 71, 107, 110, 153, 155, 158, 159, 161, 165, 166, 174, 176, 179, 181, 182; called 'lord of Mann' 152; and the queen's coronation 37, 40n, 121, 132, 135, 140n, 141n, 146, his petition 123; clothing & liveries 141, 184; as godfather to Prince Arthur 35, 103–5; his company 33, 115, 116, 169 (*listed*)
Staple, mayor of 120
Steward, Lord (steward of the royal household), *see* Sir Robert Willoughby, John Radcliffe
__, Lord High (Steward of England) 3n, *and see* Jasper Tudor; commission for office 23, 37, 121–2; coronation duties 136n
Stirling (Scotland) 161
Stoke campaign (1487) 23n, 25, 29–33, 80n, 111–18, 170n; creations at 31, 49, 59, 128n, *and see under* knights, bannerets; independent sources 29; reports of the king's conduct 29–31, 115; the battle 29, 30, 31, 59, 117, 118n, 120n, 127n, 128, 134n
Stoner, Sir William 105
Stony Stratford (Buckinghamshire) 167
Stourton, William (d. 1523), Lord Stourton 146, 177
Stowe, John 64, 100n
Strange, Lady, 'the elder' 103
__, Lord & Lady, *see under* Stanley.
Stratford Priory 15
Suffolk 109
___, duke & duchess of, *see under* Pole
surnap 82, 145, 154, 158
Surrey, earl of, *see under* Howard
Sutton, Cecily (née Willoughby), Lady Dudley, wife of Edward Sutton 134, 147
__, Edward (d. 1532), Lord Dudley 37, 167
__, John (d. 1487), Lord Dudley 107, 111, 159
Swan, Harry, rebel 184

Tadcaster (Yorkshire) & Tadcaster Bridge 73
Talbot, George (d. 1538), earl of Shrewsbury 30, 32, 41, 71, 81, 112, 117n, 146, 156n, 157, 158, 162, 163, 176, 179, 184
__, Humphrey, marshal of Calais 171
__, John (d. 1453), earl of Shrewsbury ('the good Talbot') 181
__, Sir Gilbert (d. 1518) 147, 161, 162, 181
tapers, torches & torch-bearers 103, 104, 144, 108, 180n, 181, 184
Tate, Robert, mayor of London (1488) 163
Te Deum Laudamus 80, 98, 100, 101, 105, 108, 128, 155, 163
Tewkesbury, battle of (1471) 14, 35
Thames (*Temys*), River 37, 129, 163, *and see* pageantry
Thirsk (Yorkshire) 56, 166
Tickhill (Doncaster, Yorkshire) 169
Tiptoft, John (d. 1470), earl of Worcester and Constable of England 14
Todd, William, mayor of York (1486–7) 120
Toison d'or King of Arms 11, 18, *and see* Jean le Fèvre
tournaments 10–12, 15, 120n, 144n, *and see* Smithfield, *Pas de l'Abre d'Or*; narrative accounts of 19
Townsend, Sir Thomas, justice knight 89
travers 102, 105, 164, 175
treasurer of the household, *see* Henry VII, household
Treasurer, Lord/Lord High (Treasurer of England), *see* John Dinham
Tremayle, recorder of Bristol 92
Trent, River 3, 116, 170n, bridges of 71
Trinity, Trinities: Holy Trinity Priory (York) 74; order of the Holy Trinity (France) 182; Trinity Sunday 92;

Worcester pageant 86–7
Tuchet, James (ex. 1497), son & heir of Lord Audley 103
___, John (d. 1490), Lord Audley 103
Tudor, Jasper (d. 1495), duke of Bedford 32, 37, 38, 89, 111n, 146, 153; as Lord High Steward 121, 122–7 *passim*, 132, 136n, 140–1, 151; clothing & liveries 140–1, 136
___, Katherine (née Woodville; d. 1497), duchess of Bedford 141, 145, 147, 151–2; clothing & liveries 34, 136, 141
___, Margaret 71n, 72n
___, Mary, *see* Mary I
___, royal house of 61
Tunstall, Sir Richard 147, 165, 170, 171
Turbervill, Sir John, knight marshal 82, 103, 144, 148
Twelfth Night, Twelfth Day, *see* Epiphany
Tyrell, Humphrey, of Kent, coronation petition 125
___, Sir James, lieutenant of Guisnes 147, 171, 172
Tyrwhitt, Sir William 32, 49, 59

Underwood, Malcolm 41, 42
Unicorn Pursuivant, of Scotland 99
Urswick, Master Christopher (d. 1522), king's almoner & dean of York 111n, 164, 165, 166, 184
Uvedale, Sir William (d. 1525) 177, 178, 180

vagabonds 114; vagabond heralds 2
Vampage, Sir William, sewer 119, 149, 154, 158, 182
Vaughan, William, yeoman of the Crown 102
Vaux, Nicholas 32
Vavasour, recorder of York 74
Vere, John de, earl of Oxford & Lord Great Chamberlain 28, 37, 71, 107, 121, 132, 146, 152–5 *passim*, 156n, 158, 159, 162, 171, 174, 176, 179, 184; as godfather to Prince Arthur 35–6, 63n, 100, 101n, 103n, 104–6; at Stoke 30, 32, 110–16 *passim*; called Lord Scales 152; clothing & liveries 81, 136, 140; coronation petition 60, 122–3; his company 32, 112, 167–8 (*listed*)
___, Margaret de (née Nevill; d. 1506/7), countess of Oxford 134, 141, 147, 151, 153, 154
Vergil, Polydore (d. 1555) 18, 29, 31n, 111n
void 82, 134, 144, 159, 157, 174, 184

wafers 78, 79n, 96n; waferers 126–7, *and see* Thomas Say
Wales, Prince of 22, 34, *and see* Arthur, Edward
Walker, Robert, yeoman of the Crown 102
Wallingford Pursuivant 20n, 22, 49, 58, 179, *and see* Thomas Wriothesley
Walsingham 29, 110, *and see* Our Lady of Walsingham
Waltham (Essex) 69; Waltham Forest 183
Wansworth, Dr 164
Warbeck, Perkin (d. 1499), pretender 111n
Warkworth, John (d. 1500), chronicler 18
Warr, de la, Lord & Lady, *see under* West
Wars of the Roses 18
Warton (ex. 1489), rebel 33, 170
Warwick 120, 128
___ Herald 9, 14
___, earl of, *see* Edward Plantagenet, Richard Beauchamp, Richard Neville
Water, John, York Herald 19, 59
Welles, John (d. 1499), Viscount Welles 41, 71, 89, 115n, 152, 154, 167, 172, 180, 182
___, viscountess, *see* Cecily of York
Wells Cathedral, dean, *see* John Gunthorp
Wentworth, Sir Henry 72, 149, 166, 171

INDEX

West, Elizabeth (née Mortimer; d. 1502), Lady de la Warr 134, 145, 147
__, Thomas (d. 1525), Lord de la Warr 72, 103, 146, 157, 181
__, Thomas (d. 1554), son & heir of above 177
Westminster 68n, 99, 132, 151, 163, 180–2; Abbey 16, 98, 121, 135, 136n, 137, 139, 140, 179, 180–2, dean 163, font 180; Bridge 98; Hall 134n, 135, 140n, 141n, 177, 179, 184, king's bench 179; Palace 39, 69, 98, 134, 140, 162, 173, 176, 178, 182, great chamber 99, 151, parliament chamber 178, 179, St Stephen's chapel 98, 144, 156n, 178, 184, star chamber 179, White Hall 36, 122, 140, 179, 180, 184
White Hall, Westminster, *see under* Westminster Palace
White, William, mayor of London (1489) 176
Whitsuntide 5, 26, 56, 83–88, 111n, 161, 171
Willoughby, Sir Henry (d. 1528) 32, 119, 148
__, Sir Robert (d. 1502) 110, 148; as Lord Steward (from 1488) 160, 161, 162, 170n, 184; called Lord Broke 56, 160, 161, 162
Wiltshire 173
__, earl & countess of, *see under* Stafford
Winchelsea (Sussex) 15
Winchester 34, 35, 36, 99, 101, *and see* Hyde Abbey, St Swithun's (prior of)
__ Cathedral 34–6, 101–6, 157, *and see* St Swithun's shrine; font 101
__, bishop of, *see* Peter Courtenay
__, earl of 6, 15, *and see* Louis de Gruthuse
Windsor (Berkshire) 110, 160, 171, 173
__ Castle 29, 30, 40, 80n, 82n, 154, 155, 161–2; chapter house 25, 82; hall & great chamber 25, 157, 158. *And see* college of St George

__ Herald 7, 25n, *and see* Charles Wriothesley
wine, sweet wine 98, 106, 144n, 155, 174, 181
Wingfield (*Wyngfeld*), Sir Edward 166, 182
__ (*Wynkfelde*), Sir John 148, 167, coronation petition 123
Woodstock (Oxfordshire) 161
Woodville family 35, 104n
__, Anthony (ex. 1483), Lord Scales & Earl Rivers 6, 11, 16, 19
__, Elizabeth (d. 1492), queen & dowager queen 7n, 16, 39, 108n, 123, 130n, 131n, 132, 135n, 136n, 140n, 145n, 175; as godmother to Prince Arthur 35, 103n, 104, 105
__, Mary (née Lewis), dowager Countess Rivers, widow of Anthony Woodville 141, 153, 154, 159
__, Richard (d. 1491), Earl Rivers 71, 81
__, Sir Edward (d. 1488) 30, 32, 35, 56, 103, 112, 114n, 157, 158, 159; death 56, 161,170n; funeral achievements 172
Worcester 26, 83, 88n; Cathedral 88; pageants 23, 83–7, 90n
__, bishop of, *see* John Alcock, Robert Morton.
__, earl of, *see* John Tiptoft
Worksop (Nottinghamshire) 169
Wreyton, Piers of, gentlemen/yeomen usher 64
Wriothesley, Charles (d. 1562), Windsor Herald 51
__, Thomas (d. 1534), Wallingford & Garter 10, 51, 58, 61; as Scribe B 49, 50, 55, *and see* Scribe B; hand & monogram 14n, 49–50, 161n
Writhe, John (d. 1504), Garter King of Arms 4, 19, 20, 51, 59, 61, 115, 158; and court ceremonial 37, 40n, 49, 130n, 135, 140, 144, 154, 159, 175, 180, 183, 184; as Scribe C & supervisor 48–9, 50, 52n, 55, 57, *and see* Scribe C; hand 48–9, 50, 62n, 63; on

225

diplomatic missions 21, 40n, 58
Writhe's Book of Knights 8, 49
Wychwood Forest (Oxfordshire) 161

yeomen: in the company of Northumberland 27, 72–3; of the Crown 35, 62, 64, 102,103, 181; yeomen ushers, *see under* Henry VII, household
York 22, 26, 27, 71, 73–82, 88n, 109n, 111n, 117n, 118n, 120, 153n, 169, 170; civic records 28, 31, 76n, 115n, 117n; Cony Street 77, 78; mayor, *see* William Todd, William Chimney; pageants 75–9; recorder, *see* Vavasour; sheriffs 73
__ Herald 19, 25n, 51, 59, 164, 184, *and see* John Water, William Dethick
__ Minster 26, 79–8, 80n, *and see* St William's shrine; dean of, *see* Christopher Urswick

__, archbishop of, *see* Thomas Rotherham
__, duchess of, *see* Anne Mowbray
__, dukes of, *see* Richard Plantagenet, Richard of Shrewsbury
__, royal house of 4, 12, 27, 35, 38, 104n, 129n, 134n
Yorkshire, high sheriff of, *see* John Savile
__, North 27, 33, 59, *and see* North Yorkshire rising

Zaintes, Sir Waleran (*William*) de, bailiff of Senlis 173, 175, 183, 184
Zeeland 110
Zouche, John de la (d. 1526), Lord Zouche 182